THE FIVE SENSES

Also available from Continuum:

Aesthetics and Politics, Jacques Ranciere
After Finitude, Quentin Meillassoux
Art and Fear, Paul Virilio
Being and Even, Alain Badiou
Conditions, Alain Badiou
Desert Screen, Paul Virilio
Infinite Though, Alain Badiou
Logics of Worlds, Alain Badiou
Negative Horizon, Paul Virilio
Theory of the Subject, Alain Badiou

THE FIVE SENSES
A Philosophy of Mingled Bodies (I)

Michel Serres

Translated by Margaret Sankey and Peter Cowley

continuum

Continuum International Publishing Group

The Tower Building   80 Maiden Lane
11 York Road   Suite 704
London, SE1 7NX   New York, NY 10038

www.continuumbooks.com

Originally published in French as *Les Cinq Sens* © Éditions
Grasset et Fasquelle, 1985

Published with the assistance of the French Ministry of Culture – Centre
National du Livre

British Library Cataloguing-in-Publication Data
A catalogue record for this book is available from the British Library.

ISBN 10: HB: 0-8264-5984-6
          PB: 0-8264-5985-4
ISBN 13: HB: 978-0-8264-5984-8
          PB: 978-0-8264-5985-5

Library of Congress Cataloging-in-Publication Data
Serres, Michel.
[Cinq sens. English]
The five senses: a philosophy of mingled bodies/Michel Serres;
translated by Margaret Sankey and Peter Cowley.
    p. cm.
Includes index.
ISBN 978-0-8264-5984-8
ISBN 978-0-8264-5985-5
1. Perception (Philosophy) 2. Phenomenology. I. Title.

B828.45.S4713 2009
128'.3–dc22

2008015270

Typeset by Newgen Imaging Systems Pvt Ltd, Chennai, India
Printed and bound in Great Britain by MPG Books Ltd, Bodmin, Cornwall

Contents

Sense and Sensibility, *Margaret Sankey, Peter Cowley*   vii

Acknowledgements   xiv

Introduction, *Steven Connor (Birkbeck, University of London, UK)*   1

1. Veils   17

2. Boxes   85

3. Tables   152

4. Visit   236

5. Joy   311

Notes   346

Sense and Sensibility: Translating the Bodily Experience

Margaret Sankey, Peter Cowley

Serres the polymath and Renaissance man has the European literary, artistic and philosophical traditions at his command, as he does the world of science. The full extent of his intellectual reach is displayed in *The Five Senses*. His philosophical familiars are the ancient Greeks, Descartes and Leibniz are his bedrock; the Bible, the Catholic Mass and liturgy figure prominently; Montaigne and Pascal haunt the text, Stendhal, Diderot and Verne are more substantial apparitions. What is more, mythology, fables and fairy tales are deployed with the same analytical seriousness as their more disciplined conceptual counterparts. The text references the European visual arts, architecture and music. In short, the reader is left wondering if there is anything beyond the range of Serres's erudition. In *The Five Senses* we read, for instance, about *The Lady and the Unicorn*, Bonnard's veiled figures, Cinderella and her slipper, the myth of Orpheus and Eurydice . . . And at the heart of the book, in a sparkling analysis of the root meanings of sapience and sagacity, Serres conjures Don Juan, the Last Supper and Plato's *Symposium* out of the contemplation of a fine Château d'Yquem.

This mingled patchwork is isomorphic with Serres's overall philosophical project, which seeks to establish a topology, rather than a geometry, of knowledge. The manner in which, here as elsewhere in his writings, his analysis moves from the physical sciences to fable, for instance, or from philosophy to myth, stems from his belief that to operate within one field of knowledge alone is to remain landlocked. An intolerable situation for a sailor whose preferred navigational metaphor is the North-West Passage.

Serres, who was indeed a naval officer in his youth, is most easily categorized as a philosopher, although the label is one which sits ill with him, as the reader will discover. Nonetheless, this book presents as a philosophical text – its subtitle is *A Philosophy of Mingled Bodies*. It thus awakens certain expectations, such as the orderly and logical development of an argument leading towards certain clear-cut conclusions. However Serres's project is to subvert philosophical discourse through a critique of the Cartesian world view. He does this on the one hand by arguing against the dualistic tradition and propounding the importance of empiricism and the senses as a means to knowledge, and on the other through the nature of his discourse where the association of ideas rather than logical development becomes the motor of his text. Like the human body he describes in it, Serres's text is a hybrid; and its connectivity and cohesion is as much literary as philosophical.

The book's five chapters do not represent a linear progress through the senses. 'How could we see the compact capacity of the senses,' he asks, 'if we separated them?' As the book develops its argument the reader quickly understands that no such separation can be possible. The hybrid body, basted together according to circumstance, is lovingly embraced, and turned inside out.

> The skin hangs from the wall as if it were a flayed man: turn over the remains, you will touch the nerve threads and knots, a whole uprooted hanging jungle, like the inside wiring of an automaton. The five or six senses are entwined and attached, above and below the fabric that they form by weaving or splicing, plaits, balls, joins, planes, loops and bindings, slip or fixed knots.

This image of the receptive body (subtle, as he calls it – and the careful reader will seek out the etymology of that adjective in order to understand why) displays his preference for topology over geometry, confusion over analysis (two of the terms he picks over at length), for folds, tangles, pleats and knots. It further demonstrates the impossibility of treating the five senses in separate chapters – how could one do so, if they are indeed as inseparable as Serres would have us believe?

But this one image, which is emblematic of his entire philosophical project and condenses how seriously he takes the question of interdisciplinarity, also embodies his poetics. Intermingling and confusion inform his work structurally and stylistically, globally and locally. They underwrite the style of his text, in which 'technical' philosophical language alternates and blends with the poetic and the lyrical; where he constantly moves between registers; where the reader is by turns lulled, seduced and challenged. Serres's contention is that music is the substratum of all meaningful language and his text is structured musically in terms of themes and variations, counterpoint and fugue. The reader will need to adapt to the rhythmic play of the text, which is indissociable from the conceptual moves it makes and to which, we hope, our translation has done justice.

***

The translation of *Les cinq sens* has been a long time coming. In the more than twenty years since its publication Serres has achieved a prominence, both in France and internationally, which he did not have in 1985. In France his appearances on television in the nineties turned him into something of an overnight media sensation. Suddenly, members of the general public were turning up to his Saturday morning seminars, asking questions and receiving the same careful, pedagogical replies they had come to expect from his on-screen persona.

We can trace the lightening of his prose style back to the same period. His early theoretical output, dense, academic and disciplined, evolved into something more lyrical and discursive. That evolution continued throughout the following decade, to the point where Serres's output today – aerated, playful, often supplemented with illustrations and clearly pitched to a more general readership – hardly seems the work of the same writer. His media presence continues also: on Sunday evenings now he presents a five-minute long radio programme on Radio France, in the form of a brief, topical excursus, often drawing on his writings and delivered in digestible, conversational style with the host Michel Polacco.

It might be said that *Les cinq sens* belongs to his middle period. Frequently lyrical and rhapsodic, it nonetheless owes much to his early work in its density and complexity. Like those earlier works, it has been waiting a very long time to be translated into English.

As it turns out, its transition to English is timely. When it was first published, Serres was criticized for his linguistic waywardness, in particular for his use of neologisms. In Chapter 2, for example, the recurring opposition between soft and hard leads Serres to contrast 'douceur logicielle et dureté matérielle'. Our now widely-accepted 'software' and 'hardware' lend themselves perfectly and unproblematically to the translation of Serres's analysis, but at the time of publication 'logiciel' ('software') was sufficiently newly- minted to raise eyebrows. Similarly (again in Chapter 2) the image of a disembodied Eurydice floating like a icon cannot but call to mind that of an icon on a computer screen, a mere representation. Serres insists that this was his original intention. Commonplace now, the metaphor must have been an opaque one in the mid eighties. These are rare and happy instances of the right interval in time allowing a translation to bring an element of the original to fruition, rather than introducing impediments.

The difficulties of any translation are manifold, and their enumeration often tedious. But some clarification is usually called for, if only to guide the reader through the complexities of the text at hand. Serres's use of language is highly self-conscious, sometimes displaying surgical precision, frequently bewildering in its opacity and its tendency to play fast and loose with the rules of French syntax and scholarly prose. It poses problems to the translator for various reasons: Serres plays on the Greek and Latin etymological substrata of French, weaves intertextual references into his argument, mines technical and dialectal language and, inevitably, puns.

ETYMOLOGY AND WORD PLAY

While we do not wish to catalogue the difficulties of translating Serres's word play, a brief notice is called for in the cases of several recurring key terms. One of these is *le sensible*. Typically, '*sensible*' means 'sensitive'. It is a classic '*faux-ami*' – a cognate or 'false friend' – the bane of the language learner. However it is used here as a noun to express everything pertaining to the senses, and we have rendered it as 'the sensible', in reference to the more specialized usage of the latter in English.

Similarly with *le donné*. It derives from the verb *donner*, to give, and is used by Serres to refer to the sensory experience we receive from the world – in essence, what we are given by the world, if only we will open ourselves up to that experience. While this is an acceptable, if specialized and often awkward, usage of the term in French, it is rather harder to pull off in English, at least as a noun, because of the primary substantive sense of 'given' as an established fact. However, due to the inordinately complex set of transformations to which '*le donné*' is subjected in the text, we determined that the wisest course of action was to retain 'the given'.

For the most part, where we have been able to do so with relative concision and elegance, we have attempted parallel puns and neologisms, and have only provided footnote explanations where (a) such a solution proved impossible and (b) the pun was not gratuitous, but integral to the development of the argument. This is the case, for instance, with '*vair*', in Chapter 1 (meaning 'fur' but a homophone for '*verre*', meaning glass) and '*percevoir*', at various points (a play on perception and taxation).

Serres draws upon etymology much more frequently than he resorts to puns; sometimes explicitly, but often implicitly. We are fortunate that

English and French share so much etymological common ground. In most instances, therefore, the resonance has been preserved, and when merely implicit we have left it to the reader – as Serres himself does – to be attentive to that dimension of the text.

INTERTEXTUALITY

Serres's text, to return to the image of the hanging skin and its exposed nerve endings, is as much embroidered as written, to the extent that hardly a paragraph could be said to be free of intertextual references, often overt, frequently more obscure, consisting of a *clin d'œil* to the educated reader. They are woven through the warp and weft of both the argument and the language, sometimes over, sometimes under. It is likely that no one reader will detect them all. In addition to references to works of philosophy, science and literature, he alludes to his own, earlier texts (most frequently to the *Hermes* series and to *Le parasite*), to nursery rhymes, to proverbs, to half-remembered paintings . . . We have taken care to translate the philosophical terms using the accepted terminology in English. In the case of the more literary texts, and specifically where there is a variety of English translations, we have sometimes used existing translations, sometimes made our own, according both to the felicitousness of the translations available and to the context. Take for example Montaigne's *branle pérenne*. Neither Florio's curious 'the world runnes on all wheeles' (1613), nor Cotton's 'the world eternally turns round' (1685–1686), nor Screech's 'the world is but a perennial see-saw' (1991) seemed to capture the nuance we were seeking and we fixed on 'eternal wobble' hoping that the aware reader would make the connection with Montaigne.

Serres's erudite text is almost entirely free from footnotes and we have considered it appropriate to preserve in the same way the free flow of the ideas and images. We have thus avoided footnoting most of the intertextual references, only providing explanations where the reference is so obscure, at least to the Anglophone reader, as to render the sense of the text difficult to determine.

***

Serres's contention is that the development of human language, and subsequently of the sciences, has veiled and militated against the glories of our initial sensuous perception of the world. Conscious of the paradox of expressing through words this transformation in man's perceptions, the style of Serres's writing seems to be a deliberate effort to combat the limitations of language which he turns against itself in order to make his points through suggestion and free association, as well as through philosophical argument. His style is thus on occasion elliptical and ambiguous and it has been necessary in the interest of comprehension sometimes to flesh out the meaning in translation, as well as providing connectives, absent in the French. On occasion this has solidified the meaning in English, as opposed to the looser, more fluid French construction which allowed a fuller semantic play. The introduction of carefully chosen punctuation has also served to clarify the text.

However we have, as a rule, attempted to preserve the stylistic peculiarities of Serres's writing: the shifts of register from familiar and conversational to lyrical and exalted; the deliberating wandering sentences; the occasional jerkiness. All these things help to preserve the play of Serres's consciousness. The text is, after all, a highly personal one in which the writer uses his sensuous experience to inflect his style and demonstrate the importance of the senses in the construction of human knowledge.

Les cinq sens might be called a homunculus. 'I wager,' writes Serres in Chapter 1,

> that the small, monstrous homunculus, each part of which is proportional to the magnitude of the sensations it feels, increases in size and swells at these automorphic points, when the skin tissue folds in on itself. Skin on skin becomes conscious, as does skin on mucus membrane and mucus membrane on itself. Without this folding, without the contact of the self on itself, there would truly be no internal sense, no body properly speaking, cœnesthesia even less so, no real image of the body; we would live without consciousness; slippery smooth and on the point of fading away. Klein bottles are a model of identity. We are the bearers of skewed, not quite flat, unreplicated surfaces, deserts over which consciousness passes fleetingly, leaving no memory. Consciousness belongs to those singular moments when the body is tangential to itself.

If, as he argues, our skin is the site of a generalized, common sense, generative of identity in the places where pliability, the lack of inhibition and a willingness to leave the beaten path, bring it into contact with itself, then by extension his text is stylistically and conceptually most itself at precisely those points when seeming to practise the very arts he extols: viticulture, haute cuisine, embroidery, acrobatics – arts of confusion, contorsion and mingling, all.

Our translation is, no doubt, less likely to draw attention to itself than the homunculus, less likely to cause offence in polite company, less flexible – less sensible. Translation inevitably flattens out the folds in the language of a text, the points of contact where its identity is formed and formulated – where it is most interesting, and most itself. But that is the price of acceptability.

Acknowledgements

Our most grateful thanks to Michel Serres for his unfailing attentiveness and patience in helping to unpack the occasional ambiguity in the text and, like a good sailor, teaching us how certain knots are tied.

We would also like to thank Barbara Hanna and Geoffrey Little for their careful and helpful reading of various drafts of the translation, as well as our colleagues in the Department of French Studies at the University of Sydney for their support and suggestions, and students who participated in our department's fourth-year seminar on translation.

Peter Cowley and Margaret Sankey
The University of Sydney

Introduction

Steven Connor

CONJUGATIONS

When it first appeared in 1985, Michel Serres's *Les cinq sens* had the subtitle *philosophie des corps mêlées I – The Philosophy of Mingled Bodies 1*. Readers assuming that this meant that the book was volume one of a series have had a very long wait for volume two. When the work was reissued in 1998, the subtitle had been removed. But this is not because Serres had thought better of his project of generating a philosophy of mixed bodies, indeed it was probably for just the opposite reason. For, as Serres himself has remarked, to constitute the complete philosophy of mixed bodies, 'You have only to add to all my other books "volume 2," "volume 3," and so on'.[1]

This kind of serialism comes naturally to Michel Serres. Most of his writing in the 1970s, which explored the conversations and overlaps between science, literature and culture, percolated into the five volumes that make up the sequence collectively entitled *Hermes*, only a selection from which has appeared so far in English.[2] Serres's writing often unwinds through long sequences like this, not because of any fondness for the slowly-wrought and systematic masterwork, but because of the opportunity they offer for the unpredictable rhythm of loops, leaps, poolings, spurts and recurrences to which he is so drawn, both in his subjects and in his own writing. His manner is not that of the curriculum, the straight race run without pause or deviation, but rather that of discourse, conceived as *discurrere*, a running back and forth, or even, in the word on which Serres reflects in the third chapter of *The Five Senses*, *concourse*, or a running-together. Serres praises the intricate structure of the ear in Chapter 2, suggesting that its mazy constitution provides an apt model not just for the workings of sensation, but also for understanding and writing

> We inherit our idea of the labyrinth from a tragic and pessimistic tradition, in which it signifies death, despair, madness. However, the maze is in fact the best model for allowing moving bodies to pass through while at the same time retracing their steps as much as possible; it gives the best odds to finite journeys with unstructured itineraries. Mazes maximize feedback. . . . Let us seek the best way of creating the most feedback loops possible on an unstructured and short itinerary. Mazes provide us with this maximization. Excellent reception, here is the best possible resonator, the beginnings of consciousness.

In reading *The Five Senses*, we must be prepared to enter the maze, and tolerate its toils and torsions. This may seem an unexpected way to conceive a book the title of which seems to promise a systematic division and parcelling-out of its subject. The tradition in which Serres writes in *The Five Senses* is one in which the senses are made intelligible primarily through the act of analysis or separation. Two things seem to be presupposed by this division. The first is quantity. It is generally agreed that there is a finite number of senses, even though there is much less sameness of report on the precise number than we might have expected. Democritus, who explained sensation by the friction of atoms of different shapes and sizes, thought that all the senses were really only variations of the one sense of touch. Aristotle distinguished only four senses, since he was anxious to correlate the senses with the four elements – vision with water, sound with air, smell with fire and touch with earth, with taste being regarded only as a 'particular form' or 'modification' of touch.[3] But Aristotle also suggested the necessity for a kind of sixth, quasi-sense, the *sensus communis*, the function of which was to mediate between the other five senses. This metasense which, as Serres observes, was made much of by Scholastic philosophers of the Middle Ages, is strongly identified in the first chapter of *The Five Senses* with the skin. Psychologists of sensation in the twentieth century have differentiated further senses – of heat and weight, for example – and, in this, they verify the opinion of Socrates who, in Plato's *Theaetetus*, observes that, in addition to the ordinarily-recognized senses, such as sight, hearing and smelling, 'there are others besides, a great number which have names, an infinite number which have not'.[4]

The second assumption embedded in the tradition of writing about the senses is that they form a hierarchy. Typically vision comes out on top, as it does (if only by a whisker) in the human body, with hearing often thought of as its sidekick or second-in-command. Thereafter, the order of merit is a matter of interesting dispute. Although Serres may seem in some respects to mime this tradition of divide-and-rank, it is in order to complicate and transform it. *The Five Senses* has five long chapters. The first two, 'Veils', a meditation on touch, skin and drapery, and 'Boxes', an exploration of sound and hearing, seem to conform to a one-at-a-time, seriatim syllabus and method. There is a little hiccup in the third chapter, 'Tables', in which it quickly becomes clear that taste and smell are to be conjoined; but then, taste and smell are so closely affiliated as often to be indissociable, so this perhaps presents no great difficulty. Chapter 4, 'Visit', duly turns to the remaining sense of vision, but vision construed in a very specific way, as 'visiting' or 'going to see'; indeed, the real concern of the chapter seems to be with place, landscape and mapping. This leaves the final chapter, 'Joy', without a signature sense. The chapter begins instead with an evocation of some of the supplementary senses that are not encompassed within the traditional pentalogy: the senses of heat, effort, lightness (including Serres' rapturous paean to the trampoline), weight and speed, all components or symptoms of the metasense of enjoyment, or heightened being in the body. This then opens on to a vision of the body transfigured in its entirety by new forms of knowledge and communication.

So, although Serres has plenty to say about each of the senses, there is much that is aslant, elliptical, episodic or to use the word to which he devotes some dense pages at the end of 'Visit', *circumstantial*, about his method of doing so. The reason for this is made clear by that original subtitle: *Philosophy of Mixed Bodies*. There is a tradition in the visual representation of the senses which shows the body as a circular city, with the five senses represented as five gates piercing the city wall, which provide five separate avenues of approach to the head or citadel placed in the centre. For Serres, by contrast, the senses are nothing but the mixing of the body, the principal means whereby the body mingles with the world and with itself, overflows its borders.

It is for this reason that Serres begins *The Five Senses*, not with the eye, but with the skin. As has often been observed, the skin can in one sense be regarded as the ground or synopsis of all the senses, since all the organs of sense are localized convolutions of it. For Serres, too, 'the skin is a variety of our mingled senses'. But there is a more particular reason for the priority of skin and the sense of touch in Serres's book. All the way through *The Five Senses*, Serres maintains a teasing, hit-and-run dialogue with the *Treatise of Sensations* (1754) by the eighteenth-century empiricist philosopher Étienne Bonnot de Condillac. In this work, Condillac sets out, like others before and after him, to understand the senses by splitting them up. The way in which he does this is to imagine a statue, which is possessed of a soul and all the internal organization of a man (a fully-loaded operating system, so to speak), but has never encountered any form of sensory stimulus. Condillac then imagines the introduction of input from each of the senses in turn, in order to explicate the Lockean process whereby simple sense-impressions are refined into complex, abstract ideas. The first sense to gain admission is that of smell, which Condillac thinks would be enough on its own to permit the development of memory and desire. This is followed by taste, hearing and sight, the order of the senses reflecting the growing complexity and abstractness of the statue's ideas. But the most original and decisive part of Condillac's analysis comes at the beginning of part two of his essay, which introduces the subject of touch. For up until this point, Condillac reasons, the statue may be able to distinguish between its sensations in more and more elaborate ways, but will have no awareness of itself as the subject of its own sensations; it will simply *be* the fragrance that suffuses it, the sound that ripples through it, the sight that engrosses its gaze. It is only with the coming of the sense of touch, 'the only sense that can by itself judge of exterior objects', that the statue will be able to grasp that there is an exterior world from which these sensations emanate and therefore that it is an 'I', distinct from this exterior world, and receiving those sensations.[5]

The sardonic references all the way through *The Five Senses* to various kinds of statue, automaton or robot will be Serres's way of demurring from the approach to the senses by way of dissection and analysis, since, he says, '[a]bstraction divides up the sentient body, eliminates taste, smell and touch, retains only sight and hearing, intuition and understanding'. Whereas Condillac's statue has a long and a difficult birth, such that it can only really be said to be born with the arrival, late in the epistemological day, of the sense of touch, Serres begins his book with a tactile birth (with renewed births and rebirths to follow thereafter, all the way through to the final sentence of the book), in the extraordinary, arresting narrative of his attempt to escape from a fire on board ship, blinded, choking and with only the sense of touch to save him. Serres's claim is that the soul does not reside in one particular location in the body – the pea-sized pineal gland, according to Descartes, buried deep in the brain, but flares wherever and whenever the body touches upon itself. Thinking is reflexive because it is enacted through a kind of autotactility. The soul comes into being, not in concentration but in convergence, not in simplification but in complication, not in withdrawal but in excursion. For this reason, the soul has no fixed abode in the body, but rather comes into being in its very coming and going. Serres finds the soul above all on or in the skin, because the skin is where soul and world commingle. The skin is the mutable milieu of 'the changing, shimmering, fleeting soul, the blazing, striated, tinted, streaked, striped, many-coloured, mottled, cloudy, star-studded, bedizened, variegated, torrential, swirling soul'.

This first chapter acquaints us with that most characteristically Serresian device, the variegated list. The listing impulse is stimulated whenever Serres evokes a complex or irregular surface, like the skin of the woman in Bonnard's *La Toilette*, which is 'mottled, striped, grainy, ocellated, dotted, nielloed, speckled, studded'. Rather than homing in on the *mot juste*, Serres allows the series of words for variety themselves to variegate, so that the soul, or centre of gravity of the sequence is to be found not in one particular location in it, but rather in the ramifying array or spraying out of the approximating terms themselves. The fan, as the convening of a distribution, will be one of Serres's favourite devices throughout *The Five Senses*, appearing first of all in the story of the peacock's tail, formed, according to Greek myth, when Hera drapes the skin of the many-eyed Argus on to the body of the bird that will henceforth recall his eyes in its ocelli. Just as Argus's vision is spread across his skin, rather than being located in one punctual locality, so his skin is spread across the tail of the peacock. The fan of the peacock's tail is itself broadcast through the rest of the book, appearing, for example, at the beginning of the chapter on taste, as the 'ocellated fan' of the landscape of the lower Garonne, and the 'streaked, blended, marled, damask, watered-silk, ocellated body' that is answeringly strewn across the tongue, both of which will later be recalled as 'the peacock's tail of taste or the glowing fan of aromas' in 'Visit'. The spreading tale of the peacock's spread tail also encompasses the many appearances of the word 'bouquet' (originally 'a little wood'), which means both a bunch of flowers and a complex perfume. Transposed into the order of odour, the peacock's tail becomes the remarkable arpeggio that Serres performs in Chapter 3 across the array of vegetable smells, from the airiness of rose, lilac and jasmine down to the earthiness of resin, mushroom and truffle. Serres doubles the work of the senses in the way he construes them, through unfolding rather than analysis, in the many radiating repertoires of possibilities to be found throughout his text.

Preferring, and performing the logic of an itinerary that scatters or diffuses across an entire field rather than proceeding directly from one point to another, Serres propagates ideas rather than simply conjoining them. A conspicuous example is furnished by the phrase *nihil in intellectu quod non prius in sensu* – 'there is nothing in the mind that has not first been in the senses'. The phrase, which became the motto of empiricist philosophy, seems to have no one identifiable author; it is often assumed to have been said by Aristotle, though the phrase does not appear in his work, while others assumed that it was first used by Thomas Aquinas and John Locke. The earliest use of the phrase detected so far appears to be from the thirteenth century.[6] Leibniz, the subject of Serres's first book, referring to John Locke's Englished version – '[t]here appear not to be any *Ideas* in the Mind, before the Senses have conveyed any in' – returned the phrase to Latin and added an important supplement – '*Nihil est in intellectu, quod non fuerit in sensu*, excipe: *nisi ipse intellectus*' – 'nothing is in the mind that was not in the senses, except the mind itself'.[7] Appropriately enough, this much-repeated phrase without an original is conjugated into many different forms throughout *The Five Senses*. Its first appearance is in Chapter 1 when, imagining a philosopher who might take seriously the relation between thinking and footwear, Serres wonders 'Would he say that there is nothing in his head that has not first of all been in his feet?' No sooner is the aphorism evoked again in Chapter 3, than it is transposed into the idiom of taste: 'We used to read in our textbooks that our intellect knows nothing that has not first passed through the senses. What we hear, through our tongue, is that there is nothing in sapience that has not first passed through mouth and taste, through sapidity.' Thereafter, the phrase continues to disseminate into different forms: 'There is nothing in our intellect that does not first cross this ground.' 'There is nothing in the senses which does not lead to culture . . . There is nothing in the intellect that you cannot see in the world . . . There is nothing in the mind that has not first of all been set free by the senses . . . There is nothing in conversation which has not first been in this bouquet.' Serres may even find a distant cousin of the phrase in Livy's remark in his history of Rome that 'neque mutari neque novum constitui, nisi aves addixissent', 'nothing was altered, nor any new thing begun, unless the birds assented'.[8]

Slowly, irresistibly, the first chapter of *The Five Senses* brings us to understand that the skin is not to be identified with touch alone, that touch itself is compound, so that one can never hope to arrive at the essential, unsupplemented skin as such: 'We never live naked, in the final analysis, nor ever really clothed, never veiled or unveiled, just like the world. The law always appears at the same time as an ornamental veil. Just as phenomena do. Veils on veils, or one cast-off skin on another, impressed varieties'. This is why Serres introduces the story of the conflict between Argus, signifying the tyranny of panoptical vision, and Hermes, who defeats the vigilant Argus by lulling him to sleep with music, in a moment which Serres represents as the confluence of at least three organs of sense, skin, ear and eye: 'Pan charms Panoptes by overwhelming his conductive flesh. Strident sound makes his eye-covered skin quiver, his muscles tremble, his tears flow, his bony frame vibrate'.

So, for Serres, the senses are not islands, or channels, that keep themselves to themselves. They do not operate on different frequencies, in different parts of the waveband, but are subject to interference – they are even interference itself. The front of the six tapestries in the 1511 series known as *The Lady and the Unicorn* in the Cluny Museum in Paris shows each of the senses emblematized on an oval island, floating amid a sea of small animals and flowers, but Serres reminds us of the complex ravellings to be seen on the underside of the tapestry, where '[t]he five or six senses are entwined and attached, above and below the fabric that they form by weaving or splicing, plaits, balls, joins, planes, loops and bindings, slip or fixed knots'. The senses are what the first chapter distinguishes as 'discrete varieties', fluctuating contusions or spaces of implication, 'high-relief sites of singularity in this complex flat drawing, dense specializations, a mountain, valley or well on the plain'. They are eyes in the storm of the 'continuous variety' of which they form a part and from which they can never be wholly drawn apart. In the fourth chapter, they will be described as 'exchangers'.

SOS

It is perplexing that a writer as prolific as Michel Serres, who has turned his attention to so many topics that have seemed central to the literary and cultural theory of the last thirty years – the body, language, communication, ecology, identity, space, technology – should nevertheless continue to be so little known in the English-speaking world and so hard to place in the landscape of French or Continental philosophy. No doubt the prodigious rate of Serres's output has something to do with this, for it has been hard for translators to keep up with him – even with the long-overdue appearance of this present volume, three-quarters of Serres's work remains untranslated into English – but then, philosophers like Derrida can scarcely be described as tongue-tied either. The variety of topics on which Serres has written must also have made him hard to pin down, though other much more well-known French philosophers have also written on many different topics – Foucault, Derrida, Lyotard, Baudrillard. I think that the principal reason for Serres's indigestibility by the Anglophone academic world has been that he declines the rules of engagement that govern academic theory, which seem to constitute knowledge as an agonistic space of conflict, hostility and critique. For Serres, the university is partly military and partly sacerdotal, constituted as it is both by a stifling urge to enforce conformity and by an institutionalized and institutionalizing belligerence. Serres will have no part of the academic phantasmatics of attack and counter-attack, aggression and defence, suspicion and surveillance. This fundamental aversion to the adversarial nature of academic life and writing may explain the absence of footnotes and explicit engagement with other writers in Serres's work. *The Five Senses* conducts a subtle and sustained conversation with the history of attempts to understand the senses, in philosophy, science and literature, but this conversation is amicably implied rather than declared, immanent rather than outward.

And yet, for all Serres's praise of the arts of peace elsewhere, *The Five Senses* is unusual, and perhaps even unique in his work, for the occasional ferocity of its antagonisms. It is surprising, for example, to find a man who has graced so many academic gatherings with his generosity and courtesy writing as aggressively of academic institutions as he does in *The Five Senses*. The whole of Serres's third chapter can be regarded as an attempt to make a space for the repressed lingual arts of gustatory discernment at the table of the worldwide 'symposium' that he so pitilessly satirizes:

> A colloquium. Its subject: The Sensible. There, a psychoanalyst only ever speaks about his own institution, a representative of the analytic school discourses on the meaning or non-meaning of discourse, the resident Marxist is careful not to step outside class struggle, each one embodies his discipline, all of the named bodies fit neatly into tombs of wood or marble on which the details of their membership are engraved. Into each of these boxes, insert a cassette pre-recorded in the discipline box. The organisers of the conference press play on the control panel and everything is underway in the best possible way in the best of all possible conferences – the different disciplines express themselves. The analysis of the contents is already 'untied' by the separation of the bodies, the totality or set of bodies being the equivalent of the totality or set of languages. As a result, our bodies are taken out of the equation. The sensible is expressed by colloquia or language. Socrates and his friends die as soon as they hold a colloquium on the sensible, long before the *Phaedo*.

The reason for Serres's savage indignation in this book in particular is that this is no simple celebration or affirmation of the senses. Serres begins *The Five Senses* with the narrative of a desperate attempt to save himself from death, at the end of which he remarks 'I understood that evening the meaning of the cry: save our souls'. And it is nothing less than the saving of the soul, precisely through the saving grace of the senses, that Serres urgently undertakes in *The Five Senses*. 'What shall it profit a man, if he shall gain the whole world, and lose his own soul?', Jesus asks (Mark, 8.36). But, for Serres, the loss of the soul and the loss of the world are the same thing, since what we are to call soul is nothing but the mingling of soul and world that is given in sense, in which 'I mix with the world which mixes with me'. To save oneself, one must save the world, must save the possibility of there being an access to and return from the world: 'I give myself to the world which returns me convalescent. I release a low moan into the world, and it gives back its immense peace'.

But from what does the soul need salvation? For Serres, the answer is, overwhelmingly, not sin, but language. Language is our great addiction, the stingy dope to which we are given over, instead of being given to the 'donné', the unstinting givenness of the things of the world. Language, Serres declares in his second chapter, is part of the great, almost irres-istible drift of the hard (the given, the actual, the particular) into the soft (the abstract, the signified, the general). Things become signs, energy becomes information, hardware gives way to software. Serres rejects the constructionist hypothesis that there is nothing of the real that is not altered or filtered through language. Against this, Serres makes his peeled, puny, but wholly impenitent profession of faith: 'Without being able to prove it I believe, like soothsayers and haruspices, and like scientists, that there exists a world independent of men . . . I believe, I know, I cannot demonstrate that this world exists without us'. The stubborn reluctance to abandon this native naivety is another aspect of the indigestible singu-larity of Serres's work and of *The Five Senses* in particular. In an era char-acterized by a widespread consensus within academic theory that language saturates the world of things through and through, Serres stakes on the senses the possibility of a return to the world, which means an escape from 'the abominable verb to be', and the associated trap of linguistic identity, along with 'the hideous, deadly passion for belonging, responsi-ble for just about all the crimes in history'. The life of the 'I' given by language is huddled, pinched and parsimonious; for Serres, by contrast, 'I only really live outside of myself; outside of myself I think, meditate, know; outside of myself I receive what is given, enduringly; I invent out-side of myself. Outside of myself, I exist, as does the world. Outside of my verbose flesh, I am on the side of the world'.

Serres must set his face as flint against anything that stuns, dims or neutralizes the world of sense, or the sense of the world. This antagonism begins in the second chapter, with the attempt to make good his escape from the deafening roar of collective sound, the sound we ourselves make, that encloses us in a circle of autogenic clamour. Endlessly alive and hospitable to all kinds of association, Serres is suspicious of the social when it takes the form of obliterating noise. The topic of noise had been Serres's concern since his books *The Parasite* (1980), and *Genesis* (1983), books which mark a transition in his work from the virtuoso explications of the ideas of individual scientists, writers or philosophers which characterized his writing during the 1970s, to more freestanding and fluidly mobile meditations. The concept of noise that is developed through these works is full of difficulty. Noise means relation, passage, variation, invention, for it arises in the spaces between fixed points and positions. But it also means excess, chaos. Noise is both the matrix of possibility and the cauldron of indifference in which true invention is ground down or swallowed up. The figure of Hermes which, as Serres remarks in *The Five Senses*, he chose as the 'totem, emblem or theorem' for his early work, oscillates between these two accents of noise. At the beginning of *The Five Senses*, Hermes appears as the defeater of Argus, as the ubiquity of sound overcomes and surpasses the geometry of vision: 'Hermes works in a medium that knows no hermetic barriers. Local vision, global listening: more than just ichnography, geometral for both the subject and object, hearing practises ubiquity, the almost divine power of universal reach.' But there is unease with this Hermetic victory, for it is also the beginning of the ascendancy of the word, of communications over things: 'Hermes, the god of passage, becomes a musician, for sound knows no obstacle.' As in all Serres's writing in the 1980s, the 'good' Hermes of connection, crossing, communication and rapid passage is back to back with the bad Hermes of noise, racket and the garrulous clamour of the indifferently self-same: 'Hermes has taken over the world, our technical world exists only through the all-encompassing confusion of hubbub, you will not find anything left on the earth – stone, furrow or small insect – that is not covered by the diluvian din of hullabaloo'.

The most toxic and obliterating form of this background noise is the babble of language. The horror at the dominion of language over the sensory body begins to gather in earnest during the second chapter, which centres on the image of the dying Socrates. Serres's Socrates, famously known as 'the gadfly of the state', is slyly anticipated by the story in Chapter 1 of being stung by an insect:

> One day I was lecturing to an audience in a marquee, as attentive to them as they were to me. Suddenly, a large hornet stung me on the inside of my thigh, a combination of surprise and exquisite pain. Nothing in my

voice or intonation betrayed the accident and I finished my talk. I do not mention this particular memory in order to boast of Spartan courage, but only to indicate that the speaking body, flesh filled with language, has little difficulty in remaining focussed on speech, whatever happens. Words fill our flesh and anæsthetize it.

Serres tacitly follows Nietzsche, who is fascinated and appalled by the figure of a thinker who can carry on affirming the ascendancy of abstract science and knowledge not only in life, but even up to the point of death. Like Nietzsche, who wishes that 'the wisest chatterer of all time . . . had remained silent . . . in the last moments of his life – perhaps he would then belong to a still higher order of minds', Serres too is appalled that Socrates, his body numbed by the hemlock that spreads through his limbs, can carry on speaking, automaton-like – like Poe's M. Valdemar, who is mesmerized to allow him to continue speaking *in articulo mortis*.[9] In the death of Socrates, the stinging words of the gadfly become their own anaesthetic.

As one of the voluble talkers assembled at the dinner party described in Plato's *Symposium* – indeed, he is the only one to stay awake until dawn – the figure of Socrates provides a bridge into 'Tables', the third chapter of *The Five Senses*. It is in this chapter that Serres's assault upon the numbing, robotic effects of language comes to its climax. When contrasted with the Last Supper, Plato's *Symposium* is 'A dinner of statues, a feast of stone', in which only 'dead words are passed about'. The Christian and Platonic dinners mingle with the banquet scene in Mozart's *Don Giovanni*, in which the dead father of Don Juan's lover attends a feast in the form of a statue:

> The Commander threatens, thunders and kills, but cannot hold his own against a drinking Don Juan. A robot with a tongue of stone, iron or wood, it speaks, cannot know thirst. We know how to build machines that talk, we do not know how to build robots that can drink or taste. A tongue can become artificial, intelligence frequently does, but sapience never does. It is in this sense that an automaton differs from homo sapiens: it has the first tongue, but not the second.

This chapter may contain some of the cruellest and bitterest denunciations to be found anywhere in the vast, joyously pacific body of Serres's writing. Serres asserts throughout the claims of the natural body against the violent and deadening artificiality of language. But there is something numbing and monolithic about the very terms of his attack, which wields uncharacteristically rigid dichotomies to enforce its allotments of praise and blame ('Peter, the stable rock, kills John, time.'). Serres complains that in Plato's *Symposium* 'the allegories drink allegorical wine, allegorically', but his own explication is stiff with the same allegorizing impulse to turn things into the effigies of themselves. His argument often depends upon the hypnotizing effects of rhetorical assertion, such as the absolute, but surely egregiously false statement that 'smell and taste differentiate, whereas language, like sight and hearing, integrates' (even as we are also apparently to believe that language, as the tool of analysis, is destructive of the exquisitely variable compounds and confluences to which the senses are attentive). Serres's writing here becomes singular, angular, jagged, programmatic, and nowhere more than in his sneers at those who 'vegetate in the absence of sapience and sagacity, anæsthetized, drugged, frigid', the 'soft and flabby' addicted to 'odourless frozen food for the spongy and obese, hidden under cellophane so that no-one can touch or taste it – watch out for germs! – can only be read and heard, on helpful labels, gigantic posters and thunderous advertisements'. The eloquent, unrelenting jeremiad against language and logic takes a sinister turn in the unlovely assault on ugliness (suggested perhaps by the tradition of the notably ill-favoured Socrates) – 'you should always be wary of ugly old men: their ugliness comes from their acts . . . Have you noticed how ugly thinking people are?' – and the queasy assertion of the 'secret agreement' about beauty: 'A culture stands out for the beauty of its women, the delicacy of its bodies, the distinction of its people's gestures, the grace of their faces, the splendour of its landscapes and the accomplishment of some of its cities'.

Serres never elsewhere comes so close to the belligerent lockjaw he despises than in these passages of impassioned but somnambulistic anathema. We should however remember that the chapter begins with wine and is fuelled with it throughout. Perhaps Serres is deliberately giving himself no choice in this chapter but to enter and enact the murderous inebriation of rage. The end of the chapter multiplies references to various kinds of monster-haunted nightmare – the hideous sensory Gehennas of Breughel and Bosch, the riotous Temptation of Saint Anthony – and so is perhaps best seen as the book's Walpurgisnacht, which, though clamorous with the howling of fiends and demons, nevertheless heralds the arrival of summer on the Mayday morning that dawns after it.

PAGANISM

Certainly, a serener mood and movement seem to be apparent in Chapter 4, which sets off with a celebration of the discontinuously local, the idiomatic, the situated, the pagan. The evocations of complex, irregular landscapes – and seascapes – recall the fluctuating skins and complex surfaces evoked in Chapter 1, though the awareness of the abstract cartographies of the monoculture set in place by language is still as strong as before. But now a new phase of Serres's argument begins to stir. Almost in passing, in a couple of sentences that are easy to skim over, Serres abruptly suggests that our contemporary captivation by language, by the exultant and reiterated annunciation that in the beginning was the word, is at its height precisely because language is beginning to lose its authority. We are in fact 'witnessing the last reverberation of the centuries-old shock which caused us to be born at the same time as language: we are witnessing it in its death-throes'. It is only a hint, a wink, a whisper, which it is easy for the glutted eye to glide over, and which will receive little in the way of amplification or explication until the final chapter, but it begins a decisive new phase, not just in *The Five Senses*, but in the work that will follow it, for, we will come to learn, language is giving way to data, to systems of information, to algorithms. Serres will make it startlingly clear in the final pages of his book that he believes that 'language is dying, my book celebrates the death of the word'. For thousands of years, we have lived in language; but now we are beginning to take up residence in science.

Serres believes that this new dispensation may allow for a healing of the split between experience and cognition which he has decried all the way through *The Five Senses*. In place of the anger and asperity of Chapter 3, the final two chapters of the book look forward optimistically to a form of knowledge that will be able to integrate the local and the general, sense and understanding. 'When the universe widens, the countryside returns. We maintain a better balance between world and place now, the particular and the general', Serres suggests, and this encourages him at least to begin to suppose that 'we are re-establishing an equilibrium between what our predecessors called the empirical and the abstract, the sensible and the intellectual, data and synthesis'.

This unexpected swerve in Serres's text inaugurates the more clement, even redemptive view of the relation between body and knowledge that will be developed in much of his subsequent work. Where *The Five Senses* laments the split between the body and language, as the privileged bearer of thought, his *Variations sur la corps* (1999), will no longer see the senses as the only route to salvation. Instead of turning away from language and the specific forms of cognition it enjoins, back to the infant, infinite subtlety of the sensory body, the body will now be taken as the versatile matrix and model for all knowledge. As in the elated intimations given in the final chapter of *Les cinq sens*, this is a moving, active body, expressing itself in exertion, movement, gesture and dance, rather than in sensibility alone. In this later work, Serres almost seems to accuse himself of that reduction of the body to the vehicle of the senses that he regrets in Condillac. And so, in *Variations du corps*, the *nihil in intellectu* formula is shuffled into yet another form:

> there is nothing in knowledge that has not first been in the whole body, which in gestural metamorphoses, mobile postures, in evolution itself, mimics its surroundings . . . vehicle, to be sure, of the five senses, but with other functions from that of channelling exterior information towards a central processing unit, the body thus retrieves a properly cognitive presence and function.[10]

This will open on to a series of works in which the sacramental hint given in *Les cinq sens* – 'The flesh is made word, the word is made flesh' – will be repeated and elaborated, so that, a quarter of a century after *Les cinq sens*, Serres will be able to represent his earlier work as a presentiment of the new body that he sees in the process of construction through knowledge: 'Once, I wrote *Les cinq sens*, and, just now, the *Variations*, not just to celebrate this birth or advent, but to mark the changes they induced, and above all to understand a body that has recently become translucid and visible, denuded finally of the cuirass of alienation which imprisoned it in the past'.[11]

Whether seeking to retrieve the sensory body that is drowned out by language, as in the first half of *The Five Senses*, or, as in the second half, looking to the condition of the body beyond language, Serres seems, as a writer, pledged and compelled to do this work by words alone, to be caught in a performative self-contradiction of singular piquancy, and yet Serres also seeks ways, through the very forms and rhythms of his writing, to contradict this contradiction. What can be said of the senses themselves must also be said of Serres's book, in which each chapter can be considered both as a quarantining of one particular class of sensations, and also as a weaving together of sensory impressions. Each chapter is a part of the whole and yet also holographically includes the whole in itself. Perhaps the same thing may even be said of *The Five Senses* as a whole, in relation to the corpus of Serres's work.

His book repeatedly finds in its objects of attention figures for its own shape and emergence. The veils, knots, boxes, fans, bouquets and labyrinths that Serres employs to explicate the workings of the senses serve just as aptly as figures for the relation of his own writing to its subject and to itself. Thus the book builds of words its own thinking body. There is, for example, the vast, intricately-chambered sentence that comes at the end of the discussion of forms of interiority and enclosure in Chapter 2. Beginning 'The social box, complex, constructed, hardware and software, often closed, sometimes open, constant and variable', the sentence evokes dizzying dozens of levels of enclosure and ever smaller noise-boxes, each one both arresting and transmitting sound, all the way to the final inwardness of 'the self-governing body-box' and 'the central, initially peripheral box, whose complicated labyrinth of synapses and axons organizes the reception of signals'. The very form of the sentence, with its grammatical encapsulations making out a simultaneous unfolding of and enfolding in itself, is a precise model of its subject.

As such, it seems a double of the one-to-one maps that are evoked through *The Five Senses*, like the map of her own skin drawn by the self-adorning woman of Chapter 1, of which Serres remarks 'Who has not dreamed that map such as this might be drawn identical to the world itself, measure for measure, the impossible dream of an ultrafine film following all the fractal details of the landscape?' In a similar way, the analogy between the space of the earth and the writing of texts is affirmed and reaffirmed through Chapter 4 by the rhymes between page, *pagus* and *paysage*.

> He composed it *pagus* by *pagus*. Now this same Latin word, from the old agrarian language, as well as the verb *pango*, dictate or give us 'page' – the one that I am ploughing with my style in regular furrows this morning, a small plot where the writer's existence settles, puts down its roots and becomes established, where he sings of it.

Serres represents his own writing as a geography, an earth-writing, a writing that mimics the autography of the earth, for, though the name 'geographer' is given to one who puts the earth into writing, 'it would be better to call geography the writing of the earth about itself. For things – resistant, hard, sharp, elastic, loose – mark, hollow each other out and wear each other away. Our exceptional style makes use of this general property.' This is surely the ultimate consensus of a book that teems with every kind of mixed body – the intermingling of subject and substance, of the intelligible and the sensible, of book, body and world.

Since the appearance of *The Five Senses*, the force and prerogative of the linguistic model have begun to wane in the Anglophone academy. One of the symptoms and vehicles of this waning has been the extraordinarily energetic revival of interest in the history, constitution and future prospects of the senses. Hitherto, readers and writers in English have not been in a position to take full account of Michel Serres's remarkable contribution to this question. Perhaps the long delay in the appearance of *The Five Senses* will be propitious, and in any case Serres has never set much store by orderly chronology. Now, with the appearance of this remarkable springy, sinuous translation, readers of English will have the opportunity not only to appreciate the richness of the conversation Serres has continued to conduct with himself over three decades on the subject of the senses but also to bring the ardour and audacity of Serres's thought into communication with our own.

1
Veils

BIRTH – TATTOOS – CANVAS, VEIL, SKIN – HERMES AND THE PEACOCK – SUBTLE –
VARIATION – VAIR – MISTS – COMMON SENSE – MIXTURE, UNVEILING

BIRTH

Fire is dangerous on a ship, it drives you out. It burns, stings, bites, crackles, stinks, dazzles, and quickly springs up everywhere, incandescent, to remain in control. A damaged hull is less perilous; damaged vessels have been known to return to port, full of sea water up to their deadworks. Ships are made to love water, inside or out, but they abhor fire, especially when their holds are full of torpedoes and shells. A good sailor has to be a reasonable fireman.

Fire training demands more of the sailor and is harsher and more uncompromising than anything that he needs to learn as a seaman. I can still remember several torturous exercises which teach not only a certain relationship to the senses, but also how to live or survive. We were made to climb down dark, vertical wells, descending endless ladders and inching along damp crawlways, to low underground rooms in which a sheet of oil would be burning. We had to stay there for a long time, lying beneath the acrid smoke, our noses touching the ground, completely still so as not to disturb the thick cloud hanging over us. We had to leave slowly and deliberately when our name was called so as not to choke our neighbour with an ill-considered gesture that would have brought the smoke eddies lower.

The breathable space lies in a thin layer at ground level and remains stable for quite a long period. Knowing how to hold your breath, to estimate the distance to the heart of the blaze or to the point beyond which one is in mortal danger; how to estimate the time remaining, to walk, to move in the right direction, blind, to try not to yield to the universal god of panic, to proceed cautiously towards the desperately desired opening; these are things I know about the body. This is no fable. No-one sees dancing shadows on the walls of the cave when a fire is burning inside.

THE FIVE SENSES

Smoke stings your eyes, it fills the whole space, chokes you. Blinded, you have to lie down. You can only grope your way out. Touch is the last remaining means of guiding yourself.

But this knowledge was academic until the day of genuine wrath arrived without warning, one winter's day at sea. The fire was rumbling, a terrifying sound like thunder. In a moment all the bulkheads were closed. I admired those who rushed without thinking into the manholes, down the ladders. I heard a lot of noise and remember nothing.

All of a sudden I am alone. What has happened? In the closed compartment the unbearable heat makes me feel like fainting. I have to get out. The door, behind, is immovably blocked, panels and levers locked watertight, firmly fastened from the other side. I choke under the thick smoke, lying on the moving floor, shaken by the movement of the waves. Then all that remains is a porthole. Get up without breathing, quickly try to unscrew the rusty flanges preventing its opening. They resist, they have not been used much, once or twice probably since the vessel was launched. They do not yield. I lie down again at ground level to get my breath. The weather conditions are worsening, as if the sea were becoming choppier. I get up again, holding my breath, trying to undo the screws that seem slowly to be yielding. Three or four times, I do not recall, I lie down again; as many times, jaws clenched, muscles locked, I work on, with the porthole closed. Suddenly it opens.

Light, and particularly air, rushes in, churning the smoke, which becomes even more choking. I quickly stick my head out through the open hole. Horrible weather, the brutal cold takes hold. I cannot open my eyes in the fury of the icy spray; my ears, hurt as they passed through, feel as though they are being ripped off; suddenly my body curls up, demanding to remain motionless in its warm retreat. I pull my head back inside, but choke, and can now hear small explosions. The fire must have reached the munitions store; I have to get out as soon as possible. I push my head through, then one arm, not yet as far as my shoulder, only my hand and wrist. The angle of my elbow is a problem in the small space between my neck and the rim of brass around the porthole. I cannot get out, I have to get out. Everything is burning and my head is frozen.

I remain there, motionless, vibrating, pinioned, gesticulating within the confines of the fixed neckpiece, long enough for me to think, no, for my body to learn once and for all to say 'I' in the truest sense of the word.

In truth, with no possibility of being wrong. No mistake about it, since my life quite simply depended on this dark, slow, blinding meditation.

I am inside, burnt to a crisp with only my frozen, shivering, blinded head outside. I am inside, ejected and excluded, and my head, arm and left shoulder are outside in the howling storm. Inside, amidst the insane fire which pushes me outwards, my head and second shoulder, half out, caught in an agonizing neckpiece, emerge, at the mercy of the storm. I am neither saved, nor even outside. I am still imprisoned, completely on one side of the window. The round hoop of brass open in the flank of the burning vessel is not as big as the compressed circle of my thorax. Still inside, even though both shoulders are out in the winter weather. The porthole compresses my chest to the limit – any further and it would be crushed. So I am going to die. I cannot get a foothold anywhere. Behind, in the burning hell in which I am still trapped, my arms are of no use, pressed against my body. I am a wisp of straw caught in a hole, unable to go forward, with no hope of going backwards, I will choke to death. Is it worse to breathe in the smoke, or the icy blast, or stay in the rusty iron collar, I can't possibly decide.

Then a big wave, coming suddenly from the side, violently jolts the neckpiece towards my suspended ribs. God be praised, I am out. I breathe the cold air and almost faint. To my horror, the sea, still more relentlessly, hammers randomly at the bottom of the boat which tilts over on to the other side and I am inside again, rammed again into the iron circle up to my chest. It felt as though the hull were passing over piles of stones. The shock on one side freed me; a shock from the other side imprisoned me again.

I was inside, I was outside.

Who was this 'I'?

It is something everyone knows, unemotionally and as a matter of fact. You only have to pass through a small opening, a blocked corridor, to swing over a handrail or on a balcony high enough to provoke vertigo, for the body to become alert. The body knows by itself how to say I. It knows to what extent I am on this side of the bar, and when I am outside. It judges deviations from normal balance, immediately regulates them and knows just how far to go, or not go. Cœnesthesia says I by itself. It knows that I am inside, it knows when I am freeing myself. This internal sense proclaims, calls, announces, sometimes howls the I like a wounded animal. This common sense apportions the body better than anything else in the whole world.

THE FIVE SENSES

If I slide a leg through, I am still inside, while my leg, thigh and knee are outside. They become almost black. My pelvis goes through, my genitals, buttocks and navel are most certainly outside but I remain inside. I know what it is to be a man without legs; I know for a moment what phantom limbs feel like. At a precise moment, the very moment when the totality of the divided body shouts *ego* in a general toppling movement, I slide out and can drag through the remainder of my body, pull through the pieces that have remained inside, yes, the scattered pieces that have suddenly been blackened in the violent overturning of the iceberg.

The random jolting of the vessel as it heaves to throw the I to the left and right of the window of hope. I dwell inside, I dwell outside; the I inside the boat finds itself outside, in the icy gusts of wind. The movement of the waves pushes or pulls the thorax a few millimetres in either direction, a tiny distance. My body is aware of this deviation; it is able to appreciate the movements around it. I am delivered or debarred, breathing or asphyxiated, burning from the fire inside or stripped bare by the biting wind, dead or alive. I go under or I exist. There is an almost identifiable point which, in the spatial experience of passing from inside to out, is proclaimed by the whole body. The I as a whole leaps towards this localized point and moves decisively from one half of the body to the other when the point slides, in contact with the separating wall, from its internal to its external surface.

Since my near shipwreck I have become accustomed to calling this point the soul. The soul resides at the point where the I is decided.

We are all endowed with a soul, from that first moment of passage when we risked and saved our existence.

I understood that evening the meaning of the cry: save our souls. Saving this point is enough. I found myself outside, in the horrifying cold, when the point passed the threshold of the constraining collar. I was still inside until that moment. Descartes is right to say that the soul touches the body at a particular point, but he was wrong to locate it in the pineal gland. It hovers around the region of the solar plexus. From there it illuminates or obscures the body, in bursts of light or dark, making it translucid or epiphanic, transmuting it into a black body. It is somewhere in that area for everyone, according to the dictates of each individual's body. We all retain it, marked and definitive, where it was fixed on the day we were born. More often than not, it is forgotten and left in the shadows of internal meaning, until the day when the sudden fury of nature causes us to be born a second time, through chance, pain, anguish or luck. It is not such a bad thing, *pace* Descartes, that on that youthful day, piloting a ship, we were to discover that a pilot says I for his whole vessel, from the depths of the keel to the tip of the mast, and from the quarter to the boom, and that the soul of his body descends into the soul of the boat, towards the central turbines, to the heart of the quickworks. To free yourself from that vessel, you have to search for your soul in the hold, where the fire is at its most dangerous – one perilous day.

TATTOOS

The soul inhabits a quasi-point where the I is determined.

Gymnasts train their soul, so as to move or wrap themselves around it.

Athletes do not have one, they run or throw; but jumpers do, and hurl themselves over the bar pole and beyond; they gently curl their bodies around the place where it projects itself forward. The difference between athletics and gymnastics, with the exception of the long jump, lies in the practice of the soul. The fixed bar, somersault, rings, floor work, trampoline and diving are useful as exercises in experimental metaphysics, like the passage through the small porthole, where the body goes searching for its soul, where both play, like lovers, at losing and finding each other, sometimes leaving each other, then coming together again, in risk and pleasure. In certain collective games, players have lost their souls because they entrusted them to a common object, the ball: they organize themselves, spread themselves out, wrap themselves around it, collectively. The metaphysical exercise is transformed here into a manoeuvre in applied sociology.

Lose your soul in order to save it; give it away in order to regain it.

The soul, not quite a point, reveals itself through volume, with precision in a ship, in the space traced by unusual displacements. Can we find it superficially now? A more difficult study.

I am cutting my nails.

Where is the subject determined? As a left-hander, I take the tool in my left hand and place the open blades at the tip of my right index finger. I place myself in the handles of the scissors. The I is now situated there and not at the top of the right finger. My nail: awkwardly placed along the steel blade; my hand: agile and clever in managing the cutting. The left-hand subject works on the right-finger object. The left hand has something of the nature of the self, bathed in subjectivity, the right finger is the world. If the scissors change hands, everything changes or nothing changes. The I stays in the vicinity of my left index finger, the nail of which knowingly and shamelessly caresses the sharp blade, just touching it. The handle of the tool grasped by the right hand is abandoned by me. An external motor drives the machine and my proffered index finger determines the exact limits of the cut to be made. On the one hand, I am cutting a nail, on the other, my nail is cut. The presentation of the finger to the blade, its flexibility or rigidity at the moment of cutting, the precision of the process, are sufficient for the external observer to determine the state of the soul, the place where it is now in a state of equilibrium, as it were. The soul of the left-hander is on his left side, on his right side he is a dark body, a hybrid when forced to write with his right hand.

But that changes and varies. In the case of toenails, the reversal does not take place. So far away, it is still the body, or the world. So far away, the soul is absent. No toe touches the blade the way my left-hand middle finger does. That's enough about tools.

I touch one of my lips with my middle finger. Consciousness resides in this contact. I begin to examine it. It is often hidden in a fold of tissue, lip against lip, tongue against palate, teeth touching teeth, closed eyelids, contracted sphincters, a hand clenched into a fist, fingers pressed against each other, the back of one thigh crossed over the front of the other, or one foot resting on the other. I wager that the small, monstrous homunculus, each part of which is proportional to the magnitude of the sensations it feels, increases in size and swells at these automorphic points, when the skin tissue folds in on itself. Skin on skin becomes conscious, as does skin on mucus membrane and mucus membrane on itself. Without this folding, without the contact of the self on itself, there would truly be no internal sense, no body properly speaking, cœnesthesia even less so, no real image of the body; we would live without consciousness; slippery smooth and on the point of fading away. Klein bottles are a model of identity. We are the bearers of skewed, not quite flat, unreplicated surfaces, deserts over which consciousness passes fleetingly, leaving no memory. Consciousness belongs to those singular moments when the body is tangential to itself.

I touch my lips, which are already conscious of themselves, with my finger. I can then kiss my finger and, what amounts to almost the same thing, touch my lips with it. The I vibrates alternately on both sides of the contact, and all of a sudden presents its other face to the world, or, suddenly passing over the immediate vicinity, leaves behind nothing but an object. In the local gesture of calling for silence, the body plays ball with the soul. Those who do not know where their soul is to be found touch their mouths, and they do not find it there. The mouth touching itself creates its soul and contrives to pass it on to the hand which, clenching itself involuntarily, forms its own faint soul and then can pass it on, when it wishes, to the mouth, which already has it. Pure chance, each time.

The body cannot play ball, at all times or in all places. There are zones where this contingency does not come into play. I touch my shoulder with my hand. In relation to my hand or mouth my shoulder remains an object in the world. It needs a natural object, a rock, tree trunk or waterfall in order to become a subject again. The shoulder has no soul, save in relation to what takes place outside the body. Now determine where the soul is, by putting your elbows on your knees, by placing one part of your body on another.

There is no end to it, the only limit is your own suppleness.

Metaphysics begins with, and is conditioned by, gymnastics.

Let us now draw or paint. Isolate, if you can, the chance encounters of corners or folds, the small secret zones in which the soul, to all intents and purposes, still resides. Then isolate as well, if possible, the unstable zones which are able to play at souls with one another as if playing ball. Surround also the balls or blocks, which only become subjects in the presence of objects, the dense or compact regions which always remain objects or black, soulless deserts, in themselves, or in relation to those zones which turn them into objects. Drawing rarely defines compact zones. These explode, burst forth and escape along narrow corridors, form passes and chimneys, pathways, passages, flames, zigzags and labyrinths. Observe on the surface of the skin, the changing, shimmering, fleeting soul, the blazing, striated, tinted, streaked, striped, many-coloured, mottled, cloudy, star-studded, bedizened, variegated, torrential, swirling soul. A wild idea, the first after consciousness, would be to trace delicately and colour in these zones and passages, as in a map.

Tattooing: my white, constantly present soul blazes up and is diffused in the unstable reds which exchange with other reds; deserts lacking a soul are black, and fields where the ochre, mauve, cold blue, orange and turquoise soul very occasionally settles are green . . . This is what our complex and somewhat frightening identity card looks like. Everyone has their own original card, like their thumbprint or dental record, no map resembles another, each one changes through time. I have made so much progress since my sad youth and bear on my skin the tracks and paths traced by the women who have helped me in the search for my scattered soul.

Those who need to see in order to know or believe, draw and paint and fix the lake of changing, ocellated skin and make the purely tactile visible by means of colours and shapes. But every epidermis would require a different tattoo; it would have to evolve with time: each face requires an original tactile mask. Historiated skin carries and displays a particular history. It is visible: wear and tear, scars from wounds, calluses, wrinkles and furrows of former hopes, blotches, pimples, eczema, psoriasis, birth-marks. Memory is inscribed there, why look elsewhere for it? And it is invisible: the fluctuating traces of caresses, memories of silk, wool, velvet, furs, tiny grains of rock, rough bark, scratchy surfaces, ice crystals, flames, the timidity of a subtle touch, the audacity of aggressive contact. An abstract drawing or painting would be the counterpart of the faithful and honest tattoo in which the sense impressions are expressed; if the picture imitates readymade illustrations, icons or letters, everything is reduced to a mere reflection of the social. The skin becomes a standard bearer, whereas it is in fact imprinted.

The beginnings of a drawing changing amidst caresses: naked, stretched out, curled up at my side, tiger, cougar, armadillo, you seek to guess the secrets of my historiated, liquid, shimmering skin. Our soul expands, we are not monochromatic.

The global soul: a small, deep place, not far from the region of the emotions. The local, storm-prone, surface soul: a viscous lake, ready to flare up, on which the multiple, rainbow-coloured, slowly-changing light plays. A sharp point and peacock feathers, the soul pricks us and struts about.

It is there that history truly begins. How can two such complicated labyrinths meet, be superimposed and complement each other? Ariadne is lost in Theseus' labyrinth, Theseus is lost in the avenues and roundabouts on Ariadne's mountain. One would have to imagine the relationship between two species, genres or kingdoms, tiger and peacock, zebra and jaguar, ladybird and poppy, centipede and chalcedony, a chameleon on marble. Miracles happen, ligers and tigons, although there are not many of them, and they are rarely long-lived. Otherwise, Ariadne has to turn white, and Theseus to wind back onto his distaff all the threads that entangle and divide up her bedizened body. Failing a miracle, our surface soul is an obstacle to our amorous activities. It is as if we were wearing a tattooed breastplate, unless we lay it down, melt the map of pathways and crossroads, and redeploy our soul or make it burn with a different light, so that the flames mingle.

When the soul comes to an organ, that organ becomes conscious and the soul is lost. If my finger touches my lip and says I, my mouth becomes an object, but in reality it is my finger that is lost. As soon as the soul settles on it, it takes over. When I lift these bricks, stones, concrete blocks, I exist entirely in my hands and arms and my soul in its density is at home there but, at the same time, my hand is lost in the grainy body of the pebbles. The object is reduced to a black body and the soul to a white void. The soul, as transparent as an evanescent angel, whitens the places where it alights; the skin, imprinted elsewhere with the varied colours of history, is brighter, lighter and correspondingly whiter at these points, because it has become alive. Behold: the skin of his face was shining. Behold: he was transfigured before them, as white as snow. The soul, in patches, shapes the tattoo, the set of crossed lines drawing a force-field: the space occupied by the formidable pressure of the soul in its efforts to erase gently the shadows of the body, and the major entrenchments of the body to resist this effort. On the skin, soul and object are neighbours. They advance, win or lose their places, a long, hazy mingling of the I and the black body, resulting from time to time in a peacock's tail of mingled colours. The struggle ends with the alabaster-white, mystical body. I am no longer anything. Or with the cybernetic body, a black box, another total nothingness.

The ecstatic transfiguration, the loss of the body into the soul, removes the tattoo. The totally flayed man, the perfect automaton, also replaces the body with a total black box. Thus the mingled body finds itself in the middle, between heaven and hell: in everyday space.

All dualism does is reveal a ghost facing a skeleton. All real bodies shimmer like watered silk. They are hazy surfaces, mixtures of body and soul. It seems simple, although perverse and laughable, to tell of the loves of a larva and an automaton, or of a phantom and a black box, but the loves of the composite and the many-hued are consummated wordlessly.

I have only described tattooing in order to show the traces of the soul and those of the world. We always believe that we know something better when we have seen it, or that we can explain better by deploying shapes and displaying colours. To be sure, seen and visible tattoos, imprinted with a hot needle, have their origin in this gaudy thing that is the soul, a complex labyrinth of sense striving alternately towards the internal and external, and vibrating at the limits of each. But I have drawn, coloured or painted tattoos only in order to reveal the tangible: an abstract picture of the sense of touch. Abstract insofar as it abandons the visible in order to rejoin the tactile. The shimmering, vaguely fluid and, as it were, elastic identity card, obeys the tender map of touch.[1] It favours topology and geography over geometry. Neglecting point of view and representation, it favours mountains, straits, footpaths, Klein bottles, chance borders that are formed through the contingencies of contact. It turns the skin into a generalized thumb. The skin can explore proximities, limits, adhesions, balls and knots, coasts or capes, lakes, promontories and folds. The map on the epidermis most certainly expresses more than just touch, it plunges deeply into the internal sense, but it begins with the sense of touch. Thus the visible tells more than just the visible. There is no word corresponding to touch to designate the untouchable or intangible, as there is for the invisible which is present in, or absent from what is seen, complementary to it, although abstracted from it, and incarnated in its flesh. However, the sense of touch is keen, sensitive and subtle[2]. The soul is intact, in that sense. The intact soul entrances touch just as the topological invisible haunts and illuminates the experiential visible, from within. In the lavish luxury of tactile sensation, I feel as though I am touching a new abstract, at least on two sides, one of mixture and coloured patterns, and the other being one where the geometer abandons his measuring-stick to assess individual shapes, ridges and corridors.

Many philosophies refer to sight; few to hearing; fewer still place their trust in the tactile, or olfactory. Abstraction divides up the sentient body, eliminates taste, smell and touch, retains only sight and hearing, intuition and understanding. To abstract means to tear the body to pieces rather than merely to leave it behind: analysis.

I retreat in the face of difficulty by erecting a palace of abstractions. I baulk at obstacles, just as many fear the other and his skin. Just as many are afraid of their senses and reduce to nothing, to the *tabula rasa* of the inedible, the sumptuous, virtual, folded peacock's tail of taste. Empiricism plunges one into a many-splendoured reality that requires great patience and intense powers of abstraction. What is left to hope for after the events of birth and self-recognition have taken place?

Body and soul are not separate but blend inextricably, even on the skin. Thus two mingled bodies do not form a separate subject and object.

I caress your skin, I kiss your mouth. Who, I? Who, you? When I touch my hand with my lips, I feel the soul like a ball passing from one side to the other of the point of contact, the soul quickens when faced with such unpredictability. Perhaps I know who I am when thus playing my soul like a musical instrument, multiplying the fine threads of self-contact above which the soul flies in every direction. I embrace you. Pitiful, cruel and hurried lovers that we are, we had only ever learned duelling, dualism and perversity. I embrace you. No, my soul does not fly around the fine thread that we both wind securely around the contact. No, it is neither my soul, nor yours. No, it is not so simple or cruel. No, I do not objectify, freeze, ensnare, or rape you, or treat you as that tedious old marquis would have done. And I do not expect you to do as I do. For that you would have to become a ghost or an automaton. For that you would have to become a larva or a lemur, and I to change into a black box. In reality, this limit case can occur through illness or tiredness. In all other cases, I almost always set a brown corridor against your opaline zone, or a light region on a violet area. All depends on time, place and circumstance. It is the beginning of patience. And infinite exploration. We feel our way in the thicket of circumstances like a congenitally blind man deciphering Braille, as though we were choosing colours of wool in the night. Anxiety and attention teeter, new and refined. Black on black, clear on confused, dark on a blend of colours, a rainbow on the whole spectrum of colours, images necessary for those without a sense of touch, a mountain pass on a plain, a mountain on a valley, a promontory on a gulf or strait – figures. The pallid soul flees and hides, withdraws, dons masks and appearances, makes itself visible from afar and takes refuge, leaves in its wake a cloud of ink or a wave of perfume, constructs glades, basins and marble pathways; becomes bold, advances, attacks gently, smiles and reveals itself again, waits, recognizes the territory, imposes itself, negates itself, shouts or falls silent, murmurs at length, and suddenly, in a corner of the wood, along the corridor, against the chimney, in the roundness of a curve or at the point of a zigzag, white Ariadne appears unexpectedly on the path of the inde-cipherable labyrinth: your radiant white soul, transfigured on the mountain and enveloped in immaculate dawn.

Death produces the same flat engram on corpses.

The variety of colours, forms and tones, of folds, flounces, furrows, con-tacts, mountains, passes, and peneplains, the peculiar topological variety of the skin is most economically described as a developing, amorphous, composite mixture of body and soul. Every individual place, even the most ordinary, creates an original combination of them. One could say that when these mixtures come into contact, they analyse each other or give rise, from their composition, to simple elements. As if, suddenly, one pole attracted the soul, and the other took charge of the object. In a free state, they are combinations, hand and forehead, elbow and thigh. In a state of contact or contingency, they react in relation to each other and give rise to those simplicities that we commonly think about in terms of zero and one, soul and body, subject and object. These simple entities are rarely seen in nature, one only ever encounters the indefinite spectrum of their compounds, one only knows simple entities as admixtures and through their reactions to one another.

No-one has witnessed the great battle of simple entities. We only ever experience mixtures, we encounter only meetings. The pure body, the black body or the candid soul, is more than improbable. Alabaster and jet are miracles.

I embrace you: here and now our contingency creates nuance on nuance, mixture on mixture. Brown on grey, or purple on gold. One card on another, or cards on the table. Two alloys change in composition, the cards are shuffled, jumbled, redistributed. A storm bursts over both fields. The lines of force, contours, slopes and valleys are redesigned. The warps change weft. When yellow is mixed with blue, the result is green. The titles of mixtures change, as do the titles of alliances. I embrace you as Harlequin, I leave you as Pierrot; you touch me as duchess and you withdraw as marchioness. Harlequin of this zone and marchioness of that place. Or, I embrace you as brass and leave you as bronze, you embrace me as argentan, you leave me as vermeil. Like the philosopher's stone which transforms alloys and transmutes titles. Nothing is more abstract, learned or profound than this immediate meditation on combinations, nor more subtle or difficult to understand than this local, complex recasting, than this complete conversion or these unstable reversals. No doubt we have never said anything about change, or transformation in general, which was not entirely caught up in our contingency. We cannot think about change except in terms of mixtures; if we try to think about it in terms of simple entities, we merely arrive at miracles, leaps, mutations, resurrections and even transubstantiation. This is a change through titles, alloys, fabrics and cards, this is a change through drawings and reactions, one watered silk on another, hybridity.

One day some barbarian will be able to tell us what prodigious chemistry is at work and an under-barbarian will try to bottle it. Horror of horrors, we shall see these tattoos again, but this time reproduced artificially. Yes, singularity is in motion there, its Brownian movement produces variations in colouring, our emotion leaves its precise signature. We were so moved that we changed colour, a peacock's tail on a rainbow, like spectra suddenly becoming unstable. You embrace me mottled, I leave you shimmering like watered silk; I embrace you as a network, you leave me as a bundle. We caress each other along our contour lines, we leave each other with various knots, in embraces that have changed shape.

If you want to save yourself, take risks. If you want to save your soul, do not hesitate, here and now, to entrust it to the variable storm. An inconstant aurora borealis bursts forth in the night. It spreads, blazing or bleeding, like those footlights that never stop blinking, whether they are switched on or off. It either passes or doesn't, but flows elsewhere in a rainbow-coloured stream. You will not change if you do not yield to these inconstancies and deviations. More importantly, you will not know.

In these lavishly renewed undulations, fluctuations and versatile caprices brought about by countless changes of skin and direction, there will sometimes be sudden simplifications, and saturation or plenitude: all colours of every tone will come together as white; all possible lines, passing in all directions, will form a surface; the knot will become a point. In this place summation will occur – totalization. Carte blanche, smooth fabric, dawn light. On this spot, the intense meditation culminates in an apex, in the blinding apparition of the singular brought about by the saturation of presence, the transfiguration of the many-hued tattoo into a pure soul. The I is rarely revealed outside of these circumstances. I am, I exist in this mixed contingency that changes again and again through the agency of the storm that is the other, through the possibility of his or her existence. We throw each other off balance, we are at risk.

At the saturated summit of the mixture, the ecstasy of existence is a summation made possible by the contingency of the other. My contingency makes possible the same encounter for her. A white summation of all colours, a starry centre of threads.

At the empty and null bottom of this same mixture, death, white also by subtraction or abstraction, is flat.

Without the experience of mingled bodies, without these tangible riots of colour and mitigated multiplicities, we had long failed to distinguish life from death. The misunderstanding wherein death resembles glory, where life is only happy in the tomb, had turned metaphysics into a preparation for murder.

When in fact it is an art of love.

CANVAS, VEIL, SKIN

In the 1890s, Pierre Bonnard painted a bathrobe; he painted a canvas in which a bathrobe is depicted, and a woman amidst leaves.

The brown-haired woman, seen from behind, half turning to the right, as if she were hiding, is wrapped in a very long, voluminous piece of yellowish-orange fabric entirely covering her standing figure, from the nape of her neck to her feet. All that can be glimpsed are her nose, the tip of one ear, one closed eye, her forehead, hair and a sort of chignon. The bathrobe veils the woman, the fabric veils the canvas. Studded with moons and half-moons, grained with crescents darker than itself, the material vibrates with interspersed light and dark areas. The half-moons, set at different angles, but at regular intervals, create a monotonous effect. An effect of patterning rather than vibration has been sought. The impression of printed tissue is more important than the optical effect: the eye is cheated. A night dress, an eyelid lowered, as if in sleep, the light of moons.

The loosish garment occupies the space. The canvas, vertical like a Chinese scroll, rises along the length of the body. Foliage fills the background, impinging ever so slightly on the material, so that ultimately the picture is reduced to the fabric. Why did Bonnard not paint directly on to the bathrobe, why did he not turn the bathrobe into a canvas, paint its material instead of the canvas? Why does he not now paint on fabric but on another surface?

If you removed the leaves and the bathrobe, would you touch the skin of the brown-haired woman or the canvas of the picture? Pierre Bonnard is not so much appealing to sight as to touch, the feeling beneath the fingers of films and fine layers, foliage, material, canvas, surface, defoliation, undressing, refined unveilings, thin caressing curtains. His immensely tactful and tactile art does not turn the skin into a vulgar object to be seen, but rather into the feeling subject, a subject always active beneath the surface. The canvas is covered in canvases, veils pile up and veil only other veils, the leaves in the foliage overlap each other. Leaves lying beneath the pages. As you are reading, you are no doubt focussing your gaze on these pages on which I am writing about Bonnard. Remove the sheets, turn the pages. Behind each one, still another, covered likewise with monotonous markings. In the end the eye encounters nothing more than that. All that remains is to touch the delicate film of the printed sheet, the bearer of meaning; the sheet, page, material-fabric, skin, the canvas itself of Bonnard's woman. I leaf through the layers of the bathrobe.

It covers the skin, accumulating layer upon layer.

The Child with the Bucket, painted five years later, is part of a screen, the third of its four leaves. The child glimpsed on one leaf is playing on the loose fabric of one of the panels which are set at angles to one another, with the aim of concealment. A shelter in which to undress, upright so that one can throw one's bathrobe over it, a canvas stretched like a garment away from the skin, a new veil.

Dressed in a double-breasted, printed smock, the child floats on the material of the screen, on Bonnard's canvas, in the fabric of his dress or envelope, and is veiled by as many skins. A round figure crouching on the sand, he appears to be filling his bucket under a round, leafy, orange tree: the small tree in a pot, a small human near the bucket, both originating in sand or earth, both surrounded by those subtle variegations that cover them, overlapping leaves, lattice-patterned material. Bonnard's canvas is printed with canvases and expresses veils.

What wind will whip up the smock, make the foliage quiver, make the screen shudder, what wind on your skin?

Thirty-five years later, the same Bonnard produced a *Nude in the Mirror*, also called *The Toilette*. A naked woman, in high-heeled shoes three-quarters turned towards the mirror, is looking at herself in it. We do not see her image face on.

Two mirrors and nudity, the hidden front view or stolen image, the second mirror as empty as the first, everything impels us to feel the prestige of the visual, to discourse yet again on eroticism and representation. No.

She is naked, look at her skin: covered in tattoos – mottled, striped, grainy, ocellated, dotted, nielloed, speckled, studded – even more than the old bathrobe, and layered with less monotonous patches, like watered silk. Her epidermis is painted in an extremely odd fashion. She has taken off her dressing gown and the pattern of the material appears to have remained on her skin. But the half-moons of the bathrobe are distributed over it in a regular, mechanical, reproducible fashion; live impressions are layered randomly and inimitably on the cutaneous garment. The model is recognizable. The last thin skin, the painted one, is not printed smoothly, homogeneously or monotonously, it spreads and shines in a chaos of colours, forms and tones. No other woman has the specific skin of that woman. You have recognized her.

In the mixture of shades, in the chaos of marks and strokes, you recognize the *Belle Noiseuse* whom Balzac thought unimaginable: in fact, she has no reflection in the mirror and cannot be represented. Here the body rises above disorder, here Aphrodite rises above the waves, even more complex in her skin than the nautical sound of waves breaking. No, the old painter of the *Unknown Masterpiece*[3] was not going mad, but was anticipating more than a century of painting. Balzac was dreaming of Bonnard, sight projecting touch, reason and order musing on the chaos of singularity.

Now it could be said that the frontal reflection in the half-seen mirror, or the image of the woman in the mirror, is reduced to a sort of curtain, a bathroom hanging, itself tattooed: ocellated, shimmering, mottled, studded and layered with colours and tones. Mixture for mixture and chaos for chaos, the skin's image is the curtain, its reflection a canvas and its phantom a sheet.

But the canvas as a whole – the window, wall, plate, table, fruit, draperies, scattered towels – could serve as a screen, poster, leaf or veil: a patterned curtain, a tattoo, like the skin.

The woman with the lavishly decorated body, facing the richly decorated reflection of the curtain, is holding in her hand a shawl: is it a piece of curtain, a fragment of canvas, a bit of her skin? It is a rag seamlessly joined to the scrap of material stuck to her.

Pierre Bonnard's *Nude in the Mirror* is underpinned by the equivalence or equation of canvas, veils and skin. Nudity is covered with tattoos, the skin is printed, impressed. The nude is pulling on her bathrobe or the child his smock, plain or brightly coloured printed fabrics which express inaccurately, rigidly or conventionally our individual impressions. The painter places marks on the canvas, supposedly in order to express his impressions: he tattoos it and reveals his fragile, private and chaotic skin.

This one exhibits skin, that one canvases, another luxurious veils.

The naked woman in the mirror is standing at her washstand like the artist at his palette and she often has as many pots at her disposal: tubes, bottles, brushes, sprays, soaps and makeup, nail polish and creams, lotions, mascara, the whole cosmetic apparatus. She washes, adorns and paints herself. She puts foundation on her face and then the surface tone, just as the painter prepares his canvas. The skin is identical to the canvas, just as the canvas above was identical to skin. The model does to herself what the artist does with her; to be sure, they have in common the virtuosity of optical effects, but they also work on a common variety over which their touch passes. Their hands sheathed in skin linger on skin.

Cosmetics and the art of adornment are equivalent expressions. The Greeks in their exquisite wisdom combined order and adornment in the same word, the art of adorning and that of ordering. 'Cosmos' designates arrangement, harmony and law, the rightness of things: here is the world, earth and sky, but also decoration, embellishment or ornamentation. Nothing goes as deep as decoration, nothing goes further than the skin, ornamentation is as vast as the world. Cosmos and cosmetics, appearance and essence have the same origin. Adornment equals order, and embellishment is equivalent to law, the world appears ordered, at whatever level we consider phenomena. Every veil is a magnificently historiated display.

Superior to the physicist, the naked woman in the mirror imitates the demiurge. She constructs the order of a veil: prepares her skin, decorates a layer, a variety of world, submits it to law. The artist reveals the order of the world in the order of appearance, as does she. We can hear all that in the discourse on the deceptive or superb effects of sight and bedazzlement, which forgets how the variety has been worked on: canvas, veil and skin that the hands have woven, coated, softened or fortified.

And objectified. The naked woman at her toilet, in front of two mirrors, is busy with her self-portrait: an artist in her studio. She paints her face, neck, and would have put makeup on her breasts in times gone by, she manicures fingers and nails, removes overlong hairs from her fur, shapes a mask, in the Indian or African manner, gives herself an identity. Paints the skin of her face, paints a mask or paints on a mask; her skin becomes a veil, then a canvas, as if the cosmetic fabric had received the imprint of her face, as if the so perfectly contrived finish could be torn off, as if the still damp fresco could be detached like a mobile canvas, as far removed from the body as the bathrobe or smock, as the leaf of the screen – a hovering, floating object. An impression or imprint made on an opaque area formed by perfumes, lotions or makeup. The skin of the subject is objectified, it could be exhibited in a museum. Just as a thumb makes its mark on a page, a chaotic or ordered, but nonetheless individual fingerprint, so the face imprints on this gossamer mask its indelible relief and personality. The naked woman with cosmetics, as she mixes tones and pastes, prepares to cast the mould of her impressions.

Let us enter the world of the *fêtes galantes* where so many masks and fantastical disguises whirl and dance: they display themselves and spread out, hide, fall, change places with each other. At one moment the skin is lost, the person strays, the sloughed skin flies through the air. At the feast of love, the dancers shed their skins. The skins that pass, vital, sprightly and delicate in the thin air, as though they were spirits, are visible only momentarily. Watteau and Verlaine noted them. A tiny spark of dangerous joy in which the cosmetic, an adornment prepared to last barely an evening, flies off towards beauty, for eternity.

Cosmetics approaches æsthetics in the sense of art theory. In the streets of Paris things just as beautiful as those created by Bonnard, Boucher or Fragonard can be seen. Sometimes women's adornment is so well adapted to their nature that our breath is taken away, just as when we gaze at the world; but cosmetics becomes an æsthetics of sensation, because of a particular harmony: the naked woman in the mirror tattoos her skin, in a certain order and according to precise laws, she follows exact pathways; she emphasizes the eye and the gaze, accentuates with colour the place to be kissed, crowning the zone of words and taste, underlines hearing with an earring, traces bridges or links of colour between the wells or the mountains of the senses, draws the map of her own receptivity. With cosmetics, our real skin, the skin we experience, becomes visible; through adornment the particular law of the body is revealed, just as by means of crosshatching, colours or curves on a map, the ordered world displays its landscapes. The tattooed, chaotic, unruly nude wears on her skin the fleeting common place of her own sensorium – hills and dales on which currents from the organs of hearing, sight, taste or smell, ebb and flow, a shimmering skin where touch calls forth sensation. Cosmetics reproduces this summation or mixture and attempt to paint them, differently according to different social conventions, instinctively tracing these temporary tattoos. Masks left to museums can be understood in this way; to each his cartography of sensations, to each his cosmetography, if I dare so express myself, to each his facial imprint, or, very precisely, his personal impressions – another way, in our Latin languages, of saying his printed mask. I imagine that the reason why we do not have a ring hanging from our nose, as other peoples do, is that we have forgotten the sense of smell.

No, woman does not wear a duplicitous mask, as moralists say, and is not repairing the irreparable as young men claim. She traces the Tender Map of touch, as well as the streams of her hearing, her rivers of taste and the lakes of her listening, all of these mingled, quivering waters, from which her constant beauty arises. She makes visible her invisible identity card, or impressionable body. Her sensuous world is covered with a map, to the exact scale of its surface; detail for detail, eye for eye.

Who has not dreamed that maps such as this might be drawn identical to the world itself, measure for measure, the impossible dream of an ultrafine film following all the fractal details of the landscape, the cosmic dream of an exquisite cosmetic on the skin of each thing which one would remove, spread out and exhibit, after unrolling or unfolding it, to make visible the wine-dark sea and its light breezes, finer than wrinkles in the corner of a laughing eye, the pastel mauve of the lilac, the patch of sky, the tilted, moist corolla, the cosmos in all its order and adornment?

The Garden pulls, hides and smoothes out this transparent covering which is infinitely invaginated on each object. It objectifies the face of the landscape, the membrane of its mask.

A tangible medium is necessary before form, colour and tone can exist. Skin, covering, veil or canvas. The image is formed on an unfurled variety, the map is drawn and printed on a page.

Bonnard loved all sorts of media: stage sets, posters, papers, materials, fans, vellum in books, cardboard covers, sheets or screen panels. He produced the masks for *Ubu roi*. Before the eye sees, there is the texture of the canvas. The eye has no weight to impose, it imprints nothing. On the subject's front line is the skin. Everything is enveloped in a film. In the beginning, touch; at the origin, the medium.

The painter, with the tips of his fingers, caresses or attacks the canvas, the writer scarifies or marks the paper, leans on it, presses it, prints on it. There is a moment when seeing becomes impossible, when the nose is touching, sight is cancelled by contact; two blind people who can see only by means of their canes or walking sticks. The artist or artisan, through his brush, hammer or pen, grapples at the decisive moment with skin against skin. No-one who has refused contact – who has never kneaded or struggled – has ever loved or known.

The eye, distant, lazy, passive. No impressionism without an impressing force, without the pressure of touch.

With his fingers of skin, Bonnard makes us touch the skin of things.

The Garden of 1936 traces an almost diagonal path to paradise. There is no perspective, depth, or restored relief to lead one to suspect that the viewer's gaze has been staged. Bonnard throws a bouquet in our face. The dark-haired woman was covering herself with a bathrobe, the screen was hiding who knows what. The only things reflected in the mirrors were the curtains, screening nudity, the eye is cheated. Here paradise disappears out of sight, hidden by a curtain of foliage or trees that form part of paradise. And it is offered with great generosity. Whoever decorated this garden dress, this printed veil, this leaf, must have plunged naked into the flora and bathed at length in the colours and tones.

In the same year, the *Nude in the Bath* appears. Immersion. I cannot say that I have seen this nude, I cannot claim to know it, I try to write that I know, that I am living what Bonnard attempted to do. Immersion reveals, close to the sensitive skin, close to the apparitions or impressions in which it is enveloped or bathed, a sort of membrane, a fine film which inserts itself, or comes into being, between the medium or mixture and the male or female bather, a variety common to the feeling and the felt, a gossamer fabric which serves as their common edge, border or interface, a transitional film that separates and unites the imprinter and the imprinted, the printing and the printed, thin printed material: the bath reveals the veil.

This canvas gives us the key to Bonnard's secret and, finally, that of impressionism. The bath tests sensation, it tests it in the sense of a laboratory experiment. This is the experience of sensation, or rather, this *is* experience or sensation. Bonnard throws himself naked into the garden swimming pool, bathes himself in the world. Naked bodies, exposed by centuries of painting, are not aimed at voyeurs, but reveal what belongs to the realm of the senses. They are all female bathers. Not models to be painted, but models of what it is necessary to do in order that one might one day paint or think: throw yourself naked into the ocean of the world. Feel this membrane, this fabric forming around yourself: this invisible veil.

And draw it back gently, tactfully and delicately, from this laminated corridor between the skin and things, stretch out, unfold, spread, exhibit and flatten it; slowly smooth the thin veil, cosmic in the garden and cosmetic on the skin of the *Belle Noiseuse*, as she steps out of her bath, take special care not to tear the veil – this is the canvas.

The Garden depicts the subject stepping out of the bath. I cannot decide whether it reveals the fabric of things themselves or the flayed epidermis of Pierre Bonnard, the subject of the impression or the impressed object. They are brought together by the bath, into which the subject plunges, imprinted with foliage and flowers.

A shroud, or winding sheet, is a cloth the purpose of which is to wipe away sweat, the sweat of the dying man. The skin is covered with perspiration, it exudes and becomes mottled, beaded and a blend of different colours, like that of the female nude. The shroud materializes the liquid veil, the mask streaming with sweat or blood: the fabric flows like fluid, but is also solid because of the deposits left behind, almost ethereal through evaporation. The film between the skin and the bath is the site of transitions and exchanges. The bathrobe, in the bathroom, amidst the steam, could be called a shroud.

In Turin one can visit the shroud that enveloped the body of Christ in his tomb, the veil of his face. Plunged alive into the most painful tortures, covered with sweat, blood, spittle, dust, scarified by flagellation, pierced by nails, run through by spears, his corpse was rolled in the linen fabric, a thin layer between the atrocious world and the printed skin. He was buried beneath this veil. Removed gently, stretched, unfolded, flattened, exhibited, the veil becomes a canvas and displays the traces of the body and face. This is the man.

According to tradition, Veronica was the name of the holy woman who wiped the crucified Christ's face, covered with a liquid mask, dripping with sweat and blood. In ancient languages this name means the true icon, the faithful image. True, faithful because imprinted, impressionistic.

Veronica becomes the patron saint of painters; her eyes full of tears, blinded with grief and pity, she made with her hands the imprint of the skin, the mask of pain, a holy woman of contact and caress, her hands open and her eyes unseeing.

The Garden of Bonnard is like the bathrobe: the world is more luxurious and more happily endowed than a regularly printed, woven veil; the garden enlarges the dotted skin of the nude at her toilet to the scale of the landscape, with more exuberance and greater richness in the tones and patches of colour. This is the shroud of the artist emerging dripping after bathing in the world, a true image of the garden.

Some look, contemplate and see: others caress the world or let themselves be caressed by it, throw themselves into it, roll, bathe or dive in it, and are sometimes flayed by it. The first, their large eyes embedded in their smooth, flat skin, are unacquainted with the weight of things. The others give in to the weight of things, their epidermis marked locally and in detail by the pressure, as if it had been bombarded. Their skin, therefore, is tattooed, striped, striated, coloured, beaded, studded, layered chaotically with tones and shades, wounds and lumps.

Their skin has eyes, like a peacock's tail.

It sees, is seen, varies, unfurls and displays itself. Pierre Bonnard gave us, over half a century, his successive cast-off skins and flayed tunics. We believe in images but do not find them here, the mirrors empty themselves and we have fine, sensitive skins. An exhibition of trophies and scalps, hanging on the wall.

The garden-paradise unfurls a happy, sloughed skin.

Bonnard's bathrobe, Bonnard's nudes, Bonnard's gardens display skins in full bloom.

The eye loses its pre-eminence in the very area in which it is dominant, in painting. At the limits of its endeavour, impressionism attains its true original meaning, contact. The nude, ocellated like a peacock, reminds us of the weight or pressure of things, the heaviness of the column of air above us and its variations. Tunics, curtains, scarves, leaves, bathrobes are printed like books, using strong pressure. The skin, a hard and soft wax, receives these variable pressures according to the strength of things and the tenderness of the area. Hence the tattoos, traces and marks, our memory, our history and the parchment of our experiences. Our cutaneous garment bears and exhibits our memories, not those of the species, as is the case for tigers or jaguars, but those of the individual, each one with his mask, or exteriorized memory. We cover ourselves with capes or coats from modesty or shame about revealing our past and our passivity, and in order to hide our historiated skin, a private, chaotic message, an unspeakable language, too disordered to be understood and which we replace by the conventional or exchangeable impression of clothes and by the simplified order of cosmetics. We never live naked, in the final analysis, nor ever really clothed, never veiled or unveiled, just like the world. The law always appears at the same time as an ornamental veil. Just as phenomena do. Veils on veils, or one cast-off skin on another, impressed varieties.

The ancient Epicureans gave the name of simulacra to the fragile membranes, which are emitted everywhere, fly through the air, are received by everyone and are responsible for signs and meaning. The canvases of Bonnard and others fulfil, perhaps, the function of simulacra. To be sure, they pretend to do so. But above all: between the skin of the painter and the fine envelope of things, the veil of the former encounters the veils of the latter, the canvas seizes the momentary junction of the sloughed skins. A simultaneous simulacrum.

Painters sell their skin, models hire out their skin, the world gives its skins. I have not saved mine, here it is. Flayed, printed, dripping with meaning, often a shroud, sometimes happy.

HERMES AND THE PEACOCK

Let's talk about the peacock, a doubly monstrous bird, which has so many long feathers that it cannot fly, as if evolution had erred through excess; displaying a hundred eyes which you can imagine watching you even if you know they cannot. When it struts, it displays an ocellated tail, revealing eyes of feather or skin.

Mercurial, but limited to earth-bound displays of flightiness, one day the bird crossed Hermes' path. Argus, the man who could see everything, is said to have had two pairs of eyes, one on the front of his head, like everyone else, the other behind. No blind spot. Others say that he had a hundred – fifty in front and as many on the nape of his neck – or that he had an infinite number of eyes all over his skin. Said to be clairvoyant at first, then pure gaze, then a massive eyes-ball, and finally skin tattooed with ocelli, fantastic proliferation gone mad. Growth and phantasm often go hand in hand. Argus sees everywhere and is always looking: he only ever sleeps with one pair of eyes shut or with his eyelids half closed; half asleep, half awake; the best of all watchers, whether earth-bound or aloft, deserves his nickname of Panoptes, the panoptic.

An excellent example of perfect sight and lucid skin, just as the previously mentioned painter was an example of vision and perceptive tattooing.

Panoptes would have been highly valued, nowadays, in the study of the world and experimentation. He would have been a leader in laboratories or observatories, or in the field; he would have kept watch marvellously well. We need always to pay constant attention to things, in science or in our travels.

Back then, in those mythic times, Argus was employed in surveillance. Panoptes spied on the extra-marital loves of Zeus, at the instigation of Hera, the jealous wife, who had him spy on the conjugal relationships of the gods and at the same time on Jupiter's amorous adventure with a nymph.

There is an immense difference between the observation of things and the surveillance of relationships: two worlds, perhaps, are in opposition here; two kinds of time, that of myth and that of our history.

Myth is not concerned with the careful examination of objects. Argus is the precursor of the private detective. Endowed with a hundred open eyes while the other hundred are resting, he becomes a policeman, screw, prison warder: all devoted to shadowing.

Cultures mature when they transfer their focus on relationships between people to innocent objects. A more relaxed collective life tends to improve our morals, such as when men turn their attention away from the anxious, uncomfortable loves of their neighbours, towards the trajectory of a comet. The society in which surveillance dominates ages quickly, becoming old-fashioned and abusively archaic. The past lurks there like a monster, harking back to the age of myth.

Surveillance and observation. The human sciences keep watch, the exact sciences observe. The first are as old as myths; the others are born with us and are as new as history. Myth, theatre, representation and politics do not teach us to observe, they commit us to surveillance.

Panoptes sees everything, always, everywhere: for what task do the gods employ him: for surveillance or observation?

THE FIVE SENSES

In the Greek sense of the verb to see, he incarnates theoretical man, an omnidirectional ball of open eyes. Of what use is theory? To monitor relationships or to examine objects?

I shall call anything lacking an object poor. Myth lacks an object, as do theatre and politics.

Once, a long time ago, not so long ago, we had few objects. Thing-deprived humanity lingers in our consciousness. With so few things, our wealth consisted of ourselves alone. We spoke only of ourselves and our relationships. We lived in and through our relationships. So I shall call myths poor, because of their lack of objects, and likewise theatre, theories and politics; poor and wretched our philosophies, and wretched our human sciences.

We remember so precisely this wretchedness that we cannot fail to recognize it when we find it here and there among the nations of the world, and in stories or abstract discourses. We are barely emerging from places, families and collectives deprived of things, in which we were for a long time trapped in relationships and condemned to an experience of the world that was limited to talk. Deprivation leads to surveillance and betrayal; the villages of my childhood were alive with lucid, talkative Arguses. Everyone knew everything about everybody as if, in the middle of us all, there was a panoptic tower keeping watch, an indiscreet social contract or inevitable police report. Little or no attention was paid to things, each person monitored the relationships of everyone else. I have known societies composed entirely of sociologists. They were unbelievably talented, both in watching and reporting. We have barely left that Antique age, not all of us have emerged from the poverty that lasted from the mythical ages until quite recently. I recall mythical societies entirely caught up in representation, hibernating in language. Poverty is not only measured in bread but in words, not only by the lack of bread but by an excess of words, an exclusionary prison. Language spreads when bread is lacking. When bread arrives, speaking is out of the question. The mouth, long starved, has too much work to do. We have learned to love objects.

There is no place for things on the boards of a theatre. We provide plays and words to those who have only words. Our theories are bereft of objects, they watch over relationships. So if you ask philosophy for bread, what you get are nice words and representations. If you ask it for bread, it has only circuses. It lives on relationships, on the human sciences, in myth and antiquity, without leaving the village of our childhood; it has no world, produces no things, provides no bread. For how long has it been poor and starving, as was our youth?

A prosperous, productive philosophy would provide more than enough bread for all those who passed by.

The growth of objects, the exponential flood of things, have made us forget the time of their absence. And that time seems so far away from us now! Archaic, antediluvian and indeed mythical. Myths and philosophy recount that time to us. Memories of places where lovers were kept under surveillance, and pursued as far as the Bosphorus, in an empty, sonorous space, with no-one thinking to eat. Thus philosophies without object – nearly all – thus philosophies, aged and poor, which take their values from the human sciences alone – almost all – appear so ancient to us that we read them as myths. As though they were politics, theatre or magic. When they come across an object, they change it, by sleight of hand, into a relationship, language or representation.

They pull us backwards. On the whole, the observant person is better than the surveillant, detective or policeman; and the astronomer who falls to the bottom of a well is better than the woman who, behind his back, mocks him to her friends. Who has a grasp of reality, he who gapes at the stars or she who hides in the background, making fun of him? Do the washerwomen know that a well makes an excellent telescope and that, from the bottom of this vertical cylinder, the only telescope known in Antiquity, one can see the stars in full daylight? What have they to laugh about, not knowing that the scholar descends knowingly into the abyss. Did they know this, the authors of fables that still make us laugh? Did the philosophers? It is better to go from relationships to things, a demanding innovation, than to return from objects to relationships, an easy practice: from science to theatre, from work to politics, from description to myth, from the star thing to the theatrical representation. The exact sciences came after the object had emerged, they foster its emergence. The idea of going backwards is frightening: when objects are replaced by relationships, issues, fetishes and goods. These are all forms of regression. A little bit of naivety is better than suspicion.

Inundated with objects, we dream of relationships as of a lost paradise. That paradise made for a very ordinary hell, peopled with voyeurs and volunteer policemen, slimy with suspicion, and where laziness rivalled politics. The philosophy of suspicion gives rise to the oldest trade in the world. Communities, still deprived of objects, whether voluntarily or through the cruelty of others, indulge in the delights of policing and political imprisonment, and condemn themselves to the hell of relationships. Conversely, their masters do not want objects. Proof that things liberate one from surveillance and that observation frees one from suspicion.

Sciences that are not acquainted with objects can only rely on sleuthing and policing, they are caught up in myth. Objective knowledge creates present history whereas the human, ancient sciences lead to mythology. The observer weaves in the light of day what the surveillant undoes during the night. Which is more frightening?

Hermes will kill Panoptes: the bearer of messages will triumph over the watcher, surveillant or observer. Communication and information kill theory. How?

Zeus, the king of the gods, loves Io, a beautiful nymph; Hera, a princess, suffers from jealousy. A jealous person lives in a place of thorns, where surveillance begins: a vantage point from which to see. Zeus deceives Hera by cheating: he transforms the nymph into a heifer. What, me, love an animal? The heifer shines, however, with a wonderfully white, smooth coat.

Hera suspects something, she is suspicious of the bull circling around the cow. As she is able to metamorphose beings as easily as Zeus, she sends a gadfly, her own prickly envy, that stings the female and maddens her, forcing her to leave.

Io, a wanderer, gallops through Europe, gives her name to the Ionian Sea, running along the shore, always fleeing, and passes into Asia at the place now known as the Bosphorus or Cow's Step; a vagabond, she suffers and complains, unfortunate to have been loved by a god, in as much pain from wandering and love as the crucified Prometheus from vengeance and immobility.

Hera guessed correctly, Zeus was indeed hiding behind the appearance of the bull.

The queen, foiled, calls Argus, whom nothing escapes. Panoptes guards the cow, even Zeus can do nothing about it. The king is foiled in turn.

Jealous panoptic theory sees all from the top of its tower.

Method in the human sciences, which deal only with relationships, apes police and inquisitorial suspicion. It spies, shadows, sounds hearts and minds.

It asks questions and remains suspicious of the answers, it never asks itself whether it has the right to act as it does.

It is said that God is not deceitful in the exact sciences, where the innocent object remains loyal and trustworthy. God does not deceive, he establishes the rules of the game, and remains within them. Man deceives in the human sciences, and worse still, he cheats. In the exact sciences, if God does not deceive, there is all the more reason for him not to cheat. Man deceives in the human sciences, and worse still cheats – not only subtle, complex and refined like the God of the exact sciences, but hiding his game of deceit, by feigning a different strategy, suddenly changing the rules, and cheating offside. Man cheats in the social sciences, where breaking the rules is law. Where changing the rules is law.

The exact sciences construct subtle theories that are at once honest, elegant and stable. In them, a cat remains a cat: the identity principle. The human and social sciences describe theories even more underhanded than fraud, more duplicitous than cheating, in order to outsmart their object. Here everything becomes possible; a cow is a woman or a god a bull, even the identity principle is unstable. Reason watches while reason sleeps, reason sleeps while it watches, a hellish world of relationships in which stability itself fluctuates.

The human sciences are necessarily involved in the worst kinds of double dealing, whether from beneath the table or behind your back. The term hypocrisy describes this procedure quite well: here method is critical – hypocritical – by undermining or backstabbing objects or relationships. It tricks tricksters, deceives deceivers and hides behind those who cheat (those who cheat do it behind the players' backs), it robs robbers, plays policeman to the gendarmes, teaches the most famous detectives a lesson, subjects the grand inquisitor to searches, keeps voyeurs under surveillance, betrays liars, studies the weak and miserable, exploits them by taking from them information, their little secrets, their last possessions.

The hypocritical method consists in always placing oneself behind, and this immediately creates a queue. One must therefore get quickly behind the last person in the queue, stand behind the last one whose back can still be seen, then hide one's own back for fear of being caught in turn by someone who has understood the game. Thus the rules of the method: set a liar and a half to catch a liar, a more depraved person to catch a depraved one, the pluperfect, or more-than-perfect, as we used to say; a theoretician to catch a voyeur.

The movement has no end and constructs long, monotonous, difficult chains of reasoning that seek closure. In other words, philosophies which draw on the human sciences try to find sites which, in the final analysis, escape criticism, the last link of the chain, or the end of the queue. They indulge in reasoning based on extremes, just as in the classical age philosophies that drew on the nascent exact sciences appropriated the divine extreme, the non-deceptive God of philosophers and scientists. God can neither be deceived nor deceive us, that was the endmost point. Here the limit would be, at the opposite extreme, to cheat or deceive so much that all imaginable cheating would already have been anticipated. The extralucid and inescapable panoptic has already seen everything.

Did the traditional theology of knowledge and evil foresee these closures at the extremes? Here we have God and the Devil.

Does our age of social sciences set up the Devil as a new extreme, in opposition to the God of philosophers and scholars, the God who dominated the classical age and the emergence of modern science?

God neither deceives nor cheats. Objects in the exact sciences remain stable. Man deceives and cheats, so much so that he disappears sometimes, like Zeus beneath the skin of the bull, like Hera behind the sting of the gadfly.

Now it could be said that he who cheats and deceives does so because he wants to win. So the first attribute of God consists in being indifferent to winning.

Detach yourself from notions of winning or losing, be indifferent to victory or loss, you will enter into science, observation, discovery and thought.

Here two extremes are defined: a stable apex of trust; a maximum of distrust. To the stability of the object corresponds the lability of relationships.

God has guarded the exact sciences since the classical age. Some say he appropriates them, some that he favours them. The Devil dominates the human sciences, a deceitful trickster from the outer limits of evil. It is said that he deploys extreme and exquisite cunning to foil God's power and goodness and to win or regain the place of God. God deploys no cunning and refuses conflict. The war between the Devil and God never took place, one wants to win, the other does not.

Indifferent to winning or defeat, beyond the scale of victories and losses, beyond the scalar podium, beyond metrics, God is infinite. Here infinity is defined by indifference to the battle with evil, the battle to end all battles.

Free from the hell of relationships, God is devoted to the object, and thus creates the world, the complete set of objects. Everything derives therefore from his refusal to be part of the game.

Hera and Zeus play chess, play at deceiving each other or winning, devil against devil, their cheating reaching the extremes of evil. The Devil is the god of myths, or of the human sciences, our god. Our thinking takes place under his regressive reign.

Is it possible to conceive of a new man who would have no time for cheating or deception, who would be set free from the animal podium on which victory is all that matters?

Panoptes sees everything and knows everything, from his extremal site. Nothing escapes him. Using falsely naïve images, myth provides an excellent description of concepts that we have difficulty in forming. The aim of the game is to find foolproof moves. Hence the construction of extremes: God, the Devil, Panoptes himself, Hera the queen and Zeus the king. The strongest pitted against the strongest, like rutting wapitis.

Zeus attempts to deceive his wife who tries to catch him, and therefore cheats: where you see a cow, it is really a woman. Hera cheats and the gadfly flies and stings according to her will. The goddess positions herself behind the god, who positions himself behind her: he undermines the goddess who undermines him. In this game with no rules, the back of each is turned towards the other, offering up a weak blind spot.

Let us look for a third, all-seeing man. Let us imagine someone with no back: an insomniac, without a blind spot, never inattentive or unaware, intensely present, nothing but face, an omnidirectional ball of eyes, an interlocking geometry of indestructible facets, waking and sleeping in flashes of light and dark, like a lighthouse on the coast or, more accurately, like a set of lights and signals, controlling a particular zone and filling the night, it stares or signals at random. This is Argus. Here at last we have total theory, the unassailable method that can conquer everything. There is no getting around Argus. Here at last is the right position for those who desire to be first or last, critical yet never subject to criticism, an observing presence with no observable opacity, always a subject, never an object. No-one takes Panoptes from behind, he has no underside or back, he is a sphere made for scanning.

Those who deal with men and rule over them always stay in the black, blind, impotent spot of the active or present subject, behind his back. Illness plays a minor role, as do sleep, misery, linguistic poverty, the residual unknown of collective relationships, or childlike hope. The doctors of bodies and souls, economists, politicians and rhetors, inhabit this weak spot, sheltered from blindness, in the dark of the unconscious or on the edge of tears. They see without being seen, each one finding his two-way mirror or his shuttered window. The philosopher who sums them up, integrates and reflects them, becomes panoptic: inescapable and unassailable like Argus.

You who look at everything through your perpetually open eyes, is your lucidity never bathed in tears?

Here is the state of play: Zeus himself is in check. The queen beats the king using the panoptic rook-tower. Zeus then calls on his knight, Hermes enters. The king orders his angel to attack and to kill Panoptes.

It is impossible to approach him or take him unawares. There is no surprising a surveillant: consider the pre-conditions of this strategy of always more. The knight must circumvent the all-seeing tower. How?

Hermes sends Panoptes deep into a magic sleep by playing the syrinx, as others charm snakes. Hermes invents the syrinx or Pan-pipes for this battle.

A new combat between extremal sites: Panoptes has total and complete vision. In the realm of sight he leaves his adversary no opening. Hermes therefore quits the terrain on which Argus is unassailable and moves into the realm of sounds by taking over the entire spectrum: hence the name of Pan's pipes. Pan against Panoptes. Consider the pre-conditions for the strategies of total war. Listening and looking in confrontation, a strange conflict of the faculties of sense: hearing against sight, or ear against eye, one totality opposed to another, armoury for armoury, the sum of sound-waves balancing the sum of evidence. The geometral plane of messages against the ichnographic plane of intuitions, a fabulous struggle in an inconceivable space, the system of harmony enveloping the theory of representations.

Suddenly these fantastic gigantomachies, the all-powerful against the all-powerful, the Devil and God, Jupiter and Juno, Pan and Panoptes, are reduced to an apparently simple confrontation. The syrinx sends Argus to sleep, the cobra writhes, inoffensive, to the tune of the Indian flute. Whence come these magics of fascination? Enchantment comes from chanting. What effect can the ear have on the eyes, what effect can sound have on sight, listening on looking?

A visible event is localized and locatable in its distance and angle, coordinated with the surrounding visible; we occupy a point of view, perceive profiles, sight defines a place. The panoptic myth seeks to force this place and exceed its definitions. Just as Leibniz added together the different views of a thing in order to obtain its ichnographic or geometral dimensions, so Panoptes totalizes the body's points of view, adds together the sites from which he sees. God alone, for Leibniz, reveals simultaneously all the profiles of a thing. Spherical Argus alone presents himself as a God-like eye made of eyes – facetted vision like that of flies. A real, but minor or limited benefit, because the best of all watchers, the geometral subject, far from perceiving a geometral-object, sees space as the sum of places, while still seeing each thing according to its profile. His body, still linked to a place, behaves like a lighthouse, round like its lantern and sending out into the surrounding area shafts of light while at the same time receiving the brilliance of things at every point on its sphere.

A sound event does not take place, but occupies space. Even if the source often remains vague, its reception is wide and general. Vision provides a presence, sound does not. Sight distances us, music touches us, noise besieges us. Absent, ubiquitous, omnipresent sound envelops bodies. The enemy can intercept radio transmissions but does not have access to our semaphore; sight remains unintrusive, sound-waves will not be contained. Looking leaves us free, listening imprisons us; we can free ourselves from a scene by lowering our eyelids or putting our fists over our eyes, by turning our back and taking flight. We cannot escape persistent clamour. No barrier or ball of wax is sufficient to stop it. Practically all matter, particularly flesh, vibrates and conducts sound. Hermetic to light, the black veil blinds and other bodies may obstruct other passages, but Hermes works in a medium that knows no hermetic barriers. Local vision, global listening: more than just ichnography, geometral for both the subject and object, hearing practises ubiquity, the almost divine power of universal reach. Singular optics, total acoustics. Hermes, the god of passage, becomes a musician, for sound knows no obstacle: the beginning of the total ascendancy of the word.

We are speaking of magic, but at the same time of philosophy, common sense and the world as it is. Pan charms Panoptes by overwhelming his conductive flesh. Strident sound makes his eye-covered skin quiver, his muscles tremble, his tears flow, his bony frame vibrate. The clairvoyant ball is covered by a lake of tears. Argus collapses with excitement. The global triumphs over the sum of sites. The sound-wave has immediate access to totality, so fruitlessly sought by adding together places or points of view and juxtaposing eyes. Have you ever encountered a work, accomplished effortlessly and on the first attempt, that you could never achieve, even in a hundred thousand attempts, over your whole lifetime? Did you not weep? Argus collapses. However panoptic and lucid this bright sphere is, it remains differential and pointillist, analytic of micro states or dwarf scenes. However vulgar a sound is, it succeeds immediately in imposing itself on the surrounding area. The victory is virtually magical, as it were, and of a sensuous order. Sound undoes sight, or charms it: the latter focuses itself at the endpoint of a narrow beam of light; but what else do eyes usually do except focus on that point? Sound puts sight in its place.

Thus Leibniz, eternally running after the untotalizable sum of ichnographies, succeeded in closing his system with Universal Harmony. Representation, even if panoptic, falls asleep when Harmony resounds. Better still, if we can form an idea of a world, of God, or merely of a system, if we accede to totalities, it is never because we are led there by partial or endless representations, we only ever get there through harmony, metaphysical Pan-piping.

Whether we read this myth literally, or as magic, or philosophy, we obtain the same result: Pan overturns Panoptes. It sums up in simple, perfectly dove-tailed acts what we disperse across discourses and disciplines. But the world around us angrily screams this result: by which I mean that the environment that we have prepared or constructed plunges us into an inextinguishable din. We have long been sleeping, drugged with sounds and music, no longer seeing anything or thinking. Hermes has taken over the world, our technical world exists only through the all-encompassing confusion of hubbub, you will not find anything left on the earth – stone, furrow or small insect – that is not covered by the diluvian din. Great Pan has won, he has expelled silence from space. If you pity me, tell me where I can go to think.

Pan's flute prods and disturbs. Once on a June evening, in those long-gone years when the ends of days sank into silence, I was waiting for a total eclipse of the sun on a terrace facing a garden, overlooking the foliage of a maple tree. It soon became dark and an eclipse wind, like a wave, had risen when suddenly from the neighbouring house burst forth a sort of wild dance, with the strange, biting, astringent sound of Pan's pipes. Young people were celebrating some festival, they had confused shadow with twilight and were playing as night fell. However much one knows about it, the veiling of the sun's light is disturbing and transports one to another world. Pan was taking me there, I knew that he had blinded both the sun and my sight, sweeping over the space in a wave of wind and covering appearances in orange, purple and green tones which set my teeth on edge. Horrified, I heard the approach of what might have been complex, cruel Aztec gods.

Here is the second state of play: Hera herself foiled. The king takes the queen's rook by moving his knight. No-one speaks of Io again, as she moves weeping towards the Caucasus, close to Prometheus in chains, a virgin standing at the foot of the cross. No-one speaks of her except those who weep for the misfortune of the world. Hermes has put Panoptes to sleep and killed him: everyone is talking about the murder.

All sites are local to Argus for as far as he can see. As a subtle analyst, he totalizes the information about a place flawlessly and faultlessly. Hermes intercepts all information, in all places; sites of transport and translation, interference and distribution, he occupies passages. Argus occupies a tactical position. Hermes invades strategic sites. One will win the battle, the other the war. Argus, intensely present, detects every presence; but one who is everywhere does not need presence and is absent through ubiquity. Police no longer need to shadow anyone, they simply set up road blocks. They do not need watchers, here and now. Everything changes when presence is no longer the primary consideration.

Panoptes possesses light's clarity, Hermes seizes the arrow of its speed. Classical philosophy until recently placed its trust in illumination, contemporary philosophy is discovering the rapidity of the lightning bolt. The speed of light is more important than its purity. Consider the novelty of this victory: the principal quality of a theory or idea, its oldest value, clarity, is overtaken by the speed at which it travels. Pan or Hermes kills Panoptes: the swiftness of a message is of more value than the lucidity of a thought. We are speaking here of the new state of knowledge. We are speaking of common sense and philosophy and at the same time we are describing our world. Having no centre, the network of communication makes presence superfluous and surveillance obsolete. Audiovisual or computer circuits make a mockery of the watchtowers of the last war, borrowed from the ancient Roman camps. Sailors pass by without looking at lighthouses, their safety ensured by sonar and radar. Those who control the regulation of codes and their circulation in space allow the watchers to let down their guard and sleep on the consoles of their ships, listening to music. The hum of passing messages numbs the dog, spy and informer, and anæsthetizes the prison warder. Space is better contained and prison more secure because of the telephone, television and telecommunications.

THE FIVE SENSES

All Panoptes' avatars, all those figures who remain present to presence, in short, all the successive figures of phenomenology are put out to pasture. Present everywhere, Hermes, the spirit, suddenly descends into the spatial realm.

Hermes, the network, replaces all local stations, all watch towers juxtaposed in space, all successive figures in time: his take on geometry rules phenomenology out of court.

We are speaking at one and the same time of our common sense, of listening and hearing, and then of the word and code; of music and singing; of drugs and anæsthetics, because we have forgotten presence or lost our intuition. We are speaking of newspapers, periodicals, policing or politics (the struggle of Pan against Panoptes takes place in these every day); of the new state of knowledge. We are speaking of relationships and objects, knowledge and surveillance, competition and society. The computer world takes the place of the observed world; things we know because we have seen them give way to the exchange of codes. Everything changes, everything flows from the victory won by the table of harmony over the tableau of seeing. Gnoseology and epistemology change, but also daily life, the mobile niche into which the body is plunged, as well as behaviour, and therefore morals and education.

Observation, the idea of clarity, the function of intuition tied us to things themselves, like anchors or mooring ropes. Theory, by its own admission, was distinguished from the act of seeing, and the phenomenology of appearances was left to optics. The mooring ropes break. The message itself becomes the object. The code states the given, all we are given is data and the data bank has taken the place of the world.

Or rather: the message becomes the given again, as it did during what I have called Antiquity, when the collective fed off its relationships and messages, disdaining and disregarding objects. Relationships return, bringing with them the whole of mythology, the formidable and regressive burden of conflicts and fetishes. Ahead of these, science rushes headlong towards its premises. Wealth returns us to poverty. Increased productivity leads to a state of misery. Pan kills Panoptes: the age of the message kills the age of theory. Will the human sciences engulf the exact sciences, as they did in antiquity? As the myths tell us?

The war that will take place will therefore always be more savage in the sciences. We shall see secrets and trickery blossom again, jealousy's reach extend sky-high where the gods, elderly lovers grown senile, are still engaged in their age-old struggle to the death.

Is the hell of relationships returning, fed by rigour and efficiency?

Tired of deceitful games and cheating, dreaming that our brief lives might escape this monotonous age of blood and death, we live in hope of returning to a state of trust without deception or cheating, to a theory of knowledge that brings together the exact and the human sciences. A new knowledge and epistemology, a new man and a new education. It is only on this condition that we shall escape collective death.

Hera, the loser, is still a player in spite of everything. She strips dead Argus, takes the panoptic skin of the watcher, a shredded, billowing rag of shut eyelids, and lays it on the plumage of her favourite bird, the peacock. All that is left of the omni-directional ball of intense eyes is the dual colour of the ocellations and the brilliant pattern they make, a fascinating, silky fan. The motionless fowl, squawking harshly and tunelessly when Hermes plays on the flute, limping low to the ground when Hermes flies past, has only dead theory to display when it spreads its tail. Sight gazes without seeing at a world from which information has already fled. Representation, a still ornamental species in the process of extinction, provokes gawking admiration in the public parks and gardens where onlookers congregate.

Touch sees a little. It has heard.

In the towns, only our fellow men see us; no doubt they consider us as we consider them, height, weight and corpulence varying little. Bull's-eye windows, shutters and panes gaze sightlessly.

In the countryside, peacocks with ocellated tails pass by, as well as cows, flies, dogs, hares and glow-worms. They have large, glaucous eyes, or small many-facetted visual apparatuses which reflect back to us minute, detailed, colourless, striated, striped, shimmering giants in countless fragments.

We consider the landscape, as a whole and in detail, it considers us as a landscape.

We are merged into it and its variety.

THE FIVE SENSES

Our skin varies like a peacock's tail, even though we do not have feathers. It is as though it could see. It perceives confusedly on its whole surface area and sees clearly and distinctly by virtue of the hyper-acute singularity of its eyes. Everywhere else on it there are vague kinds of ocellations. The skin forms pockets and folds and, refining itself at a given site, creates an eye. The obvious concentration of ocellations here is found merely in diluted form everywhere else. If it forms a hollow – a rimmed, pleated, hollowed, half-oval fan – it becomes an ear where hearing is condensed. Everywhere else, be it an ear-drum or drum, it hears more widely and less well, but it still hears, vibrating as though auricular. Our skin resembles that of jaguars, panthers and zebras, even though we do not have fur. The pattern of the senses is displayed there, studded with subdued centres and spotted with marks; the skin is a variety of our mingled senses.

The skin, a single tissue with localized concentrations, displays sensitivity. It shivers, expresses, breathes, listens, loves and lets itself be loved, receives, refuses, retreats, its hair stands on end with horror, it is covered with fissures, rashes, and the wounds of the soul. The most instructive diseases, the sicknesses of identity, affect the skin and form tattoos that tragically hide the bright colours of birth and experience. They are calls for help and advertise their misery and weakness; we must learn to read the writing of the enraged gods on the skin of their victims, as on the pages of an open book. The alphabet of pathology is engraved on parchment.

The organs of the senses form knots, high-relief sites of singularity in this complex flat drawing, dense specializations, a mountain, valley or well on the plain. They irrigate the whole skin with desire, listening, sight or smell. Skin flows like water, a variable confluence of the qualities of the senses.

Interior and exterior, opaque and transparent, supple or rigid, wilful, present or paralyzed, object, subject, soul and world, watcher and guide, a place where the fundamental dialogue with things and others happens and where it is most brilliantly visible, the skin bears Hermes' message and what remains of Argus.

SUBTLE

We no longer know why, when it is acute, or refined or delicate, we describe a sense or a thing as subtle. We have lost the memory or secret of it.

In the Cluny Museum six large tapestries, originally from the Château of Boussac, have been given the collective name of *The Lady and the Unicorn*. They show or illustrate the five senses.

Each scene takes place on a blue, oval island. Well-defined and self-contained, the island is dotted with sprigs of flowers. It portrays a group: one or two women, the principal one and her attendant, two main animals, the lion and the unicorn, three or four trees, pine, holly, oak and orange, covered with foliage and laden with fruit, a host of small animals, monkeys, lion cubs, herons, magpies, jennets, cheetahs . . . plus specific objects, a mirror for sight, a positive organ for hearing, a sweet dish for taste, a plate or basket of flowers for smell. Touch has no specific object. The island of each sense stands out against a red, orange or pink background. The background is also laced with twigs, leaves and flowers and dotted with animals.

The balance of open and shut, or the contrast of one to the other, is achieved through colour and density. The fauna and flora, life, crowd together on the island and are diluted on the background, as if the fabric were dilating the scene or receiving a lighter animal and floral cloud from the denser source. Stronger and warmer impressions on the plateau on which the trees grow, their blue outgrowth projecting on to the red; a less dense, less compact and colder configuration against the background.

Exact and faithful outlines: each organ is drawn like an island, eye, ear, mouth, nose, an abundant, teeming complex of sensations, the skin stretches out its background canvas and is tattooed by these fiery centres. The island is woven from canvas of the same texture as its background, the organ is made from puckered skin. One notices in the scene that touch alone has no need of a special tool, its skin becoming at will both subject and object.

A neat question, an easy one too, arises in the case of the sixth tapestry, the only one with a written cartouche. Have we five senses, or six? Scholastic thought in the Middle Ages divided our *sensorium* into external and internal. Hearing, sight, touch, smell and taste were reputed to be external. In fact, the mirror reveals the image of the animal and not that of the subject: it shows the neck and nose of the unicorn and not the face and neck of the young girl who will utter her desire; the bonbonniere offers the mouth the taste of sweetmeats; and as this sense remains weak and unrefined, the island adds a shelter here, a trellis on which roses climb, to indicate the extent to which smell contributes to taste; the crown or necklace combines the smell of roses with carnations, giving the double meaning of the word bouquet; the hand tactfully caresses the stiff pole or erect horn; hearing listens to the pipes vibrating to the action of the bellows. This is the exterior world, flowers or sugars, animals or music, wood or ivory; the woman does not see or hear herself, does not feel or touch herself. Indeed a sixth sense is necessary, in which the subject turns in on itself and the body on the body: a common or internal sense, indeed a sixth island was necessary, a doubly enclosed island for the body itself.

A tent represents this interior, the intimacy of the body, and begins to construct the common body of these different women, this one smelling entirely of rose or carnation, that one quivering with harmony, a third displaying graceful images, yet another turned entirely to sugar or honey . . . the pavilion encloses their totality.

The tent consists of a blue veil, blue like each of these insular organs, but in addition woven and draped, with many folds and richly decorated. Each island is flat and enclosed but open to the space around it, a well-defined external sense but open to events in the world. The new blue pavilion is doubly closed, to the island and in space; it is closed on itself. And it is veiled in drapery.

The entire description is equally valid for tapestry and body. Each insular sense organ forms a dense singularity on the diluted, cutaneous plain. The island is woven of the same fabric as the background, each sense organ is invaginated in the same skin, spreading around it. The internal sense is draped in its tent, a new veil, a new fabric, but the same carpet and the same skin. The internal sense is veiled in skin.

Touch seems to have the upper hand. It comes together with the common sense, the sum of the first five, and weaves their tent. Standing alone, it required neither tool nor specific object, neither mirror nor organ, neither flower nor sweetmeat. In addition, before smelling the flowers gathered into a circlet, the woman touches them, singling out each one between index finger and thumb. The woman representing sight holds the handle of the mirror with her right hand and, with the left, caresses the neck of the unicorn. The one representing taste offers her fingers to the bird as a perch, as in the art of falconry. The one representing hearing touches the keyboard of the organ. The hand serves five times as a common factor and a common sense develops there.

Touch will win the day. With his large paw, the lion turns back and raises the tent hanging; with his cloven hoof, the unicorn raises and turns back the fabric flap of the pavilion; with both her hands, the woman lifts and twists the material which seems to cover, hold and cradle the precious jewels, enfolding them in their casket where they will soon be out of sight in their closed jewel box. She touches the girl, touches the animal, touches the monster.

Touch has the upper hand, the pavilion, an internal sense or the body itself, closes its veils as the body does its skin. The organs of the external senses are open veils or envelopes. Through these doors we see, hear and experience tastes and fragrances; through these walls, even when they are shut, we touch. The fabric of the pavilion, or the skin of the body, can either open or close, the external sense retaining its integrity. The internal sense is clothed in skin that is either impermeable or pierced with windows and forms its tent or pavilion, its habitat or tabernacle.

Touch ensures that what is closed has an opening; the body of the woman occupies the space of the open doorway and closes it. The hangings and the veils of the partly open tent will fall and close on the woman-summation, on the common sense, the totality or mixture of the five others, on the internal sense, the closure of their externality.

Touch has won the day through the equivalence of veil, fabric and skin. Its palette combines flowers, fruits, leaves, birds and animals. The world is printed on the wax garment that surrounds and clothes us, that now offers us an intimate habitat. A factor common to four external senses, an open and closed sense in itself, it protects the internal sense and begins to construct it.

The whole description applies to the final tapestry, to the woman's body and to the sensorium in general. The cloth of the island is woven of the same fabric as the cloth of the tent and the background. The fall of the veil or cutaneous garment implies something new – their tattooing is different. The pavilion sets an ordered geometry, dotted with regular tongues of fire, against the sometimes dense, sometimes extensive, but always chaotic scattering of the patches of skin.

The tent opens and closes, as does the casket – two black boxes. Black or white? Light illuminates the interior of the pavilion, shading into the darkness of the interior surface of the box's lid. White and black? We know and we do not know. Are they opening or closing the tent, is the maidservant preparing to close the chest? We do not know and we know.

Our body is covered with skin, is imprisoned within it. It opens on to the senses. It closes on the internal sense, remaining slightly open. Touch continues to predominate, it is well acquainted with these juxtapositions of white and black, of openings and locks.

The sixth tapestry constructs the body: the feminine body? There is no male in the Cluny Museum, no male and no sky.

Touch therefore has the virtue of closing and outlining an interior. In the tapestry that expresses the sense of touch, the lion and the unicorn each wear around their necks a shield attached by a belt, a monkey remains prisoner of a neckpiece chained to a roller. The dog, the hyena and the jennet are held on a leash and the other monkey is held by a belly-band. Yes, touch surrounds and encircles. I rest my case.

The roller has its own significance: impression. The cylinder imprints on the exterior world, just as the necklace makes an impression on the skin of the neck. It could not be better said, it could not be better demonstrated or written.

All the tapestries are silent except the last.

The woman signifying sight lowers her eyelids, the unicorn contemplates its own image in the mirror, and the lion, its eyes wide-open, looks at us: specifically animal sight. The woman with the necklace of flowers is satisfied, at a distance, with touch; the monkey smells a rose: specifically bestial smell. The monkey again raises a sweetmeat to its mouth while, absentmindedly looking away, the woman barely touches, as though at a distance, the sweets in the bonbonniere. Taste is also animal, the lion pokes out its tongue. The young girl signifying hearing plays and does not sing, she hears. She forms a message at a deeper level than her voice, a colourless or sense-free harmony, before the sense of language. The constituent women, each one dedicated to a single sense, keep their distance from language. It could be said that, incapable of speech, their efforts are confined to pure animality. The external senses share muteness with the flora and fauna, and with a few objects.

The resulting woman, having constructed her body or pitched her tent, accedes to language, which crowns the open-closed pavilion of the internal sense, imprinted with tongues of fire.

The naïve external senses abandon themselves to leaves and branches, to rabbits, herons, foxes and to the young, hornless unicorn, ever defenceless against poisons. They have the wild status of thyme, goat and holly. Bleating, caressing the light air with their wings, sweet-smelling and tasting, and of undoubted elegance in form and colour, but mute like brutish animals or tree branches. Open and abandoned to the world like a flat island to the sea. Unstable also because they are mingled: indefinable shades of colour, mixed bouquets, tastes with variable fragrances, touch quivering with sense. Plunged into the variable and the mixed, tattooed. Multiple also: scattered, studded or dotted, never single. The chaotic whirl-pools of the senses never achieve singularity, conservation or identity. Hence these tapestries, studded and spangled with every thing in the world.

The internal sense speaks at last and for the first time. The tent is printed with burning tongues and crowned with writing. Language arrives.

The pavilion opens and shuts, contained but facing the outside. The woman is standing in her doorway, turned outwards, attentive, her body is given over to what is given. It is necessary to write the dative: TO.

Defined by the closing of the volume on itself, the slightly open tent reveals itself. The body can write or say: MY. My body, my belonging, which behaves like a circle and turns in on itself.

Monadic, the pavilion stands isolated on its island. Shut, open, it is revealed as singular. The body can say or write: ONE.

Solitary belonging gives itself to itself and to what is given.

Dense and blue, the body burns with stray languages. Empty like the tent, it leaves behind its jewels and regrets their absence: DESIRE. At the end of the fifteenth century, this term retains its Latin meaning, nostalgia, more than it embodies the contemporary meanings of lust and covetousness.

I leave behind my jewels, those that my body was wearing, those displayed by my partial bodies when they were a scent of roses, a shiver of sounds, a simulacrum in the mirror . . . I carry them and shut them in the casket. I miss them. I am nostalgic for a lost world, a lost paradise, an island between two seas, where the senses sparkle like a lake of gemstones. I speak now and shelter in the tent of language or writing. The tabernacle closes, its flaps are lowered. I live now in the prison of my language and the jewel-box closes. Having withdrawn beneath the veils printed with tongues of fire and beneath the crown of the written cartouche, the body which has left the world mourns it, the woman who leaves behind her jewels misses them, the beauty of the five senses lies in the black box while we sleep under the blue hangings engraved with fire.

Solitary belonging, devoted to itself, no longer devotes itself to what is given, except to what language gives us – to what is said or dictated.

TO MY ONE DESIRE

This is the first sentence, the originary, primary proposition, as original as the fault committed in the past by a girl on a paradise-island, as original and permanent. These are the first words uttered by the body when it becomes an interiority endowed with a voice, and is enveloped in flames and imprinted with signs, when the skin-tapestry or the skin-pavilion no longer bears on itself lilacs or cheetahs but geometry and letters. This is the sentence that causes the world to flee and the necklets to be abandoned, that excludes rabbits and goats and that chased us from paradise, these are the words which cause the senses to withdraw into a black box. Our only desire is that it be reopened.

The woman-summation bids farewell to the world, takes the veil beneath the tent of language.

This is the first *cogito*, more deeply buried although more visible than the thinking *cogito*. I feel, I have felt; I have seen, heard, tasted, smelt; I have touched; I touch, I enclose myself in my pavilion of skin; it burns with languages, I speak; I speak about myself, about my loneliness and the nostalgia of lost senses, I mourn the lost paradise, I regret the loss of that to which I was giving myself or of what was given to me. Since that phrase was written, I desire. And the world absents itself.

This is the first, self-contained proposition, literally circular, the first stable unitary philosophy of identity. My desire identifies with writing, I exist only in language. The identity principle shuts itself off and is blind to the unstable, multiple, mingled, invisible senses, hidden in the jewel-box in the tent.

The girl, having laid aside her regrets, will turn back, will enter once and for all the tabernacle of language. We have always dwelt there with her, we have never left it, we have never seen, known or understood the Cluny tapestry.

I cannot tell or write of touch, nor of any other sense. I live in the tent crowned with the cartouche and clothed in tongues. Those who are in the tent with me demonstrate categorically that no-one can go outside, has ever gone outside. You will not find, they say, any language to tell or write things – flowers or fruit, birds or rabbits, sounds or shapes, tastes or smells – to write or tell the world before the emergence of language. You will only find a tapestry in the Cluny Museum. You find yourself foreclosed. They are right. I cannot write or describe the five tapestries, for if I describe or write, I only speak of the sixth. The original language has come into being, we can do nothing about it.

It is said that the horn of the unicorn is a protection against poison. One merely has to grind it to a powder, and mix or dissolve the powder in a beverage, in order to mithridatize oneself against harmful pharmaceuticals. The unicorn liberates us from drugs.

One day I was lecturing to an audience in a marquee, as attentive to them as they were to me. Suddenly, a large hornet stung me on the inside of my thigh, a combination of surprise and exquisite pain. Nothing in my voice or intonation betrayed the accident and I finished my talk. I do not mention this particular memory in order to boast of Spartan courage, but only to indicate that the speaking body, flesh filled with language, has little difficulty in remaining focused on speech, whatever happens. Words fill our flesh and anæsthetize it. It has even been said, and written, that the word was made flesh. Nothing makes one more insensitive than words. If I had been looking at some image, listening to the sound coming from an organ, smelling a garland of flowers, tasting a sugared almond or grasping a pole, the hornet sting would have caused me to cry out. But I was speaking, balanced in a groove or enclosure, protected by a discursive breastplate. You want to anæsthetize a patient completely? Get him to speak with passion and vigour, ask him to talk about himself, and himself alone, of his one desire, demand that he prove something or that he convince his audience. He is intoxicated with sonorous words, the hornet is powerless. Militant egotists, we speak in order to drug ourselves.

We seek the pharmaceutical, the fabulous animal which can free us from the hardest of hard drugs, language. We find it in the Cluny tapestry.

The lion and the unicorn raise the veils or flaps of the doorway, the lady emerges from the prison, flecked with tongues of fire, takes cascading necklaces of gems out of the black box with the open lid: they pour from the box as the woman frees herself from the veils and is reborn. Then, accompanied by the monster, she visits the island paradise amidst the oranges and cheetahs, the same world of five continents or aspects. She participates in the banquet of things, to our joy and hers.

Always accompanied by the unicorn even when we evoke her name . . . the fabulous is always with her: stories, poems, mythologies. To accede to things themselves, let your tongue be still.

When the shuttle moves on the tapestry loom, the thread of the weft passes under the threads of the warp. Thus sense becomes entwined in the fabric, as does melody, sometimes, in sonorous flesh, and deep thought in vowels. The dazzling display of the figures and colours on the worked canvas corresponds to a thousand ties and knots on its other side, events on the *underside of the canvas* which, by hiding them, obscures the roots of the adjective 'subtle'. The secrets of the tapestry are knotted beneath it.

This is the secret of the unicorn: the secret of the five or six subtle senses. The skin hangs from the wall as if it were a flayed man: turn over the remains, you will touch the nerve threads and knots, a whole uprooted hanging jungle, like the inside wiring of an automaton. The five or six senses are entwined and attached, above and below the fabric that they form by weaving or splicing, plaits, balls, joins, planes, loops and bindings, slip or fixed knots. The skin comprehends, explicates, exhibits, implicates the senses, island by island, on its background. They inhabit the tapestry, enter the weaving, form the canvas as much as they are formed by it. The senses haunt the skin, pass beneath it and are visible on its surface, the flowers, animals and branches of its tattooing, eyes that stud the peacock's tail; they cross the epidermis and penetrate its most subtle secrets.

Displayed beneath our gaze since the Middle Ages, the enigma of the unicorn can be read, without representation, as the secret of subtlety; the tacit ascendancy of the tactile.

VARIATION

Bonnard's nude with cosmetics, and the myriad-hued garden, display varied canvases, skins and appearances. Let us consider the sense of variation. Varied means multiple: a thousand shades and tones, a thousand forms enhance the woman's tattoo and the floral exuberance of the park. Likewise, the remains, the cutaneous rag of panoptic Argus, laid at his death on the peacock's tail, is dotted with varied ocelli: the pavane does not sound monotonous, the feathered fan sparkles with many colours. Finally the blue island of the senses and the red background surround the lady and the unicorn with diverse flora and varied fauna: nothing plain, but on the contrary diversity, abundance, proliferation, number and difference.

The field is covered in flowers and grass: the tufts on the ground and the threads of the fabric are juxtaposed. We shall speak first of all of discrete or distinct variety. The fruit of the orange trees is clearly distinguished from the acorns, as are the carnations from the roses and the goats from the lions. The skin of the nude is tattooed in a variety of ways; the woman has turned pink, probably from the smell of the roses, but she has been affected at the same time by quite different causes: modesty or caresses. The traces and marks of all the senses are mingled: we shall call it continuous variety and describe her skin as variable. Woman is often variable, like the sky and the weather. Next to the lady of the Cluny Museum, the unicorn combines a goat's beard on a horse's body, with strange cloven hooves and a narwhal's horn. The discrete and continuous variety on the tapestry is not averse to mixing. It is not known whether the legendary beast symbolizes a mixture of the senses or the jumble that the senses cause us to perceive, but the important fact is that the monster varies in itself. Thus the tail of the peacock, silky to the touch, seems to see. It has been killed by listening, a mixture of three senses scattered on the fan.

Everything that precedes this and that comes after is a variation on the idea of variety.

Our skin could be called variety, in a precise topological sense: a thin sheet with folds and plains, dotted with events and singularities and sensitive to proximities; discrete and panoptic when the eyes make regular holes in it; but also continuous when tattooed, like that of the naked woman at her mirror, in reality a compound like the unicorn.

Fable once again speaks the truth. The total woman or completed body, the internal or common sense, the sixth or totalizing tapestry, the skin of the final tent, in other words you and I, are manifested in the reality of your daily life or mine, in the form of a suit, cobbled together with its seams visible. The circumstances of our lives, be they tragic or opportune, and our will, are responsible for this. The variety of sight, basted with large tacking stitches on to the variety of hearing, these sewn temporarily to each other, and each one separately and both together tacked on to those of taste, smell and touch, piece by piece and in no particular order, working towards the definitive garment which never eventuates, forms components which are seen and which, on occasion, clash with the resulting variety or with a neighbouring one: the goat's beard beneath the nostrils of a horse attracts attention, the neck beneath the narwhal's horn causes surprise. This is how we originate and how we are formed: a slapdash piece of work, subject to the vagaries of time and the blunders of brief opportunities. At times our skin, a hasty and untidy construct, happy from some fortunate encounter, resembles the chimera, with inexpertly attached fragments: a chin adorned with strange hairs, or pasterns not matching the hooves. Our upbringing or environment, the chain formed by the chance assembly of our genes, makes weird half-breeds of us, variables on a globally stable pattern. Our time does not end in a system, but in a rough-cut and patchwork rag. All women differ, the goat, mare and narwhal differ, all women come together in the woman in the sixth tapestry, the mare, narwhal and goat come together, the unicorn brings about the required totalization, the woman wears the animal skin. We are all dressed in fabulous skins, assuming the guise of enigmatic sphinxes. The skin varies, discrete, continuous, inexpertly sewn, horned. It varies: woven, historiated, tattooed and legendary.

The construction of the body proper is like the fiction of the unicorn.

What is revealed here about the skin can be said more generally. It is presented and lives as a discrete variety, with separate islands, but also as a continuous variety, with mingled regions or states. It totalizes and adds together these two sorts of varieties: it mingles or juxtaposes the juxtaposed with the mingled. What results from this is called variable.

The senses vary, the feeling and the felt vary. To measure their appearances according to the criteria of truth or falsehood is obviously inappropriate: one must first of all think in terms of the variable.

The horse variety joined together with the goat variety and mixed with it produces a very ordinary monster that juxtaposes and mingles places: witness the issue of tigers and lions, ligers and tigons, thus named according to the species of the male or female. There is protest about genetic manipulation. But any genesis is party to such manipulation, any individual, any organism can call itself a sphinx or unicorn. Who, after all, would dare affirm that they were not of mixed blood? On the blue island or red plain you see a rabbit, leopard, or a heron in flight. The identity that you attribute to them is a sign of your ignorance: each one is the result of cross-breeding. I reproach myself for not knowing enough about the varieties of rodents, waders or panthers; about hybridization. The marvellous thing about the tapestry is that it consists entirely of crossings, otherwise how could it be woven?

We have to come to terms with a difficult idea that shakes our notion of identity. The unicorn is, and is not, at the same time, in the same place and in the same relationship, a horse, goat and walrus. Again, that can be said of the goat, walrus and horse. I have said this about the skin, about variable and mixed sensation, about the engendered organism or about the completed body itself, a heterogeneous structure hastily cobbled together with sticking plaster. I also say it of myself. I am and am not this or that, here and now, in the same relationship. Half-breeds in our own thought, do we not all know this? Hybrid in our existence, do we not all think this? Changeable, diverse and varied? I do not know or feel this or that, here and now, in the same relationship. But if I have to describe it, I am positively obliged to feel or know it. In addition, if I promise or write it, I feel, know or am it without a shadow of doubt.

I, feeling, unicorn: a horn in the middle and tattooed everywhere else, with a fluid identity.

Suddenly I know why the unicorn has only one horn. The chimera with the varied body, its sundry parts hastily cobbled together with sticking plaster, loses its identity because of all the joins in the rag. Its deviation from the identity principle consigns it to fable, imagination and legend. Yet in this impossible location, in this cutaneous excrescence springing forth from the centre of its forehead, its identity is successful. It is there only that it is a unicorn, and it is to this that its name refers. In every other respect it can be said that it is a goat or horse. Rather like an ordinary animal or man, one can speak of right or left, or one can speak of left or right. Plus a weld, a seam in the middle. Plus a perineum, as Plato, seeing a trace of tacking, was wont to say. But a chimera accentuates seams, it makes them blatantly obvious. In the middle, where the skin is welded together, grows an enormous horn, skin itself. Neither right nor left, nor even rift or leght, but exactly in the centre, like Polyphemus' eye. This is where the very concept of chimera takes form, the very meaning of the unicorn, its impossible or characteristic organ, its name. Here the otherwise impossible mixture is successful. Here the sensible is successful.

And suddenly I understand why, according to the legend, by dissolving the unicorn's horn in liquid and drinking the potion, one is mithridatized against poisons. To understand the single horn, one must understand the mixture, make and drink it. Scientists from the Royal Society in London who once drank, as an experiment, a solution of rhinoceros horn and concluded, in the absence of consequences, that its supposed effect was myth or legend, did not understand that they had already understood. The legend simply expresses the mixture, as the horn does the seam. Conversely, the mixture can so far only be expressed in myth or legend, like the sensible.

VAIR[4]

The prince seeks a queen. What is to be done in a principality, unless he can find a shoe that fits? He sends out the town crier, he wants to see all the women.

To see? Come, come, would a king's son be so lacking in taste, and not know that seeing tell us very little? A seer isn't worth much. No, he asks the candidates to try on a vair slipper, and here begins the mystery.

A story often proposes two riddles, that of the things said, and that of the narrative: for example, the riddle that the sphinx poses Œdipus and that he solves; then the one posed by the myth to all who hear it, and which remains for a long time without an answer. It is necessary to understand that Œdipus' name signifies that he knows feet, that he is acquainted with, or can resolve everything relating to feet. Thus the narrative explains the riddle and anticipates the solution. Likewise the prince solves his question: the vair slipper belongs to Cinderella; as he is ruler and has the means, his method is as expensive as possible. He makes such a thorough review of all the women that he is guaranteed not to overlook any. But the riddle of the story remains: why is the slipper covered in vair, why use the word vair, just as we might ask: why give the name Œdipus to the one who unravels the riddle?

What can be said, first of all, about a slipper? Incidentally, would you please give credit to a book of philosophy which at last asks serious questions – what can one say, I ask, about a slipper? It gently sheathes the foot, like an invaginated pocket: an awkward pleat, a sort of bonnet or the finger of a glove. You can feel its shape, an open and shut tent, made by and for the touch, skin on skin in places where it suffers, pathologically sensitive. What intelligent leader or captain would admit that our feet are the site of the greatest sensitivity? Would he say that there is nothing in his head that has not first of all been in his feet? The prince, however, begins there. Just as humble, Cinderella began with *Cucendron*.

Touch the vair slipper, caress its warm, soft, gentle fur. A higher, sparse layer of long, thick hair protects another lower layer of fine, short hair. All fur reveals and conceals a similar double property. The skin of the foot is protected by a skin that is protected by another layer, protected in turn by yet another. Quadruple, quintuple variety.

Give no credence to the glass slipper: it is the wrong word, devoid of meaning, inappropriate for dancing, solid, brittle, hard, cold, transparent. Glass is seen or reveals, clearly and distinctly, vair is touched and hides, soft, not hard, loose, not tight, extremely pleasant to feel, and gentle, velvety and voluptuous to the eye, leaving the dancing foot free. Now look closely at vair: a colour lacking in homogeneity, white and black, not black or white, distinct and separate, but with somewhat mingled colours, not grey, but precisely squirrel, a mixed ash-grey colour. In the language of fur, or that of the furs of heraldry, vair indicates a varied colour.

Now, in an ordinary sense, it could not be said that the prince discovers the poverty-stricken woman. He does not unveil Cinderella beneath rags or finery, revealing glimpses of her adorable body: the rags already express admirably ocellated nakedness. No, the prince discovers his queen, sitting almost naked amidst the ashes, by encasing her foot in the vair slipper. Recognition works by touch, not sight, by the stereospecificity of that which fits perfectly. Exactly the right size, the slipper moulds itself point for point to her foot. The skin precedes the gaze in the act of knowing, vair wins a victory over glass. Is it a fairy story or a letter on the blind[5]? Or true love whispered with a grateful caress?

Vair designates a varied colour, soft, double fur, a slipper that allows the foot enough freedom to dance, a variable shoe.

A glass slipper, constant and rigid, calls for a fixed and rigorous concept, valid for a stable world: an accurate measure for a foot that does not grow, walk, run or waltz. A flexible slipper is better in a world, in a variable environment, where rats change into footmen, where things whirl around under a fairy godmother's magic wand, where unrecognizable horses are transubstantiated into lizards.

When in proximity to cinders, the world varies: a fairyland where pumpkins become carriages that after midnight become cucurbits again, alchemy that transforms rags into crinolines; the servant, miraculously, becomes a princess. Meanwhile, for the Prince, things are immutable; just as for other women, stepmothers or false sisters, balls and societies, nothing changes. For Cinderella, things fluctuate, volubly.

The reasons for the alliance between a fairy who in a trice changes things, and an overburdened victim, are not to be found in resentment alone or in the impotent dream of the persecuted. Those who are excluded or beaten concentrate within themselves the power of metamorphosis or apotheosis. Society considers them to be pestilential and then suddenly adores them as gods. This has been a common phenomenon since the dawn of history. The hearth, to which the stepmother consigns the poor ash-covered girl – just as in times gone by the scapegoat was burdened with the refuse and sins of the world – is the antechamber of palaces. These two values or positions, misery and glory, oppression and royalty, murder and power, Tarpeian rock and Capitol, close to each other but opposed, are ordinarily the hallmarks of all stories with sacred content. They are the two sources of the in no way exceptional, and in fact quite ordinary, double worlds of anthropology, politics and religion. The victim and the Prince are separated by nothing more than the twelve strokes of midnight or the touch of a magic wand.

But Perrault's story attempts to say even more. It traces the path of a value to its dual other, from the cinder value to the gold value, from the hearth to the palace, from one source to the other, from the place where power oppresses you to the place where it belongs to you; it traces the path of variation. The whole century is looking for the same road: the distinction between good and evil, falsehood and truth, power and misery, never poses a very difficult problem – you could even say that it is a distinction that we make almost naturally. All our hatreds lead us to it, all our violence impels us towards what is supposed to be a rational, or sacred division. But the path from one of these positions to the other, the continuum that links them, or the gulf that separates them, poses a much more formidable question for which neither our culture nor our resentments prepare us. The whole century is seeking the path of variation.

Things vary, volubly. You always arrive at a crossroads at which, to your discomfort, the coach in which you are travelling morphs into a pumpkin, where gold, between your fingers, is reduced to ashes. Yet the slipper is the sole object amongst these changing appearances that resists the wave of instability. Midnight chimes, noble luxury collapses into ignoble banality, the shoe remains unaffected by the transformation. It does not become an ignominious clog, as it should. One vair slipper remains at the palace, a hostage of the prince and a witness, while the other slipper returns to the scullery: there is an invariant in the variation, one in each world. A unicorn's horn. A place of seams, mixture and marriage.

We were not expecting, either, to see things, or hear the word. Things vary, the word says so. Vair designates the varied or variable but does not itself vary. The whole secret of the tale is contained therein: the foot of the chosen beauty in the shoe, the king's business, a subtle sense in the designation, the business of science. The age-old dispute about glass and vair, the one transparent and the other a veil, has long pointed to the nub of the matter. Glass breaks, fur varies. The root of the word vair goes back to varied, which suits us nicely. The root of the word varied, *varus*, knock-kneed, lame with two odd slippers, suits the Prince. He was looking for a knock-kneed woman, because he had always understood that they make marvellous lovers. A limping gait gives an uneven and therefore varied beat. Clearly there is no getting away from the foot of the *Belle Noiseuse*, the only stable or unvarying element in the striped, striated, chaotic and varied painting of Balzac's German painter. Here, I encounter it again as the invariant variable element, in body and in name, just as in Œdipus' riddle.

The slipper grips the foot and is the correct size. The foot designates the unit of measurement. The unit, of course, must not vary, the slipper which envelops it and is the correct size, is the hallmark of the variation. The vair slipper, the parameter, becomes the variable. At the same time as Perrault was writing his stories, Leibniz was introducing into mathematics, and into the same French and Latin languages, the notion of the variable, and giving variety as a criterion for the reality of a phenomenon.

Variation requires one to think both the stable and the unstable simultaneously, not pure instability, which is strictly speaking incomprehensible, but the invariant in the variation. The whole voluble world refers to the stable measurement of the foot, the whole path of change is travelled by means of the variable slipper, another seven-league boot.

We come back to the unicorn's horn, a large excrescence of skin, the synthesis of the right and left horn crushed to a powder and dissolved in a liquid, blended into a potion so that left and right are to be found indissolubly at the same time, in the same place and in the same relationship. We once again encounter the unthinkable mixture. In the impossible horn the chimera at last achieves the union prefigured over its whole skin by vague meanderings and bizarre juxtapositions.

So with the vair slipper. Flexible but specific, with the potential for all shapes but fitting one only, individual and voluble, open and shut, holding the foot firmly but allowing it to dance, it obliges one to think in the same place, at the same time and in the same relationship the stable and the changing, the one and the multiple, reference and variation. Quite precisely, vair designates the variable.

In the prince's hands, the slipper leads to the irreplaceable princess and tomorrow we shall go to the queen's wedding: a unique key opening only one door. For us, absorbed in the story, the word vair gives the meaning, the key to language: to what is a variant sense to be referred?

Sight is pained by the sight of mixture. It prefers to distinguish, separate, judge distances; the eye would feel pain if it were touched. It protects itself and shies away. Our flexible skin adapts by remaining stable. It must be thought of as variety, like the vair slipper. It apprehends and comprehends, implicates and explicates, it tends towards the liquid and the fluid, and approximates mixture.

MISTS

I like to live in the dark, in a material as well as a moral sense – the man in the public eye enjoys no freedom. I practise seeing in the dark. Often light appears harsh, aggressive and at times cruel; wait for night, take pleasure in the twilight, light the lamp rarely, let the shadow come. The night shines like a black diamond, it shines inwardly. The body as a whole sees the close proximity of things, their massive night presence, their tranquillity. Bright light removes them forcibly from that peace and takes away mine. My shadow body can evaluate shadows, it glides amongst them, between their silences, as though it knows them. Shadows excite the closest possible attention and are even subtly revealing; our whole skin comes alive. Even on the darkest night almost anything can be done without the faintest extra gleam of light, you can even navigate the middle of a sunken lane on a moonless night. The soles of your feet begin to be more aware, your shoulders brush against the branches, the stone in the ditch gives off a peaceful light. One can do almost anything without light, except write. Writing requires a glimmer. Life is satisfied with shadows, reading requires clarity.

Night does not anæsthetize the skin, but makes it more subtly aware. The body trains itself to seek the road in the middle of darkness, loves small, insignificant perceptions: faint calls, imperceptible nuances, rare effluvia, and prefers them to everything loud. Things wandering in the silence and shadow help it to rediscover practices long since lost through forgetfulness and habit. Technical prostheses date from such a recent time in our history that our humiliated bones rejoice in playing once again from an ancient score; our tendons and muscles, the garment that is our skin, sing with joy when we throw away our sensorial or motor crutches: wooden legs, lamps, automobiles. Our technology is often like orthopædics for a healthy limb, which, as soon as it is replaced or lengthened, so theory has it, becomes ill or impotent. Let us keep what augments us and spurn what diminishes us.

But the world provides more than just night or shadow to frustrate the skill of the attentive person. Even if darkness envelops us, it does not attack the skin as mist does. The anguish into which fog plunges us comes not only from the blindness it provokes, but from the way in which it trails and crawls, in layers, over our arms, shoulders, thighs, stomach and back. What does it mean to veil, how does a veil cover things? Shadow awakens our limbs, intensely present when sight is veiled; they hasten to take over automatically from the eyes. When mist veils sight, it lulls the body to sleep, saturates it, anæsthetizes it, our skin makes a concerted effort over its whole surface to resist its compresses. Impression fails under compression. Our skin loses the freedom to back up our hesitant gaze. Fog tears out our back-up eyes, it blindfolds or cocoons us. Mist multiplies veils. Veils are invisible at night.

The large, relatively stable trihedron which traverses and orients us, left-right and up-down, is left unchanged by the shades of night, which also maintain the distribution of the large surrounding masses. They allow what little remaining light there is to emerge, and there is always a little. The markers and relationships by which our skin relates to the surrounding volumes are removed by mist. In order to learn that in such circumstances one loses confidence in even the most reliable instruments, you have to have passed through a bank of mist so thick that you lose the person next to you, even though you may be touching elbows. Aircraft have been known to come out of the clouds upside down, or ships stray off course on irrational orders from the officer of the watch, thrown into a panic by the fog. Fog removes the skin's potential, its extension and ascendancy, it creeps into every corner and progressively fills every part of space, it blankets or sticks to flat or curved surfaces, it fills crevices. Global shadow, local mist. Night suddenly flares up from afar and the surrounding volume remains empty. Mist lurks and creeps and spreads slowly, from place to place, filling or skirting around neighbouring areas. Night is empty or hollow, fog is full; darkness is ethereal, mist is gaseous, fluid, liquid, viscous, sticky, almost solid.

Darkness is concerned with optic space and retains Euclidean volume; shadow, like clarity, preserves the order of common geometry; fog occupies a variety of topologies and is concerned with the continuous or ragged space of touch. Its tatters invade the by-ways. When dense and compact, it accumulates; when insubstantial it rarefies and vanishes like mist. Thus shadow retains the features of the world, whereas mist transforms them continually by homeomorphism, causing distances, measurements and identities to be lost. On an open bridge, swamped by a pea-souper, you retain the tactile certainty of being situated between the captain and the watch, phantom neighbours like phantom limbs, but you lose the sense of their size, the shape of their profile, and your feet, like their bodies, vanish into the unfathomable distance. Shadow leaves everything invariable and mist makes everything variable – continuously, whether broken or unbroken.

Dry Greece remains the kingdom of geometers, all born there, in blinding light or in darkness, and empty enough to make you believe that the dazzling truth will appear if you merely lift a veil. Optics, also, has its beginnings in these places. The damp Atlantic carries yellowish banks of mist that tower above you like cliff faces, as do the Baltic Sea and others to the north. Topology could never have originated in Sicily or Iona, where everything is known in terms of distance and measurement; one has to go beyond the Pillars of Hercules to have some idea of it, through the seas where there is no guarantee that the hazy fog-shrouded distance is subject to the same laws as what is in close proximity, itself subject to distortion. Veils, there, are too numerous to count.

THE FIVE SENSES

Skin attaches itself to a treacherous membrane, to an irregularly-shaped tatter, canvas or veil, followed by thousands of others, every one different. The whole environment loses its invariance, reliability and faithfulness. I am speaking about sensation, culture and science, about philosophy. Filling space in a random fashion, mist resembles both the medium and objects, what covers and what is covered. Darkness does not betray, nor does shadow: in them a thing remains a thing, veiled or not, visible or not, always accessible through touch. Fog betrays, completely fills the environment with potential things. Whether they are objects or vapours – we cannot tell. Night unsettles phenomenology, mist disturbs ontology. Shadow reinforces the distinction between being and appearance, mist blurs it. Thing or veil, being or non-being, that is the question.

COMMON SENSE

Sensation, receptive to any and every message, controls the skin better than the eye, mouth or ear . . . The sense organs appear on the skin where it is soft, fine and ultra-receptive. At given places and sites it is rarefied to the point of transparency and opens and stretches to the point of vibration, becoming gaze, hearing, smell, taste . . . The sense organs cause strange variations in the skin which is itself a fundamental variable, a *sensorium commune*: a sense common to all the senses, forming a link, bridge and passage between them: an ordinary, interconnecting, collective, shared plain.

We bear on our skin the complex singularities of which it is composed: germs, pimples, navels and inflorescences, folded, drawn and ocellated, like the bezels of rings. Just as flat or irregular fabric becomes islands, hems, flounces, frills, gatherings, sewn decorations, so does our skin form the continuous backdrop, the base note of the senses, their common denominator. Each sense, originating in the skin, is a strong individual expression of it.

Conversely the skin, the plain to these mountains, receives all the senses together. Rather more transparent, vibrant and concentrated, sharper, higher in altitude or in performance, the senses are more specialized than the skin and, therefore, cruder. The skin displays them collectively, unfolds their density, opens out and exhibits things deposited by them in a central place, dilutes and thins them down. The plain is made of the sands that wash down from each mountain along the rivers, just as the face is made by the erosion caused by tears and laughter lines. Our wide, long, variable envelope hears much, sees little, secretly breathes perfumes, always shudders, draws back with horror, withdraws or exults at loud sounds, bright light, foul smells. Shivers when it sees white and when it hears high notes, and flows smoothly beneath every caress. We are bathed in things from head to toe. Light, shadow, clamour, silence, fragrances, all sorts of waves impregnate and flood our skin. We are not aboard a vessel, ten feet above the water line, but submerged in the water itself.

Exquisite sensitivity – normal sensitivity – does not mind dense messages but prefers subtle ones, feeds heartily on quantity, but delights in the places where quantity withdraws, leaving only traces: quality, a gentle beginning, the barest of traces. Thus does faint evidence of the visible and the audible linger on the skin, chiaroscuros and whispers; on it remain the invisible side of the visible, the inaudible sounds of music, the heavy caress of the light wind, imperceptible things, like remnants or marks of loud, harsh energies. Skin is haunted by the gentleness of the sensual.

I come to the conclusion, furthermore, that the sexual organs, recognizable on the skin – tertiary as in the angle of the elbow, secondary as in the adornment of hair or the tessitura of the voice, primary, unnameable because of the shame of everyday or scholarly words – are sense organs, singularities on the common plain, remarkable sites, folds, seams, buds, hems or seeds, mountains and wells, springs irrigating the whole landscape, as do the others. They emit and receive, recognize and vary.

I have certainly not the skill, competency nor specialized knowledge to conclude thus. But I regret, as a gentleman, that physical love is ponderously described today both in supposedly learned discourse, and in ordinary usage, only in pathological terms. As though it were dramatic, fateful or painful. Thus denominated, sex indicates the illness of separation, of being cut off. The pathetic or pathogenic grimace fades when the senses joined together form de facto particular cases of the skin-variety. Skin translates the amorous caress into arousal, subtly displaying desire and diluting listening and seeing to the point where they almost disappear. It bears the signs of the one and the signals of the other and the energy and information of both. Odours beguile love, which then calls for champagne. Love shines amidst the five senses and is their happy summation. Love knows no separate zones, nor specialization.

Alcohol swells, burns and corrodes the epidermis, thickens and hardens it, gives to those that it drugs the appearance of heavy pachyderms; an elephant man or mammoth woman moving about under anæsthetic. The primary sense of the French word *blaser*, a northern term, refers to insensate body armour. The learned, humpbacked idiot, Master Blazius, discourses much and drinks copiously, having become indifferent through an excess of words and mediocre wines. The maker of phrases has made his skin blasé.

In the year 1692, during the month of July, Leibniz published in the *Journal des savants* a brief conjecture – whether good or bad, true or false, on the whole it was quite profound – on the origin of the word *blason*, which means a mark in old Celtic and Saxon. Or otherwise, indicates a sign. The author quotes Scandinavian, Icelandic, popular speech, Greek and English slang. We believe today that *blason* and *blaser* both come from the Dutch word meaning to swell. The noble carries a sword and the ignoble displays his overripe paunch, swollen with alcohol or importance, or sometimes both together. But why separate the two values: the *blason* and toughened skin can be confused. Each is a sort of callus.

Leibniz, again, compares the French *blesser*, to wound, with the English *bless*, in both cases meaning to mark with a sign, defamatory and painful, or fortunate and salutary, two values for whomever receives it, marked with a beneficial or deadly seal, and sometimes both at once. The Greek *blaise* means bandy-legged, the opposite of knock-kneed: he who points his feet outwards. Poor Blaise, still marked by his feet. Leibniz goes further and claims that French *bleu* and *blanc*, English *blot* and German *Blitz* belong to the same group. Blotch, colours, lightning, scarifying the sky.

The baron and the alcoholic, blessed and wounded, master and slave, king or victim, marked out for glory or sacrifice, armadillo,[6] taboo, bear the sign and are marked with the seal. But why carry values to extremes? All in fact bear a mark and name: they are all tattooed.

Admittedly, it must be understood that the language of the blazon codifies a prior tattoo. Originally both the heraldic and the ordinary shield were covered in skin. But also, I believe, before coding and even before any voluntary lesion or benediction, or imposition of the written or spoken name, the individual tattoo of each person acts first of all as a sign, marking and naming him. A wart here, a scar there, flaming red hair. We are born emblazoned, our skin imprinted. Nicknames come from the impressions left on our skin by our personal histories.

But even greater understanding is needed; there is an obscure relationship between naming – the mark, sign, scarification, writing of the proper name on the parchment skin – and anæsthesia. The voluble array and mixture of colours express fluctuations in time and history, and deposit our identity there. If we try to stabilize it in order to have an invariant, identifying, constant, compact sign, then we are blasé about what surrounds us.

We must either feel or be named. Choose. Language or skin, æsthesia or anæsthesia. Language solidifies meanings.

The argumentative, Latin-speaking scholar on his mule is drugged with wine and good words. How many impressions and how much time have I wasted inscribing so much writing in a sort of heraldic code on paper skin? Unstable stripes mingling in patterns on watered-silk skin would make a better page. I have no code for it, nor pen, but I am attempting to make a tracing of it.

Was my grandfather trying to turn me into a writer when he would mutter: 'Don't bite your nails, child, how else are you going to scratch your little girl friends when you're playing?'

Hippopotamus or horned rhinoceros skins, the protection of armoured warriors impatient to throw themselves naked into battle, chitinous skins of beetles, bearing sagittal arms, skins of soldiers or drug addicts, what do you know about anything? Skins without doors or windows, coats of mail, bullet proofing, what do you feel?

And what do you feel, equipped with techniques and formulae, protected by exact, rigorous language?

No, war is not the mother of all things. Battles produce nothing but new battles, hence no productivity. Yes, dialectics loses its way. Not totally erroneous, it enjoys occasional successes, exceptionally or as counter-examples, but it is always invariably, mathematically false. Show me a single thing produced in and by conflict, a single thing and I shall be converted; show me just one invention induced by polemics. I offer my possessions and my time to anyone who can reveal a single success. As battles produce only battles, dialectics is reduced to the identity principle, to repetition, to null information.

Dialectics has enjoyed great success. How is it possible for such an error to have invaded not only philosophical reflection but also education? Who amongst the public doubts the generally accepted notion of the benefit of battle, who amongst publicists is ignorant of the fact that the word 'struggle' fascinates us? The younger generation has imbibed the idea of quarrelling with its mother's milk and reaches adulthood ready to destroy everything through a belief in the beauty of wars it has not experienced. And when it has gone beyond that age and those misfortunes, it will find itself old, like the generation that preceded mine, mourning the waste of lost lives. It will have waited too long to discover the error of dialectics.

THE FIVE SENSES

Nothing is constructed, made or invented, except in relative peace, in a small, rare pocket of local peace maintained in the middle of the universal devastation produced by perpetual war. Dialectics owes its success only to hominoids' passionate love of quarrelling. They rejoice in murder and destruction, talk about them endlessly and rush to gape at them as at a theatrical performance. Most do not know how to construct, invent or produce a thing or an idea. They want to win, they want to fight. In a choice between creation and destruction, those few who hesitate can be counted on the fingers of one hand. All run to the abattoir, stupidly confusing energy and aggressiveness. They adore therefore any theory that assures them that creative work is born of battles, even if they never see it proved, even if every significant work is only ever born of an improbable island of silence and peace.

I call them hominoids because this conduct resembles that of primates locked into their relationships, drugged on domination, physically and materially, and who pass or waste their time ensuring that this one occupies the first place, and that one the position of lieutenant, one step down, and so forth down the pecking order. Hominoids fight to remain primates. Static equilibrium in the animal groove. War is the mother of animals. Battle produces the society of monkeys, which produces battle. Conflict stabilizes the archaic bestiality in us. Dialectics describes the logic of anthropoids. Man comes into being when he sees the falsity of this.

That happens if he has survived the struggles to become a grand old man to whom wisdom comes at last. Listen to him, the returned soldier dissolved in tears and having difficulty digesting his wasted life, lamenting his former thick-skinned, gorilla-like aggressiveness.

Combat – either political or scholarly, involving either language or the body, bare-handed or armed, individual or collective – and thus hierarchy, power and glory count amongst the hardest drugs, the chemical and pharmaceutical composition of which is dictated by dialectics. These drugs give us a monstrous skin, as does alcohol. Squamous, sclerosed, rigid, insensitive. Blasé.

Avoid struggles that masquerade as works in progress, avoid battle-productions and drugs, save your skin. Refine it, while you are waiting for whatever will happen, for the birth of creativity.

Endowed, supplied, afflicted with a quivering envelope, a tender onion-skin disturbed by wrinkles like a fragile lake, naked, nay flayed, these are the ones who are unsuited to the battles of crabs. It appears that life evolved from animal forms whose soft parts were inside, covered by a hard external casing, into other forms, such as ours, in which everything hard is interiorized as bone, cartilage, skeleton, while the soft is expressed as flesh, mucous membranes and skin. Those who love to fight are unevolved leftovers from a very ancient past, from the dark time when we were armoured. The newcomers amongst us become gentle, wrinkle-bearing: we bear imprints. We are clothed in soft, warm wax, we are tarnished mirrors, a warped, scratched, blotched, diverse surface in which the universe is reflected a little, on which it writes and on which time traces its passage; clothed in wax tablets, an ancient image of the soul, clothed in our intelligence and memory, engraved in a different way from the world, with a network of longitudes, latitudes and contour lines expressing our longevity, suffering, broadness of views and generosity. The skin receives the deposit of our memories and stocks the experiences printed on it. It is the bank of our impressions and the geodesic panorama of our frailties. We do not have to look far, or search our memory: the skin is engraved and imprinted to the same extent as the surface of the brain, and perhaps in the same way.

Beauties of Asia, fine and delicate creatures that you are, where do you place your remembrances, you whose tireless skin, devoid of such markings, conserves its freshness for so long?

Everyone seems to believe that our point of view, our point of vision, is up in the dress circle, eyes sitting at the top of the trunk on a swivelling, mobile head, like a lighthouse lantern. Our skin would be the stone base of the lighthouse, with no relation to the lights and signals, a simple raised structure ensuring that the gaze will travel. The lighthouse guardian would be the pupil of the eye, or at least ensure its movement. I assume that the official in charge of the concept, like the chief engineer in charge of Lighthouses and Beacons, runs things from his office in Paris, the brain or central processing unit. An expert trained at the Ecole Polytechnique, he pays a few quick visits to the sea illuminated by his department, when he has time. The centre is preoccupied with important things. For the rest, it suffices to telephone; to send or receive messages, to make language circulate.

The soul, and perhaps also knowledge, glides up and down the structure, on the surface of the tower. There is a kind of softness in the way it presents itself, like naked skin to sea water, a softness strong enough to resist circumstances or to seek them out boldly when the opportunity arises, but a strength subtle enough to pick up discreet calls, a hard and sensitive softness, a delicate balance, sometimes off-balance, between the delectable and the heart-rending. We learn nothing, really, except what marks the wax, which is soft and warm but cold enough for the tracing to endure, adaptive to the point of death but stopping short of it; to write, I read from my flayed skin rather than copying parchments from the library. These days I trust this memory more than data banks. An author speaks for himself. I write on my skin and not on that of others who would answer for me, as Bonnard paints on his and exhibits it without shame. I decipher my wrinkles, the engravings of time, written with a stylus; my soul haunts this inscription-covered hide.

It seems to me that the brain is a local concentration of this place of knowledge. The thinking I quivers along the spine, I think everywhere.

If everyone exhibited, as painters do, their cast-off skins, their moults, and imitated the writer and the exhibition of his scarified parchments, each one with his labarum, shroud or winding cloth, we would see a fine sight. Wrinkles, scars, tough old hides, corns, psoriasis; work, pain, memory, secret perversions, tattoo the skin and determine it even more than its natural colour or high-class shades of brown, acquired on beaches – where no-one is naked, because clothed in their tan, a thin veil waiting for cancerous growths, sun-bathing. Bits of rag, marked, tattered and torn, heavily embossed, on display for all to see, feeble confessions or occupational stigmata, are we really anything but those rags? Are we anything more than these ghosts?

This is how souls wander in limbo and in bookshops.

One of the last thinkers in the French language, Henri Bergson, left his successors with several questions to resolve, among which is that of varieties. Like mathematicians of his time, he distinguished between discrete varieties: contrasting flowers juxtaposed in the fields, animals scattered over the islands; and continuous varieties: a painter's palette, a garden paradise, a vair slipper, shades of modesty or emotion on the skin. He situates the first varieties in space and the second in time; he groups space with intelligence, and time with intuition; he classifies intelligence under science and intuition under philosophy. This discrete positioning shows the limits of his intelligence. It could be thought that he left the question of time to his successors. One must, before toying with that idea, go back to his assumptions; the distinction between both families of varieties. For topology has never stopped exploring spaces, trailing continuity in its wake. The only philosophical mistake committed at the outset is in fact concerned with those spaces; it was believed for a long time that Euclidian or metric space, that which we consider usual or everyday, was the only space conceivable. In fact, since the time of Bergson's thesis, geometries, and with them, spaces, have proliferated. We no longer see why the continuous should be alien to them, why it should be necessary to classify it with time. We can no longer confuse space and metrics, space and discreteness.

Subtlety goes behind the canvas. A certain figure appears on the front. Behind, a forest of knots conditions it, prefiguring a computer circuit board. The medieval tapestry shows the five senses; whereas we believe we are manufacturing artificial intelligence. In the same sense, the *Lady and the Unicorn* weaves a subtle, artificial sensorium. The subtlety enmeshes the warp and weft, one over the other, or underneath it, high or low-warp. The interlacing designates an analogous, even more subtle situation. Can we place a third thread between the other two. Where would it go? Under, over, beside: what does 'side' mean?

Juxtaposition of the discrete variety assumes distance between elements or seeds. The distance which separates and distinguishes between two neighbouring flowers, animals, or even threads; the gap, however small, allows one to insert a third element or seed between the other two. This possibility initiates a sequence, which reproduces the old question of the third man: no one knows if, and when, it finishes: between the first and second seed and the third, can a fourth or fifth be inserted? You can imagine the direction of the series and its simple law.

Before rushing headlong towards infinite things and appealing to time so as to be able to think about dense accumulation, we need to return to the situation in which insertion occurs. Indeed the third, at any point in the series, gets its bearings between the two preceding ones. This intercalary situation is subject to several constraints. Where is the third seed to be placed – between the two, or in the middle of them? What are we placing between the two elements, a thread or a plane? What inclination will be given to the plane? At this point, either a finite or infinite series of new seeds can be aligned on the thread, or the said plane gradually filled with them, or the said space saturated with them, etc. In other words: the situation 'between' describes a sequence along a straight line separating the seeds, or permeates the space in which they are both immersed. To be more precise: this situation also, and especially, deploys a great multiplicity or variety of paths or ways crossing this thread or space. Indeed, at each level at which the question is again posed, the choice of the intermediary situation of the new seed can take place in a different dimension. It's something that all women know – dress-maker's apprentices, spinners, knitters, or weavers: over, under, etc. None of the paths thus obtained runs in a straight line, none remains in the same dimension, all twist and curve.

Since many braids and curls are involved, an inextricable tangle presents itself. Metric measurement and its rigidity, so often confused with rigour, disappear. Distinction is distinguished from distance, the number of ways from here to there increases inexorably, and the paths overlap. The body, armed with its hundreds of degrees of freedom, used to live flexibly and still lives in this situation until topology teaches it to us again, or teaches us a rigour different from that of a wooden automaton. It is immediately obvious that a knot, in the common sense, is formed as soon as a space-between presents itself. It presents itself discretely, as well as continuously, and more often in the first guise rather than the second. Could separate elements join together more easily than inseparable ones?

The distinction between continuous and discrete varieties no longer appears so clear. Could each be reduced to the childish gesture of Alexander the Great cutting the Gordian knot with his sword in order to take control of the Asian empire? Separation ignores the knot or tangle that lies between separate things. Since Alexander, we have forgotten Eurasia. A lack of subtlety prevents us from seeing the forest of knots beneath the canvas or behind the tapestry, dazzled as we are by the representation of intelligence. To be sure, the tapestry displays a sort of discrete mosaic, but to analyse it properly it would be necessary to undo by hand the tangled threads behind. What a job it would be indeed to separate out this mixture! Before infinity or time separate the discontinuous from the continuous, the knot ties them together. The practice and concept of connection precede many others.

The situation described here remains a naïve one. We are only talking about seeds and threads. It quickly becomes necessary to generalize it. Where and how is a thread to be slipped between two threads, what path is to be taken through what space? One has to move up through the different dimensions in order to have a better understanding. Where and how is a sheet of paper to be slipped between two others, what path is to be taken, through what space? A knot traces a one-dimensional path in a three-dimensional variety to connect elements to one, two, zero or three dimensions. It is necessary to imagine foldings, invaginations, exquisitely complex situations that generalize the practice and the idea of the knot to all imaginable dimensions.

The set of elements situated between two others can follow the straight line that separates them; their metric distance can fill the whole space into which the two elements have been plunged, but more generally it describes a subtle and supple path, curved braid, curls and garlands going from one, and meandering through every dimension, before joining the other. The number of such paths increases indefinitely. In the first two cases, the middle situation is described – a point situated at an equal distance from the two others or a global series that surrounds or encompasses the latter – in the third, a state of mixture.

This is the spatial or conceptual situation of the knot. Of course knots can exist in all imaginable dimensions: smooth or crumpled fabric can also pass, via an edge of fabric, on or under another canvas and so on. This situation marks the limits of the analysis. In a discrete variety, sorting always appears possible, it is a matter of patience. The seeds or discrete elements, too subtle, light and imperceptible, and the complex paths that describe their situation in relation to each other, are not taken into account. In continuous variety, these paths have gained strength. Bergson expected us to wait until the sugar had melted in the water. He never required us to wait for the mixture thus formed to separate out. Readers would have had to wait until the end of time. A mixture is not easily analysed. Work, heat, light, a thousand pieces of information are necessary. If I wish to drink this water, I also have to drink the sugar, if I want the sugar, I must swallow the water, if I want one constituent, I have to pass via the result as well as via the other constituents. The continuous is unanalysable at any given moment, and so are mixtures. It could be said that the sugar and water are tied together by a knot that we cannot always untie. It is common knowledge that the term analysis comes from a Greek verb which, as it happens, means to untie. Analysis requires that a knot be undone. We believe that analysis demands only one cut: the cook's knife cuts the tendons, sinews, and muscles, the analyst is satisfied with having separated the bones. As if bones alone were sufficient for the animal to live. In discrete variety, sight that divides, the vision of the division, is blind to the light, tenuous knots that unite the respective situations, as if a given situation, with given bearings in relation to the other elements, mattered not at all. The elements of a jigsaw puzzle in a box tell one nothing about the design which becomes visible after the correct assembly of the pieces. In some ways the analyst always carries a knife, always imitates the young Alexander and knows no bonds.

There are only varieties tied or bound by soft or hard, cobweb-thin, or thick bonds, knots that analysis undoes with ease or difficulty. This situation is better described as a mixture than as a medium.

And as a veil rather than a solid. And as skin rather than sight. And as the body rather than its tongue.

Fabric folds, crumples, turns on itself, is knotted at will. Skin wrinkles, adapts, reigns between organs and contains complex paths that link them; more than just the medium of the sense organs, our skin is a mixture of them, like a palette. The naked woman's tattoo resembles Bonnard's palette.

The organism forms a gigantic knot with as many dimensions as one could wish. It begins, in an embryonic state, with one or more sheets, folded, pleated, rolled, invaginated. Embryology has the appearance of applied topology, looks like an infinitely wrinkled skin. The organism fills with local interchangers that finally form a global interchange system, a giant knot made from small differential knots.

The body folds, curves, adapts, enjoying at least three hundred degrees of freedom. From the feet to the head or to the tips of the fingers it traces a variable and complex path between the things of the world, changing like a piece of seaweed in the depths of the water, a thousand and one exchanges or signals. Knowing things requires one first of all to place oneself between them. Not only in front in order to see them, but in the midst of their mixture, on the paths that unite them. In her right hand the lady with the unicorn firmly holds a flag strewn with crescent moons and in her left, the animal's single horn. Touching is situated between, the skin is the place where exchanges are made, the body traces the knotted, bound, folded, complex path, between the things to be known.

MIXTURE, UNVEILING

The skin is a variety of contingency: in it, through it, with it, the world and my body touch each other, the feeling and the felt, it defines their common edge. Contingency means common tangency: in it the world and the body intersect and caress each other. I do not wish to call the place in which I live a medium, I prefer to say that things mingle with each other and that I am no exception to that, I mix with the world which mixes with me. Skin intervenes between several things in the world and makes them mingle.

Mixture is a more accurate term than medium. Medium, too geometrical, is minimally useful: a centre in a volume, when it is reduced to an intersection, or the volume itself, when its tendency is to surround. A point or totality, singular or almost universal. A contradictory and inflexible concept.

Everything has its place in the middle when the medium is concentrated, everything meets and joins together in this complex place, in this knot, through which everything passes, like an interchanger. It makes me think of the solar plexus of a thwarted left-hander, of an unwilling ambidextrous person. Everything still has its place in the medium when it expands to fill the volume. Everything meets there. How? By chance. Where? In proximity to one another. All right, here is mixture. Confluence, unfurling, occupation of places.

A medium is abstract, dense, homogeneous, almost stable, concentrated; a mixture fluctuates. The medium belongs to solid geometry, as one used to say; a mixture favours fusion and tends towards the fluid. The medium separates, the mixture mitigates; the medium creates classes and the mixture, hybrids.

Everything meets in contingency, as if everything had a skin. Contingency is the tangency of two or several varieties and reveals their proximity to each other. Water and air border on a thick or thin layer of evaporation, air and water touch in a bed of mist. Earth and water espouse each other in clay and mud, are joined in a bed of silt. The cold front and the hot front slide over each other on a mattress of turbulence. Veils of proximity, layers, films, membranes, plates. We live on slow, inexorable moving footpaths, thousands of metres beneath our feet.

The theory of knowledge is subordinate to its choices, by which I mean the examples it uses. It could be said that theory and intuition belong to the order of vision, and that strictly speaking they belong to the solid. I have long been moving towards the fluid and have encountered turbulences in the past and, more recently, mixtures. Thinking about fusion without confusion, I shall come soon to liquidity, difficult to conceptualize but the future resides there, and I shall come to mingled bodies.

Meanwhile I am seeking the best model for a theory of knowledge, less solid than a solid, almost as fluid as liquid, hard and soft: fabric.

The skin, more topological than geometrical, does without measurement. Topology is tactile. The skin, multisensorial, can pass for our common sense.

We have just left classical theory, subordinate to the solid and to sight.

We cannot claim to be so exceptional. We are not the only ones, surrounded by boundaries, to throw ourselves into contingency, the only adaptable ones who can turn our hand to anything.

The world is filled with complex veils.

According to one tradition truth is an unveiling. A thing, a set of things covered with a veil, to be discovered.

If it could be reduced to this exercise, philosophy would be equivalent to a rather boring variety of illusionism or juggling. Science would lose its complexity if it were only a question of discovery. That seems puerile.

THE FIVE SENSES

No, there is no thing under the veil, nor does the woman dance under her seven veils, the dancer is herself a complex of fabrics. Nudity reveals more pleats and wrinkles. Harlequin will never arrive at his last costume. He undresses infinitely. There are always more peacock marks, ocelli and tattoos.

The state of things becomes tangled, mingled like thread, a long cable, a skein. Connections are not always unravelled. Who will unravel this mess? Imagine the thread of a network, the cord of a skein, or a web with more than one dimension, imagine interlacing as a trace on one plane of the state that I am describing. The state of things seems to me to be an intersecting multiplicity of veils, the interlacing of which bodies forth a three-dimensional figure. The state of things is creased, crumpled, folded, with flounces and panels, fringes, stitches and lacing.

Unveiling does not consist in removing an obstacle, taking away a decoration, drawing aside a blanket under which lies the naked thing, but in following patiently and with respectful diplomacy the delicate disposition of the veils, zones, neighbouring spaces, the depth of the pile, the talweg of their seams and in displaying them when possible, like a peacock's tail or a lace skirt.

This medium or mixture would be our model for the state of things, thinkable or intuitable, or sensible, like a heap of fabrics, a thousand possible arrangements of veils.

Sensible to sight like an aurora borealis, for anyone who finds themself in the vaporous, honey-combed, incandescent, draped, light, fragile underpinning of the dawn light; tangible like the topology of surfaces and their events or circumstances; audible like waves of the sea or sound, or batiste handkerchiefs floating in the air; sapid without a doubt, I feel my tongue sheathed in a fitted rag when I taste; the state of things is the medium of the senses, or rather their mixture. The skin mixes them and also veils them.

Weavers, spinners, Penelope or someone like her, once seemed to me to be the first geometers, because their art or craft explores or exploits space by means of knots, proximities and continuities, without intervention from measurement, because their tactile manipulations anticipate topology. The mason or surveyor anticipates the geometers in a strictly metric sense, but she or he who weaves or spins precedes them in art, thought, and no doubt in history. We had to dress ourselves before building, clothe ourselves in loose garments before constructing solid buildings.

Generalizing this hypothesis, it can be said that fabrics, textiles and material provide excellent models of knowledge, excellent almost abstract objects, primary varieties: the world is a heap of clothes. Where knowledge was concerned, woman was for a long time ahead of man. Pierre Bonnard's naked woman, the goddess with the bird, the girl and the unicorn or the wretched creature in her slippers.

The hand moves rapidly on the loom and distaff, around the needles, it creates the thread, twists it, threads it through, folds and knots it, the hand deftly splicing and lashing, unfailingly finding the gap underneath that the eye cannot see, it strays across the frosted glass, levelling the seeds sown by chance, prickles that it alone knows how to identify, on the sand it traces loops or braids, happy amidst the leaves and garlands the hand dances, enjoying its degrees of freedom.

Touch is topological and prepares the planes and smooth varieties for a relaxed, metric, Euclidean gaze, the skin covers with a veil what the eye cannot see. Molyneux's problem – whether a person blind from birth, who has just been operated on, would be able to recognize with his new-found sight a cube or sphere that he was previously able to identify with his fingers – raises more questions about the geometry of those whose vision is not impaired rather than it does about the theory of knowledge. Why not experiment on a nightingale or a lilac branch, an emerald or a velvet skirt, which exist, rather than on abstract volumes, which do not exist? Who among us has ever seen a cube or a sphere? We have only ever conceived of them in language. So if you give the blind man a ball and a cobblestone, he will by touch be able to appreciate the continuous deformations, the jagged edges and particularities, he will soon ask you if you are able by sight to tell the difference between a ball and a sphere, a cube and a cobblestone. He will laugh sympathetically at your discomfort.

Are we aware that writing requires the most complex nervous and muscular skill? No other form of manipulation brings into play as many nerve endings. Those who know how to write could do anything with their ten fingers, peoples who learn this refinement, learn at the same time all possible manual trades, cruder and simpler than this one. They who invented it revealed to humanity the path towards everything that was practically possible. But conversely, the female embroiderer, sewer, spinner or even surgeon operating under a microscope, still stitch together seams with loose links, compared with the fine knots and the intricate paths of writing. They have their hands in hard things while she who writes immerses her hands in the soft sign. A link so subtle that it is attached to nothing, a knot so tenuous that it is already passing into another order.

Pure touch gives access to information, a soft correlate of what was once called the intellect.

2
Boxes

HEALING AT EPIDAURUS — THREE KINDS OF AUDIBLE — SOFT AND HARD —
PASSAGES — CELLS

HEALING AT EPIDAURUS

For the last two hours this morning I have been tasting the sun in the theatre at Epidaurus, alone, reclining against one of the steps. During the winter solstice the deluge of tourists slows to a trickle: a truce in a new war. Peace in the transparent air, yellow and blue. Silence. The countryside awaits the gods – it has been waiting for two thousand years. Silence. The gods will descend, healing will come.

A question mark on the sky's axis, visible from passing planes, an immense ear bathed in the precisely tuned acoustic properties of the amphitheatre. I listen, I wait, in the dense silence. Even the insects sleep, ever present in the muteness of summer. Diaphanous, the world calms the turbulent noise of my body. My organs fall silent – health returns. Illness comes upon me when my organs can hear each other. Silence in the great theatre, in the capital of healing. The body no longer listens to itself, adrift in the pavilion of the immense ear of the gods. When a body will not remain silent, what voice do we hear? Neither voice, nor language; cœnæsthesia emits and receives thousands of messages: comfort, pleasure, pain, sickness, relief, tension, release – noises whispered or wailing. Æsculapius quietens these messages, and slowly erases them. We are healed better by leaving noise behind than by diving into language.

The silence within the theatre and in the surrounding scrub seeps into my skin, bathes and penetrates it, vibrates and drains it, in the hollow of the empty ear. I give myself to the world which returns me convalescent. I release a low moan into the world, and it gives back its immense peace.

Horror. Here comes a group. I can hear it in the distance, coming this way. It projects itself across space as filthy noise. It is deafening, disturbing the transparency of the air, even before I can see it from my vantage point, coming out of the tunnel of green branches. Two, ten, forty people are encased in a shell of language and then in a rumbling outer hull which precedes, flanks and follows them like the prow, sides and stern of a bulky ship. The sea vibrates around the vessel, overwhelmed. It is here. A whole orchestra. They talk, squawk, discuss and exclaim, admire out loud, call to each other, give explanations, point out this, describe that, read the guide book, lend a distracted ear to its explanations and test, for the hundredth time, the location's exact acoustic properties. A din in the great ear of society. The fearful gods have fled from this eruption, as have healing, and the harmony between our organs and the things of the world. Its cries exhausted, the group moves on, trailing a long train of language behind it; and its fractious wake, still vibrating in the buffeted air, evaporates in turn, the stain disappears, and the smooth silence returns like offended modesty.

What did they really see? They heard: cries, words, echoes. But certainly saw rather little – all the more so as their cameras saw for them. But what did they hear that they did not already know from their language-memory? Did they come to Epidaurus at all? They arrived ill, indisposed by the murmuring of their organs, surrounded by their collective noise, and they departed in that clamorous ship without ever really arriving. If they had talked, shouted, conversed with each other in Boston or Aachen, they would have made the same journey, but for the rain in one or the snow in the other. Alone on this step, sitting in silence for the last two hours, little by little the world gives me its gods; immersed in the social ship, I would only have picked up stray bits of language from the people around me. The group carries its gods around in bags and walkmans. In its sects and libraries.

Silence returns like a modest veil. Slowly. The immortals are hesitant to descend to such an easily sullied place. The gods pass us by, weightless, insubstantial, flanking non-existence, evanescent spirits; the least wrinkle in the air will chase them away. They have long since fled our deafening world.

The collective only believes in its own noise. Living aboard this boat and travelling without leaving it, the collective believes that the world is given to us at the outer hull of language, or possibly at the water rippling around it. That the world is given to us in the midst of pandemonium. Immobile, in the sunshine, on my step, swimming in the yellow and blue transparency, I learn – slowly – that the given comes upon you like a state of grace. Evanescent spirit, lightness scudding through the limpid air. The gods will meet suddenly in a corner of the forest, that is where we must await them, timid and fearful like a small animal, but patiently: I have often felt like a statue from immobility and waiting. I listen. The given approaches me quietly. I listen. My ear grows to fit the dimensions of the amphitheatre, a marble pavilion. My hearing flat to the earth, on a vertical axis, tries to catch the harmony of the world. It awaits the birds coming in on the wind.

Amphitheatre does not mean a space where people speak, but one where many see. A sacred word will silence those assembled there; it need not even be a word, sometimes a wordless gesture is all it takes to render them silent: a kind of ritualized mime, and silence overtakes the collective hearing as all eyes focus as one. Transfixed, one's organs are at peace: this is healing. Sometimes music is all it takes, and nestled in the hollow of hearing the orchestra listens and watches, the assembled throng heals itself by listening to its own harmony, observing it in silence, nestled inside the immense marble ear; what it hears is its own social contract.

The actor – tribune and teacher – listens to this silence passionately, explores its volume, recognizes its quality, evaluates its grandeur. The grandeur and musicality of his own words are produced not just in, but also by this cathedral-like calm.

It is time to begin. The smallest thing, a sign, a gesture, an attitude is all it takes to detonate peace. The voice in the centre sings this tranquillity; describes and produces it; makes it, yes, but receives it also. This is a circular movement, like mouth and ear for a single body, and this cyclical return is what produces theatre itself, its form and its structure. Eloquence comes from silence alone, and perfects it. Speech has the quality of stillness, the grandeur of its volume; stillness has the quality of eloquence, and the social contract answers silence with the silence of what is said. The gathering hears and recognizes itself through a word that emanates from its own silence. What is said can be cancelled out between the two large, heavy blocks of stillness and peace, its cause and its consequence; should the spoken word be silenced, then the gods will come.

Speech catalyses and propagates the silent harmony from which it can then be removed.

But the collective is quick to bury its harmony, grinding it up in the chaotic noise of applause. The gods are broken into tiny pieces in the palms of our hands.

On solemn occasions the theatrical circle of gesture, word and – rarely – silence, is closed. During this ritual the group is not so much encircled as imprisoned by its own shouting and arguing. The swallows flee at such vociferation. Just as the nightingale sings in order to define its nest and mark out its territory, so do we occupy and at the same time empty out the universe with our thunderous techniques. Like the submerged cathedral of old, the earth is engulfed by noise.

More than patient waiting, it is distance that is needed for the flighty given to reveal itself in all its timidity. Is it possible to step back and measure one's distance from the very collective to which such measurements owe their existence? Can we break the circle of this theatre, open a doorway in the hull of the vessel, break free of its wake, when the whole universe resounds with our fury? Being enclosed in a group condemns us to language and language alone, since even social silence produces it. Being enclosed in language stops us from seeing that the noise that it makes veils and overwhelms the things which compose our world, and causes them to vanish.

The world, heavy, yet light, is frightening, yet easily frightened off; it imposes itself, yet vanishes into the shadows; it is necessary, yet fragile.

Hermits are familiar with the distance that must be crossed before the fleeting given becomes audible. Anchorites and reclusive scholars have had the same goal. And others; not just those who love God, or the truth, but those who are simply attentive. Hunters, too, will observe silence so that the observed world might come to them.

Immersing yourself in silence is a form of healing; solitude releases silence from the control of language. If the world fills with noise, then who will seek it out? Language gave us the sciences, and they made possible a thousand different techniques which, in turn, generate so much noise that we can finally say that the world is riotous with language. Language is our reason. At Epidaurus, during the winter solstice – in the off season – I seek shelter outside of this reason.

The given is only given to us beyond this first threshold: that of living alone. If you should come together in the name of research, all research will flee. As the word descends into your midst, all focus will evaporate. It is not a lone thinker we find in the ivory tower, but a gathering. Groups surround themselves with a compact wall of language. The only thing anyone can attend to is words. I have never come into contact with this ivory when working alone. When I am in the midst of the collective, I see it, I hear it, I touch it, it smothers me. This hard, smooth, insurmountable wall is built from their language. Groups imprison themselves behind their language of wood, wind and ivory.

Bathed in silent air, yellow and blue, alone, outside, I give a chance to the given, which the collective ruckus expels; I give a chance to those senses anæsthetized by language. The group devotes itself to its own din, revels in its own roar, notices little outside itself. It resembles a sick body, rumbling from the clamour of its own organs. What health would it recover if it were one day to fall silent? Is it only the good health of individual bodies that depends on silent organs? Had I come to Epidaurus as part of a group, I could never have healed. Aboard its ship buzzing with communication, the collective is not so much ill as intoxicated: drunk on language, drugged with noise, deprived of beauty, anæsthetized. Morning and night, each one of them treads the same paths in the same relationships with the same people in the same channels with the same words. They cannot not do it, rather as though they had to rebuild a crumbling section of wall over and over again, to restitch a tapestry which unravels every night. Distracted. Insensate. I live no differently from these drugged individuals. I am devoted to language, which anæsthetizes all five senses. Every group I am part of, needs it or lives by it. This is the healing I seek from the god Æsculapius on a winter morning: not just the silence of my organs, in harmony with the silence around me, but even more than that, the silencing of language within me. My very first, and hardest, detoxification treatment. The first step in constructing an æsthetic is to pray for the disappearance of these anæsthetics.

Alone in the immense amphitheatre, under the intense blue sun, I want to purify myself, unlike my ancestors. In the ruins of tragedy, I wish to tune out my own static.

Sitting down alone, in silence, on a marble step at Epidaurus under the winter sun, far from the throng, focused for a few hours: this is a necessary, but not a sufficient condition. Doubtless much more is required to achieve the sufficient condition, in order that the world give itself to the healed body; in order that what is given, gracious as it is, should come and sit next to me; in order that I might actually observe something. The given might indeed be given to us beyond the first threshold of solitude and silence; we can only be certain that it will do so after the second: can I measure my distance from it, locate it? Can we step outside our language?

The god I am waiting for never announces his visits. Will I even recognize him if he comes? All I know of Æsculapius the Healer is a name, a figure, designations and descriptions – this is already too much knowledge, he will not heal me.

Just before dying, Socrates wished to settle the debt of his recovery by sacrificing a cock to the god of healing. 'Crito, we owe a cock to Æsculapius. Remember to pay this debt.' His body was already half cold when he uncovered his face to pronounce these last words. He thought he was going to get better. Death is the last stage and objective of the cure. Must death come at Epidaurus? Socrates wanted to die. There he lies, on his bed, cold, delivered. How heavily life and body must have laid upon him, that he should ask the god to heal both! The final silence of mouth and organs.

For as long as he thought, he remained ugly. Is it truly possible to think without arriving at beauty, without penetrating the secret place where life bubbles up, without the transfiguration of the body? Once a certain age is reached, a thinker must take responsibility for his face; his knowledge and thinking must take responsibility for his body. Socrates, hideous. What a thing to admit! His body, wizened. What a symbol of hatred! The deformity of the man reflects the infirmity of his philosophy. He loved death; he so wished for it. See how he displays it, behold the tragedy: in the midst of the wailing and the tears, such delight over this gnome's corpse, laid out centre-stage; the sublime dialogue, the flute music, the weeping relatives, the wine drunk to its dregs, the sobs, the applause. He did not know how to die alone, he turned the most banal, unavoidable, private and solemn moment of our short lives into a performance. Twenty-five centuries of weepy, plaintive philosophy follow in the steps of this circus freak. To which squalid, monstrous god does he sacrifice himself? To which hideous god – god of loathing, death and ugliness – does he owe his apotheosis; which of these put him centre-stage in our theatre of philosophy?

What do his friends do, hearing him speak while he lies dying? Are they distracting him by making him speak of the soul? Are they anæsthetizing him to pain and fear? Is this dialogue as good as a drug, a narcotic phial? A narcotic for Narcissis? What am I to make of this death, these words, if I am to get better?

Ever since those dying words in the tiny cell-like theatre in Athens, becoming a philosopher has meant taking one's place in the necromancer's circle – standing, sitting, leaning against a stone step, fascinated by this sacrificial body, decomposed now – eating Socrates' corpse and resuscitating him, his narcotic forever on one's lips.

He would not stop talking, right up to the moment of death. Even in such a private, solemn moment, he could not stop talking. Socrates wanted not to abandon the prison of iron and stone, could not, even for a moment, escape the fortress of talk, nor leave the ivory jail of Law and his peers, could not leave behind the word, any more than he could forget his dialogue, or his language; a flying insect colliding with the window-pane of the answer and ricocheting into the wall of the question. The prison vibrates with noise until death, it all ends with the sacrifice of the rooster, words, more shouting when the body is half cold. Of what polemical illness are Socrates' friends cured by his death, Socrates who was apparently sacrificed to the Law?

I see and hear them this morning, from where I am perched on the stone steps, locked into their dialogue, stuck in their language, more securely than if they were in prison. Whereas earlier I was distracted, so intent on listening to the silence and waiting for the gods to arrive that I failed to recognize the group come to test the acoustics of the site with their shouting and vociferating, now I perceive Socrates' entourage, rehearsing the same scene for over two thousand years. One of them imitated the crowing of a rooster in order to hear its echo in the immense amphitheatre, the others laughed. The oldest among them, exhausted, lay down in the centre of the tympanum; all his friends crowded around him. Silence. There is a brief emotional moment during which tragedy returns, furtively, to this intense, solitary place. More laughter. Were they healed when they left?

See if you have anything else to say, said Crito. Crito leaned over Socrates and said to him: see. See what you still have to say. But Socrates' gaze was fixed. Upon seeing that, Crito closed his mouth and eyes.

The fixed gaze no longer sees what remains to be said, proof that normally it keeps an eye on what needs to be said. It sees neither cock nor rook, but it sees that cock remains to be said, rook to be spoken; words and categories absent from the farmyard. The dead gaze was drained not of light, images, things, colours, shapes or nuance, but of language. Crito saw that Socrates saw no more, with his own eyes he saw in his master's eyes that there was no more to say. Upon seeing that, he closed his mouth and eyes. His eyes, in other words, his mouth.

To see is to know, and knowing is saying; saying or living, and living or saying. There is nothing left to say, and the gaze is still: nothing to see beyond the sayable, there is nothing beyond the sayable. When you are silent, you see no more; all that remains is to die.

What do you see, you who are drunk on words? I see your sight, still and empty.

THE FIVE SENSES

A still gaze does not necessarily signify death. It may be the result of some narcotic. Haggard, anæsthetized, drunk, drugged, the vacant stare of lunatics.

I can recall hearing philosophers in dialogue, screeching and quarrelling at the foot of beautiful mountains, on ocean beaches, in front of Niagara Falls, they had the fixed gaze of those with something to say, and I can testify that they saw neither the snow of the glacier, nor the sea, that they heard nothing of the crashing water: they were arguing. They never left the prison of laws, each threatening the other with a term of confinement; should one of them win through force, the other would be killed. So much the better if the other is the only one killed. Dangerous people. I fear those who go through life drugged, less than I fear those under the edict of language.

Language dictates. We are addicted.

Stretched out on a divan, Socrates speaks of the soul, he associates the soul with language, words with healing. In the midst of his friends, at the centre of the theatre, he talks of the immortal soul up to the very moment of death, associating death and recovery. Without the slightest opening between speech and death, no window, no doorway, not so much as a minute's gap, nor the slightest fissure between discourse and death, no way of leaving the collective, just suffocation behind closed doors, strangulation under the triangular yoke of death, recovery and language of the collective.

The mouth has spoken, drunk, tasted the bitter draught. It is not only language that can kill or intoxicate us by passing our lips. It is a sinister wisdom which tastes nothing but the cup of death; a bitter wisdom which has haunted us for two thousand five hundred years.

Crito, Phaedo, Cebes, Simmias, Echecrates, Socrates: they all speak, screech, argue, exclaim, admire, call out to each other, advise each other, exhibit themselves, point things out, describe a world they do not see – invisible, intangible, colourless, odourless, tasteless – promise each other a better future in Hades. The prison of speech only leads to hell, or to the ideal heaven. Already half cold under the effect of the pharmaceutic draught, the hero is prostrate in the centre of the orchestra, humming with language. They rush towards him to ask if he sees, if he sees anything else to say. Numb, Socrates dies in noise, at the theatre. He has drunk the formula.

This morning I am in full possession of my faculties; and I declare it my unambiguous wish that people remain silent when I am dying. I want no drugs, neither pharmaceutical nor linguistic. I want to hear who is approaching.

Who am I now, alive, at a distance from the seething group and its competitive cycle, who am I, seated here in the sunshine for more than two hours now, motionless, upon a marble step, giving myself over to the transparent air through which rooks fly; who am I, made up of languages dead and living, French and Greek, trained by culture and drawn here by the prestige of the names Epidaurus and Æsculapius and their promise of healing, a statue fascinated by this small group, this representation of the large collective, playing out a larger drama in the amphitheatre built to display it? No matter how far I travel, poor subject that I am, I never manage to put any distance between myself and the droning of the language that shaped me. What merely resonated within my mother's womb is a clamour in this stone conch, and finds itself echoed in my innermost ear. The threshold that I imagined remains impassable, I am made up of the others I claim to have left behind, even alone they make the same noise in my chest, residually. Can I leave this drugged subject behind in order to sit and wait and observe? I must keep my distance from myself. That is what we call ecstasy.

I try to split myself in two. As though, on this marble step, there remained a corpse made up of language, Socrates, dead, a memory filling up the space of my head and body, my passions and my thoughts, a subject with a fixed and vacant stare, its eyes always riveted on categories, heaven and hell. As though a listening attentiveness, white, empty, pure desire and gift, projected itself beyond this set of memories, keeping its distance, the counterpart of the subject of language.

If we always talk, then we suffer: drugged, anæsthetized, addicted, under the edict of language. Drunk on words, as once one was said to be drunk on God. Unspeaking, I go towards silence, towards health, I open myself up to the world. The sensitive, delicate, receptive, refined feeler detects another echo and withdraws hastily, waits, observes, unsteady, outweighed by the mass of language, like a rarely-extended antenna, waits for the unexpected, recognizes the unrecognizable, expectant in the silence. Patient watchman, upright, searching for a peephole, crack, fissure, hole, window in the densely-packed wall of language, motionless watchman bent under the chaotic weight of night, waiting for dawn, occasionally ravished by the sight of this wordless dawn exploding out of nowhere along the breadth of the horizon, thirty-thousand feet above the ground.

Without this dark vigil I do not exist: my body of history and memory, stable within my language, prone, coiled up, asleep in the box bed of words and propositions, in their logical and combinatory lodgings, or in the immense amphitheatre. This subject of language dreams. Dreams cut a fake window in the wall of language. This subject of language and memory does not exist, sleeps, has the same dreams as everyone else, the same ambitions and struggles, in the ivory tower of language; dreams during performances, just as at the theatre, at Epidaurus, or watches television and computer screens, drugged by words and politics, addicted to what is said. A submissive subject, subjugated, prostrate, trampled, flattened by the enormous burden of language. Crushed to death.

By extending myself precariously I exist, outside of the stability where the other subject remains asleep or dead. Along the giddying crest of language run the battlements patrolled by guards. Frightened, shivering, horrified by the wind or arrows flying in the middle of the day, some watchers sit down, their backs against the battlements framing the crenellations. Walk with me; I recognize my stable, sleeping body along the way, cradled by dreams, in a stupor of language that reaches all the way into its unfulfilled desires. I recognize it in the watchman who looks inward, whether facing the battlements or with his back to them. Here on the other hand is my existence: sharp, agile, vigilant, frantic, gripping the battlements and leaning out through the crenellations, unbalancing into vertigo, ecstatic. Existence, or ecstasy, throws itself outwards, projects itself, unsure-footed; expectancy, a gift to space, a vertiginous risk, deliverance from oneself. First stability, then existence. Propped up by language, then delivered from it. First, aligned with landmarks and points of reference, then far away, with neither landmark nor compass. First security, then abandon. The I only exists outside of the I. The I only thinks outside of the I. It really feels when outside of itself. The I within language is reducible to the sum of its mother tongue, to the collective, to an undefined set of others, to the closure of the open group to which it belongs. It is set in its habits: caught in the I of language almost always and almost everywhere, our whole life long we do not live. I only really live outside of myself; outside of myself I think, meditate, know; outside of myself I receive what is given, enduringly; I invent outside of myself. Outside of myself, I exist, as does the world. Outside of my verbose flesh, I am on the side of the world.

The ear knows this distance all too well. I can put it out the window, project it far away, hold it distant from my body.

Lost, dissolved in the transparent air, flowing with its every variation, sensitive to its shallowest comas, shivering at the slightest breeze, given over to the world and mingling with its outbursts, thus do I exist. My body has fallen so silent that over-convalescence has turned it into an angel. Ah! Good news! Our humiliated bones are exultant, our flesh has become sensitized.

Tragedy returns in more mundane arenas.

Condemned by the judges of Athens, Socrates condemns himself to death out of a desire to be healed. On the tribunal sit men who have the power of killing with a word. Their sentence is executory: speech equates to act. As in the prison of language, so is there no interval here between saying and dying. Outstanding performance. Forbidden access to the theatre, to the prison, to the tribunal, the world cannot come between language and action. Philosophy is most comfortable when experience cannot stem the power of words; comfortable in representation, within a cell, in groups, in judgement. Language can kill an actor in the theatre at Epidaurus, it kills without reprieve in a tribunal.

Enter the judge. He pronounces sentence. Socrates is condemned, here and now. I prick up my ears, I listen, I hear the sentence – curiously, I hear it in another dead language: *Socrates addictus*. Socrates, convicted by law, whether spoken or written, convicted through deliberation, is condemned by and through these words. This procedural term is performative, as deadly as hemlock. It matters not whether you drink poison or have these words in your mouth. It is not the case that philosophy becomes involved in questions of law and justice, where speech is action, at the end of the eighteenth century. It does so from its Platonic beginnings. Since that time it has enjoyed saying that to say is to do; it loves speaking about language. On the day he died, convicted by the words of a judge, but equally condemned by his own, Socrates further demonstrated that it is better to die, if we thereby deliver ourselves from this corrupt world and from this unspeakable body. Doubly *addictus*.

For the second time I hear the same word echoing around the steps of the amphitheatre. Without knowing it, the group below has acted as though the theatre had not long ago lost its role and purpose. Dead now, open to the world outside, submerged in limpid blue and yellow, surrounded by shrub, green even in winter, stretched beneath a pale sky in which crows wheel and turn. Plants, animals and wind have invaded this closed place, just as a wedge splits a log, opening up a wedge between what is said and what is given.

As at the theatre, the group is locked into its lines. In the midst of his friends, Socrates remains in a dialogue to the death. Life's tourists will see nothing of the land of the gods, occupied as they are with talking; none of them wants what is simply given, none wants to receive or accept it, all are condemned to their sentences: addicted to diction, anæsthetized, drugged, *addicti*, sentenced to the gaol of words.

The English language says *addicted* of a person whom the French language would call *adonné*. Such a person is *given to* meditation, study, pleasure, gaming, drugs. The distance between the two languages, the translation across that distance, traverses a passage, an interstice in language. In one we speak of what is given, in the other of what is dictated. Is to have experienced the given, the same as having spoken it? There is no word in French derived from *addit*, as though French were leaving room for the given, or fashioning an opening onto a strangeness outside of itself, as if the addicted person could be given to something other than language; as if the word *addicted* somehow stoppered up that opening in English, closed the door of the language on a deaf and dumb – a tacit – porch, or threshold, or horizon. Can an experience of the given be reduced to its utterance? With this question comes that of drugs – lingering around the body, around language, around the group and the world, lurking in the very knots that bind them together. Yes, I have come to be healed. We are addicted to what is given just as we are dedicated to speech. Do we now live dependent on the world, the free source of the given; and in the future, will we live equally code-dependent, addicted to the universal data bank? Is the choice of our addiction all that we are left with?

The Latin root of this utterance is to be found within the space of the tribunal, which like the amphitheatre is cut off from the world. His gaze fixed and vacant, Socrates is drugged, condemned by his sentence, by reason, by the *logos* in general, by the utterance turned thing, hemlock: addicted, *addictus*. Hemlock: drug, remedy and poison, sentence. Enter the judge, exit Socrates. The judge enters into speech, Socrates exits life. Socrates exits his life of words, his life of logic.

Enter the judge, exit Socrates. Henceforth it is the judge who holds the floor. A performance upon a stage is a simulation. It kills for a laugh, it kills to heal, and everyone goes away relieved. At the tribunal, speech is action, speaking performs the action, it kills for real. Since philosophy entered the tribunal, it has put itself in a position to act – to kill. It has in fact killed millions. By what right?

By what right does it grant itself this right? Remarkable in its formulation, this question replicates both the judge and the law itself. When we ask someone 'by what right' we are in fact asking that person to designate someone else who can act as guarantor. But exactly the same question can be asked of the latter and so on indefinitely. As though a third man might appear behind the second's back, and a fourth behind the third's: an endless line. In philosophy and elsewhere there is a class of questions dealing with existence and non-existence, questions which relentlessly pursue this third man.

A group entered the amphitheatre below a little while ago, huddled around its eldest member or its guide. Socrates appears behind him. The judge appears behind Socrates. And so we ask of him: by what right? And behind him stretches a long chain of shadows.

The guarantor is summonsed. Now, when dealing with this class of questions calling upon a third man, philosophy has always sought to determine if the chain has an end, a last member whose existence would legitimize each preceding link. If he exists, let him appear before the tribunal.

The judge exits.

The judge exits. Enter the praetor.

The praetor opens the judicial proceedings. First magistrate in terms of seniority and rank, he opens the proceedings by uttering the first words, the fundamental terms, which end all debate about a third man. He cannot be asked 'by what right', since the law cannot be spoken before his arrival. He gives everyone the right to speak. First, originary, he initiates the time of law.

The praetor speaks, and says: *do, dico, addico*. I give, I say, I confirm or award. Of course, no-one really understands *addicere*, the source, root or origin of both sentence and addiction, the verb which lurks behind Socrates' words and actions, just as the judge stands behind the philosopher and the praetor behind him. *Addicere* further means to vow, to dedicate, to dispose of (as in to sell), to award, to legitimize a transferral of property, but also to sentence. The praetor's first three words, the *tria verba*, pertain to language, law and religion. They are the beginning of judicial action: once they have been spoken, words *are* actions. The praetor gives: he gives the formula, the action, even the judge; he speaks: he speaks the law, he rules on proceedings; the praetor approves and confirms the will of each party. I could go on and on refining the translation of this word, but it would get us no further: the essential thing is to enter into language and assess its weight, to give it its full force. Which proves that before the praetor we were outside of language.

Let us consider the development of this formula, as though the first two terms were there to give rise to the third. The addition of saying and giving equals addiction.

THE FIVE SENSES

We know many things about saying, about its logic and anthropology, we know so much about it that surely everything we know is through it, with it and in it; it is all we know. We know many things about giving, about the logic of exchange and its anthropology, we know so much about it that it is surely only because we are submerged in the network of exchange that we live at all. But we know nothing about the addition of these two, their synthesis, their mixture; about addiction. About what makes the death of Socrates the foundation of our philosophy, Socrates condemned by speech and poisoned by hemlock, poisoned by speech and condemned to hemlock. We know nothing about how giving might be taken over by saying; about how the given might be anæsthetized by speech; about the price speech pays for the given, which was free in the first place; about how speech sells out the given; we know nothing about the gift of speech, the gift of languages.

Addicere: to speak and to give approbation through saying; or, to give oneself the right to say through saying; or, to give speech the right to give. That is how Festus defines it, using the third verb to close the circle in such a way as to break away from the recurring question, always referring to a third man: *by what right*? Behind us is Socrates, and behind him, the judge; or, behind the play, the tribunal; behind the judge, the praetor; or, behind the law, its foundation in language. That is where the series stops. The praetor gives to the praetor and to no other the primary right to speak and to give that right to others. He gives himself as first man, the first to say: *addico*.

Addiction, the first diction, the first word, confirms all others. The addition of saying and giving trumps everything else, it is the convergence and summation of everything else – try to find an exception.

Addicted: drugged – addicted to speech as to a drug. The philosopher drinks endlessly from the cup of hemlock, from the crater of words. *Addictus*: sentenced. Socrates the philosopher sentences himself to death. To understand and trace the origin of this sentence, this addiction, we need to look to the very first addiction and synthesis of language and the given. As if, somehow, it were that first decision made by the praetor, the almost algebraic addition of the given and speech through the *tria verba* – as if that first identification of the given with speech produced, out of death and drugs, the sacrifice of philosophy. It is behind the stage, behind the tribunal, that the originary tragedy is played out: the actual death of a man from the poison of language, and life carries on, as we drink from the same narcotic. Asleep at Epidaurus, even our dreams are not safe from language. As death nears, healing flees. The price of adding saying to giving is death and narcotics.

Shadows seem to be dancing behind the praetor's body, behind his words. Might his claim to speak before all others be a lie?

Before the foundation of knowledge, or of law and approbation, even before the foundation of speech, it was decided, according to Livy, that nothing could be changed or instituted *nisi aves addixissent*: without the *addiction* of birds. This is the feral, non-historical origin of the city.

A wake of vultures swoops behind the praetor's back; now a murder of crows. Exit the praetor, enter the haruspex.

The greatest empire the world has known, the longest-lasting in our history was, when all is said and done, governed by the flights of birds. This was the most profound political decision ever taken. You who read this now, you who have just learned this, stop what you are doing and tell everyone; tell the general commanding an army, tell the great economist managing a crisis, tell the President's advisors, tell the ministers, tell the head of state in person, and tell anyone you know who votes. No battle was ever entered by Roman legions, no cargo of wheat allowed to set sail, no law amended, no matter of significance ever decided at that time until the soothsayers had received the approbation of birds; whether this took the form of how they flew through the sky or the way they pecked at grain, nothing was done without the *addiction* of birds. Rome, as we know, won more victories than any other empire in history, devised the most stable legal system, adopted the best possible policies, made, for the most part, the best decisions. As we know, it remains the greatest empire of all time, and it put its fate in birds. Have you ever heard better news, do you know of a single philosophical idea finer and wiser than this one? Is there anywhere a simple fact more likely to teach the great and mighty a lesson in true humility? Or more likely to show the frivolity of our supposed insight, our reason and knowledge, our discourses on economics, strategy and politics, our illusory sciences: the humanities and social sciences. They who were more successful than anyone before and since paid no heed to language, but watched birds fly; they listened to no experts, but observed chickens pecking. I would love to see those who claim to hold the destiny of the world in their hands, whose images we see and whose voices we hear ten times a day, in these times when politics has been reduced to publicizing the State – I would love to see them down in the farmyard, their brows furrowed, meditative. Oh, to see them thus, standing and gaping in anticipation!

The tragedy of speech collapses in laughter.

THE FIVE SENSES

Exit the magistrate, enter the seer. No-one has ever heard a soothsayer speak, no-one has ever understood what one was saying – when he seemed to be speaking, that is. Out of place in the amphitheatre, he chooses instead to race up the steps and leave, to exit the tribunal, to escape from prison; he wants nothing to do with tragedies, has no need of killing – he watches the sky.

Birds do not speak, entrails say nothing, the flight of vultures leaves no writing on the sky.

Apollo was the father of Æsculapius, master of this place; his mother was a princess, the nymph Coronis. It is said that while pregnant she granted favours to another man. Apollo discovered this and killed her, but not before ripping Asklepius from her womb prematurely. How did this imbecile come to learn of her infidelity and commit this heinous crime? By observing how strangely the crows were flying. He had seen their *addiction*.

Thus did the god of divination beget the god of healing and medicine. But in their midst a human sacrifice took place. The theatre is still encumbered by the mother's body. This tragedy is an affliction of ours that we really must treat.

Philosophers mock them, but I admire the rituals of augury, the close attention that haruspices pay to the meaning that traverses or resides in the world, prior to our intervention, whether physical or spoken; the very first observation, wherein perception precedes the utterance or evaluation of language. The praetor cannot say *addico* until the seer has observed the flights of birds. Vultures fly, crows swoop by and chickens peck for food, all without consulting us: it is we who consult them. It is if, and only if, an action has been approved by the birds that the first speaker permits or forbids it. Augury opens a window in the sky that leads in to the prison of language, to Socrates' gaol, to the theatre and the tribunal. This temple, this sacred space fashioned out of the air, is the fissure through which language comes undone, the interstice through which it breathes, the sense with which it begins, its pre-condition. It is the condition and the limit of experience.

It is via this aperture that our eyes turn towards the world, our hearing heeds sounds other than those of language, noises other than those of vocalizing. The sounds of scratching or pecking, or the soft caress of feathered wings in the turbulent air – not even Rome could be founded before this movement was heard.

The dictator talks, the general commands, the praetor pronounces and endorses the law, the philosopher speaks, but the soothsayer listens and sees, before the king, dictator, praetor or philosopher can speak. He comes before speech, in silence. He observes silence in order that the birds might come and be observed.

Tribunals are idealistic, and speak the world exactly as they represent it to themselves, employing performative language; they tell us that saying is doing, and they *do*, obliging others to act as though saying *were* doing. The king, the dictator, the general and the praetor, even the priest, the exacting philosopher, the rigorous scientist, the scrupulous historian, all remain idealistic, everything in the world seems to transpire according to their representations of it. Their speech is performative, it commands. They will all tell you that saying is doing and, under their command, everyone seems sufficiently naïve or obedient to believe them and to act as though it were true. The price of this belief – of this obedience – is tragedy, and death.

Death alone, the presence of a corpse, proves how serious speech is. It is an act of faith, an act of law and an act upon a stage. It is the only guarantee that he who speaks does not do so for nothing. Only death can close the window of language through which the truth might vanish, flying away like a crow. It ensures that language remains a closed system, from which truth takes its traction. Death alone counts as proof. Speaking men, dead men.

The death of Socrates shuts down his language and at the same time validates it, endorses it – I almost said *addicts* it. The death of the word validates the word, and at the same time redeems the things of the world. Death alone underwrites language, the veracity of science, its fidelity to things, its astonishing efficiency. Hiroshima is the foundation of contemporary science, just as the death of Socrates is the foundation of modern philosophy, just as the death of the word is the foundation of the very language which makes us human. Death alone sits centre-stage.

It is not my own immortality I seek, in this place where I have come to be healed, to drink ambrosia from the cup of immortality, but that of the species, in immediate danger. Our race as a whole needs to be cured of death. The human race needs to be given ambrosia, the drink of immortality, not hemlock. Here in the ruins of this ancient, lost culture, I try to understand how and what it is that drugs each one of our cultures, and to what fate they are condemning themselves. I seek to know how I might contribute to healing them, and giving back to them their innocent and immediate vitality.

Soothsayers presuppose a world pre-existing the speech of kings and judges, a world beyond the linguistic enclosure of the collective, and independent of weapons and prayer, a world where uncomplicated sense emerges. They presuppose that this meaning manifests itself without us. In observing the flights of vultures across the sky, or the behaviour of sacred fowl, or the entrails of victims, they are already acting like scientists. Observing, watching. Observing the world as though it were not something brought into being by the collective. Those who practise what are known as the experimental sciences also presuppose a world removed from men and independent of them, and things which exist in a distinct state. Meaning occurs in this world, meaning which cannot be given exact utterance in the language we use, nor precise utterance in the language of our exchanges. This meaning traverses the space beyond our languages, as a flight of crows or vultures. Like scientists, soothsayers observe meaning, with nothing at stake, without fetish, without merchandizing – without having to speak in those terms. It is said that the books of augury were incomprehensible; secret, sybilline and indecipherable, written in a language foreign to all others. My intuition tells me that they contained the ancient algorithms of our physics. Just as ancient Greek foreshadows our language, so must these formulae have been written in the ancestral algorithm of the equations we write today.

Philosophers used to ask if soothsayers could look at themselves without laughing. Indeed, philosophers never laugh, certainly not when they see themselves: they gnash their teeth. They cannot bear to see themselves speechless.

Without being able to prove it I believe, like soothsayers and haruspices, and like scientists, that there exists a world independent of men. No-one knows how to demonstrate the truth of this proposition, which we might like to call realist, since it exceeds language and thus any utterance which might demonstrate its proof. Realism is worth betting on, whereas idealism calls for demonstration. The affirmation that there is no world beyond what we can say about it, is an affirmation rigorously of language, and a rigorous affirmation of language. Then there is the assertion, an illogical one for our logic, an unspeakable one for our language, that there are things, facts, a world beyond language and logic. These propositions, autological one and all, proclaim the autism of language. This is our illness. Thus do philosophers scoff if someone pokes a hole through the transparent wall of language, reaches a hand through, jumps through it on horseback and heads for the forest, leaving the clearing behind. Philosophers laugh at this because philosophy is contemporaneous with language, we acquired them together, invented them together. Suddenly I understand why mathematics dates from earliest Antiquity: it never leaves the clearing of language; and why physics was such a latecomer: everything about the culture of the word mocked it. Greek philosophers mocked soothsayers in the name of the logos, just as the Roman cardinals condemned Galileo in the name of scripture, just as we still condemn the tenacious belief in the subsistence of the world. We always forget that the world bears our immortality.

I believe, I know, I cannot demonstrate the existence of this world because books written by means of other books teach nothing worth knowing, yet we recognize those that come from the world.

I believe, I know, I cannot demonstrate that this world exists without us. Who would not rather take dictation from its formidable silence, joyously and in good health, than write under the judgement of some tribunal?

At the top of the amphitheatre, the coping is crumbling away, here and there, producing irregular crenellations, occasional windows through which crows come and go.

I thought I had found an inaugural lecture. Yet these augural observations, as usual, came camouflaged. The priest's knowledge came from a prior text. Observation cannot be detached from interpretation. Language and code stick to the given facts; mouths are imperious and marks are stubborn, keeping meaning in check, never giving it free rein.

The nymph was killed by the *addiction* of crows before the god of healing could be born. The knowledge of language always comes first. And it is always accompanied by death, the sordidly tenacious tragedy. The theatre is always with us.

Drugged by knowledge? I love that knowledge gives us life, cultivates us; I love making my home in it, that it helps me to eat and drink, to stroll, to love, to die, sometimes to be reborn; I love sleeping between its sheets and I love the fact that it is not something outside me. Yet it has lost this vital quality, so much so that we need to be cured of knowledge.

Broken down into tiny fragments, each rush feeling just like the first one, quickly becoming monotonous, and just as quickly outdated, subject to inflation rather than actual growth, the knowledge that comes to us through articles, theses and academic journals has taken the same form as the information thrust at us by the media in general, newspapers, radio and television; the same form as a wad of banknotes or a packet of cigarettes, divided into units and sorted at the data bank, encoded. We no longer live addicted to speech; having lost our senses, now we are going to lose language too. We will be addicted to data, naturally. Not data that comes from the world, or from language, but encoded data. To know is to inform oneself. Information is becoming our primary and universal addiction.

The aforementioned intellectual activity is the same as a drug fix: be careful not to miss your regular information fix or you will lose touch. The latest announcement renders all preceding announcements outdated. Such is the law of drug-taking: the next fix is the only one that counts. Neither information nor a drug fix ever gives any happiness when you have it, but will make you miserable when you don't. Science no longer teaches detachment from the worst of our evils – competition, mimicry, envy, hatred and war – but instead presents itself in a guise which worsens and exasperates them. Cutting-edge knowledge quickly devalues all the rest: this edge cuts deep, causes pain, subjugates.

Knowledge gives. Quickly, abundantly. In the form of data, it becomes the given.

Knowledge says. Quickly, abundantly. In the form of code, it replaces language.

It replaces the given, it becomes language.

It gives, it says. Approves, sentences and subjugates.

Exit the praetor. Enter the oracle. The praetor, the first man; then the oracle at the real beginning. Before even the praetor.

Exit the oracle. Enter the scholar.

In turn, the scholar says: *Do, dico, addico.*

I am doped on knowledge.

Silence in the centre of healing, silence far from information. Giving up drinking seems easy, giving up smoking seemed a heroic gesture not so long ago; throwing out the papers, switching off the radio, leaving the television screen blank, that is the truest, most elementary form of detoxification. I came to Epidaurus for even more than that. Not keeping current, as they say, with science; not swimming in that current is what delivers us. The end of the hardest drug of all, the beginnings of wisdom.

This wide-spread idea that everything must be said and can be resolved by language, that every real problem is a topic for debate, that philosophy can be reduced to questions and answers, that one can only cure oneself by talking, that discourse is the only way of teaching anything, this theatrical, garrulous, publicity-seeking idea, lacking shame and modesty, is oblivious to the real presence of bread and wine, their unspoken taste and odour, it forgets how to raise infants through barely discernable gestures, about connivance and complicity, and things that go without saying, unspoken expressions of love, impossible intuitions that strike like lightning, the charm that lingers behind someone's outward bearing; this judicial idea condemns the timid, those who are not always convinced of their own opinions and those who do not know what they think, researchers; this didactic idea excludes those who do not attend classes, humble folk, inventors, the hesitant and sensitive, men of intellect and labourers, the grief-stricken and the poor in spirit; I have known so many things without texts, so many people without grammar, children without lexicon, the elderly without vocabulary; I have lived so much in foreign lands, mute, terrified behind the curtain of languages, would I have really tasted life if all I had done was listen and speak? The most precious things I know are embedded in silence. No, neither the world nor experience nor philosophy nor death will allow itself to be locked up in a theatre, or a tribunal or in a lesson. This true idea overlooks physics and life, science and literature, modesty and beauty.

Wise knowledge heals and moulds the body, it embellishes. The more alert and inquisitive I am, the more I think. I think, therefore I am handsome. The world is beautiful, therefore I think. Knowledge cannot do without beauty. It is a science of beauty that I seek.

Once it reaches a certain point in its history, science must answer for its face, for the beauty it displays and produces. I have deserted knowledge in its present form because it makes men and things ugly, because it is not ageing well and has failed to mould our children. It brings ugliness and death, the twisted mask of tragedy.

After a certain point, science must answer for our children. Exit the scientist, behold the child.

We moved towards each other, underneath the sun, he did not speak, I had stopped speaking, we joined hands, we left the amphitheatre, furtively.

THE FIVE SENSES

It is neither hot nor cold, the wind caresses our faces and arms as though drawing a map on our skin, the gentle breeze engages the foliage on the trees in a quasi-musical dialogue, *sotto voce*, the first pungent odours are coming from stems around us, there is grass between our teeth, we chew on its astringency, the landscape of the gods unfolds in the valley below in small ploughed patches, yellow and blue, like an ocellated peacock's tail, as far as the rocky austerity of the hills, come come, I would like to pass on to you the perceptible things we have lost, the secret coming together of the composite world and the harmonizing body, I will leave you wisdom and shrewdness, and the tastes and perfumes of delicacy, come, and once we have stitched together our patchwork skin, like a garment, then I will tell you of the ancient ruins of my language, my beautiful, dying language, born of water that wrinkles like silk, and of the rustling of the sessile leaves of poplars, the gentle voice of things, come to the abandoned remains of the two forgotten, ransacked gardens, the garden of senses destroyed by language, the garden of my language destroyed by codes, come while there is still time, I did things badly the first time around, we are going to start again, come, the last child of men to be able to hear and see, come feel and touch, you will learn science quite soon enough, rest assured that you will.

THREE KINDS OF AUDIBLE

Treatment at Epidaurus consisted of sleep and dreams: the patient was required to hear the sounds his sick body was emitting. He left healed if he had silenced his organs. The primary source of noise is within the body, whose subliminal murmur our proprioceptive ear sometimes strains to hear: billions of cells dedicated to biochemical reactions, the likes of which should have us all fainting from the pressure of their collective hum. As a matter of fact, we do sometimes hear it, and we call that audibility illness. The hubbub spreads across the nested levels of integration that form a black box full of black boxes – molecules, cells, organs, systems – and gradually, over boundaries and through twists and turns, resolves into information. Through this succession of rectifiers thrown up by the complexity of the black boxes, it ends up as healthy silence, and no doubt also as language.

Between the extremes of vision and blindness, sight disintegrates, blurs, fades into a milky cloud: disorder will overcome the obstacles that the body puts in its path. Should it overcome them completely, then darkness reigns, and total blindness is upon us. Likewise, what the deaf hear are neither signals nor voices, but tinnitus; hellish shrieks; high-pitched, strained, monotonous cries that drive you mad. This dreadful torture condemns them to a life of music. Their lives become a tricky balancing act, as they strive to maintain an equilibrium between the layer of music and the chaotic bombardment of noise. When harmony gives way, like the breaking of a dike, I will die, my eardrums punctured by the screaming flood. The moment of death is marked by the final victory of the multiple.

The second source of noise is spread over the world: thunder, wind, surf, birds, avalanches, the terrifying rumbling that precedes earthquakes, cosmic events. Soothsayers used to listen to the beating of wings in the air, outside of the theatre and before its advent, outside of the social or the political, and before their advent. This noise also resolves itself into information via the neatly complicated box of the inner and outer ear, but we often build equally refined boxes around our bodies: walls, cities, houses, monastic cells. Sounds reach the monad softly, through doors and windows.

The last source of sound comes from the collective, surpassing the others by far, often to the point of cancelling them both out: silencing the body, silencing the world. An unusual set of circumstances is required for a group to consent to be quiet: Carthusians, Trappists, Quakers, all attentive to another word; loud, garrulous Gascons, twenty-five thick in a dove-hunting blind and silent as the dead while they await the inaugural shoot of the season. These are exceptions that prove the rule: society makes a colossal noise, the latter increases in direct proportion to the former, the town rat can be distinguished from the country rat by its immunity to this din. Our megalopoli are deafening: who would put up with this hellish din if we didn't simply expect that with a group comes a racket? Being part of one means not hearing it. The better integrated you are, the less you notice it; the more you suffer from it, the less well-integrated you are. Shouts, car-horns, whistles, engines, cries, brawls, stereotypes, quarrels, conferences, assemblies, elections, debates, dialectics, acclamations, wars, bombardments, there is nothing new under the sun, there is no news that is not news of yet another racket. Noise is what defines the social. Each is as powerful as the other, each multiplies as quickly as the other, it is as difficult to integrate into one as into the other. The transition from chaotic rumbling to information – no matter if it is meaningless provided it appears organized – or from a din to music, even if only awful music, dictates the social contract, a document lost to us. You will never find any sense to it, it has as little as melody, rhythm, information or rumbling. Hermes defeated Argus by showing how sound, through its very ubiquity, unites space in its entirety and makes of it a single phenomenon perceptible to all, whereas sight always remains multiple. The audible occupies ground through its reach, power belongs to whomever has a bell or a siren, it belongs to the network of sound transmitters. Even armies used to make their drummers march at the front: the most closely knit of all collectives, united through violence, advertises the strength of its bonds to any potential adversaries, as though it were preceded by its definition, or its signature. In any event this noise, words, motors or music, for the most part overwhelms the call of things and the soft rumbling of our organs. Is the given thus only given to us through speech? Why certainly! Furthermore, it is given in and by the hubbub of its constituents, a racket the singular progress of which is sometimes illustrated by our language.

For the most part we do not know how much we frighten the world, nor the dark holes in which it seeks refuge from us. Tigers roam the jungles, eagles retreat to escarpments, foxes into trenches and wise men to certain islands, all in terror of this noise. All these are endangered species now, dying because we have learned how to broadcast our noise more efficiently. Soothsayers must make their pronouncements before the battle – what bird would risk coming near it? Ask the inhabitants of Hiroshima what they heard of the world one summer's day in 1945.

Do we have an ear for the collective din?

I will never be able to show how grateful I am to the friend who took me to Pinara. A soaring cliff-face makes up the back wall of an immense, almost closed circus of mountains, which one can only reach on foot these days through a narrow pass. You would swear it was the face of some steep continental shelf preventing ships from reaching the shore, just as it does at Fécamp – one hundred metres of shallow water, then a sheer drop. And it is pocked with tombs, up and down, length-wise, in uneven lines, in columns. Vertical burials. Open windows, dark, giving on to the world beyond this wall. What sovereign power will show itself here, on a thousand balconies, to the acclamation of the circus? If all these corpses were to rise up suddenly, we would find ourselves looking upon the façade of a cathedral, busy with immobile statues, studded with ghosts all the way up to the coping. Ten thousand dead eyes watch the ruins of the old city built on a hill below, watch over it, small and crumbling. A bewildering and constant vigil, death keeping watch over life, the time of history carrying on, beyond the extinction of history, beneath the unseeing and multiple gaze of eternity. And Pinara is located in the centre of the world, almost Greek and already European, Asian because it is Turkish, its tombs evoking India, but African in its replication of Dogon cliff dwellings. Time stands still where space folds in on itself.

Facing this solemn wall, on the other side of the city, diametrically opposite the tombs, lies the Greek theatre. Anyone who sits there does so in the expectation that everything will be audible, amplified by echoes: the dignified silence of the entombed, sheltering from the clamour of the city at the very back of their crypts, the words and the music of the tragedy on the decaying stage, the applause on the crumbling steps.

The theatre at Pinara does not face the countryside, or the sea, as though in defiance of the wind and the musical diction of the surf. On the contrary, it is enclosed by the social circus, homothetically. One has the same form as the other, its scale model. The whole landscape is an amphitheatre: the funeral cliff-face rises at the back, the city is the stage, the circle of mountains terraced seating; the constructed theatre is only a small part of the whole. Behold Il Campo in Siena, the main square in Bazas, or Notre-Dame in Paris, closing the social circus with its cliff-face of the dead, just like Saint Peter's Basilica. Everyone sees the town hall or the church, and the public edifice sees each passer-by – as though the social contract, which cannot be spoken, could still be constructed. An institution of stones and statues. The theatre provided the model for the square, and the square the model for the amphitheatre. So simple, so banal, the circle is closed. Yet everyone seems to be fixated on *seeing*. Everyone on the steps and on the slopes sees everyone arranged on the cliff-face and everyone sees at once the spectacle of death, or the foundational tragedy. The more we immerse ourselves in this space, the more we see and the less we hear. And the more we withdraw from it, the less we see and the better we listen. Better still: the better we see that it is a matter of hearing. Of a sound stage, or a noise trap. Of the immense, transmitter-receiver, social box.

In the centre, the speaker or singer hears the silence of the audience which hears its own silence and the voice that comes out of it, a perfect, temporary circle which will soon collapse under the wave of applause, or the shouts and cat-calls of failure. Within a single sentence, inside a single space during the course of a single action, we find rhythm and music, silence and singing, the chaotic crackle of noise, everything that precedes language, and the transformations of one into the other, as though we were dealing with a box both sonorous and deaf, tempestuous, attentive and tacit, capable of changing one acoustic system into another, just as

I described it happening within the body, both the transmitter of its own noises and the receiver of its pains and fits, its pleasures and joys; an empty box during times of good health, manufacturing language out of warm vibrations. The only echoes that come back from the mountains at Pinara are of social acclamation; we will no longer hear the howling of wolves in this place. Except as forebears of cities.

The group listens to itself as we do. It emits noise, colossally so, hears it, refines it and transforms it during this feedback loop into stereotypes, stubbornness, the droning of poetic stanzas, tragic verse, political analyses, social sciences . . . and another noise, background noise, waste-product or residue from the process of transformation, acclamation that grows louder at the perfection of the resulting music, then sends out speech and clamour once again, for its own sake, through the very same process of transformation and sets up yet another feedback loop for a new, but still repetitious transformation and so on, thus do we keep recounting its myths, music, chants and religion, its hidden gesture and its recent history. Thus does the group constantly send out and receive information about itself, its noises, wars and stories, crises and tragedies, its languages and its conditions, all in multiple cycles.

Under the oppressive sun of Asia Minor, Pinara is astonishing for its pure and abstract geometry: the theatre orients its pavilion towards the detailed rumblings of the lively city, although for the most part it is directed at what is being broadcast in the background from a thousand shadowy mouths, tombs that blacken the tall, sombre cliff-face; the lingering moan of the dead still audible in the circus two thousand years after the death of the city. The theatre relates epicyclically to the hemicycle that starts and finishes at the tombs. It is as though the former keeps going around, on or within the latter, multiplying the loops, creating performances beneath the continual hum of eternity, its politics and its history. Together, people listen to their dead: the cliff-face, an immense radio transmitter or television screen.

We can neither speak nor sing without the feedback loop which guarantees the audibility of our own voice. The ear guarantees and regulates the mouth, which emits noise in part for the speaker, in part for others, who in turn guarantee other feedback loops. Intuitively we imagine a large prostrate body, buried underground, the marble pavilion of its ear jutting out, its dark mouths speaking and shouting for millennia through the plunging cliff-face.

Our myriad cells shout out: a proprioceptive ear, often deaf, listens. Multiple loops regulate this racket which no doubt transforms itself into our pleasures and discomforts, our fits and silences, the beginnings of language. Our mouth shouts out; the child who does not speak, cries and screams: the ear ensures these messages; dialogues will regulate them. We can draw cycles which unify the body's transmissions and reception. Why not simply call them self-awareness? More often than not closed by these cycles, yet open.

Our myriad dead shout out; in the theatre, the audience, noise; the collective is deafening. Whoever listens to this din with his whole body calms it, provokes it, regulates or masters it – sometimes, not always, for it can crush you, dismember you. We can draw a thousand cycles unifying the group's transmission and reception, as well as the constant maintenance of this movement. Speeches, music, constructions, media, performances. Why not call the circulation of this thunderous flux, meaningful or meaningless, the social contract? Or for each one of us: concern, passion, enthusiasm for belonging. More often than not closed by these cycles, rarely open.

Myriad things shout out. Often deaf to unusual transmissions, our hearing is astonished by the shouts of things which have no name in any language. The third cycle, which begins with a rare attentiveness and requires turning a deaf ear to oneself and to the group, interrupting the closed cycles of consciousness and the social contract, might simply be called knowledge.

Every possible kind of audible finds sites of hearing and regulation.

It is as though the body were constructed like a box, or series of boxes, through which these cycles pass. As though the collective forms itself into a box or boxes through which these flows circulate. And as though knowledge, a world crying out for more attentive hearing, constructs the largest white box of all.

The task that remains is to describe this last kind of audible, which I will call soft or hard.

And to open a few black boxes: houses, prisons, infernos, ships.

And finally to describe some of the passageways that are difficult to negotiate for these flows and cycles: corridors controlled by Muses, Sirens, Bacchantes, women all.

SOFT AND HARD

When a highway is in disrepair, it can be fixed: you fill in the pot-holes, go over the new bitumen with a steamroller, reinforce it at considerable expense, both physical and financial. But there is another solution: put up signs which read 'Road under Repair'. This is the preferred solution of administrators; it is cheaper, and panders to their tendency to communicate by memoranda. Not so long ago engineers argued, with the figures to prove it, that the act of reading the sign, accompanied by a few jolts to the chassis, was enough to force drivers to slow down, thereby drastically reducing the number of accidents: safety. It's as though they imagine the car skidding on the sign itself, rather than being shaken by the actual ruts in the road.

Breaking rocks, transporting them by the tonne, compacting their sharp edges into a solid mass, demands an energy output measurable in horse-power. On the other hand, drawing letters and crosses with a brush, red on white, recognizing their place within a code, makes energy demands that are not even comparable. The former is measured on the entropic scale, the latter on the informational scale. The former is manual, the latter digital. It is the latter that is preferred by philosophers, who love signs and words, icons and notices, language, writing. A childhood spent breaking stones no doubt predisposes me to prefer the former. With time, progress is shifting from one to the other; I know full well that history passes from reality to language, from things to signs and from energy to information: from hard solutions to so-called soft ones. I merely ask that we remember hardness.

My ears still ring from stone-breaking.

The philosophy of language is our reason, and always will be; it has converted us, and is winning. There is no doubt that it has the upper hand over phenomenology; we must declare it the winner. Loyally, and without reservation.

Hoping for a return to things themselves, it was my naïve wish to hear, see, visit, taste, caress, smell; to open myself to the given. How can we do this without also saying it? How do we divest ourselves of flesh which has been speaking for millennia? Is there a single given independent of language? If so, how do we apprehend it? The discussion is over as soon as it begins: no-one knows how to say what is given, independently of language. Any description of the aforementioned thing is merely present-ing data in relation to the language being employed. The thing itself flees along the infinite asymptote of utterance.

Behold the world: it is filled with propositions and categories, in the tiniest nooks and crannies, pebbles, roots, crickets, in hidden recesses, mines, pockets, tunnels, under ground or under water, in primitive for-ests and at the fringes of distant galaxies; no space is left unoccupied.

Is it language and language alone that gives us the given?
The former stone breaker cannot believe his ears.

The given I have called hard is sometimes, but not always, located on the entropic scale: it pulls your muscles, tears your skin, stings your eyes, bursts your eardrums, burns your mouth, whereas gifts of language are always soft. Softness belongs to smaller-scale energies, the energies of signs; hardness sometimes belongs to large-scale energies, the ones that knock you about, unbalance you, tear your body to pieces; our bodies live in the world of hardware, whereas the gift of language is composed of software.

The difference between the softness of software and the hardness of hardware is perfectly sensed when we locate it unambiguously outside of language. The difference is of course one made by science, and thus once again by language and software, but even though we formulate it in the language of energy – whether thermodynamics or information theory – our body perceives and endures it via things. Tacitly, the body understands the softness of meaning, and that one's retinas are never burned out by discourse, one's back not broken, one's skin not flayed. Looking through a window and seeing that tree down there seems as harmless as *saying* 'tree', but looking at the sun which illuminates it is a little harder on the eyes; even more than that, staring at that same sun at midday, in the middle of the Sahara, or being surprised by the flash of a thermonuclear explosion, will end your sight for good. Even if the murmuring of zephyrs through the tree tops seems divine, wind can knock you about and make you stumble – the north wind can, at least; you will never be blown over by the word 'wind'. Our bodies are aware of this discrepancy, or more precisely, live as though they understand it, or even better still, *survive* because they understand it. If we proceed in wilful ignorance of it, we injure ourselves; we die.

Life, as such, exploits this distinction, moving from hardness to softness. Its momentum carries it from hardware to software, from energy to information. The sensible moves in the same direction. It is through the sensible that the body recognizes the interval between the two and the direction in which we are carried.

It is not always the gentle delights enjoyed by holiday-makers as they stroll innocently through a man-made Arcadia between lake and forest that the environment holds in store for us. We might mistake the return to things for a return to the simple life, or a beach holiday, but conversely he who never gets beyond the local bookshop, where the wind only stirs on the morning of Pentecost, or who never leaves his advertisement-saturated neighbourhood, tends to overwhelm the given with language. There are so many filters, cities, posters, medicines, techniques and assurances, protective casings and customs, erected by history around the reasonably well-to-do contemporary Westerner, entirely caught up in the small-energy software covering our screens, running across walls and through our work, that hardness is a rare commodity these days. Empiricism is not enough to wake us from this new sleep, we need an eruption, a large-scale seismic event, a major cyclone, a new Hiroshima. But no: the ocean rises up on our screens, voluptuously.

While it is true that, more often than not, what we receive is a gift of language, a breach in the wall of software that surrounds us can sometimes let in an overwhelming force. The given can knock us off our mount, and it is not always a loud utterance. A rough parpen or sharp-edged brick will cut our hands, our retinas are defeated by bright light and our ear-drums by cannon-fire, a sailor will be knocked over if too close to a water-spout in a cyclone, our backs ache from the distance between hands and soil. Nausea is not always the product of writing, a heavy swell will send us for the nearest bucket without a word being said – sea-noise, noisea. Yes, sometimes the given can be hard, whereas it is always soft when it comes through language.

It would seem that there are two kinds of given: one is gentle, conveyed by language, a suave kingdom, satin-smooth, syrupy, soft, exquisite, logi-cal and exacting; the other is unpredictably hard, a mixture of hard and soft, giving no warning before waking us with a slap in the face. Faced with this mixture, we must identify the given which resists being named by language and which is still without concept. This mingled given, stud-ded with sharp thorns, wakes us from the sleep of language when the soft membrane of our box – our gaol – of sound is lacerated by hurricanes.

Hard, material forces surround us, threaten us, sometimes shelter us, are a condition of life; we know how to pit hard against hard. The natural sciences deal with the elementary conditions of our existence: large-scale energies.

There is a sort of tide, or current, or drive from hard towards soft: it is history, of course, but evolution as well, and time, no doubt. Energy resolves into information: the former supports the latter, the latter taps into the former. Hardware becomes software, force becomes meaning.

Our body, warm, powerful, resistant and therefore hard, an object on the entropic scale, mingles its hardness with the softness of small-scale energies: information first, meaning and language last. It is as though life were a stage in this process. Our body mingles soft and hard and thereby produces and receives the same mixture. A state in the middle of this process or progression. Our undertakings themselves are getting softer and softer.

Yet this flow encounters obstacles, twists and turns, walls and filters; negotiates, traverses, follows and skirts them. The passage through which it percolates is an obstructed one.

Eloquence begins by standing on coarse sand, facing the chaotic ocean and breaking pebbles in your teeth, and ends with the sublime. We should define sublimation as the passage from solid to gaseous, a softening.

I do not know if talking of filters will help us understand how thunder, noise, the vibration of sound waves (whether audible or felt through our skin), subtly become meaning. There is no reason to discount the hypothesis.

The question of knowledge, of the sensible and of language is located somewhere on the graduated spectrum of this fan, somewhere in the range it encompasses between hardness and softness, this partitioned, compartmentalized distance, strewn with obstacles, twists and turns, and clear pathways. A box within boxes where the sound of cannon-fire gradually transforms itself into a whispered confidence.

At what point on this path do we leave behind hardness for permanent softness? When? The time is not far off for us.

Large-scale energy overwhelms small, the wind swallows voices, carries away cries; small sometimes controls and captivates large. The distinction between the two comes after their mingling, rather than before it, the given comes to us however it can, amidst jolts and signs; an upbringing or a life without the former marks the beginning of the reign of the latter. Sensation gets just what it needs from this mixture. Philosophy has all the more difficulty conceiving of the former because it is disgusted by the latter. Sensation, never pure, filters energies, protects itself and us from an excess of it, encodes and passes on information: it transforms hard into soft.

This transformation, which occurs against a background of differentiation and mingling, clearly cannot be understood without science, and therefore at the most basic level without language, but once more the body manages it, the organism lives it, the living body survives because of it, and will die of it. Children and animals understand it without language.

THE FIVE SENSES

What remains now is to think about mingling itself; the softening, the levelling, the planing, the smoothing out of hardness into softness. It is time to write about mixtures, and filtering.

Voices get through. Raucous, low, full, pleading, vulgar, sharp, cutting, jovial, harmonious, commanding, harrowing, seductive, explosive or irritated, a virago's, a virgin's, a fishwife's or whore's voice, an overbearing victim's, a passionate, imperious lover's, shouting out the dreary obstinacy of true passion, a maternal, sisterly, counselling, pious, infantile, rasping, insolent, egalitarian voice, a team player's voice, a voice of encouragement, of destructiveness or caresses, an ironic or aggressive or cynical voice, an old alcoholic's cat lying in the gutter, denying the arrival of spring, a voice that is vile, veiled, velvety, noble, high-pitched, servile, majestic, ample, sick, affronted, clothed in silence, echoing with the sea or forest, undercut by the twittering of birds, howling like a wild beast, street cries reflected off walls and town squares, a piercing, plaintive voice, asking questions and saying come here, an alarming voice, broken, sobbing – along what paths has your voice not flowed, off what surfaces and what rocks has it not echoed, extending the carillon of senses, intuitions and implications beneath language?

The human voice will get through the obstacle course, whether yawn or prayer, prophecy or screech. Waterfall, sandstorm, torrent, it sweeps away gradations, the chromatic spectrum that runs from obscure loathings to purest love, from bestial growls to flights of mysticism, from the inert noise of matter to the perfect syllogism: mixture, life.

Grammar ignores physics and biology, plus human passions and all literature. Behold the voice of philosophy, which moves from litanies to theorems, from experience to invocation, from adamantine rigour to cries of pain. It abandons sublime and rapidly idiotic inflexibility so that language might not die – from the smothering of meaning. Its voice, like any other, traverses all possible Fourier equations to expand the stained-glass window in which meaning shines out, gold, lead, blood and passion.

Language speaks, gives us gentle meaning, proves, but also blows, thunders and shreds us with its screeching. It may leave traces and marks, but it requires light to make and read them: writing is obliterated by night, it assumes perpetual daylight, a summer solstice on New Zemble. Meaning and proof are made on waves of sounds and light, require energy and, soft though they may be, spill over on to the hard scale of entropy, music, rhythms, cries and noise, sun or lightbulb. Léon Brillouin exorcized Maxwell's demon with a similar remark. Language must be paid for, in energy at the very least; it is never free. We will need to determine after this if it gives the given. Meanwhile, they're not exactly giving it away. And if you believe they are, you might as well believe in perpetual motion.

Once again, the body is aware of this dependency. Uterine, it thrilled to hear its praises sung in its mother's tongue, breathless with desire for it, and three thousand years ago, upright in a storm of siren song, lashed to a mast, felt fear, fled or danced, fascinated – would have given anything for this beautiful language. It has always known, without needing it explained in language, that language is soft and hard, it has known since birth that the given is a mixture of soft and hard, that sensation transforms hardness into softness, how could it not know difference and transition?

The philosopher of language would like everything to stay soft. Let him build, let him navigate, let him break stones, let him abandon for a while his rigorous languor, his felt, his logic and his fleecy lining.

PASSAGES

First nuptials. If, one summer's day, you should ever climb the hill to Pratz-Balaguer, a small, dying village atop the spur of a deep valley in the western Pyrenees, you will have the good fortune to find a little silence as you leave behind you the noisy crowd, the vulgar war which first industry, and now tourism, wage on space, beauty and the countryside. Tranquil places are disappearing, a few old men haunt the ruins, black ghosts, too weak to repair the stone walls crumbling under the force of snow and passing time, wander the laneways in search of the screeching children who, some seventy years ago now, ran around a village square that used to hum with gossip. Space is stopped in its tracks by this valley, history has run its course here. Perched vertiginously above the gorge, a few sections of wall remain of the ancient chateau, the cemetery is disintegrating behind the locked church. No more nobles or warriors, no more religion or priest, no more shepherds, the only thing that ever passes through is the tramontana. This slower than slow death is shrouded in silence.

Our morning trek up the mountain ends there, a drowsy siesta begins here, on a path invaded by wild oats. The wind plays through the moving leaves of the poplars that line it. Music? It is barely audible. Rhythm? More of a quasi-period, which the gentle gusts of wind lift out of the multiple trembling of sessile leaves. Rumbling? Friction, chance caresses, the

merest stirring of barely perceptible currents, background noise. Music –
no, nor rhythm, nor noise; might this be the voice of God?

Far from the collective, able to hear and touch it, our body perceives the
divine. Our body is familiar with the ancient union chased away by the
filthy noise of social ritual. The religion of the collective despises the religion of the world; a place in which messages are shouted out can have no
connection with the world of things. Where are we to find the smallest
island of silence now? Alone with the ghosts of this dead village, not so
much prostrate as submerged in the wild grass of its pathways, saved from
the mindless rumble for just a moment, I hear the branches mingling with
the first stirrings of the tramontana, their harmony, the gentle conversation between trembling leaves and wind, softer than gentle, secret, modest,
silken, almost sleek and uniform, a caress with a veil. Through the foliage
we can detect the small grains carried in intermittently on the transparent
gusts of wind. You need to sink even deeper into an almost-sleep to further fine-tune your hearing, your attention, letting the slow and gentle
gusts of the wind's currents stir your body's tissues and lift their leaves to
dance.

What does it say, the mild, gentle voice of this union?

In some music, the melody expands and rises like bread dough to
become the sound wave itself, just as the woven image of a tapestry bur-
ies itself in the textile surface. This thread is not sewn on to the tapestry,
that song does not sit discretely on the bed of harmony, philosophic
thought does not exhibit itself, alone, above and exterior to the tonality
of speech, like a meta-language or caption; rather the thread blends with
the fabric, the meaning dissolves into the story, the threnody sustains the
sound. Aphrodite manifests herself as watery flesh and the ocean sparkles
with infinite possibilities. Audible language trembles from the multiple
meanings contained within it.

What did the voice say?

That this was how we must write. Like the fractal gale blowing the
almost livid leaves. Far from speech, before any words are spoken, augural
observation of the hard sonorities of the world contains multiple dimensions of meaning. The haruspex had to choose from this myriad density
of possibilities. We must write as close as possible to this moving, dense
proliferation, to the full capacity of the senses which is opened up in this
place and given to us by the sensible. By this I mean the sensible that is
designated by the infinite capacity of sense.

The sessile leaves of the poplars write the sensible, say the sensible, to
be read here, and heard too.

The sensible envelopes hybrid multiplicity, the potentiality of sense: fluctuating stock and capital, a well, capacity or source. It envelopes them without containing them, like an overflowing cornucopia.

What did the voice say? It manifested itself as different voices, whispered words, which is something voices are capable of when they come from faces we can imagine. I will not fear death if, through force, or over time, I can manage to etch the outline of this face in the sand. Clear and distinct meaning – spoken, heard, exchanged, on which some agreement can be reached – draws this face in profile, an instantaneous harmony of multiple voices, a partial and perfect rendering of this masterwork, inaudible yet audible on a summer's day beneath the poplars, when a thousand filaments of breeze ripple a thousand mobile stems, slim and slender, in every possible direction in space. Potential becomes actual, the sensible becomes sense, a single note emerges from the din. I seek the well of noise.

What did the divine voice say? It gave us the palette on which shades and colours combine, the interplay from which tones are drawn to the surface, the inaccessible totality of meanings, it gave us – quite precisely – a common sense.

Which the generalized eardrum of our skin received.

The wind, sensible, passes for wit, provided we listen between the lines.

Voices make noise, so do things. These were clashing clamours, once. A prophet's voice needed nothing less than a desert to be heard. Mountain dwellers called to each other across great distances; sailors would overcome the howling of the wind and the tongue-clacking of the waves to hail each other; the Gauls passed news along from one hillock to the next, often only to have it intercepted by the wind. My father and brother were shy, like all the men in my family, but living next to the hungry belly of a stone crusher they were also incapable of speaking without shouting. Eloquence had its beginnings confronting the crashing of the waves, with a mouth full of pebbles, so as to learn how to dominate the roar of a crowd. The exercise was performed facing the thundering ocean, tongue, teeth and palate full of stones, not tropes, and only afterwards before an assembly. Before it submits to the rhetor, with his grammar and his logic, our tongue is a physical thing – Stentor's was said to be like a trumpet.

Ours is an age without trumpets. We can now receive the gift of language, because we have silenced the world. Our amplifiers blare out in a desert, where dogs obey a new master's voice. Motors reign everywhere, the background noise of town and country alike. You need to make your way as far as Patara, another dead city, to see the converse situation, an amphi-theatre invaded by sand: the beach has filled Demosthenes' mouth and ears, a human voice smothered by the flowing of an hourglass. At present, the five oceans have been vanquished by the assembly of humanity. Language, previously soft in a hard world, learned the hard way how to overcome that obstacle, and these days counts as the only hard thing left in a world softened to the point of muteness. It has silenced hardness. The philosophy of language is winning because language is winning, and it does so physically first and foremost. In the last fifty years, who suffers from the sound of thunder or tornadoes; who has *not* had their ears blasted by loud-speakers? There is no longer a single recess left in the world, peb-ble, root, cricket, no secret place, mine, pocket or tunnel, underground or in the seas, in the rainforests or in the middle of the desert, which is not smothered by filthy noise.

Before making sense, language makes noise: you can have the latter without the former, but not the other way around. After noise, and with the passage of time, a sort of rhythm can develop, an almost recurring movement woven through the fabric of chance. The sea gives birth to a tidal flow, and this flow to Venus: a rhythmic current emerges from the disorderly lapping of waves, music surfaces in this place. In turn, this layer of music, universal before the advent of meaning, carries all meaning within it; distilled, differentiated language selects the meaning or mean-ings it will isolate from this complex, and then broadcast.

Whoever speaks is also singing beneath the words spoken, is beating out rhythm beneath the song, is diving into the background noise under-neath the rhythm. Meaning trails this long comet tail behind it. A certain kind of æsthetics, a certain kind of physics take as their object this brilliant trail, which light or the grammar of meaning leave in their wake. Writing lends itself to a similar description, clarity replacing noise: Brillouin exor-cized Maxwell's demon by remarking that no-one can read or write in the dark.

It is through the voice that the first act of seduction passes between interlocutors, *sotto voce*, a tension that is rhythmic and musical, calling for consideration, pleading for attention. Some virago repels us with her insistent nagging, some self-important windbag bores us with his endless monologue: too much noise, not enough rhythm, no melody at all. Throw out any book that fails to grab you with these right from the start. It is the first chord that captivates, fascinates and enchants us. Pull out all the stops for your introduction, make it abrupt if you seek to wake up your readers; long, gentle and floating if you seek to disarm them. Music always comes at the head of a parade, so that from far away the first thing we hear is the drumming, before the procession of long rhetorical divisions. Dialogue can only begin if there is an end to the petty squabbling where no-one listens to anybody else, and where everyone has a bone to pick with everyone else. Visit the museum of Rhodes and you will see an ancient vase on which two men, above the vase's mid-section, appear to be having a pleasant conversation. They seem to be engaged in gentle dialogue, each seated upon on stool located at the vase's swollen belly, but hidden on the underside, underneath each seat, is a monstrous animal, lying in wait. Our bestial relationships, of bickering and dominance, barks, cries and braying, show themselves in the very foundations of dialogue. The two beasts under the seats watch each other, ready to snap. At conferences you hear words that yelp, growl, bleat, wail, ululate, trumpet, moo, whistle, yap, bellow – this is how sessions begin, with jungle noises coming from underneath the seats. This is how dialectics strikes, like rutting billy-goats, this is the struggle of the political animal. This is how language and theory begin. It is often said, glibly, that their origins are lost to us in the mists of time, irrecoverable, but here they are, thunderous, with us every step of the way. On the contrary, it is a miracle if we can distance ourselves from them at all. How many conversations do they keep at bay, each like a guard dog, gnawing away at its own little truth, or howling the howl which has for so long guaranteed its dominance; how few words there are in these hard signals, how rare is reconciliation between the boisterous animals that precede language, and how improbable that any new meaning should come out of this scripted rut. Let us first of all tame the animals crouching under our seats.

Rhythm manages to do so, like a hammer evening up crooked teeth; so does music, having as they say a civilizing influence, putting Argus to sleep and reducing him to tears, the hammering out of the cadence suddenly taking wing. Orpheus, tamer of wild animals, sails into the sirens' pass, the Argonauts rowing furiously behind his lyre. Ulysses follows him. Anyone who would attempt to create something must brave the same peril.

Fantastic animals perch on the rocks where the waves break, hang on with their claws and screech out. We must pass through the clamour of the ocean, then defy the beasts, all talons and beaks – what do the soft feathers of these women have in store for us? Before there is any chance of dialogue, there is the roar of the ocean and clamour of the menagerie; no-one can come before them without fear and without having heard from afar the din which shakes you in your skin till your solar plexus vibrates and your legs tremble; and yet they draw us in, seductively, towards this theatre, into the hollow of its splayed legs. We know how to construct the body of the great animal, we know how to get into its black resonance box. From the first note of music, a religious silence. Before a single page is possible, you have to get past the wailing of the body, tinnitus, sobbing, inflamed desires, then the sharp-toothed hounds which forbid creativity in the corridors of institutions and the channels of false glory; after this, the hard song of the world seems so gentle.

Here, directly ahead, is the Sirens' pass. Ulysses enters it, but cleverly avoids it too. Once again, he becomes no-one: he slips in, immobile, lashed to a mast, in the wake of his sailors who swim through the choppy waters, their ears sealed with balls of warm wax. In myth, the monad-ship, with neither door nor opening, has already discovered Leibniz' solution. It sails past the obstacle of noise, neither transmitting nor receiving, and cancels out the Sirens.

Orpheus, all ears, his lyre or cithara held before him, is more than a match for the noise. Ulysses succeeds, making it through the pass in silence, but cheats by suppressing all noise, danger or temptation. Orpheus precedes him bravely, confronting the problem and resolving it with music.

Orpheus transformed noise into music. And no doubt invented it too in this dangerous place.

Music, which comes from all the Muses, cannot be held to be an art; it is the summation of all the arts. Without music, not one of them can achieve its goals; music watches over them all, it is the condition of their existence. Without it, poetry is at best pedestrian; architecture, a pile of stones; sculpture, inert matter; and prose, mere noise. Eloquence deprived of rhythm and the modulations of singing evocation collapses into gibberish and boredom.

Orpheus understood this. When Apollo offered him the old seven-stringed lyre, music was still an art among others, one Muse among nine sisters. Orpheus gave the new lyre nine strings, one for each sister, and since then, music has incorporated the instrument, becoming the first amongst the arts by bringing them together. Strings, arts, Muses, come together as a spray of flowers, a spindle of thread, a weft of fabric.

There is no single Muse devoted to music, which is shared by the nine sisters. What a fit of jealous rage there would be, between those who found themselves deprived and isolated from music, and the one who would seek to federate her deaf and disconnected sisters. Music resides in their midst, constitutes their milieu, intersection and coming together. It is the ensemble of the Fine Arts, and their precondition, it can be equated to the Muses' continual dialogue or conversation, their harmony; it built the house of the Muses, maintains their collective existence, expresses their social contract in its secret language. History brings time to this language; and the surveyor-architect brings stone, iron and glass to this language, each his share and each his version; the landscape architect brings glasshouses and fountains and garden paths to this language; poetry, tragedy and eloquence add languages to this language, and astronomy even adds science to this language bereft of language and underneath languages, lacking ideas and knowledge and yet underlying all knowledges: music expresses what transcends the arts, sciences and language.

Our languages have meaning. Beneath language, beneath all languages, universally so, music lives beneath meaning and before it, its pre-condition and its physical medium. Meaning presupposes music, and could not emerge without it. Music sounds the transcendental in language, the universals preceding meaning. It inhabits the sensible, it carries all possible senses.

It vibrates in the secret recesses of our conversations, continually underpins our dialogues, our exchanges presuppose it, it knows in advance our harmonies and discords, it built our house before we were born as speaking beings – and not only in the vibrating enclosure of the uterus – and paved the way for our collective existence; the social contract, hidden from all languages, can be heard indistinctly in its orchestration.

Anyone who seeks self-improvement and growth, hopes to be able to compose: may I achieve this before dying.

Before we can exchange meaning, even false meaning or the trivial nonsense of clichés, before we can create something new together, an event so rare as to be miraculous, we must shape these universals, in order to turn ourselves towards a common meaning, draw closer to it and tame it. The transcendental dimension of our communications is woven from music.

Beneath language, this layer of music covers the chaos that precedes it with universality. Language needs music, its essential condition; music has no need of language. Music needs noise, its essential condition; noise has no need of music. The latter softens the jagged edges of the tumult; suddenly, music is so undifferentiated it can no longer carry any specific meaning, but carries all, and none. Thus do the Muses guard the corridor of universals, the mandatory universal passage between noise and meaning.

There are two local passages bordering this global passage. Upstream, the Sirens control the mandatory local passage between noisy din and the beginnings of music: crashing waves, bird song, the Siren song of women. Has it ever occurred to anyone that, downstream, a college of women, neither beasts like the Sirens, nor goddesses like the Muses, might oversee the mandatory local passage between music and meaning? Noblewomen excelled at the French art of conversation in the *salons*, their grace presiding over this manifold and delicate traffic with tact, taste, perceptiveness and acuity. Let us say that women – Sirens, Muses, noblewomen, Graces – thus have perfect pitch, the three kinds of hearing required for the three passages from sharp-toothed chaos to the soothing layer of harmony, and from universality to the subtleties of meaning.

What do the Sirens say, shout; what is their song, what is their rhythm? The Odyssey does not tell us, nor do the so-called Orphic rituals, nor does anyone who passes through this place. Cunning Ulysses plugged his companions' eardrums, we have no testimony from them. What if the rhythm of the bird-women's squawking in fact resembled the song of the *Odyssey*, precisely the one Ulysses hears when his ship passes the Sirens' waters, and which – all ears – he learns, in order to be able to sing it afterwards at the King's banquet? And what if they screamed in Orpheus' ears when he attempted to pass, this Orphic sort of ritual in which the body ends up torn limb from limb? When I was navigating in those parts, they had reduced communication pathetically to a Leibnizian, mathematical calculation, having become entirely mithridatized to Ulysses' solution . . . The Sirens perform the incantation that enables creativity and screech the price that must be paid: life and health caught up in a giddying spiral, near-shipwreck, thought swallowed up by background noise; then emit the noise out of which the work is created, conduct the first customs and quarantine check, impose the first toll. They ruin your work by forbidding it, rupture it by speaking it.

They have made astonishing progress, equipped with transistors, hi-fi systems, colour televisions, calculators, autotimers and word processors, the waters are filling with sound waves, amidst the noise of motors. We no longer need to seek the dangerous passage that they used to guard, long ago – they come to us now, and fill the space around us. The world is filling to saturation point with bird-women, thunder, rhythm and music. There is nowhere left, not a rock, nor a corner of a house, nor a square of luzerne, nor a copse under a canopy of trees, not a hidden recess, desert, hole, mine, tunnel, well, unbreathable summit at fifty-five thousand feet altitude, that escapes the fractious control of the media. Only the Sirens sing of the Trojan war now, Orphic poetry is only chanted by the Bacchantes, by the Thracian women who dismembered Orpheus, the screeching of birds fills the sky as far as the horizon, no-one need enter those frightening narrows again, no-one comes through them stronger for not having perished, we are under the influence of the Sirens' cries. The world – box, ear and mouth – resounds.

Victory for the Sirens, woe betide creative man.

Orpheus passes the Sirens, the crashing sea noises and the cries of beasts. He managed to tame the wild beasts, hyenas and leopards following in the wake of his cithara or song. The most savage animals are reconciled. Orpheus calms the bird-women, the crashing waves remain – he calms them too. How?

Ulysses passes the Sirens, deafens his shipmates by stopping their ears with warm wax, and remains quiet, immobile, tied to the mast; he travels underneath the din, his solution minimal or non-existent – no effort required. Those on board who can move hear nothing, he who can hear cannot move. Whether rowing or manoeuvring the vessel, the ship's sailor-engines do not tremble with desire, nor with fear, but carry out their orders, come what may, since they cannot hear them countermanded. Before reaching the vile straits, God-Ulysses has already dictated everything that will follow to his monad-sailors. Thus the helmsmen on our ships blindly follow the course dictated to them, not the route they can see before them; language, and not the given; the orders given, not the world they perceive. Ulysses' companions steer their course from memory, can still hear their previous orders: they receive orders through the language of their captain, and nothing at all from the deafening world of the Sirens. Even flying women, who can make them tremble with desire, cannot lure them away from the realm of language.

The best of all solutions, the greatest efficiency for the least effort; Homer has anticipated Leibniz, shutting off these monads, programmed to swim in a straight line, from any direct communication. The Siren-given vanishes.

What do the Sirens sing here, what do they shout? The ordinary world, a mixture of the enticingly soft and the repulsively hard.

Thrifty and miserly, Ulysses uses cunning; Orpheus is happy to spend. Accompanying the latter, the Argonauts, all ears, can choose at any given moment between the troubling song of these women and the harmony of the cithara; they are free to change their heading. Ulysses negates time, Orpheus plays it, creates it, improbable. Composition confronts the noise of beasts and invents harmony in close proximity to their song; the music that issues forth always carries within it the trace of the screeching that preceded, heralded and inaugurated it. Thus did Demosthenes use his voice, his ears filled with the sound of the waves and his mouth full of pebbles, so that his eloquence might spread forcefully over the noise of the throng. Ulysses sails through the straits once, he will not tempt fate again; Orpheus, on the other hand, has another attempt. He attempts to get past the Bacchantes, but fails. Wins against one din, loses against the next. His body is torn limb from limb, music dissolves, collapsing into noise. Ulysses, careful and calculating, always wins; hero, composer, Orpheus does not.

In order never to lose, all communication must be cut off. Ulysses blocks noise out, Orpheus drowns it out. Ulysses-Leibniz suppresses all noise; hardly surprising, then, that his messages are heard. The monads recite the lesson imprinted on their memory at birth by God; as one they row against the pull of the Sirens, united in deaf solitude, while their inner ears hear the pre-established harmony. Science presupposes a world without noise. It wins.

There need only be noise, and the world will blossom with Sirens' passes. Ears open, carrying his instrument before him, waxen heart bared to the winds, Orpheus confronts the chaos, he rushes, defenseless, towards the beasts and women, into the breakers, attempts the maximal, dangerous, spendthrift solution, the solution that produces music. To get through this, you need to compose, sing non-stop, never lower your shield of harmony against the confounding clamour, conjure an improbable curvature, like the prow of a ship dancing through the waves, project a new time ahead of yourself. Orpheus does not always win and exhausts himself in this task, a musical offering laying down his own time. But he leaves himself open to the risk of collapsing into noise. For without the universals of music, without its transcendental aspect, chaos will carry the day, no-one will make it through the channel. Leibniz presupposed a world without noise, his solution required no effort, for him the universal resided with God. But as there is in fact noise, philosophy is obliged to invent a solution bound to Orpheus, just as Leibniz is bound to Ulysses. Before there can be successful meaning and communication – the precondition of logic and language – it must presuppose a music which is victorious over noise, must invent it, must risk composing it, discovering in the process an improbable time.

Even in his optimal or null solution, achieving perfect results with the least output, Leibniz had admitted the precedence of music: he attibutes to God, and eternally so, an authority or function which he calls harmony. I have scarcely altered his words. The precondition or foundation of optimal communication, and of the sciences, is equated with music or harmony, an already transcendental condition. A mysterious and mystical score heard by the deaf monads, its job is to explain why they move in time through the silence.

Alas, we do hear noise, we can no longer act as though we and God alone inhabit the world; we are assailed by moaning, shouting, sobbing and supplications long before we arrive at meaning; we must therefore compose music at every moment in order to survive, feel, take part in conversations – as we do so we must expose ourselves to beasts and Sirens, to the dispersal of things, of the group and of our very limbs, to the Bacchantes. Without this background production containing the background noise, nothing else will hold together; nothing in the world, no-one in the collective; not the senses, not the arts, not the parts of the body. Music precedes philosophy, no-one can give themselves over to the latter without passing through the former.

Orpheus soothes the beasts, lions prostrate themselves before his cithara, harmony smoothes out the sharp and jagged. The waves die down, the bird-women sheathe their claws: dog will no longer eat dog, they are reconciled. There is a truce in the wars of things and men, malaise is banished. Music smoothes out the serrated edges of noise, dulls claws and fangs and horns, polishes the coarseness of chaos, softens the hard.

Three-fold hardness is thrice softened: in the messages of things, groups and the body.

Orpheus the son of Calliope – the muse with a beautiful voice, patron of epic poetry and eloquence – sings. Song casts language over the material framework of music, covers hard acoustic wings with the downy softness of meaning.

The blanket of music softens the hard. Conversely, it presents meaning with the hardness of the soft.

Sometimes, beneath song, like a smothered, stifled, veiled, flattened, timid meaning, the phrasing seems to speak a forgotten language from before the time of meaning, so ancient that it speaks to our flesh. It makes audible the material framework of language, its energy, like its walls, support structure or habitat; it builds the nest of meaning.

THE FIVE SENSES

The softest part of hardness, after the ordeal of the Sirens, and the hardest part of softness, while passing through the Muses.

Music-variety thus shows two sides or faces: the soft side smoothes out jagged edges, the hard side flattens out meaning. Twice universal with two inseparable faces.

Our skin, hot and strong, defends us quite fiercely, but at the same time, warm and delicate, gives itself over gently to be tattooed with one thing and another, and with its own emotions. We listen to the double-sided musical variety with our whole, similarly double skin. Naked, we nestle in its nest.

I do not know if the given is only given through and in language, but in such a case everything would happen as though it were given in advance in and through music, as though it were forgiven by the latter. By music I mean all the Fine Arts. The writer who merely goes for meaning does nothing but calculate; he can only be said to write when all the senses tremble within the flesh of language, semi-soft, a double variety for sight, touch, smell and taste. The nine-string cithara is always to be found between wild animals and recitative, between death and knowledge. Our language – vowels, syntax and precision – must be bathed in music lest it die.

The musical variety or layer flows or slips between us and the world, between us, within us. If any harmony should transpire between our body and the world, between the individuals making up a group, or within my body on the verge of being torn apart, then its arrival is conditioned by this music.

Hardness in softness and softness in hardness, a form of transition, the music of my language nonetheless prevents me from calling it either sord or haft.

How does sensation work? What must we learn in order to understand the workings that underpin our knowing, its foundation or its precondition? This question, too, belongs to the category of problems which systematically invoke a third term or man. There is no science that does not in some way presuppose a preceding sensation, even if it has sometimes, often, almost always – always, in fact – been necessary to expel the senses from the field it occupies. Not only does sensation stand behind the knowledge that presumes to speak of it, but what is more, it finds itself ousted by what we know at any given point. The philosophy of language still wins out in these places, breaking the cycle of referrals to a third science.

Whatever sensation may have taught us, we know nothing about it.

Take a black box. To its left, or before it, there is the world. To its right, or after it, travelling along certain circuits, there is what we call information. The energy of things goes in: disturbances of the air, shocks and vibrations, heat, alcohol or ether salts, photons . . . Information comes out, and even meaning. We do not always know where this box is located, nor how it alters what flows through it, nor which Sirens, Muses or Bacchantes are at work inside; it remains closed to us. However, we can say with certainty that beyond this threshold, both of ignorance and perception, energies are exchanged, on their usual scale, at the levels of the world, the group and cellular biochemistry; and that on the other side of this same threshold information appears: signals, figures, languages, meaning. Before the box, the hard; after it, the soft.

We do not know sensation: we might as well say that it occupies this black box.

The most honest description we can give of it, made up more of ignorance than actual claims to knowledge, tells us no more than the insinuations of a hundred mythical tales. The black box has two sides: the hardness of softness, the softness of hardness. Place, space, volume and finally variety where energies move from one scale to another. A soft black box for high energy, a hard box for the very low.

Sensation-variety, the set of its boxes, insinuates or places itself between us and the world, between us and within us. If any harmony should transpire between our body and the world, amongst the people who make up a group, or within my body on the verge of being torn apart, then its arrival is conditioned by sensation: harmony requires a change of scale.

Sensation guides and defends us, without it we would die, our bodies exploded, torn limb from limb by physical forces, the power of the social and intimate grief. Like a nest, it surrounds us with a lining, a closeness, supple but with hard thorns, and in its hard hollow it carries soft sense. The latter leaves that hollow and flies away.

Hardness in softness and softness in hardness, a transitional threshold. My language, so soft to hear yet so hard and fast in its rules, prevents me from calling it either sord or haft.

Sensation has the same status as music.

The traditional term 'æsthetic' has two senses. It designates discourse on fine art, and equally discourse about the given. These two layers of words do not always reach their object, as though beauty tended to flee as far from our utterances as the things we sense. In the major European languages, philosophical texts tend to keep these two senses of the word separate; the most famous ones formalize their divorce. Here, now, are their nuptials.

Music, considered the summation of the arts, hard and soft, soft and hard, makes felt its double-sided variety, the double lining of its box.

Sensation, a black box, soft and hard, hard and soft, installs the double lining of its variety between high energy and low.

It joins with the arts; æsthetics has only one sense.

Music sings before language, before sense, is the condition of that which remains always soft. Sensation and the sensible allow and condition sense, they preserve its softness. Language remains outside the unitary sphere of æsthetics. The arts of language owe their beauty to their proximity to that which resides outside language.

The rediscovered unity of an exceptional and familiar place gives great joy: the world displays itself as beautiful. We need beauty in order to live.

Eurydice dies from a snake bite while fleeing Aristaeus, the first and best beekeeper. Fangs and stings. The lovely material contours of the woman fade away, Eurydice becomes a shade, a name, image or memory to be evoked, an inscription on a tombstone or the proper name written or read this morning. The Underworld used to be inhabited by the very same phantoms that we moderns believe we carry around in our hearts and heads, by those spirits that we have in our own spirit, by those words that we, these days, believe we carry around subconsciously or else collect in libraries or grammar books or data banks. Historically they vary, the names that we give to black boxes, in which hard is transformed into soft, or into understanding or writing, inward soul or Elysian Fields: the same darkness, grief and labyrinths, a similar verbal tenuousness, but what does it matter what name we give to these hinterlands? Eurydice, tangible and receptive to caresses, descends into the darkness of the shades, her physical strength now a simulacrum, her voice frozen in an epitaph. Death speeds us from the volume of things to the space of language.

Orpheus descends to the Underworld, leaves behind the physical for phantoms, abandons hardness in order to abandon himself to softness, enters the library, or his head, or his own music box, the lyre. Philosophers know how to go down this path: they open black boxes, traverse infernal secrets and labyrinths, visit consciousness or understanding, reason itself, as much at ease as if they were in a bookstore, and act as though it were in fact a bookstore.

Orpheus pacifies the monstrous guard dog Cerberus. He arrests Tantalus' greedy but futile gesture and the boulder of Sisyphus in the middle of its ascent. Everything stops, frozen images remain. The lesson here is the same: the softening of hardness. Let us fear snarling fangs no more; the hellhound is as gentle as a lamb, the verb *bite* has lost its teeth, the word *cynical* has neither bark nor bite. Beasts are transformed into animal posters decorating a corridor; Tantalus has gone into advertising.

But Orpheus' task begins at the precise point where the lesson turns back on itself; with his second act, the mirror image of the first, the changing of softness back into hardness. Ulysses descends to the Underworld, so does Orpheus. One is a visitor, the other a conqueror. Ulysses meets acquaintances, converses effortlessly with them, crosses the field of pale shades fearlessly, visits the history shelf of the library and consults, compares, discovers, settles himself down in the box where bodiless phantoms make sentences. He risks nothing, goes in and out, leaves the box just as he entered it, but with new information. Orpheus on the other hand takes risks, not wanting to leave as he came, but wanting more: energy, a body. He wants Eurydice alive. He tries to convert the voice-woman, the word-woman, into body.

Music would tear Eurydice away from the Underworld, where her dress, body and charm are stripped away, where she is reduced to software; the death of the body has turned her into a pallid icon floating through the Fields of Asphodel, a soft shape with neither body nor outline, which her lover can no longer caress; how do we resuscitate this inflation of the voice, this engraving?

Death turns us into words, words turn us into dead people. An epitaph-sentence under which things are buried. Those who deal with words deal with the dead, and like to look as though in mourning for the world. From the time we are baptized, our names seek a formless immortality, a gentle trace that will linger after our disappearance. In death we are reduced to our name alone, fragile, weightless, fleeting, defenceless, covered over by the customary handful of dirt. Beautiful, ample, warm and vibrant, Eurydice dwindles into her soft name. This is how death softens, as do music, and language. Orpheus cries out under the vaulted roof of the Underworld, 'Eurydice'! The hard voice is already enough to carry her name. Beneath this infernal cathedral, Orpheus sings 'Eurydice! Eurydice!'. He sings, and music carries the cry. Orpheus gives his lover's name the weight of his call, his vibrant hardness, he fills the sunless valleys and the gangways of the Underworld with these echoes.

Music sets out to turn soft into hard, to harden Eurydice's name, to remove her from the realm of epitaphs and marble etchings, it seeks to deliver her from the minimal prison of the written, spoken, sung name, from the congealing gaol of two-dimensional images. Eurydice, Eurydice, Eurydice, come down from the painting where you lie trapped, step out of the immobilizing icon.

She leaves the word. Arises from her name. Frees herself from the cartouche. Removes herself from representation.

Rediscovers movement, solidity, her dissolved flesh and vanished radiance, the material volume of her body, the delicate, satiny texture of her skin, the variable, clear, coloured light of her gaze, the horizontal agility of her gait as it adapts to the ground, the weight of her chest, hips, shoulders and neck, her hard skeleton. She steps softly out of shadow, image and word. The word is made flesh.

Evocation: something, flesh, emerges from voice.

Orpheus invokes, his voice and strings tremble, he calls out, shouts, sings, chants. He composes both music and Eurydice.

The ghost-woman reawakens, she follows her vocation.

Voice makes the name flesh, delivers words from death, lights dispels the darkness, music adds flesh, hardens what is soft: how far does incarnation go?

Just as the hard beasts trail softly behind the lyre's harmonies, just as the dark forests soften their sharp thorns and needles, in concert, so does the soft evocation of Eurydice follow her husband in hardness through the complex maze of creation and birth towards the propylæa which it is forbidden to cross in this way. Eurydice hardens. As the lion advances towards the cithara it becomes image, shadow, phantom, it is more verbal and nominal. Eurydice's progress, on the other hand, becomes flesh and blood, her name finds voice, her voice finds harmony, harmony a throat, her throat a head, head and flowing hair emerge from her shoulders, she springs forth from evocation, torso, armpits, waist and breasts rising out of darkness as Aphrodite once emerged from the sea, as each of us did from the uterine black box, from sensorial virginity and ignorance, as each of us emerges from the cold. Light and warmth soften skin wrinkled by frozen darkness. Orpheus composes, constructs a living Eurydice, piece by piece and sense by sense. Stand up and walk! Go on, speak!

The length of the labyrinth shows how much patience is required to achieve incarnation. Creation emerges from the Underworld where words, concepts, images, names and shadows flit about, it incorporates them through enchantment or by summoning them; frigid, drugged, the nominal awakens. Construction. Each book is released from the library, the deadliest of traps.

Orpheus sets himself the most difficult of tasks. Nothing is easier than taming hyenas or jaguars, or softening the hard: merely head downhill, follow on the heels of the entropic processes of dying, towards disorder and fragmentation; go from things to representations; name, describe, reduce an object to a set of words and phrases. Nothing is more difficult than climbing back up in the opposite direction, the vertical path towards life, creation or incarnation. An immutable law points us towards the Underworld, no-one ever comes back, you who enter this concept, abandon all hope. Like Ulysses, Orpheus succeeds in softening. But he fails in his attempt to drag Eurydice up to the very top of the incline, in the very last act of making flesh; his lover collapses back into her own shadow: head into throat and throat into harmony and harmony into voice and voice into name, instantaneous involution, reversion to epitaph. The supreme achievement, rare and grandiose, is giving life to speech; the banal, everyday gesture, the easy one, is substituting a word for a thing. Creation tries to break through to the world itself, not even Orpheus can manage that. A maternal act, always undone at the last moment.

This tells us quite plainly that the only thing under the sun that is easily achieved is philosophy. Nothing quite so easy as naming, describing, conceiving. Our passion for these things is fed by gravity and death, the law of least expenditure favours the sharpest drop: a rapid decline towards the Underworld, grammars, dictionaries, libraries, data banks, *facilis descensus Averni*. Do not seek an object, name it. Seek neither woman nor beast, cite the proper names which name them. Conversely, the insufferable law of maximum output requires the drawn-out patience of the vertical path, the endless summoning of shades so that they might dance, carnally, in the light, such hard work, such a long time, such totally inaccessible power that the most patient will give in to impatience, that the wanderer on this pilgrimage is always too quick to believe that he is emerging from limbo at last, and that she whom he is leading out is finally being delivered from this place. Now he looks back, too soon, she is still following, the suffering of her deliverance not yet ended, only half her body torn from death, she collapses brutally into a flattened image, a floating shade, her name, a tomb, down the sharpest slope, quickly, in free fall. She returns to concept as she does to equilibrium, at the bottom of the well.

They who have no talent for life do philosophy. Life takes time to emerge out of concept, word or name, it takes time for a child to break free of code. Even Orpheus cannot extricate himself from the enchantment of software, but he can point out the pathway of creation, the exit from the Underworld.

THE FIVE SENSES

A pathway that is always lost in the end. Infinite. Exhausting. Abruptly bringing us back to the dead on their bookshelves.

In the streets and the valleys, all that we hear are ideas, words, names, borne on cries and sobs. Eurydice! What is life to me without her? I sought to create a body, here, now; all I have left is pure abstraction, this soft product of the voice: Eurydice, Eurydice, Eurydice, I so wanted to give you life and all I can do is write philosophy.

Awoken in the intimacy of the night, ripped from the protective sheath of dreams, extracted from the blanket of sleep, pulled up from the well of sheets, from the depths of your berth, emerging with a start from the warm, dark cabin, emerging from these holes by jolting painfully from one section to another, pushing aside one curtain after another, crossing one bulkhead then another, obliged to get dressed quickly, on the hop, in silence, called by the watchman hammering on the door for you to take over the watch, opening your eyes and ears, wedging the cleat in place, opening the hatch and passing through the airlock, lurching down the gangways panting for breath, gripping at ladders, attentive to the dull echoes of the tossing hull, sliding upwards, deck after deck, arriving topside and opening a hatch, lee side, present, conscious, external now, through the bulwark and brutally delivered up to the terrifying wind, the screaming, whirling squall, outside, defigured by blue ice, torn by the blast, deafened, bombarded, stung by rain, contorted, having to decide on the spot, amidst the shouting, the whistling, the thundering orders, your skin all goose-flesh, unbalanced by the rolling of the ship, your whole body revolting against this ascent from the belly of the vessel towards the gangway open to the elements but itself silent, dying from the joy of being alive, now you know how every single one of us dealt with the ordeal of being born.

What we learn in the middle of the night is that the world makes us flinch, and that we would do anything not to hear it, to keep it far from us, were it not for that tiny pinch of bitter but magnificent joy that draws us to it. Our horror of sensations predisposes us towards staying in our bunks, wrapped in words, dreaming.

One night the Thracian women tore Orpheus limb from limb. Why? We do not know, or we know only too well. Some say that after losing Eurydice, Orpheus turned away from women, who in turn grew resentful.

Then there are those who say that he invented homophilia. Others that he introduced mysteries from which women were excluded. Others still that he had been cursed by Aphrodite. Explanations abound, and all of them follow the same groove: a thousand and one times over, we hear that the reason was sexual. What remains true is that a group of women, Bulgarian or Thracian, running through the mountains in some sort of sabbath frenzy, threw his limbs into the void, and his head into a river, whose current carried it far out to sea. The same old myths of diasparagmos.

This explanation has been with us since Antiquity, and diverts our attention from the diasparagmos itself. Using sexual urges as a justification has precisely the same effect as a sexual urge, grabbing us and flaunting its logic shamelessly, as we can see in advertising. To add value to something, you surround it with women, lots of partly naked Bulgarian women. Our attention is diverted from the worthless thing in question to the superb abundance of nudity. This diversionary tactic is all the explanation that is necessary: we speak of Aphrodite and homosexuality, we forget all about the dismembering. Before we attempt to justify or understand this in terms of anything else, let us consider it in its own right. We throw a hundred explanations at the crime, just as the Thracian Bacchantes threw stones, arrows or projectiles at Orpheus to tear him apart or bury him. We call this analysis: the explanations of the diasparagmos take the form of another diasparagmos; one is quite real, the other critical or judicial – an application. The first hard, the others soft. It's the same thing.

Orpheus, a musical body, is torn apart by a crowd. Harmony falls to discordance, disintegrates. Do we need to analyse that? But that is precisely what analysis is!

We learned the language of France by conjugating the verb *aimer*, to love; we learned to read the mother of that language, Latin, by declining *amare* – again, to love. We used to learn Greek, the language of science, by studying the verb to loosen. The first verb of a Greek grammar lesson means to chop up, to break up, to take apart – this is analysis. In our study of letters, we were raised from childhood to love in our everyday language and to destroy in the language of ideas. Now that we have forgotten this language, or simply do not know it, it has returned to take its revenge. We are unshaken in our belief that thinking and knowing consist in destroying, disconnecting, undoing, disarticulating, explaining – this is analysis. The opposite of constructing or connecting. It sends Eurydice back to the Underworld of dictionaries. The Thracian women, as though speaking Greek, attack Orpheus in order to learn or know, to think or explain music. But music is composed; if we analyse it, it evaporates into notes and fragments. Diasparagmos is analysis, analysis is diasparagmos.

THE FIVE SENSES

The Bacchantes explain texts to pieces. Analysis: the articulations of Orpheus' body are undone; harmony is divided; the crowd of Bulgarian women pull apart his lyre, string by string, we no longer have a single, global art, with nine Muses and nine strings, we will be left with nothing but disciplines. We will have no more sensation, we will be left with organs.

The women who dismember Orpheus do not descend upon him in silence. Perhaps they remained silent while hiding in the woods, waiting for the singer to pass by. Their harmony is silent, which further deepens it, enabling them to hear the gentle lyre approaching from afar.

Deaf, mute, the monadic world develops harmony. God is or creates prior music which organizes the sonorous emptiness of the world. Music produces silence, which in turn reduces music to its elemental self, almost perfect. Music produces silence like a beautiful musical singularity, a rare example of harmony. To my ears this is also a sensible truth: when hard noise ceases, soft silence carries the promise of the most complete of all the arts. Music surrounds or envelopes or includes silence, carrying no single meaning in order to elevate all meanings. When music ceases, in turn, silence reappears, naked, and is reborn, sublimated. It has two sides, one turned towards the great din, the other towards words and meaning.

Health comes from the silence of our organs, social harmony from the silence of the Bacchantes, it is where the Desert Fathers know happiness. The soft-hard side of silence protects us from chaos, its hard-soft side lifts us up towards meaning, deliciously so.

All reception occurs within silence. Transmission will always win out, hands down, over reception. Here is neat proof: we cannot know that someone has received a message without asking for confirmation. Further transmission is therefore required in order to confirm reception. Sensation, receptive, is bathed in silence. You can take that as a sensible truth, as the truth of the senses, as a metaphysical truth. Our senses are bathed in muteness. May this book of mine inhabit the joy of such silence. To remark upon it is to acknowledge it. Thus, when the philosophy of language says that the given is only ever given through and in language, it is the perfect illustration of this structure. Sensation is acknowledged by language, and transmits confirmation that the latter is receiving, thereby speaking of its silence. Sensation remains deaf and mute, almost monadic, tacit for as long as it acts as a receiver. Afterwards, reception confirms itself, transmits, and thus speaks.

Silence builds a nest, sensation's habitat. Without the latter, we cannot have the former.

The women who dismember Orpheus do not throw themselves on him noiselessly.

They hear him coming from afar, in the murmuring of the forest, for the otherwise motionless branches bend towards him as he advances, holding his lyre, amidst the usual assembly of beasts, now reconciled. Orpheus does not escape their claws and teeth, like Daniel in the lion's den, but the lions and wolves escape the wolves and lions, through the music and singing which reconcile the irreconcilable and replace the fury of combat or sacrifice with softness. Once again, here is the unwritten social contract. Beasts, hard towards one another, become soft. Man is no longer lion or wolf towards man, anharmonically, as though a different species, but becomes man, recognizable. The collective takes many names – pack of wolves, herd, forest, crowd of women – music each time providing their rare and unstable harmony, rare like silence, unstable like the music of genius, always at risk of collapsing into noise. The social contract is inherently unstable, like the softness of women and the sullenness of wolves. Orpheus advances through the concord; as he proceeds, the man-wolf recognizes another man in the lion, or in the branches of a tree, or in woman. Harmony. Recognition unfolds across space, above individuals, like melody.

Orpheus stands in the clearing, the forest becomes soft to the animals, the lions soft, the women soft, the wolves soft; hear the almost silent harmony, as they each hold back words, cries and breath itself in order better to receive. But the branches tremble slightly, the foliage starts to rustle, the breasts growl softly; now the first screeches of the advancing Thracian women are heard, challenging music's claim to the acoustic space. Fragile harmony, disintegrating under the first arrows of commotion; its hard-soft side, fragile, shattering beneath the sharp projectiles launched by the uproar. Following a dangerous and unstable equilibrium, harmony is overtaken by tumult, breaking apart and exploding in our ears, beasts turn against each other, tree-trunks bow under the force of the tornado, here is analysis, harmony shatters, herds scatter, Orpheus is undone.

Music's unstable and rare equilibrium is held precariously high. The first shout or swipe of a paw, the least gesture of applause will destroy it, bringing it crashing to the ground, broken, analysed.

Each lion or wolf believed it heard a note, separate from itself, coming from the lyre, as did each woman, without suspecting that they were that very note. Each lets out a discordant cry, each knows that that cry is unlike others. Each lion or wolf believes itself to be carrying off a piece of Orpheus, as does each woman, without suspecting that she, or it, is that very piece or member.

Each one of us, applauding enthusiastically, shatters Orpheus in the palms of our hands, crushing him as we reduce the music of triumph to a vile noise.

Orpheus is singing on television, the lions, standing on their hind legs, press their paws against the screen, the glass shatters into tiny pieces, the image vanishes when the surface breaks. But remains visible everywhere else on every other set.

Orpheus only ever existed in myth, outside language. He represents the comprehensive integrality which music propagates across space, the once rare harmonization of non-integrable elements; a fragile summation. But he exists powerfully now, indestructible. Harmony is no longer defined as producing one from the multiple; it has succeeded in accessing the multiple as a way of encompassing everything.

Music was not resistant to analyses. Once, the Bacchantes explained Orpheus' scores. It is to their scores that we listen, now.

Analyses dominate language and the Thracian women control what remains of music, invading our spaces with their cries.

Touch involves stitching together, place by place. Pointillist, if you like, or impressionist, moving between sections and localities, it creates maps, varieties, veils.

Global, integral, already abstract hearing, seeking unity, fills volumes: boxes, cases, houses, prisons, theatres, cities, circuses, hells and forests, marine expanses on which the musician's severed head, forgotten, detached, drifts on towards distant islands and sings, pervading the wind that sweeps between sky and waves. And my whole body, a music or language box, resonance chamber, resounding gong; and my local group, an assembly sometimes found in the theatre, for contemplation.

CELLS

A black box is ignorance, interrupting a chain of knowledge or creating a void in a transparent volume. We understand one thing up to a certain threshold, another thing and what follows it starting from another, but between one point and the other, this threshold and that one, we neither know nor comprehend; how this thing becomes that thing is quite beyond us. On any given scale, the box receives one thing and transmits another, hiding the mysterious transformations within its walls. The black box would appear to correspond to our definition of ignorance.

Objection. We observers may know and understand information transmitted by the box, its output, just as we might understand its input. How might we understand or know what occurs in the vicinity of that input-threshold? The box does of course receive, but what are we to make of that reception? We must receive it – yet the reception itself is not transmitted. We must therefore be located inside the supposedly closed box, the walls of which must as a consequence be moved. But whenever we talk about reception, the same irrepressible logic reasserts itself. So let us add a small black box, on the threshold of the large one, sitting astride its input side. However this is another of those questions like that of the third man – so we need to suppose a third box astride the side of the second, and so on as far as you like. Boxes upon boxes, proliferating leftwards.

We do not understand reception, except insofar as it coincides with observation. Do we understand observation? Once again, the answer escapes us. Transmission trumps listening, we know how to project a sound and how it spreads, we know how to relay it, we are not good at receiving. Science and philosophy both reproduce, in their respective disciplines, the brutal imbalance typical of dialogues where everyone talks and nobody listens, and of those animated groups in which each member produces as much noise as possible to the great discomfort of everyone else, with each person's suffering finding expression in a cry whose intensity seeks vainly to compel the attention of others, but to no avail since they in turn respond by giving voice to their suffering through wailing. Tomorrow, we will come to love reticence, which speaks rarely and prefers understatement. Monadic solitude grows in the space of messages, solipsism is taking on greater gravity in the world of so-called communication – Hermes' empire accentuates subjectivism.

Transmission trumps listening, we are no good at receiving. Whether we are dealing with a black box or the very simple scenario linking a transmitter to a receiver, the pole which perceives or feels is encased in a series of black boxes. Listening is rooted in silence and deafness.

Communication is vanishing. Either there is a private dimension, in which case there are no objective messages; or the latter are in fact in circulation, in which case there is no private dimension. So study mathematics and drink cold water.[1]

That's my last word on the subject.

Or my first.

The objection destroys both my book and any hope of describing reception, while at the same time it starts constructing something we might call an abstract receiver. Everything leads to the conclusion that sensation is organized, or trapped by us, within, by and through a similar set of embedded models. We create boxes in order to hear, we connect our ear to a conch to hear the sound of the sea, we build spaces with the express purpose of listening, or hearing each other: town squares, vaults, walls, churches, theatres, narrow passageways, alleys, ears of stone. We favour echoes and rhymes. Robinson Crusoe visits the desolate valley, a narrow gorge where the last word of the verses he reads out are echoed back to him: 'my soul', my soul, my soul, reverberating into silence, the manifold mirror of his cogito. He manages to find an alleyway where his footsteps will be echoed by its walls. Knowing nothing of the creature in question, certain that it will flee and disappear, we combine spaces through which sensation can pass, hoops, nets, mazes that the fish will thread its way into, unseen and unheard by us, swimming in circles, trapped, ensnared.

Captive reception.

Through touch, through our skin, we depicted tattooing, variable and varied imprinting, a singular variety for each of us, a universal covering. The painter makes us see through touch. I was not able to describe every last detail of each isolated or interconnected ocellus, stripe or streak, knotted and interwoven, original, repeated . . . a fluctuating web, inseparable from the surface of the warped sheet that enfolds us. These globally contingent traces of tangency – mixture, labyrinth, interlacing – structure the great snare of touch.

Rarely selective, reception occurs in a configuration in which input, which is mobile, is highly susceptible to feedback. It can become output and vice versa, in short cycles: as reverberations, echoes, reflections on screens, down narrow pathways, passages, gorges, defiles, impasses, frequent and unexpected bifurcations, circuits – think of a scrambled computer chip – creating specific points where the captive energies are lobbed back and forth. Reception is structured as self-transmission, it tames the unfamiliar, just as we repeat new words to ourselves in order to assimilate them. A liminal consciousness stirs there, in the folds of self-contact, through the repetition of reception; iterative and self-contained reception, whose prefix is apposite.

Tattooing works the same way. But I also imagine that the much repeated or embedded structure of what I have called the abstract receiver can be found in this interlacing. Our skin receives by constructing these undefined black boxes within its supple and flat surface. Which is why it is impossible to describe individual traces or projections in detail.

Whereas touch involves local patches activated or created by contact and brought together into an ocellated fragment, and skates about in the flattened out dimensions of irregularly shaped patches and imprecise tacking, sound, on the other hand, occupies volume and expands into the global, requiring of listening yet another dimension. Just as the abstract receiver, with its boxes within boxes, projects multiple networks or labyrinths on to the flat, uneven surface of the skin, like a model, so the same projection into the auditory spatial trap requires folds and sculptures in space, exquisitely chiselled contours. From touch to hearing, from map to landscape. The labyrinth raises its walls, digs its tunnels, lays down its corridors. Like the black box, hearing, by its very nature, is the multiplication of boxes.

But before that, the whole body or organism raises a taut sculpture or statue of skin, vibrating to the voluminous sound, open-closed like a cylindrical drum, trapping what traps it. We hear through our skin and feet. We hear through our skull, abdomen and thorax. We hear through our muscles, nerves and tendons. Our body-box, strung tight, is covered head to toe with a tympanum. We live in noises and shouts, in sound waves just as much as in spaces, the organism is erected, anchors itself in space, a broad fold, a long braid, a half-full, half-empty box which echoes them. Plunged, drowned, submerged, tossed about, lost in infinite repercussions and reverberations and making sense of them through the body. Sometimes dissonant, often consonant, disturbed or harmonious. Resonating within us: a column of air and water and solids, three-dimensional space, tissue and skin, long and broad walls and patches, and wiring, running through them; moorings receptive to the lower frequencies, as though our bodies were the union of ear and orchestra, transmission and reception. I am the home and hearth of sound, hearing and voice all in one, black box and echo, hammer and anvil, echo chamber, music cassette, pavilion, question mark drifting through the space of meaningful or meaningless messages, emerging from my own shell or drowning in the sound waves, I am nothing but empty space and a musical note, I am empty space and note combined. The moving statue finds its balance in the din as a fish does in water. The body remembers its previous, aquatic life, guiding itself through the sound waves by instinct and force of will. Humanity in shoals swims through these waters.

THE FIVE SENSES

The body stands and walks through the space of messages, orients itself within noise and meaning, amidst rhythms and rumblings. As it hears through the soles of its feet, through the sites where muscles, tendons and bones are attached and articulated, and finally in the space where the inner ear connects with the canals which control our balance, it can be said that our whole posture is linked to our sense of hearing. Our most intimate gestures move to sounds, we dance. Or rather, this is where dancing begins. We twist and turn, fascinated by different cries and melodies, like snakes charmed by a flute or Argus facing Hermes.

Geometers and topologists, we inhabit spaces in dimensions and proximities, tears and continuities; we live in gravity, strong, vertical, symmetrical; but our submersion in sound waves prompts our attitudes, supple, oblique, lop-sided, strained, restless. Time begins here, with rhythm. We are still fish, evolving in an environment where at each moment we find our balance through our hearing, an accurate calculator and computer. Proprioceptive hearing controls our gait, weary or lively; ordinary hearing commands flight, alertness, wakefulness, sleep; societal hearing dictates deportment. Those who live in ecstasy amidst notes, style and rigour sometimes have a secret, fourth ear which guides them through musical currents or spares them lapses in good taste by giving them true harmony.

In many languages, to listen is to obey: seduced by a voice, the body follows. It follows its vocation. Horrified by noise, muffled or dissonant, it drowns itself. Thus do we see huge processions herded or led by a breath or a rumbling from which they receive their sense of belonging and direction, shoals of fish suddenly redirected en masse, this way or that, by a perfunctory signal. They call this the spirit of the times, if it occurs to them.

The large consonant and dissonant box, trapping messages through posture, gesture, dance, orientation and movement – but also trapped by those messages, which balance and unbalance it, in turn – now gives them audience in and through a second box, straddling one wall of the first and attached to its petrosal bone. We find the same delicate outline of interlacing, corridors, screens, bottlenecks that defines the two-dimensional labyrinth of tattoos, but in three dimensions now, another vestibule of sound. Inside this new trap, the hard is made soft: deaf to whatever lies beyond its range, the box is protected; the membrane of the eardrum presents skin to the outside world, mucus to the inside, the skin harder, the mucus softer, kept separate within the membrane itself by a more resistant armature; the sound wave produced by a physical shock is transformed into a chemical signal carrying electrical information towards the centre . . . Which centre? Does the box receive or emit? To listen is to vibrate, but to vibrate is to emit. Unfold the cochlea, for instance, and you will see an inverted piano with tiers of high and low notes running from left to right. But a piano produces sound, it does not hear. The same logic dogs us: the ear needs a more central ear to hear what is transmitted by the three others, outer, middle and inner, which hear each other, each in turn. The hearing centre. Which centre? Move the partition. Partition after partition, black box after black box – this is a projection of the abstract receiver.

Sound is transmitted here in non-linear fashion, travelling from hardest to softest; here, at each stage, it submits to loops, circuits or feedback. The box receives the captive energy, organizes the repetition anticipated by the prefix, it traps noise, sound and message, makes them circulate quickly, brings them to rest, makes them vibrate in themselves for themselves, and through these circular movements transforms transmission into reception, resolving the contradiction that besets hearing.

Let us change the discourse on method, let us optimize our journeys another way. We inherit our idea of the labyrinth from a tragic and pessimistic tradition, in which it signifies death, despair, madness. However, the maze is in fact the best model for allowing moving bodies to pass through while at the same time retracing their steps as much as possible; it gives the best odds to finite journeys with unstructured itineraries. Mazes maximize feedback. They provide a very long path within a short distance and construct the best possible matrix for completing a cycle. The best possible method for all kinds of reception, they are often to be found in sensation, whose problems they solve clearly.

Underpinned by metric theory, the discourse on method finds ease in shortness, simplicity in speed, prefers the minimum. It flies straight and talks straight. Metric theory and its method will thus always seek to escape from the labyrinth by optimal means, in the briefest time, via the shortest path. Drawing on information theory and topology, I would put forward as optimal the figure which is diametrically opposed to such projects. Speed is of no consequence when we are dealing with fast-spreading phenomena such as light, sound and even touch, which is transmitted instantaneously from one end of a stick to another. Sensation cares little for metrics, you see. Let us find other ways of optimizing journeys. Let us seek the best way of creating the most feedback loops possible on an unstructured and short itinerary. Mazes provide us with this maximization. Excellent reception, here is the best possible resonator, the beginnings of consciousness. We see, finally, that the design of a labyrinth traces a series of boxes, non-concentrically embedded in each other, one straddling the wall of the next and so on – the abstract receiver again.

Knots and weaving gave us a topological description of touch by supposing it to be made up of one-dimensional threads and intertwining them. To describe hearing, more global than local, through body, head and thorax, inner, outer and middle ear, fossa triangularis, auditory canal, cochlea, vestibule, all of them more or less well-embedded boxes, according to our abstract model, the topology of depth requires varieties in every dimension, hollows them out, folds them, creates edges, mountains and valleys, passes, chimneys, tubes and lobes; architecture, landscape. Tattoos dye the warp of our skin, which acquires volume; boxes are fashioned out of veils.

Hence my (poetic) resistance to the conviction that we would hear just as well with no pavilion at all or that our hearing would not be impaired by a flat pavilion. The lovely carved design of our outer ear, a final series of little boxes or dimples, combining helix and counter helix to make one last maze, must receive messages which are still unknown to science. We wear two questions marks, one on each side of our head like placards, two treble clefs, with neither repercussions nor answers.

Love potion. The prisoner in the tower loves the gaoler's daughter. The tower rises above the castle, the dungeon is embedded in the tower and the cell in the dungeon, a nest of structures; to reach the cell, you need to make your way through endless walls and doors, climb stairs or cross chasms via fragile aerial staircases, pass through hundreds of grilles, even a chapel. The real cell, carved out of wood, adds another box of timber framework and beams, its floor raised, within the stone walls and ceiling. No, we have not yet reached the final box in this nest of boxes: the governor has had a shutter installed in front of the window of this cubby-hole, a window through which only rats could enter; he has had every crack sealed up with oil-paper. The honoured prisoner resides behind numerous impermeable walls, thick, blind, opaque, fifteen layers of partitions.

Opposite the dungeon, below, the castle wall opens on to an aviary, boxes, cages, cells where birds are caged, birds which the gaoler's daughter tends. We do not know what twisting paths she takes to reach them. A love story is unfolding there. From inside his semaphore house, behind a small peephole, her lover speaks to her in signs or letters. She responds, letter for letter, amidst the twittering and birdsong. She will soon swear never to look at her lover behind lowered eyelids. Later, she will hear him preaching, in tears.

Is it an angel or devil passing through the veils of these boxes, what message traverses a thousand walls, to be exchanged between which instances of the self, confined within, transmitting and receiving? What cry, appeal, light – animated, mobile, intense, sharp – has the power to send out energy which can force its way through the maze and be refined as it filters through?

The dungeon-body maintains its distance from the desired chateau-flesh. The window-eye beseeches behind the eyelid-blind and the ear hears the song of the bird-soul through its tympanum of oil-paper. Timid lovers, isolated underneath their multiple skins or rigid walls, stiff and horrified behind their battlements, whose beautiful love will be lost if ever the prisoner escaped and who will hasten to maintain their distance and throw up new obstacles, as though the only love possible were the effect of the walls surrounding lovers crashing into each other, or echoes reverberating between boxes, interferences, vibrations, harmonies, thuds; the citadel forming a giant organ. Two phantoms thrashing about inside music boxes constructed like gaols. This is the traditional notion of the body, and no doubt also that of science.

The love stories which so astonish our supple, naked bodies, painless and nearly mute, were stories of knowing, long ago. Just as the call of love circulates through the corridors, grilles and vaults of the chateau-body, haunting them, so do sense data pass through the obstacles placed into a kind of statue or automaton with twenty layers of armour, a veritable Carpathian castle, their energy purified as it makes its way through successive filters towards the central cell or instance, soul, understanding, conscience or transcendental I, to which very few gaolers hold the key.[2]

We appreciate the exquisite delicacy of a design in which one filtering station follows another, in the service of knowledge or love. Few have earned the right to penetrate the dungeon or holy of holies, the last box behind or beneath other cells: it took a priest, or a judicial figure. This is what it was to know or to love. It happened rarely. Under surveillance. Through hear-say. By twists and turns of a labyrinth.

Sensation is held in a black box, and functions like one. Both the former and the latter precede knowledge, just as each, misunderstood, comes after, envelopes or punctures it.

Through sensation the hard becomes soft. Sensation protects and guides us. Without it, our bodies would explode from the screeching attacks of the Bacchantes, would disintegrate like Eurydice, half out of her black well or box of shadows, would be torn limb from limb by tornadoes, would decompose under the scorching sun or be shredded by sounds beyond the range of our hearing: Orpheus is mutilated by lions, women and branches.

145

THE FIVE SENSES

We multiply our skills and strategies to avoid the deadly fate of Orpheus: we will turn away, flee in horror, sweat, shiver, cover ourselves with veils, lie low; produce variations on the box, enlarging and reinforcing it.

An aid to knowledge, the box supports life. I am that box. I inhabit it.

We are soft, and construct softening boxes.

Behind a courtyard, its grills and portals closed, withdrawn, in front of the high walled garden, the house collects itself within its walls. Distant, protected, holding the world at bay. Inside, the hard stone or rough concrete is covered in gowns, envelopes, ever softer membranes, ever finer textures, smooth plaster, refined paper or liquid paint, decorated, historiated, floral wallpaper; the house multiplies layer upon layer, starting with the rough and ending with pictures. On the vertical plane, the same multi-layered progression: plumbing, girders, floorboards, carpet, rugs. Finally, embellishments and plasterwork. The house closes up its openings too: shutters, windows, double-glazing, stained glass, net curtains, drapes, decorative pelmets, and until not so along, doorways and windows with deep alcoves. Built to be closed, the box has labyrinthine openings. To open our dwellings so brutally, as we have done recently, we needed to shed our fear of the world and believe it criss-crossed by nothing more than signals. The house functions as a space of transformation where forces are calmed, like a high energy filter, or converter. Outside reigns harsh spring or unrelenting dawn, inside is the dream space of calm pictures which do not hinder conversation, inside the space of language is created. Like a skull, a brain. The box transforms the world into coloured pictures, into paintings hanging on walls, changes the landscape into tapestry, the city into abstract compositions. Its function is to replace the sun with heaters and the world with icons. The sound of the wind with gentle words. Cellars turn alcohol into aromas.

In such a house, the philosopher writes and thinks and perceives. Inside. Through the window I see an apple tree in flower, he says. He searches for the origins of knowledge and places himself at its beginnings. He discovers a garden in this Genesis, naturally, and in this garden only the apple tree interests him, tempts him: he can see its flowers. Long dissertation about the tree, the picture of it he might draw, the image he has of it or the word he finds and writes in his language – something that is absent from every orchard. He forgets the window, the alcove, the curtains, the opaque or translucent glass and, depending on whether he lives in the north or south, the sash or casement window. Forgets the house, and the opening through the house, in front of the apple tree. In strong wind, in driving rain, the tree houses squawking birds at night in the branches where they nest; one thing to prune the tree, outside, another thing to describe it, inside. Beyond the reach of water, beyond wind, cold, fog, light and dark – even beyond noise, in the past – the house protects us just as the belly of a vessel separates us from the cold of the sea. Second skin, enlarging our sensorium. Still a box, but now an eye also. Hearing and pavilion. The house observes the apple tree through the window. The house-skull quietly contemplates the tree through the porthole-eye. We might call the window a medioscope, mesoscope or isoscope. Thus did Captain Nemo, behind the scuttle of the *Nautilus*, descend slowly into the classification of fish, into taxonomy, the dictionary of natural history, more than he plunged to the depths of the sea. The scientist observes the naturalized butterfly beneath glass, or peers at Linnaeus' table from behind his spectacles, or microbes under his microscope. From behind the window-pane, the image of the apple tree is disciplined even though the window preserves its dimensions. The philosopher cares nothing for its fruits and flowers – acacia, maple? Behind the glass there is a phantom, just as we say that the soft replica of an object is formed on the retina, behind the pupil or crystalline lens. Tempest becomes moan as it crosses the shutter-eardrum, information as it works its way through hallway and winding staircase.

The house stares through its windows at the vineyards and tufts of thyme, ornamental oranges take shape on its walls, a tissue of lies, oranges and liemons. The philosopher forgets that the house, built around him, transforms a plantation of olive trees into a Max Ernst painting. The architect has forgotten this too. And is happy if the next harvest, outside, is transformed into a *Virgin with Grapes*, inside. The house transforms the given, which can assault us, softening it into icons: it is a box for generating images, a cavern or eye or *camera obscura*, a barn which sunlight only illuminates with a slim shaft piercing through the dust – an ear. Architecture produces painting, as though the fresco or canvas hanging on the wall revealed the ultimate cause of the whole structure. The aim of architecture is painting or tapestry. What we took to be mere ornament is its objective, or at the very least its end product. Walls are for paintings, windows for pictures. And padded doors for intimate conversations.

The philosopher holds forth about sensation, yet he inhabits it already, dwelling in a kind of sensation, a part of his house as the pupil is part of his eye. The writer forgets the window, its position and the passive work it does, and observes the painting. Or, if he contemplates a painting, thinks he is dealing with a porthole. He forgets the house, the soft box which ends at the window. Sees the picture, vaguely contemplates a few icons, now abstract, destroyed by a wave of iconoclasm, looks at his page of language where he discovers the given.

The house is a picture box, like a skull or an eye. The philosopher inhabits his own problem. In the past, the world was called God's sensorium. Let us say that the house is man's sensorium. The heavens are filled with God's glory, the house is filled with our small energies.

Within the house, the bedroom encloses a box within a box. When people got into box beds, in Ouessant, or four-poster beds, in Rambouillet or Versailles, you could add yet another box to the list, this time a slightly darker one inside the still illuminated larger one. Sheets add another pocket to the nested series, and rarely do we slide between them naked. O! frozen time of our childhood when no-one went to bed without their woollen sleeping bag. The empiricist is astonished by the number of layers, strata and partitions from rough concrete to bed linen, the number of skins until we reach our real skin. We have already counted the box of veils, of garments. No, we do not live as beings in the world the way books tell us, we cannot possibly make such a claim, there is no way we could tolerate it, but rather as a variety of mammal or soft primate which, having lost its fur, invented the house and promptly filled it with boxes within boxes. Only the external house is exposed to the world; the multilayered apartment is merely exposed to the city. Language weaves the last protective wall in front of our delicate skin, just after images and paintings.

Radio and television would have us believe that they bring the world itself into our homes. .

The house constructs an orthopædic sensorium around us; conversely, the sensorium constructs our little portable house, our fragile vessel, a soft membrane ready to burst open under the assault of the smallest thorn. The philosopher forgets the house he inhabits, but also this house of sensation, the last softening box. There is always a third box in this question.

Our softening houses, built to house pictures, constitute the common sense. Unmoving, the windows watch the trees. It used to be said that God's gaze was always with us, until the final box, even though it be as dark as a tomb: the painting depicts Cain seen by Him.

Our houses were built in a peaceful world, where music only had to overcome the roaring of lions and the furore of the Bacchantes. The invaginated set of walls and pockets surrounding my vague soul cracks and falls apart under the terrible din of noise pollution. I no longer inhabit my house or my skin, panting, defenceless, racked, dismembered by noise. But no matter if it should cause my soul to fade away, my mouth to vomit, my body to faint – what if it were to be the death of music itself?

The social box, complex, constructed, hardware and software, often closed, sometimes open, constant and variable, defined by walls as well as by ideal or carnal attachments, created by the town planner, the architect, the mason and the bridge-builder, in thrall to different networks and media, organizes the manifold and almost ubiquitous hearing of its own noise, by sometimes allowing the world's background noise to filter through, when we hear our cheering in stadiums and theatres, churches and meetings, in public squares, in the streets, once narrow and winding to better capture or channel sound waves and turn them back on themselves, nowadays wide and straight because of the greater power of transmitters ensuring sounds are heard everywhere and echoed by newspapers, radio and television, in circulating rumours, all of these messages constructing the box and sealing it as securely as a wall, a powerful social box whose walls, ever present and reflecting sound waves, surround, protect and penetrate the house-box, soft and hard, enveloped, made of concrete, plaster and paintings, vibrating with words, or the ship-shell, the arrangement of which enables a more careful hearing of the rumbling coming from outside, crashes and news, wind and commerce, sounds of the world and society, but also the cries of children and the moaning of the sick, the clamouring of bodies or insignificant acclamation, during festive meals, from the smallest group, hiding, discrete, isolated by this music box, porous but nonetheless full of smaller noise boxes, but whose frame and tiles in turn envelope and protect the box of veils or clothing, hardware or software, fabric and decorations, the defence of which can terminate in the bedroom where tattoos can be displayed and whose dermal support surrounds and protects the body-box, soft and hard, sculpted from bones and codes, resounding and adjustable, out there in the fields where noises and sounds are propagated, its semi-conscious circuits listening with the most refined system to its own jubilations and complaints, as it does to words whispered nearby, audible thanks to the complex of discrete boxes, and to the public racket, bringing down the barriers erected in front of it; but also to the background noise coming from crude things, low, silent, abyssal detonations preceding earthquakes underneath the foundations of our houses, the clamour of waves in a gale, protects the self-governing body-box, choosing and sometimes not choosing between these transmitters and filters, piled up, overlapping, each straddling the outer wall of another, reinforcing or blocking one another, long parasitic chains, as invasive as metastases, bifurcating and feeding back into one another, but amidst hesitations and sidetracks, protecting, surrounding and penetrating the ear-box, multiple and complex, acoustic and codified, whose maze controls the sensible, physical hearing of messages within its range, perceived in the theatre or bedroom, on the beach or in confidence, and transmits them, softened, to the central, initially peripheral box, whose complicated labyrinth of synapses and axons organizes the reception of signals, preparing the sense which has been protected by language, itself protected by music or light, and diving headlong into noise, sense and language whose grip intersects with the range of the social box, enchanting and linguistic, enticing and cruel, ubiquitous like meaning and proclamations, multiple like approval, and penetrating ear and head, orientation and consent, the whole body, movements, posture and bearing, the house, the city and the world, where the noise coming from shadowy mouths is quelled.

The summation of hearing, hard and soft, box of transmitter-receiver boxes, runs the course of the labyrinth thus described, quickly and over long, difficult passageways; a labyrinth which produces the maximum number of cycles, some of which remain stable for a long time, or for a short time, in which case they tend to form boxes.

What ear hears this summation or rumbling from the depths, harmony or interference? An immense sea, soft and hard, beneath languages, somehow familiar as we dive in. As we descend to the Underworld.

Whatever pain or fatigue might ail our body, suffering a thousand ills, overwhelmed by work and injury, it always manages to raise a protective wall around an untarnished space to which the instance of self, quivering with joy and expectation, can flee ever-present danger and imminent death, no matter how far or deep their blows may reach. It starts over, secreting or building a new wall each time an outer barrier is brought down or given up. Flees from box to box, from shouting towards silence.

In this sovereign, always protected space, this constant and living flame, shining with joy and intellect, dancing, leaves behind a membrane – in the same circumstances – when it flees beneath another layer, rather as a thief who has been nabbed might shed his jacket into the hands of his captor and run. Like Harlequin discarding his old costumes and skins, we frequently shed layers in this manner when confronted by natural cruelty, when fate seizes us, when hatred preys upon us. We flee behind boxes and veils.

The dancing flame or instance we might easily call the soul, frees itself, invents shapes and places, boxes of silence, a bridal gown, seeking stability.

When the final assault comes, it slips away, true to its usual strategy, once more triumphant, but has failed naively to see or feel that there was only one garment left, that the final barrier has fallen, shed at the moment of departure; at the instant of death the body surrenders the living, still thinking soul.

The soul, white doll at the end of a sequence of black boxes, final instance, mocking our advancing efforts to know it, as they demolish one dark threshold after another. The soul, deaf to their noise, singing joyfully, protected, immortal.

3
Tables

ANIMAL SPIRITS – MEMORY – STATUE – DEATH – BIRTH

ANIMAL SPIRITS

So we had bought a bottle of 1947 Yquem in the north-eastern corner of Paris, near La Villette, from an expert dealer who had acquired it from the restaurant that used to be at the Gare de l'Est, which in turn cellared its wines in long-forgotten underground tunnels – a bottle from the catacombs. It was said that the wine list was like a dictionary that aficionados would take their time poring over, sometimes without getting around to ordering dinner, or even days before their meal. The dealer went out of business, his son imports soft drink now, the restaurant has been replaced by fast-food outlets (in matters of taste, as in love-making, if you would rather hurry, better that you abstain altogether; in both these cases haste leads to nothing but regret), the dark tunnels now house only rats, until the next air raid. The three of us sat down, two friends with the gift of the gab, which is to say knowing how to remain silent.

The liquid had taken on a deep golden hue, orange-yellow with coppery tones and hints of pink: the colour of intelligence and wisdom, scented with the thrill of desire. It was like the base of a cauldron in a Flemish kitchen, polished with patience over time, half-hidden in darkness amidst the crosspieces of dark timber. The wine glowed like straw in a barn, like a windy night watch illuminated by the glow of the compass. The cork, solid, was starting to turn to liquid, just a little, dark shading into light, everything shifting phase.

It took us so long to finish this bottle that we are still talking about it.

I remember with gratitude the moment when a great wine gave me a new mouth – the day of my second communion, it says. It already existed, ill-spoken no doubt; the second mouth was born there.

Speech passes through the mouth on the day of our first communion – giving us our first mouth. The golden mouth starts to chatter, will not stop chattering. Speech reigns there, a queen in palatine splendour; the reign of language over lips and tongue is absolute. Imperious, exclusive. But speech and language cross these spaces, neither smelling nor tasting. Soft: not hard. Soft: dull and insipid. They anæsthetize the mouth, which finds the zestiest conversation tasteless. The most wide-ranging eloquence, the most sonorous poetry, the most incantatory song, the liveliest dialogue transform the palate into a musical instrument, which nonetheless remains numb to fragrant flowers, to the scent of the earth, to the powerful fragrance of musk and skin; or worse still, chases them away. Neither acidic nor astringent, sentences refrain from awakening our tongue to anything but themselves. Sapidity slumbers beneath the narcosis of speech. Frozen: frigid.

Of our five senses, this one, these two – smell and taste – seem to us the least æsthetic. I'm beginning to understand, says the golden mouth, why we reject, forget, put off their specific abilities, why I can say with such confidence that the given only gives itself in and through language: one mouth kills the other. I, a golden mouth, kill the long palate of Yquem. I will not tolerate doubt, a double tongue in my mouth, a forked tongue, me speaking, it tasting. Today, the day of the banquet, I will be kind to my victim, it says, and step aside.

And awaken the palate from anæsthetizing talk through the use of a second talent. Which discovers an æsthetics of sense in the work of a different, artistic æsthetic. The Château d'Yquem awakens the second mouth, the second tongue, reveals it through this second communion. Oppressed, too close to language, too much its twin or competitor, taste is rarely conveyed well, is often expressed in language that provokes mirth – our mouth laughs at it – as though in this place language allowed it no voice. One mouth chases the other, the mouth of discourse excludes the mouth of taste, expels it from discourse.

The second tongue sleeps; timid, it remains silent; receives what is given, all the better when it forgets its twin.

Before drinking good wine, we have never tasted wine, or smelled it, or known it, and have no chance of ever knowing it. We may have drunk, and gotten drunk; another form of anæsthesia. But knowledge cannot come to those who have neither tasted nor smelled. Speaking is not sapience, the first tongue needs the second.

We were too quick to forget that *homo sapiens* refers to those who react to sapidity, appreciate it and seek it out, those for whom the sense of taste matters – savouring animals – before referring to judgement, intelligence or wisdom, before referring to talking man. The rise of the golden mouth at the expense of the tasting mouth. But hidden within a dead language, we find this confession of the first about the dead mouth: namely that wisdom comes after taste, cannot arise without it, but has forgotten this.

Let us speak dead languages, says the dead mouth. Do you remember, O golden twin, jewel of philosophers and scholars, the common linguistic origin of the words regulations and rillettes, from the Latin *regulae*? Where are you, Descartes? Or of the words induction and andouille, from the low Latin *inductile*? Bacon, where are you? This is how the sapient tongue asserted its rights and demonstrated, in its neighbour's tongue, their joint intersection, the place where they go their separate ways.

The first mouth, all talk, was left speechless. Caught out by its own forked tongue.

Sensation, it used to be said, inaugurates intelligence. Here, more locally, taste institutes sapience. In the ancestral Latin definition of human beings, our educated but still sensible forebears are a serious demonstration that, without taste, we risk abnegating our human state and returning to that of animals. Before recreating ideas about sensation – a strange business – they no doubt wanted us to imagine the opposite: if we disdain sensation, replace it with artifice, with orthopædic forms of discourse, then we are headed towards animality. Animals wolf down their food, man tastes it. Appreciates the aromas, hunts no more. Cruelty only produces blood.

Before having received, bedazzled, the manifold and vibrant bouquet that unfolds through our sense of smell, exploding as it descends, still full of arabesques or new stars, like fireworks; before having known the complex, fringed moiré that meticulously segments the precise geographic map of the cheeks, differentiating top from bottom, and front from back, short and long palate, tracing ornamentation on the roof of the mouth, passing over and under the tongue, to the sides and back; before having known that we have tongues, and not just one tongue; before having transformed this volume into a rainbow-coloured, tattooed, ornamented, mingled space, before the unction of wine has changed the uniform into the multiple, and frigidity into tenderness, before this patient, slow, detailed recognition, we have drunk, of course, have quenched our thirst over and over again, have even been heavily intoxicated, but have never sensed; sensation never came – we were speaking. Knew need and desire; took remedies and poisons in altered states, most certainly drugged ourselves, but overlooked sensation. Anæsthetic robs us of æsthetics.

Communities which hasten to shed the naïve sapience of empiricism find themselves locked out of their destiny by drugs. Take this wine: drink, taste – you must choose. If you merely drink it, you will keep only speech, language. If you taste it, it will give you your taste by giving you its taste, it opens a new mouth in you, this is the day of your second communion, prevented by the first. The given, generous, gives more than we think. It heals impotence or the inability to receive, or other inadequacies. Æsthetics cures us of anæsthesia. It awakens us. The given often gives the subject the capacity to take what is given: here is the gift, plus its container, and ribbons too, as well as the right disposition to apprehend it. In short, it will create the function, or at least activate it, or initiate it. The first tongue, talkative, admits this: fine food and wine can create taste in the person who tastes them. Similarly, a beautiful sight gives sight to the person who sees it. It has the same word for what is smelt and the act of smelling it – but it takes a lot for the recipient to make the most of it. We know more people who are asleep than people who are awake, more who are blind than clear-sighted, more impotent people than lovers. The apprehended given does more for perception than the other way around. Fine wine works on the tongue, awakening it from its narcotic slumber.

Therefore you cannot get drunk on it. Take this wine: drink, taste, reveal your dormant sense of taste or anæsthetize it again by getting drunk, but both at once – no. Æsthetics or anæsthesia, no third tongue. I cannot sense the difference between the speaker and the drunk, says the second tongue, the taster, in both cases I am drugged and put to sleep. The guests at the *Symposium* hiccup, speechify or slump about, weighed down by alcohol, Plato has ensured that the banquet never takes place.[1] They speak of love without making love, sing of this or that without actually singing, drink without tasting, speak with the first tongue – but for all the sounds they produce, do we know what wine they drank: from Chios, Corfu or Samos? He who holds the floor and talks the most until pallid dawn, triumphs over the inebriation of the rest. Wine encourages talk, and is numbing. The first tongue, the talker, uses the mixture drawn from amphorae and mixed in craters, circulating unnoticed around the beds, sometimes spilled on the cushions or bread, to oppress the second, always asleep in philosophy. At symposia today you can still hear virtuosic talk, over cups of a weak, black beverage. But no banquet.

The second tongue tries to trace its geographic map of the tongue, as it wakes.

THE FIVE SENSES

From where might we describe it? From near or far or middle distance, it always seems to shimmer like watered silk.

No doubt because smell and taste differentiate, whereas language, like sight and hearing, integrates. The first mouth stockpiles, the second expends: words pile up in dictionaries, food accumulates, frozen, in coldrooms, like bank accounts; smells and tastes are transitory, evanescent, ephemeral. Differential. The map is refined like delicate silk, or a spider's web. With neither stock nor total, a fragment of time.

Unstable moire, mingled body.

The second tongue has humility: simple, rudimentary taste, poor like reasoning, it can barely make out four or five qualities, sweet, sour, astringent, acidic . . . It depends on smell to achieve its festive richness. Avid, empty, gluttonous, roaring, whether talking or eating, imperious as only the weak can be, the mouth relies on its nose and ears to be able to boast as it does. It is the mouths of barbarians that we hear, talking about talking, holding forth about eating, ignorant of fleeting tastes and aromas, deaf chatterboxes, gluttons with neither sense of smell nor wisdom, human funnels, eating and drinking sweet or savoury to bring the nose down to the mouth's level, reducing smell to taste and manifold refinement to crudeness. The man of sapience, whether peasant or baron, has flair and a keen ear to capture the moment; the stubborn, like the jovial, are all mouth, transmitting; whereas everything comes from subtle reception. Leave aside singing and eloquence where the voice is regulated by the ear in an active loop: in both instances, music arises when the general din beseeches hearing for its clemency; hearing in turn gives or gives back timbre and cadence. And the first tongue becomes hoarse when the eardrum becomes brittle with age. In a comparable loop or cycle, smell regulates taste judiciously. Earring, nose-ring. So our sense of smell, champion among our sensations, and our taste, excellence in culture and refinement, bestow their rare treasure together, within a shared cycle. A cornucopia emerges from nose and palate, odours and tastes spilling forth, the peacock's tail is displayed.

Here is the map.

Here is the bottle from which this fan emerges.

Here is the region of the lower Garonne, the left bank, where the forest disappears, where the tide ends, a knot of eleven confluences, here is the gentle slope, near Yquem, from which the ocellated fan can be seen: a map of the area and an expanse of taste.

156

The second tongue, in between the two others – the one that will not stop talking and the one that remains hidden modestly, and has neither spoken nor tasted yet – now requires silence and time. It never has either of these.

Take time, remain silent, taste.

The streaked, blended, marled, damask, watered-silk, ocellated body unfolds itself gently from the cornucopia or around the tufted feet of Juno's bird. Can we enumerate? Here are spring flowers, dog rose or lilac, clematis, the fruits of *Messidor*,[2] including peaches (autumn or winter ones), pears, apples, grapes, walnuts, some hazelnuts trailing in their wake, in dark, fern-covered undergrowth, here are truffles in the greyish humus, bark sticky with resin, then rare mineral fragrances, flint, gunflint, and animal fragrances, musk or amber, damp fur or the scent of copulation, and here, behind the second and first bouquets, the first one floral, the next bestial and mineral, comes the third bouquet, so difficult, like pizzicati heard beneath an orchestral storm, like cross-hatching through floral-print fabric, aromas as ethereal as acetone, try to pick them out: aromatics – mint, geranium; ambrosias – jasmine, vanilla, lime; balms like benzoin, carnation, camphor; empyreumata like coffee, tobacco; the Yquem bears traces of the persistent forest, remembers distant Armagnac, cites its neighbour, Graves; now here is disequilibrium, the outer edge of the expanse, or ocellated tail, its instability or catastrophe, repulsive combinations like mercaptan, the stench of oil, tar and sewers, sulphur; what's happening? Close the door when the East wind is blowing, the one-track reason of the highway has intruded bringing a vile and stupid horde of Huns, has uprooted the vines of Sauternes, severed the heraldic shield from its nobility, torn up the map, cut out its tongue. It cuts through the sacred vines, merely indicating them with a road sign. For those who hurry past, riding thunder and spewing a cloud of gaseous filth in their wake, the given is reduced to written language, painted on a panel. The roadmap is rectilinear, as linear as the method which passes through the forest without seeing it and which, ignobly, severs the ancient vines without so much as a greeting.

If you pass through a vineyard as a blabbermouth might cross the sea, then you will see only green or red foliage, just as the other would see only water. Bend down and examine the furrows: earth or body, streaked, blended . . . silica, pebbles, sand, clay and limestone, deposits from above or afar, carried by the Garonne. Fine silica, rich limestone, moist clay, everything comes from the mingled earth. Walk through the vines where the Muscadelle has been picked, sweetness comes from the Semillon, spice notes from the Sauvignon, the rows are streaked, striped, composite. We would have to superimpose several maps: geological, pedological, viticultural, a mosaic of yellow, pink, royal blue, bottle green, an unexpected element, as though the substratum – what a surprise – were reproducing itself on the surface, as though the old growers themselves, unwitting geologists, were revealing the dark secrets of the earth, through and in the arrangement of these maps: mingled seacharts for navigating the Bordeaux region. In the same way, through the alloy of syllables, vowels, rhythms and assonances, the writer tries to evoke the map of deep-seated deposits and brings to the surface the glittering pattern of underground veins.

The coat of arms of the Comte de Lur-Saluces, master of Yquem, should, it seems to me, bear or depict on its unified page, this streaked, ocellated body, this honourable map, in its colours, devices and charges: either a peacock's tail, or an interleaved stack of atlases. Doesn't a coat of arms typically reproduce a map of mixed blood and the manner of its enduring survival? What is a title, if not the proportions of a mingled body? The noble shields of the vineyard would thus show how, after so many quarters, wine becomes blood – or the other way around.

Now, in the silence and cool tranquility of the cellar, what different sort of mingling is at work? Alcohol and acid are balanced against sweet-smelling ester, suspended in water and sugars. The right balance comes in incremental changes. Might we guess at the various titles, at any given time? The titles of the mixture would indicate time.

I can draw a thousand maps, but I am only ever talking about time.

Mixture haunts the cellar in the art of the vigneron, runs through the vineyard – soil, layering and subsoil – fills the singular bottle, completes the mouth by closing the cycle of aromas, the same map everywhere, I draw it on the page, it is my coat of arms.

Old cellars, vineyards, bottles, seacharts, enduring heraldic alliances, ancient mouths and tongues, attentive patience of the design marking earth, flora and palate: the time of mixtures slowly ticks by.

The accumulated quarters divide the space of the shield between them; conversely, the shield displays the antiquity of the title, and the title borne by this blood. Many a vermilion cascade has flowed over the shield, thus marked: red clepsydra.

The earth of rivers, seas and forests, long ago laid bare, ravaged by tears and sterility, long unsuited to all kinds of agriculture due to an excess of sand and gravel, slowly becomes the exceptional specific of such and such a botanical palette. It takes at least a millennium of peasant stubbornness, punctuated with famines, to reach this blended picture.

Alluvial cascade, receiving or giving cascades of wine: if only my tongue were equal to these miraculous nuptials, amidst the floodwaters of the versatile Garonne, a grey clepsydra.

In a miracle of the first tongue – when it is speaking in French, at least – the word for time is also the word for weather: *le temps*. The miracle of bountiful seasons interspersed, pot-luck, with weak or barren ones. The ground, the vines and the wine itself carry traces of the clemency and inclemency of the weather; the mixture of any given vintage is an expression of this mixture of hot and cold, moist and dry, calm and turbulent that we call the weather – which we might just as well call temperament or temperance, if the world had the same moods as our bodies: weather which is typically rather mild in this temperate region. Take this great wine, taste it, the map of its temperament will be traced on your tongue, the inimitable and singular facets of a particular season. Remember that year: the autumn was immense, unmoving, soaring, endless, flecked with notes of orange and yellow, so light as to be barely perceptible. Cascades of wind, sun and rain mingled with the Sauternes, a golden clepsydra.

Now read: in the left-hand column, a simple list of calendar years, a roll-call of years gone by, none omitted, none repeated; in the right-hand column, a list of notable years, glorious or catastrophic. 1930, the year I was born, produced an unspeakable liquid and nothing better, yet 1929 (when my brother was born), has been equalled only three times since in the whole Bordeaux region, in '45, '61 and '75, once in a lifetime vintages of supernatural taste and enormous longevity. As though weather and time were intimately connected, enough to make us understand how two words could be one, two meanings – time and weather – cohabiting in a single term, *le temps*. If time flowed like a series of whole numbers, on the left, we would have known long ago that history and reason go hand in hand. But the stochastic mixture of years by which we might read the different vintages of Château d'Yquem over the last hundred years gives us a very different idea of that same history, once again drawing us a blended map. During our banquet with the bottle of '47 Yquem, an almost mythical vintage, the first tongue runs off the series of numbers, the second throws the figures to the wind, savouring the highpoints. On the left, the time of language; on the right, the time of the given. From which we can see that the two are separate, like a forked tongue. On the left, time as an *a priori* pure form – I was going to say algorithmic – on the right, the time of mixture and mingling, of which the time of the left understands nothing.

A cascade of numbers, not parallel as we might think when reading them but merging into one another, because we live; an immaterial, abstract, double clepsydra, combining a straight corridor with the irregular percolation of a fulling mill.

The unstoppable current of the Garonne is blended with tears of joy and mourning.

Three friends or enemies thus find themselves seated at the banquet, drawing maps, stirring mixtures, discovering time. Maps of watered silk trace the spaces around mingled bodies, poured together; their fusion in the same clepsydra or bottle follows the currents of duration.

Two of the friends, intimate acquaintances, want to liberate themselves from the third, enamoured of discourse. They too love speech, but want to free themselves from its absolute tyranny. The golden tongue, disengaged from the other two, travels a different path, rare and disconnected, with time flowing through a unique clepsydra. The other two tongues, enamoured of concourses, follow blended, fluidic, liquid pathways, flowing in knotted confluences.

The dominant tongue performs analysis. Successfully, convincingly so, which proves that it should continue.

The other two dare not say that they practise confusion. In the language of the first, confusion means failure. Just as success avoids failure, so has the first tongue banished the other two.

Once enemies, they find themselves seated thus together at the banquet, temporarily reconciled.

Mixture and confusion preside in the crater of Château d'Yquem. Nothing more delicious, more divine, more memorable than this confusion of gold, copper and bronze.

The two neglected tongues challenge the first to speak, to expatiate upon this confusion without maligning it, for once.

When Monsieur le Comte Alexandre de Lur-Saluces' hundred and twenty grape-pickers spread themselves across the gentle slopes of the hillside, between rows of vines, to pick the overripe Sauvignon and Semillon, one grape at a time, for yet another autumn since the first in 1785, from the glorious beginning of October until, sometimes, the heavy mists of December; when they mix the harvest from the rocky side with the harvest from the clay-rich side and then with that of the sandy side; when the must of the southern slope is mixed with grapes that ripened under a more oblique, less generous sun; when different slopes, wines, bunches are thrown together, we dream indistinctly that a word capable of expressing this confluence might be acclimatized into our tongue. We cannot say concade nor syrrhesis.

Greek abhors the term synchysis, which should describe the act of directing several currents from different sources or urns into the same channel, one confluence uniting numerous affluents. But it merely refers to confusion or entanglement, a chaos that will not be unscrambled. French abhors it equally, speaking only of confusion. What flows together seems confused to the first tongue, whether speaking French or Greek, but seems as divine as a mouthful of Yquem to the second, which receives it as an unction and can follow the map of its mixtures. We must suppose that the first has never tasted, in order for it to so despise unified streams, compound waves, entwined colours flowing into the same space; interchanges and fluid interference.

I can accept that the primary and immediate tongue should have banished confusion from thought, but anyone who does not hate liquid concourse will be taken aback that the philosophy of knowledge should as a consequence of this have canonized this blind spot. To confuse means, first of all, to pour together, to conjoin several streams into one. Taken literally, confusion sounds rather like a solution.

The metallurgy of alloys, with us since the Bronze Age; the new science of chemistry, classifying mixtures and new bodies through recombination; pharmaceutical preparations, adding specifics to broaden the efficacy of remedies; kitchen-craft, whether of baked goods or liquors – since the dawn of time a thousand noble practices, whether hot or cold, have stirred different streams together in a hundred craters for practical purposes or merely for pleasure, often for knowledge. Why are they not recognized? These actions, alloys, mixtures, brews should all be called confusions, and the philosophy of confusion should be the common ground of sapience.

The first tongue, which speaks and has the ear of reason, calls the second confused, and the latter, confused, accepts the name. It receives concourses of liquid, a hundred simultaneous cascades. A single one, like the Yquem, is abundant, hiding many and composing on the second tongue the map of mixtures, drawn in confusion, fluctuating. A multiple, vibrant, complex map, more complete than clear, detached, simplistic ideas, about which the first tongue boasts so loudly.

I remember with gratitude she who gave me my third mouth, it says. It was the blessed day of my last communion and my first union. Fragrant flowers fell from her mouth: be silent, third tongue, your discretion is your wisdom.

THE FIVE SENSES

The mouth will not enter into discussion of tastes and odours, in fact they have a fixed scale. Strong or weak, superficial, profound, rich or poor, delicious, repulsive, immediately agreeable or enduringly constant. What we call bouquet, whether accurately or not, seems as objective and precise as a numerical sequence to the initiated.

The scale or order is a descending one, going from air to earth. The most fragile or obvious fragrances, at the top, belong to the flower family: rose, lilac, lime-blossom, jasmine; lower down carnation and violet; less delicate, but still fresh is the order of fruit scents: peach, pear, raspberry, almond, apricot, cherry. Pear and peach are more resistant to wines than red fruits, and less childish. Stonefruits are better than berries. How can you taste a pear, using the chattering tongue rather than the sapient tongue? Pears really melt in the latter's mouth – Passe-Crassane, Duchesse, Anjou and Comice or Messire Jean, in increasing order of excellence. With the exception of the adorably named Lady's Thigh, sweet and flavoursome. Similarly, how can you eat plums or apples? Yes to Belle-Fleurs and Greengages, Blue Damsons and Court Pendu Plat; but modesty prevents me from eating prunes except at home. The series progresses downwards from leaves and high branches, where flowers bud, where fruits hang, towards the ground, along bark, odours of resin and dead leaves, mushrooms, truffles. Black ones, from Quercy, not hypocritical white Italian ones. Glory to the heady scent of truffle, precious, subtle, delicate, subterranean. Self-evident, this progression is not open to debate, it runs from light to dark, from trivial to serious and dense, from puerile to trained expertise. The order or series keeps descending, towards the decomposing earth where animal and vegetable remains in the undergrowth mix with the humus. All these bouquets wedded to decay: the vegetable realm discovers sublime aromas when it merges with the inert.

This downwards exploration takes places in the countryside, near its periphery, at the end of spring, at the beginning of autumn or all year round at the markets, in our part of the world. We should also take a stroll through the realm of imports, cane-sugar, vanilla, tobacco, coffee, the blended haze of spices on the docks of Bordeaux or Le Havre, in the merchant's cellar, the bazaars of Istanbul, or elsewhere in the tropics. We could not survive without mingling with other worlds. We used to read in our textbooks that our intellect knows nothing that has not first passed through the senses. What we hear, through our tongue, is that there is nothing in sapience that has not first passed through mouth and taste, through sapidity. We travel: our intellect traverses the sciences the way bodies explore continents and oceans. One gets around, the other learns. The intellect is empty if the body has never knocked about, if the nose has never quivered along the spice route. Both must change and become flexible, forget their opinions and expand the spectrum of their tastes as far as the stars. How many past adventures and sometimes even heroic deeds have served to astonish our sense of smell, how much knowledge was acquired along the way?

Just as taste is crowned by sapience, so does sagacity complete the aromatic scale. The title of every banquet should be: sapience and sagacity. Around the table, only sage tongues.

The vegetable bouquet, aptly named, decomposing into the rot of the undergrowth, leads in to animal odours, heavier and more composite, less easily dispersed, denser and heavier. The scale descends further, from violas to cellos. Floral waste mixes with filth, straw litters are blackened from dung, under the bellies of cattle; don't look away city-dwellers, sagacity is entranced by the sweet odour of cows.

This is how we recognize individual bodies, in no way are we inferior to animals in this respect; it is only practice we lack, or shame that overcomes us. It is this initial reckoning that makes for a good nurse; a doctor's diagnosis begins there; a veterinarian should find a new profession if he is offended by sweat and musk. Sagacity goes beyond intuition, or informs it: certainly it recognizes mint and lilac, orange rind and sage leaf, but it comes to know men too, weakness, deficiency, illness or explosive force, their very singularity; recognizes the beasts within that transform our nearest and dearest into parrots, sharks, birds of prey or pigs; is trusting or wary, fleeing or approaching them. Scents of hatred and indigestion, of acrid sweat and resentment emanate from this chamber, this scrutiny. Floral emanations come from spring mouths, does this mean that they speak? Love begins with consent and is only content when two conspiring bouquets combine, the scent of mingled genitals so heady that we sometimes think we might pass out. The sage knows, in the scriptural sense; what is there in our mind or consciousness which does not first pass via this sense?

I am hesitant, says the third tongue: must we be convinced that the given comes to us through language for Denis Diderot, Sophie's perfect lover, to give voice to a jewel so precious that, in the mind of our philosopher, it is equal in excellence to the mouth and lips of a kiss?[3] Speaking lips experience less happiness, tenderness and sweetness. Why do they spend so much time expatiating on love instead of, and sometimes while, sweetly making love? The given is truly given to us through soft, voiceless lips, says the third tongue, still hesitating.

No-one is ever rendered speechless amidst the aromas of foliage and flowers; the distinct odours of flesh sometimes make us gasp, leaving us breathless in the duel of mingled bodies. Sweat, shroud. Here is the frontier or catastrophe, the border which opens up or closes off what we might call instinctive repugnance: deep, pungent, dense, black aromas, underground, in graves.

Compost and soil are mixtures of bodies and plants, flora and fauna, dead and alive, organic mixtures. We like vegetable detritus well enough, animal excrement repels us, but not always, it can be heady; when it comes to game, we can appreciate the smell of meat that is high. Yet we flee from the stench of death.

Just as the most sublime sound verges on noise, so is the headiest perfume but a step away from death and putrefaction; it arises from their domain; the soul leaves its deceased body in an odour of sanctity, we burn incense at funerals.

Led by volatile spirits, we are approaching the sacred; we are verging on the unclean and purification, where sagacity seems to awaken both knowledge and the sacred dimension. Do not enter here, you will profane this place, or sully yourself. The terrain thus defined can be called temple or propriety, or dirty, clean or taboo – in any event, it is demarcated, thus located and known. The terrain thus purified sees the birth, through cleansing or ritual, of pure reason in the midst of impurity. Together, Pasteurian hygiene, our more recent aseptic tastes and the theory of knowledge take us back to ancient rites of purification. Priests in the past and scholars today make us forget the insuperable boundary, or reinforce it. They make us feel disgusted by our own noses. I sense that we are heading simultaneously towards knowledge and the sacred, we are approaching repulsive places: filth, mixture, excrement, death – the supreme filth, supreme excrement. In death my dust will mingle with sticky, slimy substances in the moist compost. This is where the limit lies: smells of life, beforehand; funereal fragrances beyond this threshold. This is where definition is born.

Earth, rocks, gunflint, sulphur, hydrogen: terrifying, primary, molar, simple, primeval – I was going to say atomic – mineral odours. Here lies our horror of chemistry, the reason our ancestors burned alchemists and sorcerers at the stake, terrified by the common ground shared by knowledge and death.

There is nothing in our intellect that does not first cross this ground.

Emanations rise, the fragrant procession dissolves into light, airborn spirits; they are quickly dispersed. Conversely, the spirit descends into density, is converted into matter and, mingled with the heavy entrails of things, finally knows. It collects itself, and plunges from flowers to the dead. The Greeks of the decadent period sometimes used the word cathode to describe this fall or descent that overturns dispersal or emanations.

Emanations flow from the air to the ground or across the water. Over the tidal expanse, the ebb and flow churns over the beach sands; seaweed, kelp, jellyfish, half-open molluscs and dead, limp fish accompany the sagacious on the surface of the sea, where their sense of smell is lost, swamped. Saline spirits or volatile iodine: the wind carries everything back towards submerged fantoms. Orpheus' head, severed by the tornado, is still floating alone, still singing, his mouth full of brine, not smelling these last spirits swirling about on the water's surface.

Orphic itinerary, descent into the Underworld; the order of odours or subtle spirits, once emitted, is a fall towards the repugnant bottom, until we reach the odourless: whether shipwreck or funeral, the nose fills with water or earth.

Foliage, a scattering of flowers, berries or fruits, bark, humus and roots, markets, bazaars, beaches and ports, sewers, graveyards, mines, ditches, Underworlds: still life.

The evaporated spirits of beings laid low: substances.

Flames, fire, oven: no matter how far our travels take us, we must return home to the hearth, where the banquet is prepared. Outside, the raw; in the kitchen, the aromas of a sublime alchemy emanate from the grilled meat.

Socrates, Agathon and Alcibiades speak of love without ever making love, or sit down to eat without actually eating or drink without tasting; likewise they enter directly from the porch, over the threshold, into the dining area, without ever visiting the kitchens. Like the Gods, slaves and women stand near the stoves, where transformations occur, while the barbarians talk.

This transformation within the flames, this passage from raw to cooked, is connected to knowledge. The fermentation of bread or wine, for instance, or pretransubstantiation. The Last Supper did not consecrate grapes or wheat. It attended to the things that were eaten, tasted, made, transformed by heat. Wine belongs to the order of the cooked: the peacock's tail, in which each ocellus exalts an island that is simple by nature, raw in its elementary composition, comes together through cooking, is organized into a whole. The flavours, more numerous than before, converge into a new synthesis. Visit the Sauternes region, vines and woodlands, resin and flowers, river and breezes: it would take you twenty years to gather through sapience and sagacity what a single drop of Yquem gives you in a single moment. In the days when our bread still tasted of the countryside, it too would be like taking a long stroll in a single instant. There is a whole lifetime in a glass of Margaux, or even in a simple cob loaf. Cooking compacts, concentrates, reduces the given, makes it converge, the raw is made more abundant by cooking, the given goes from random chance, from flighty, improbable, inconstant circumstance to habit and compactness. Goes from diffuse, chaotic mixture to dense, ordered blend. Fire cements mixtures, transforms the above-mentioned confusion into stained glass, stirs in the small, secret elements just enough to combine things that would disgust us when cold. It assists convergence, favours collusion, binds closer, enriches alloys, discovers new combinations on the spot and, through synthesis, learns how to know.

When scholarship or knowledge is reduced to analysis, the guests at the banquet lie down in distaste on their cushions, in a different order and language, keeping their distance from the hearth where some crafty genius combines, composes, blends, creates a new order, a different scale of sapidity: a slave or woman with dirty hands, pouring incompatible liquids into a single crater, as though into a stomach. The analyst gags in disgust at these messy characters, in revulsion at the bubbling broth; he prefers to vomit. Thus emptying his stomach of the mixture and confusion to which he is addicted.

And yet, there is confusion behind every recipe: bubbling away in the pot, sizzling in the embers, simmering for hours. Take this, and measure, then take that, and blend.

Nothing surpasses the excellence of cooking when one knows how to cook well, as we do in France. For once, nature does things less well than we do. Our savoir-faire magnifies the given, which belongs to a suborder when raw. The aroma of roasted coffee early in the morning makes our muscles and skin quiver with delight; the smell of roasting meat, which verges on that of burning meat, delights our spirits – although rather less so than caramel, mere sugar until it meets fire. I have difficulty understanding that other culture, of boiled food, more Nordic or puritanical, hidden beneath the smell of cabbage. I have lived downwind of a fast food restaurant long enough to know how disgusting it is to be lacking in culture.

Once again, this literally supernatural excellence emanates from mixtures and confusions. Fire fuses many things together. The raw gives us tender simplicities, elementary freshness, the cooked invents coalescences. Conversely, analysis slices and dices raw; synthesis requires flame. As a result, the latter tends towards knowledge and culture; the former remains unrefined.

What if the philosophy of knowledge had not yet begun?

Clear, distinct knowledge is the result of analyses which divide and separate, systematically distasteful of confusion. Separation and division presuppose a space, on which or in which distinction pricks out a singular location: all simple topological operations. Confusion or multiple cascades, intertwining and interchanging in confluence, also presuppose a space, but also somewhat more attention. They represent, in fact, the direct operation of division, or separation; which is a kind of summation, or multiplication. If you know how to undo a knot or pull apart its fixed strands, you do not typically condemn the person who knots the loose strands together: the same person can perform both gestures. Yet the theory of knowledge, untying knots and refusing to tie them, tolerates only one side of the equation: the analytical. Cutting, undoing, subtracting, dividing, differentiating. Destroying. To analyse is to destroy. Such a theory resembles the traditional practice of certain tribes which consisted in binding the left arm to the body in order to ensure that one would only ever use the right, so dominant is one side over the other: sinister. Nor does it tolerate confusion. Yet confusion enables fluid multiplication, where the indistinct multiplicities in play are transformed into continuous varieties. The latter flow into one another and vary in concert, subject to multiple variables. Everything leads us to the conclusion that analysis has not yet accepted these varied, complex functions with which it has been dealing for two hundred years.

We return yet again to mixture and to the concept of variety, both immediate in the rich, complex, vibrant experience of the senses and, unparadoxically, more abstract than the simple, inverse operations of analysis; or perhaps we should say that they are posterior to what we call abstraction. Here, sensation appeals to a more difficult and complex kind of abstraction than our traditional understanding of it. We can say either: that in order to be understood, the senses require a new effort of abstraction to recompose what analysis separates, or that working towards a more composite kind of abstract leads to sensational or sensual results.

Confusion presupposes a space, or series of proximities, it accesses time, which is no doubt not as separate from spaces as we think. It marks, watches, keeps time. For a long time now I have thought of time as a node or interchange or confluent of several times, each of which can be understood spatially. This multiple clepsydra is incomprehensible to thinking that is limited to inverse operations alone. Oddly, it is made perfectly comprehensible by the immediate given.

How can it be that philosophy has taken several centuries to ask that we wait a moment while the sugar in a glass of water melts? How can it be that when faced with such evidence, time itself was not immediately associated with mixture and the fusion of one body into another? Yet two streams poured forth their compound as one. Bergson, following Duhem and in the footsteps of the Greeks, invented a clepsydra with several entry points: variable inflow, communicating vessels. This was the precise practice of confusion. And solution. The intimate fusion of one thing into another, of one flow into another: generalize this to as many kinds of flow as you like.

It has indeed taken the whole history of philosophy, which from its very beginnings had nonetheless intuited mixture and chaos, to rediscover in a glass or a vessel, in a simple, naïve, almost childlike way, what was already happening in the kitchen while the guests drank and spoke of love, and what vignerons have been doing in an insanely complex manner since the very beginnings of our traditions. Remember this: confusion begins with the flood, and the Ark of the Covenant. As though the water clocks were already beginning to fill: a colossal volume of water, a stock of animals, life, seed, the first blended wines. Alloys. The old patriarch Noah, the prototype of the œnophile, makes the multiple clepsydra flow in confusion. Remember this.

Clear, distinct knowledge presents or represents a space. Confused knowledge flows and returns along fluent times. Is present, certainly, but its past floods back, and it remembers.

Take this and drink. Do this in memory of me.

MEMORY

Let us return to the immediacy of the senses.

Can we establish a sensorial base line: a point of reference? We can dream, at the very least. Conventional wisdom tells us that water functions this way: an exceptional fluid in many ways and what is more, odourless, colourless, tasteless. Elusive and almost intangible, nearly translucent, still when nothing disturbs it, noiseless. One thinks of Plato's definition of intelligible space, made when geometry was young. Yet the evidence contradicts this: water has taste, colours and an aroma that tells us where it came from, twenty different ones we can distinguish with our eyes closed: still, running, city, mountain. The base line has shifted.

The air, an indistinct mixture, has a stronger claim to being our base line. Intangible, you could almost say intact; colourless and transparent, a conduit for light and colour; odourless and a vector for smell; tasteless; soundless when not driven by heat; it penetrates our bodies, ears, mouths, noses, throat and lungs, envelopes our skin: it is the medium for every signal that reaches our senses. This neutral state or base line is not determined through sensation, but remains a thing to be sensed, at the very limit of the insensible.

The air, an indistinct mixture, light, subtle, unstable, promotes combinations: as vector of everything, it blocks nothing. Medium of the sensorium, general excipient of mixtures: principal chamber of the confused clepsydra.

Let us dream that sight and hearing give us general information relatively swiftly, somewhat abstract or universal; and shapes: a melodic line, harmonies, morphology. It is doubtless because of these properties – intuition, harmony – that philosophies of knowledge prefer to use sight and hearing as points of reference. Taste is also prone to recurrence and stability; its habits are continuous with a culture. France is divided more categorically by a preference for butter or oil than by any departmental demarcation, and along the same boundary line as *langue d'oïl* and *langue d'oc*.[4]

Smell seems to be the sense of singularity. Forms reappear, invariant or recurrent, harmonies are transformed, stable across variations, specificity is countersigned by aroma. With our eyes closed, our ears stopped, feet and hands bound, lips sealed, we can still identify, years later and from a thousand other smells, the undergrowth of such and such a place in a particular season at sunset, just before a rain storm, or the room where feed corn was kept, or cooked prunes in September, or a woman.

We have lived with overpowering odours for a brief time only: diesel and kerosene intrude on our wounded sensibilities, stenches that stand out in a crowd. Mostly, till now, we moved through air which was changing and carrying ephemeral traces. Nothing resembles circumstance more than this vapour. It mingles with the atmosphere, depending on the time (hour, date and weather), the place (altitude, inside or outside), events, positions, conditions, causes and acts, its occurrence is improbable. The smallest point of a rare apex, a highly complex compound, a blend of a thousand proximities, unstable knot of capricious currents, an aroma comes about like an intersection, or confusion, we do not smell simple, pure odours.

Forms reappear, a harmonic line is reproduced, this is already a kind of knowledge, at least a frequent, recurring recognition: a strong stability can appear again before our eyes, ring like a refrain in our ears; memory presents itself as knowledge, rhythm presents itself as habit – and before long, as law. But this rare trace in the aerial fluid, this unstable, complex mixture, this partially undone knot, trailing a thousand threads, is not subject to repetition, never achieves invariance: too circumstantial to begin beating in time, too fluid, diluted, chaotic. On the contrary, knowledge eliminates such unstable circumstance, it planes down rarity. Its catch-cry: *In the same circumstances* . . .

Improbable, blended, specific, singular odours, their time and place uncertain. Now suppose that a rare blend should appear a second time in the random turbulence of the air, that this unique confusion should recur, improbably: the knot gathers in its threads, the apex pulls up its base, the tributary subsets burst forth as they intersect, a whole world rushes in: bodily position, enchantment, colour, circumstances crowd around, rarity reappears, richly ornamented and decorated; here, for want of frequency, memory is not transformed into knowledge, but we are dazzled, ecstatically, by our proximity to this overabundant memory.

The sense, therefore, of the confusion of encounters; the rare sense of singularities: our sense of smell slides from knowledge to memory and from space to time – no doubt from things to beings.

Loving a body, that rare special thing; no other volume on the surface of the planet has more value. Love confuses us; two chambers pouring together. Lingering near the surface of skins – veils, complex and subtle tissues – this or that indefinable scent, belonging exclusively to her or to him and signifying each one to the other, in conscent. We do not love unless our senses of smell find themselves in improbable accord, a miracle of recognition between the invisible traces which scud over our naked skins, as air and clouds float above the ground. Until death there remains within us this spirit, in the chemical and mystical sense of the written and spoken word; as far as the nose is concerned, the emanations of whomever we have loved remain. It returns to haunt our skin, at dawn on certain mornings. Love perfumes our lives, aromas resurrect encounters in all their splendour.

We used to embalm the dead, so that the memory would evoke those who had been loved by our forebears.

Life itself announces its presence from afar with these balmy emanations.

It is a wise and true language that calls the exhalation of a fragrance a *bouquet*. A bouquet is not just a mass of flowers, a simple multiplicity, but a bundle tied together, held by string or thread or the neck of a vase. Each flower adds it colour and shape, spreads and diffuses its perfume, but each one vies with the others; bouquet expresses their intersection. If you pull towards you the knot, ribbon or neck, the precise place where a confusion of multiple cascades is formed, all the stems and petals will come together, the whole state of things is revived in your memory. No single component can be identified separately from the resultant. A bouquet forms a fragment of memory because of the impossibility of analysing mingled bodies: either it has integrity, or does not. A singularity reappears around the intricate intersection. Recurs. Resuscitates.

Bouquet expresses a product, an intersection that defies analysis.

The rare and organic liaison, the singular specificity that bears the name love in my tongue, how can we know it, how can we create that knot, other than through just such an intersection, through a stable or unstable circumstance surrounding the local state of things – a star; other than – speaking quite categorically – through a bouquet? How can we recognize it, if not through an odour – sensory, sensual, radiating in every direction?

I love your odour and your spirit.

In my language, the emanations from your body used to be called spirits.

The sterile language of today would called them odours; our intellectual training would balk at that and substitute perfume. Our language leads us to understand that the relationship between aroma and perfume is analogous to that between giving and forgiving. Language goes beyond the given; the sublime. When in closest proximity to a beloved body, language replaces the given with a formula. Singularity vanishes for the sake of a brand name. For the sake of a signature. A chemical equation or elegant label. Individual secrecy is lost through advertising. When the given is given only through language, labels or algorithms, we find our bed in a shop window, or splashed across a television screen. Obscene. The given is for sale.

I love your individuated spirit. We do not separate two lovers; mystical and carnal, sacred or profane, pure, impure, ignoble, noble, spiritual or fragrant, because the spirit manifests itself near the skin; but both of them, bound together, private, oppose the obscenity of public language. The wandering soul hides in continuity with our postures. Amidst the liberties we take.

Âme: soul. The French word *âme* translates the Latin *anima* which, in turn, translates the Greek *anemos*, meaning wind. The wandering soul comes from where the wind comes from.

The wind. The movement of the light, subtle, vaporous, turbulent air, rhythmic, almost periodic, chaotic; mixture and carrier of mixtures, confused, the medium of every signal that reaches our senses, penetrating body, nose, mouth, ears, throat and lungs, surrounding the skin. Base line of the senses, carrier to all of them.

Having begun in the air, the circuit of odours returns there; rising through emanations, descending towards love, death and knowledge, rising again. Having begun in the wind, in the soul, the circuit returns to the soul, on the breath of the wind. Soul: base line of the senses, carrier to all of them. I love your light, subtle, vaporous, turbulent, chaotic soul, I love that it penetrates your skin, your ears, that it reigns over your skin. Tell me the difference between soul and wind.

Do you call what circulates through the world or inside our bodies information, or animal spirits?

Confusion associates, multiplies, pours, ties knots without undoing them, neither undoes nor separates, causes the convergence of the unanalysed: this is time.

The inverse operation of distinction is carried out in different spaces; the direct operation of mixture fluctuates across different times. The spatial gestures of separation give rise to knowledge, the spatio-temporal gestures of confusion give rise to memory.

I do not really know what this word *Yquem* signifies, says the mouth. I would merely note that in Maimonides, after the Seraphim, Powers or Cherubim, the tenth order of angels is known as the Ishim.[5] The Ophanim, swift; the Seraphim, brightness; the Malachim, messengers; the Cherubim, images; the Ishim, animate.

Animal spirits flying over the eponymous hillside, myriad archangels pouring forth from the unstoppered bottle.

A philosopher friend of mine, enough of a reader and talker to take people at their word and assure you that our senses can mislead us, one day came to be inducted into the serene brotherhood of the *Chevaliers du Tastevin* – a society of wine tasters who practise what they preach. Twenty years later, he told me how one of the group had for so long proven himself to be so infallible in the recognition of wines and their vintages that the others conspired affectionately to trick him. In the greatest secrecy, the conspirators bribed a Burgundian vigneron to plant a few rows separately; on higher or lower ground, but away from the dominant vines. This he did. The years passed. The young vines aged and surrendered their product. And on a day as beautiful as today, they served their pope this wine which so richly deserved the appellation *nouveau*. They beseeched the oracle to speak. Silence. He took his time swirling the ruby liquid around the bulbous sides of the glass, observing its legs; considered it, sniffed it and, his eyes closed, tasted it. Silence. 'Gentlemen', he declared, 'I'm terribly sorry, but this wine doesn't exist.'

Cheerful exclamations – albeit secretly flabbergasted ones. '*Maître*, if it didn't exist, it wouldn't be in your glass.' My philosopher friend started to expatiate on nothingness, the others hushed him, he had forgotten he was dining in good company. 'I'm telling you it doesn't exist, and that's all there is to it! This simply cannot be from Bordeaux, nor from the Rhone, nor Hungary. I can't even tell if it comes from the Côte d'Or.' 'Come now!' was the answer from the disconcerted chorus. 'If it did exist, he continued mockingly, struck by a sudden intuition, it could only come from . . .' and went on to describe precisely the spot where the vigneron had planted those rows. Our specialist in words and nothingness was taken aback, as were they all.

THE FIVE SENSES

A laser beam from the Earth makes a mark on the moon the size of a fingernail, and we admire its precision. A good wine taster should be able to recognize a South African, Chinese or Californian wine, not to mention one from Germany, Tuscany or Chios. Yet let him pinpoint twenty-five metres of vine on a map and a single week in autumn on the calendar of history, and he is accused of having unreliable senses. He can even notice a hole in the globe's tattered viticultural garment: 'Gentlemen, I'm terribly sorry, but this wine is from nowhere.' We have everything we need to define distinctiveness, clarity, precision – qualities which we praise in ideas alone; capabilities which language claims it alone can achieve. Perhaps blabbermouths are just after publicity?

How can it be that for the last two thousand years we have commemorated the Last Supper, but merely studied divine Plato's *Symposium*? We nonetheless read the latter as a tale already anchored by a long chain of memory.

It took place, we know whose house it was, we know who was at the banquet and where each guest was seated; sometimes there are permutations, altering the seating arrangement of the guests. We even have a parallel text, plus the rich history of these banquets, plus the backwash of commentary.

If instead the roof and colonnades had come crashing noisily down on all and sundry, if all that had been found afterwards had been the unidentifiable pulp of the bodies in the ruins, we could nonetheless have reconstituted the scene, the different positions, the remarks they exchanged, diameter and dialogue, all from memory, point for point and place by place. Everything was perfectly positioned for the art of memory.

So well do we remember it. Yet we have never set a table as the Romans did for their gods, never have we dressed at night to drink like Socrates' friends drank and speak of love as they did, till dawn, waiting for a young man to enter, crowned with violets and his head flowing with ribands, drunk and supported by flute-girls; and hoping most of all that a foreign woman speaking the truth might come. Never have we done this in memory of that evening; we have read what our forebears used to read, but never commemorated.

We have made and repeated the gesture of the Eucharist thousands of times. The Last Supper incites its own repetition through the millennia, like a star casting its light before itself; as though a particular action needed to be recorded in order not to be forgotten; as though something infinitely precious and infinitely fragile were asking us to carry it through history, passing it from one person to the next.

What do we remember? At the symposium banquet it is allegories that drink: comedy, tragedy, medicine . . . They speak allegorically. This never becomes clear until one has attended an invited banquet where each chair represents an institution, where each guest is there to represent politics, science, banking, the media or public administration – the powers of the moment. The dinner mimics that of the gods – the individuals present believing that the mere loss of their individuation makes them gods. The hostess could have invited robots who would have said what they were programmed to say, at the push of a button: what an administrator or journalist says can never surprise us, they are celebrating their power. For a long time I believed that the loss of individuation was due to the wine circulating around the room and becoming a collective subject by taking on the individuality of each person as it did the rounds; and that the wine became us, objectively conveying the sum of the I's entrusted to it by each subject, lost, in an ecstatic trance; but the loss occurs differently, for each person enters like a statue. Allegory, a block of marble carved into a representation, speaks. A mouth of stone neither eats nor drinks. The Commander threatens, thunders and kills, but cannot hold his own against a drinking Don Juan. A robot with a tongue of stone, iron or wood, it speaks, cannot know thirst. We know how to build machines that talk, we do not know how to build robots that can drink or taste. A tongue can become artificial, intelligence frequently does, but sapience never does. It is in this sense that an automaton differs from *homo sapiens*: it has the first tongue, but not the second.

The individual representing comedy, tragedy, medicine, the media or public administration – statue, robot, apotheosis of allegory, long-dead automaton – speaks at the banquet but does not drink. Speaks of love, does not make love; speaks of wine, does not taste it. A dinner of statues, a feast of stone.[6] Here dead words are passed about; we study them, comment on them. The allegories drink allegorical wine, allegorically; we speak about this categorically. A symposium of marbles and circuit boards.

To comment or commemorate? What should we remember? Wine? Ourselves? Not the positions around the table, the places, the honours, the dominant relationships – just the wine, and ourselves. The wine makes its way around the group. Each person, James, Andrew or John, simple coastal fishermen, lake dwellers, fresh water mariners, small-time tax collectors, representing nothing but themselves, individuals, paupers dreaming of a catch so miraculous that they would have to wade through piles of slimy fish overflowing the sides of the boat; each drinks in turn from the chalice and passes it to his neighbour, saying nothing. No-one knows if James spoke, or John or Andrew. Peter spoke. To betray. Peter the head, the first, the pope. Petrus, rock or stone. The only one who represents. Peter, for whom the last supper is a feast of stone. The others drink for the sake of drinking. And tasting. Drink and taste in silence. The others drink for the sake of love. James, Andrew, Simon then John. A feast of love, the crater passed around, the feast of John. You who speak and create the institution, you are known as Petrus. You who drink out of love, you are known as John. An impossible banquet, between the stone statue and Don Juan, drunk on love, drinking, still drinking, on and on.

What to remember – so fragile and forgettable that we must go through the gestures of commemoration together often in order to revive its memory? Observe – the wine is passed from hand to hand. Each person receives the vessel, drinks from it, passes it to his neighbour; the wine's passage makes him both a station and an engine of circulation. Circulation describes the group, following the thread of the relationship. The crater is a quasi-object, tracing the relationships between the apostles, carrying, weaving, objectivizing what unites the group, the twelve. The chalice comes to rest in front of Andrew, James or John, and continues on its way: the group relationship stops and starts. The group dies and lives again in each of them. Each apostle takes and gives. Takes wine, drinking or tasting. And gives. Gives his individuating principle, which the wine, nonetheless, snatches from him. Leaves – in the vessel and in the wine – the very identity that the wine takes from those who taste it. The circulating chalice takes on individuations, collects subjects as it passes, all the more easily for the fact that these fresh-water fishermen or stone breakers – men of no account, peasants, sailors, wanderers, Franciscans before their time – are not so attached to their own subject that they won't gladly leave it behind: they do not keep the crater to themselves for long, passing it along like a hot potato to him, to me, to you – who are you and who am I? What is your name? That's not so important any more, I no longer notice, you do not know, he has forgotten, the quasi-object, the crater of blended wine, becomes a quasi-subject, mixing the names and pronouns lost along the way and fused into an us, confused in the chalice, giving the table its form, composing the feast, suddenly presiding over the Last Supper, the sacred subject of their relationship; the subjects became relationship, the relationship becomes subject through the intermediary of the object, of this, the wine. Fragile subject, so precarious that it teeters near death, condemned to disappear, forgotten, if we fail to repeat the same gesture, quickly; ready to be resuscitated with each gesture of commemoration.

Every morning therefore, everywhere, we must once more begin the celebration of this unstable, never quite substantial collective, always in its death throes on Friday, in all its glory on Sunday. It must be supported, we must be sustained, it must be substantiated.

This subject which transcends their various names, their place and presence, is held in their hands for a moment and handed on to the next person, with no understanding of what they do; they bring it into existence, aware of little but its mystery; they all kill it and revive it, in an instant. This, this wine which takes away their individuation which they all surrender to it, this crater of blended liquids that charts their relationship and gives them unanimity, this is the blood which circulates through the body they form, here and now, at this Last Supper. The blood which courses through this unanimous body has a beat, and a cycle. Poured, it flows.

I am you, or him, indiscriminately, you are indiscriminately the other, or me, the subject is detached from me, you, him, everyone else, Peter, James or John, from now on we live as one soul in one body in which one blood flows, circulating wine and broken bread: Him.

The bread is shared out and the wine is poured.

Qui pro vobis et pro multis effundetur: wine or blood, spilled, shed, poured forth. What should we remember? This effusion.

This division: the bread is broken or analysed into as many individuals. We know this, learn this, unforgettably. No-one has ever forgotten an act of partition, separation, rupture. Nothing endures like analysis. We remain divided, separated, like morsels of bread, broken into individualities.

This effusion. Blood flows, like wine, water or vinegar. Like them, time flows. At the wedding feast at Cana, the first banquet, water is transformed into wine at the end. At Jacob's well, mortal water leads to the promise of a drink of immortality. At the feast of Bethany, the second-last Supper, precious perfume flows from the hand of Mary Magdalene to anoint Christ's body, and the house is filled with its exquisite fragrance. At the Last Supper, wine is transubstantiated into blood. On Friday, come midday, blood flows freely, then water, at the end. The dying man was also given a vinegar-soaked sponge on which to suck. History is accompanied and dated by flow, changing and mingling, rising in excellence or falling in disgrace, wine as delectable as ishim or starting to smell of nard, intolerable vinegar, sometimes turning back on themselves cyclically: water, wine, blood, vinegar and finally water; all these streams display their form or process, this is time – remember that time.

What should we remember? The subject that dies, and that we forget, and must resurrect from the dead at every moment. But also, and especially, that time – time: flowing currents of water, wine, blood flowing and blending. Memory is ensured by this multiple passage and because of this confusion.

Time itself carries memories. It flows like currents, those rivers which pass by, stop, return upstream, or divide time, or flow into one another. Time flows like these manifold currents, so different and confused, changed, transubstantiated.

Old, new, eternal union: with what body is my body confused, with what blood my blood, with what wine my wine?

In our culture, within us, we carry two feasts. At the banquet of allegories or representations, a lectisternium, the statues hold forth in their fossilized tongue. We comment on their speeches, as though the statues of this feast of stone, of Peter, who drink to stiffen themselves with anæsthesia, had returned to seek their revenge. Who killed them, lying there? Who killed Socrates?

At the Last Supper of Christianity, the feast of John, the guests known as apostles share a name which signifies their absence from the world: sent forth, gone elsewhere, dispatched, banished. They accept that they will die, like their Teacher; the Last Supper precedes death; Don Juan perishes too. Accepting the death of their subjectivity in the hope of resurrection.

The statues, dead, refuse their death and become ghosts. They demand another death. Thus, another statue. Which will return in due course. Eternal return, passing through death or the mechanism of negation.

The lake or river fishermen accept their death, hoping it will satisfy the appetite of the stone statues, hoping that their death will be the last: the last meal of the condemned, the last men in history condemned to die.

In our culture – where we seek to commemorate this supper, as though we did not quite remember it – the banquet and the Last Supper, the feast of Peter and the feast of John, are diametrically opposed; Peter, commander, leader, always rises from the grave to kill John, who submits out of love.

Peter, the stable rock, kills John, time.

Remember time.

I dream of writing about a third banquet at which the vengeful statue would agree to drink fine wine with the one who seduced his daughter.

We suffer from lovesickness because we have forgotten ever having made love. Our bodies, sense of smell and tongue have lost all memory of such dark, ancient confusion or confluence. We feel bound to commemorate frequently. Come, my gentle confused one, plunge into time with me, let us shed our memories in the river of forgetting, and drown our amnesia in the clepsydra of remembrance.

What do we stockpile, squirrel-like? Power, before using it: dry-cell and storage batteries; dams. Money: bank accounts, insurance, capital. Codes: libraries, computer memory, data banks. Food: cold rooms for meat or fruit, grain silos, cool, dark cellars. Sperm, oocytes, embryos.

Time does not always flow. We can find or excavate places where it has frozen. Sometimes an obstacle stops it: a dam, a Closed for Lunch sign, a bottleneck, a lack of light to read by or heat to break up the winter ice fields, a cork. Time percolates, sometimes filtering through and sometimes not. The structure of percolation helps us to understand memory: things back up and create obstructions in a blocked corridor. It should suffice to imagine closures and openings fluctuating and feeding into one another randomly, in space. Here the flow is fortunately unobstructed; there it accumulates, fortunately. Two happy situations: tomorrow time will flow because today, somewhere else, it does not; better still, without these conditions, there will be no tomorrow. No, time does not flow, it percolates; better still, it flows because it percolates.

These obstructions allow us to build banks, stockpiles, dams and cellars. They allow us to access power and not waste our time in continual action. They put power within our power. Our body percolates: its phenotype follows the river of flowing time until death, its mouth; but it carries with it the static genome, in pockets where the flow of time is suspended. The organism is free to break through the obstacle almost at will, sending forth a new existence which percolates at the mercy of the manifold tide: it creates a child. It closes up shop and the stockpile lies dormant: one memory for itself, encoded in its brain; another for the species, encoded in the gametes, two chambers or cellars where two kinds of time sleep, differently; reservoirs whose sluice gates open and close at different times, continually or rarely, and sometimes never at all.

Let us have a cool drink, the organism says. A guest at the banquet, it is annoyed by all the speeches. You can only drink from one bottle, the voice drones on; the wine that you guzzle has only one memory, one bank, one cellar account, held in check by the cold. Like our body, the table is a constellation of small accumulations, amphora and craters, bottles, glasses, plates; no-one eats or drinks entirely in real time. We need intermediary stockpiles. Small lakes of memory: goblets. No, time does not flow, quite. It is extremely rare to have a pure channel, a perfect corridor, with neither sidings nor bottlenecks. The meat that you eat – smoked, dried or preserved in a cellar, protected from flies and the heat – has also percolated. Without cold, the ice that obstructs time, we would not have the heat of the banquet.

Now have a cool drink.

The body resembles the table, and the banquet, love.

The organism is studded with small memory pockets, where time hardly flows or stops altogether, unconscious; intermediary stockpiles like glasses and bottles; and larger banks, where it can remain frozen forever.

Let us drink deeply of this splendid wine, let us forget about it, deep ruby-red in its carafes; or cellar it for the pleasure of some descendant or other. The lineage of the visible sons of the hidden cellar is made up of our banquets, yours and theirs; the warm-hearted children of cold rooms. The lineage of the visible daughters of hidden leavening is made up of our loaves of bread, yours and theirs; the delicious children of inedible mass.

At the beginning of this series of phenomena lined up in a row, a stable, black memory lies in wait in the cold.

We carry within us a dormant genome, in a low pocket, suspended in the cool between our legs, outside of the overheated body which would awaken it, outside of time, which would damage it, the memory of the species; or a stock of undeveloped genomes, which come to maturity regularly, one at a time. Banks of potential beings, virtual, unreal, or forever asleep, or passing by chance, coincidence, intersection or confluence through the small, uncertain window by which we reach the great theatre of action. Created by love, lovers ourselves, children of potential and passage, of virtuality and insinuation, of non-existent capabilities and sufficient cleverness to slip through the narrow strait. The products of love are the visible lineage of hidden genomes, hot lineage derived from cold memory; love is the offspring of forgotten memory, rich and poor, virtually rich but miserable in fact and by choice; love recognizes the memory it has lost. Today we put the genome into straws at the lower than glacial temperature of liquid nitrogen; we keep it cold, outside of real time – but it has been kept cool for millions of years, like good wine in a cellar or delicacies in a cool room, just waiting to emerge into presence. To dive back into the current of time.

No banquet without cellars and larders: without memory and ice. No guest without love; no love without cold and memory.

No text without a library, no philosopher without an encyclopædia, no singular word without the bank of language where words sleep in the cool darkness. Closed books, no light. The writer is situated in the long lineage of visible children of hidden language, the offspring of the virtual and the clever passage through the window: what misery to have neither the language nor the finesse to find it again. Child of darkness or quantity, and choice or rarity.

All are children of multiplicity and singularity. Multiplicity alone guarantees secrecy, burying memory in darkness, creating oblivion or glaciation. You will never know precisely which banknote you deposited into your account. It is singularity that emerges, rare, unique, recognized, remembered.

Bring a rare bottle up from the cellar, a bottle of the best picked out from the countless rows of dusty bottoms; write the only fitting word out of the thousands of possible turns of phrase that grammar books and dictionaries put at our disposal; I will recognize you with my eyes closed – out of ten thousand: feast, masterpiece, love, children of the multiple and the one.

Children of man and woman. Of the male, manifold seed in small dimensions, incalculable male herd; of the female, large, round, monadic, voluminous, rare, unique. A memory arising from multiple oblivions.

The speaking, feeling and loving tongues seated at the banquet approach the vessel in which the liquid rests, where confusion sleeps, where time accrues and from which memory comes.

Emprisoned within for an age, an intelligent genie escapes. No-one can capture him or put him back inside, he goes forth, explodes and is transformed into a thousand apparitions and evasions. This has become that, and also something else – how can we even name him? He will not return.

Hope lies at the bottom of this vessel. Will it flood the world, overwhelmed by evils; or will it be lost?

The box bears the lovely name of Pandora: all-gifted. The given in its entirety gushes forth from the horn of plenty.

The only Pandora's box we have ever known is the world: it alone, box without sides, contained the given in its entirety.

THE FIVE SENSES

A bottle of Sauternes mimics the world, concentrates the given, delivers it suddenly: coloured, luminous, radiant, tactile, velvety, profound and caressing, suave, orchestral, a composition of brass and woodwind, spiritual. Body and world: agrarian, *floréal, prairial, vendémiaire*, wooded.[7] Time: minutes and months, decades. Spaces: countryside and peacock's tail. Gifts or the given invade the sensorium, leaving tongues behind, travel down arteries and muscles, nerves and bones all the way to the fingernails.

The bottle contains the entirety of the sensible, all at once; contains bottomless common sense. Left on the table for a week, open and empty, the course of the emanations never runs dry.

A sensorial bomb, crowned by a cloudlike plume above the neck of the bottle.

Invaded by this cloud, our body learns or achieves transubstantiation into spirit. The entirety of the given, vibrant and multiple, kaleidoscopic, comes together like a spindle, a knotted bundle, asks that it be allowed to pass, at the bottom of a chimney, neck of a bottle or nasal fossae, straw, filter, threshold, rectifier – what name should we give to this rising corridor? – tripping over itself or organizing itself as it passes, wanting to ascend, moving through; and there, is transubstantiated into spirit. Sense becomes scent, a light vapour, matter becomes animated. Soul or information.

But the work had already been begun by time: time, in the bottle since 1947; time, that year, above and below the vines; time, beforehand, in the vine stock and in the earth. Soil, climate, gravel, the darkness of neighbouring pines, the sweat of the vignerons, the heavy alcohol and the hot summers, the rains, the rot, everything hard about the world being transformed into softness, patiently. The wine says a thousand things, moving from sense to information: spiritual.

It fragments into spirits: bouquet, carillon, pavane, rainbow; multiple and subtle but nonetheless unitary intelligence – spirit. The abundant spray of the multiple, and sensual complexity, is knotted, refined, blended, summed up; flows together and passes through the narrow chimney I think I can sense in my head – why would we need to imagine that the senses require an intellect in order to be united?

Through our hands, matter can touch itself; it can echo in our ears or cause our skin to shiver; it astonishes our eyesight, fills our mouth: matter which is solid, liquid, fluid, acoustic or luminous, rough, porous or silky, bound to the inert, the *en-soi*, the objective; to substance, dark and stable tranquillity, below; rising, lightened, spirit, into scent, zephyr of the soul.

This is wine – how can we call this wine? – this is spirit, this is my blood.

My blood invaded completely, from head to toe. Wine circulates within us. And between us, bodies in communion. Here we are, united; reunited; we are one body, from now on, unanimous. The same soul circulates between us, the new blood of a collective body. Each drinks from the same chalice, each drinks till the principle of individuation ruptures, each disappears, only the passage remains. Circulation within a single organism. This is my blood.

The old ambrosia of the old gods passes into the heart of the community, immortal now, unlike mortal individuals. The blood of the new and eternal alliance.

They drink wine, pour blood, lose their singularity by pouring it into the community – alloys, mixtures, old and new alliances, confusion, still and forever more; the appearance of a new time and new promises, memories.

Do this in memory of me.

A path abandoned for the last two thousand years, a crossroads covered over by centuries of neglect – are rediscovered. Observe.

The attention given to the senses, respectfully, in their own right and not as embryonic, inchoative knowledge differentials, is best expressed through myth: Hermes, Pandora; or fairy tales: Cinderella, the unicorn; or the arts: Orpheus, the muses; or religion. And suddenly we are sitting down in the company of old friends, around the oldest table in the world, where Ulysses once sang for King Alcinous, where Jupiter made the pitcher flow endlessly, where Socrates debated till morning with Agathon, where death refused Don Juan's invitation to drink, suddenly we are sitting down to eat in Lazarus' home, where Mary Magdalene washed Christ with precious nard, thus giving him his name, we even commemorate the Last Supper, where wine was changed into blood, and constantly replicate the last meal at Emmaus, the host having long since left us, although he remains present for having given us, after his departure, the gift of tongues, by which I mean language.

The logos cannot express the attention we pay to the senses: its formulations precise or confused, always inadequate and risible; its formulations in chemistry, physiology or anthropology abstract, always theoretical – does anyone know of an æsthesiology? It forks away from the logos, and veers towards myth.

THE FIVE SENSES

There is nothing in the senses which does not lead to culture.
Not towards knowledge, but culture.
Not towards discourse, but towards what?

Here we are at the dawn of time. Sensibility dates from Antiquity, defines Antiquity. Whoever has the gift of the senses speaks ancient languages, sings dead myths in forgotten cadences and dialects. Around the old table, in front of the old wine, brought up from dark tunnels or foundations, bought from an old merchant, teller of old tales, the three tongues, white with age, the oldest enemies in the world, plunge together into the most fabulous Antiquity; attempt, passing from one to another, to plunge from word to body, from spiritual scents to the grey, stable, tranquil substance of things, and climb back up, though memory, from one feast to another, to the beginning: not, in search of sense, to the beginning of knowledge, but to the birth of our culture. They do not comment, but commemorate. Recreate the gestures, refill the glasses, but do not repeat the words. And immediately discover our most distant predecessors who already realized that an immense, inaugural act took place in the feast of wine, its preparation and storage, the attentive and fervent consumption of it. As though each banquet, integrating previous ones, easily attained the first.

Attained this act, this transubstantiation of material energy into signifying scents, into spirit; this, concentrating or summing up the gifts of the world, or all it has given, invades each person's body and circulates throughout the collective body, like blood that burns, flows and pulses. This is where the life of language is resolved, its relationship to this concentrated, totalized given, exploding inside each person's body. This is where the redemption of the body through the word is consummated, the whole body condensed there: material, inert, sensitive, living, individual, social, collective. This is where the word captured it with a word. Redeemed the world and history at the cost of its body, for the price of a word. Someone with the gift to do so could speak this inaugural act fully and rigorously, but he who did so made a solemn and unparalled pronouncement: this is my body, this is my blood. Those with the gift of the gab fall silent here: this – everything that can be designated, shown, that can make sense or be perceived by senses – is the body or blood of the word itself.

From this moment on, the given will only ever give itself in and through language.

We commemorate. As soon as we say this, the word is born, it has captured or redeemed everything. We leave behind the ancient shore and move on to the Good News – Noël! – but immediately we forget this event

184

without parallel, we forget that we are speaking, the word dies having just redeemed things and men. In that moment we move from ancient religions to our religion, from creeds of the senses to that of the word, from the body to speech, from philosophies of experience to those of language, this story is a day old, or ten years old or nearly two thousand years old, or as old as the forgotten moment when the world buried itself under language through the word of him who became man by saying it. This is the very first story: *this*. This is the body and blood of the word itself. Could *this* be a mere word?

The substantial force of the coppery yellow, pink-flecked liquid is transformed into spirit; the hard, material force of fluidic sound is transformed into this soft word, ready to die: this.

This story swims between two shores, speaks between two religions, trembles between two languages, comes to a halt between two temporalities, leaves behind two philosophies.

Could this be reducible to a word? Could these rich aromas and this complex taste, changed into soft signals, be contained by a series of propositions? And is this commemoration limited to a written contract?

Let us cross the sea, since we boast about our ability to swim, and seat ourselves at other, less outmoded banquets. The mustard is insipid, tasteless; the beer, almost non-alcoholic, is flavourless; spices are bland, coffee weak and barely roasted, fruits and vegetables monotonous to the point of sameness. We can only differentiate between foods by the name and price on the label. Wine has been transformed into milk – white. Nothing to upset our stomachs or offend us. America eats mush.

And sips the insipid – a dull palate. Frozen too, to numb the taste-buds. Thus gorges itself, because the only impediment to quantity, other than poverty, is quality. Always more. So gluttonous bodies are surrounded by an aura of flab, *homo insipiens* has an imprecise outline, swells to monstrous proportions, loses its shape, not so much fat as enveloped by pregnancy, once more an embryo. America leads the way.

The body, as we know, is becoming more and more undifferentiated. Like food, it is tending towards dedifferentiation: infantile, mammalian, it is returning to its sweet, milky origins. Roly-poly behemoths tumble out of their cars, stunted babies blown up to scale. America is looking much younger these days.

Obviously, your bread needs to be soft if you've lost your teeth or have only false ones – all the more beautiful for your publicity shot; obviously, delicate stomachs need bland drinks; and weak palates, mild spices.

THE FIVE SENSES

Progress is happening elsewhere, creating a common denominator for many cultures. Thus, anyone can sit down at the banquet, whether Eskimo, Mexican, Japanese or Slav. The cultural vanguard is reviving the archaic. Now at last everyone can evolve remembering bottle, breast, thumb, or better still, reminiscing about their foetal suspension in amniotic fluid. The common denominator, monotonous unity, shaves off sharp edges, eliminates spices, softens and dilutes, cancels out aromas and tastes. America leads a peaceful existence.

In the future, war will not break out between cultures with hard differences, but will pit against each other those, on the one hand, whose nutritional or cultural ethnology – surviving amidst ruins whose stark beauty will provide travel agencies the occasional stopover – can still be described; and on the other, those who will vegetate in the absence of sapience and sagacity, anæsthetized, drugged, frigid.

Odourless frozen food for the spongy and obese, hidden under cellophane so that no-one can touch or taste it – watch out for germs! – can only be read and heard, on helpful labels, gigantic posters and thunderous advertisements. Glass walls, supposedly transparent, are covered, blinded by advertising. One has killed the other. Writing has killed architecture. Henceforth you will live in the realm of reading. Language has killed the senses. A deluge, explosion, a tsunami of words and numbers; of messages shouted, sung and carried along in the turbulent flux of what we are surprised to hear others refer to as music. City and countryside are being swallowed up by language.

The given – forgive me – what is marketable, is only given – forgive me – is only sold in and through language.

Reason, which society gives us, has prevailed.

Triumphant, the word redeems anything that could lend taste or aroma and transubstantiates it into something seen and read and heard, the channels that are peculiar to it.

This – what you eat and drink – is the body and blood of the word.

Here – where you buy it – lies the grave of bread and wine, body and blood, dead and resuscitated as messages.

The word prohibits the senses, and most especially those that do not concern it. Triumphant, it imposes prohibition: the social organization of anorexia and disgust.

The speaking tongue kills the tasting tongue. It kills it with the collective, in the language spoken between us. This, which is spoken, is reduced to a price. You will eat words, but more often these days you will eat codes and numbers. So you will gorge copiously, and still more, always more. Nothing goes down quite so easily as code, nothing grows as well as numbers. You will gobble up quantities of them. Your body will overrun the space around it, just like the word itself, carried on the wind, just like a society founded on the word.

The theory which reduces the given to language is produced within a collective which practises and lives that very reduction, always returning to it like ideology and inflating it; through this expansion, the language and currency of the collective are imposed on the whole universe.

Resounding victory of the soft and the flabby.

The Roman Empire ruled in this fashion for over a thousand years. Overweight, flabby, unwieldy, unfocused. Nothing further from the truth than Cato's austere, heroic, hard model of ancient virtue: as false as an ideal. Every empire displays this idea of violence and harshness: through Western movies with their machismo, or urban guerilla warfare. Whereas in fact they succeed through softness.

We ought to define them as collectives whose association has nil or zero reason for being. A military group attacks or defends itself, that is its reason for being; churches or sects pray, withdraw from the world, condemn heretics, worship their reason for being; an association of common economic interests either makes a profit or goes bankrupt, the company's efforts are directed towards its reason for being. Let us suppose that the latter, transcendent, intense or mediocre, tends towards zero, is cancelled out – as we said of taste and smell – like reality itself. If so, a soft society, come together for null reason, unites itself in and through language, through a written or spoken contract stipulating its unity: redundance.

This is how administration was invented. It oversees this flabbiness or nullity, indicative of the same progress towards sameness, or leading to the same swelling. Everyone lives together for no other reason than the fact that they say so, and write it incessantly; inflationary paperwork. 'Administration' defines the corresponding institution by the performative nature of those words. It is an epithet that neatly describes the vigorous tendency to minimize, the active and gradual cancelling out of a genuine reason for being.

The Roman Empire owed its singular longevity to the reduction of all such reasons, the genial discovery of administration, the application of null reason. To the suppression of all objects in favour of language.

THE FIVE SENSES

It is in the interest of any empire, with the slightest ambition to endure, to retreat, to hide behind its administration, to leave behind reality for language.

To suppress all objects in favour of words. To suppress the word itself and its meaning in favour of codes and numbers.

To eliminate culture with currency.

At zero on the scale of reason and sense, with the nullification of taste and scent, in the absence of any point of reference, anybody, however simple-minded, adapts and is gratified.

Old cultures are familiar with two, or even three, communions. The first in held in the form of the word, a First Supper, giving us our golden mouth. We receive the second more belatedly, in the form of two quite real presences, fresh leavened bread and great wine bottled in a specific place. This communion opens our new mouth. The last, miraculous communion forgives the loving mouth; without it we would sound as hollow as crashing cymbals even if we spoke all human languages and knew all that science can know.

Hollow tongues take up all the seats at the banquet or Last Supper, destroying the other tongues; the world is like crashing cymbals, deafening everything with languages and learning. A new world with one communion alone, with just one contract, devoid of reason.

We have long waged war to determine whether all feasts are but a single feast, whether all communions are but a single one, whether substance is just a noun. Or whether bread and wine can be distinguished from the word. Do we really have just one tongue, or two, or three?

They who claim that the given comes to us through one tongue only have the clearly identifiable profile of the venerable, old, reformed theology.

Which prevailed on the other shore, and returns triumphant.

STATUE

Entering the room heavily, a statue interrupts the feast, as is customary.

Its marble exterior denies it the use of any of its senses. The philosopher who built it and leads it inside has reserved the right to open up the senses, as he sees fit, to the different impressions they are capable of receiving.

Organized like us on the inside, animated by a spirit devoid of any kind of ideas, heavy with the scent of rose, crowned with carnation, jasmine, violet and bandaged, it enters amidst guests whose spirit has come from the floral or earthy bouquets making up the peacock's tail surrounding the glass of Yquem. The statue takes it seat amidst the mouths and tongues.

Beneath the cold, smooth, untouched skin, veined like marble, the body resides inside a black box. Its master, Condillac, activates the entrances: he opens or closes a well-defined window through which a single, well-filtered, specific piece of information penetrates. He experiments on his automaton, analytically and systematically. He begins in the domain of scent, with rose, then carnation, jasmine and violet.

Which rose did he use, and which violet? Parma violets, tricoloured and hooded? Sweet violets, dog violets, common blue violets, Russian violets? As though nobody in the living world had ever picked a rose and smelled its heady fragrance. Which colour variety, from which latitude and nurtured by which gardener; we should specify the season and the exact week during the course of its flowering. One May afternoon, the weather still not really mild . . . one glorious September morning . . . having gone to the Parc de la Bagatelle to better appreciate the emotional state of Condillac's statue, I found myself laughing out loud and crying like a baby when confronted with the spatial explosion of the different hues and the speckled palette of different varieties. Did the statue find itself submerged in the delicate fragrance of Great Maiden's Blush, the most beautiful of all speckled roses, Petite Lisette, Queen of Hearts, Princesse de Venosa, the Carmosine or Jacqueminot? Not to mention the much-neglected dog-rose and other varieties. Bathed in this new peacock's tail to the point of drunkenness, could or would even the most expert sense of smell want to fall back on analysis? And would gardeners or expert perfumers from Grasse not laugh till they cried at the excessive sophistication of the experiment, where the automaton is concerned, and at its crude and profane ineptitude when dealing with flowers? The machine frightens the guests – it is imposing. One day we will construct, and respect, a computer capable of distinguishing a Sauternes from Coca Cola. We will have forgotten that the latter has a fixed formula, reducible to a finite sequence of words or codes, and that the former, unstable and individuated, is as variable as watered silk. We will have forgotten the empiricism of the gardener, the overwhelming profusion of roses and the confusion of their fragrance.

And, said the old gardener, whom the terrifying statue wanted to silence, I've never seen a violet violet, I've never been able to decide whether they were violet, mauve or any of the fifteen kinds of blue that my eyes, now weak, could once arrange into a spectrum. When my sight began to fade I slowly learned how different hues bled into one another. The peacock's tail of fragrance deploys a similar spectrum or fan. How long will the statue have to spend exploring the scent of roses across the length and breadth of such a differentiated terrain? The whole life experience of a gardener; several generations of those unwitting geneticists who cross varieties, always creating new ones. 'Make your garden grow' – that ancient adage, advice handed down across generations – in fact means: 'You will live like a god'. A god who continuously crosses and creates species in an evolutionary paradise. The scent of roses never stops changing; the statue is too clumsy and heavy to keep up. The experiment stops at the first line, in the first garden, for all eternity. Indeed, at the banquet of the gods themselves.

If it is to continue, then it is better that we put an end to this endless banquet. Come on, don't linger at the dining table, you pick up bad habits there.

Upon entering, the statue is filled with negations, long before any floral scents penetrate it; has no idea of either figure or extension, nor of anything else external to it. Therefore it sculpts an indentation of understanding through figure, extension and movement, patiently waiting to fill out as understanding; it has had no other desire. This form must be filled in.

We shouldn't laugh – there are serious matters at stake here.

In my language, an organism like ours, immobile beneath a slab of marble, is called a corpse. An immaculate stone envelope covering a body, and with a statue above it, is called a tomb. An automaton, a machine equipped with an internal phantom reawakening into consciousness, is usually called a cenotaph: a black box with holes and doorways through which information can enter and exit. White marble statue or black box in the colours of mourning. Displaying a shield or coat of arms. It's hardly surprising if the experimenter who creates a window in the funeral casket should think of smell first, and toss a spray or wreath of flowers on to the stone grave or vault.

The real name of the statue that arrives at the banquet – ghost, automaton, machine, hollow outline of reason bereft of sensation – is death. In the Underworld, the pale shades also needed blood to sustain themselves briefly, to fill out their vague forms.

Why should we have to die in order to start knowing or even feeling? By opening up these windows, the philosopher is in fact dissecting a corpse. He has killed the living, in order to turn it into a tool; to attempt to resuscitate it – as if newborns looked anything at all like ghosts.

The mouths at the banquet have scarcely begun living, the statue has come to put an end to that.

The philosopher claims that the statue fills up with the scent of roses; it used to be said that the former, with his last gasp, died in an odour of sanctity. The philosopher even begins by asking us to do as the statue does, to start existing at the same time as it does. Become a child again, but in an orderly fashion.

Life is no stranger to such beginnings, vibrant moments of rebirth. Such as when the golden tongue, forgetting for a moment its lofty words, discovers its exquisite neighbour, and the latter a love-struck sister. Nothing will ever pass through the mouth-window as it did before. The tongue regrows, triadelphic and trilobate, three people in one – what an adventure! Drawn along by an energetic life force[8] and by the enthusiasm that overtakes us at the threshold of a potential new life, who among us would shy away from palingenesy?

Yet we have not been able to do as the statue did; not through any fault of our own, but because we could not find a rose. The programmer failed to specify the scent, the variety, the precise moment during its season. All he specified was a concept. We could not know how to inhale or smell the idea of the scent of the concept of rose. The automaton fills up on words. The name of the rose has no fragrance.

Yes, here the rose is reduced to its name, and the statue to a dictionary or computer. What enters through the window, a unit of sensation, equals a unit of sense or digital information. The automaton learns to sense one word at a time, like a pupil copying from a blackboard. Hardly surprising if knowledge ensues. One word at a time, language finally comes, damn it!

If the given only gives itself through language, tell me what your anthologies smell like?

In the year 1813, at number 12, impasse des Feuillantines, in Paris, there occurred something unparalleled, which gave its chronicler the opportunity to pair rose with the obvious rhyme of morose, and to align that adjective, associated with *stupid* and *unattractive*, with a series of nouns such as dormitory, study, courtyard, classroom, pillar, schoolmaster, workbooks.[9] In a garden filled with humming and confused voices, where the shimmering surface of a pond mingled with the imprecise reflections of a silver birch, in a garden full of roses, a child ran and dreamed, beginning to exist. The principal of some school or other arrives unexpectedly: Janotus, Marphurius, Blazius, Honorius, Mouillebec. He interrupts the feast.

THE FIVE SENSES

Garden or boarding school? A fork in the road of child-rearing: the leafy, thorny shrubbery, echoing with the sounds of bullfinches or wasps, threaded with mingled odours, or the four-square courtyard, asphalted and geometric, where little kids face each other off in the atrocious first struggle for dominance? Banquet or statue? Janotus or fine wine? Copse or dictionary? Rose, or the name of the rose? *Rosa, rosam, rosae . . .* the statue-children decline the noun without perfume or hue. Language or sounds, breezes, scents, shadows and songs, shapes, ecstasy? Such an improbable event: how his mother, forced to choose between the stupid and cruel schoolyard of wild animals, and the grove behind the impasse des Feuillantines, suddenly discovered within herself a genius to equal that of her son, Victor Hugo.

For this garden of mingling confusions, the unstable corolla of his senses – note that the child becomes a rose five times over – gave him, in the short term, a sea of words: the language of France, almost in its entirety.

If you wish to train an army of statues socially dedicated to the struggle for dominance, give them a poor, dry lexicon, as hard as wood and as cold as iron, studded with technical jargon like an endless refrain, form their senses through these words, give them access to the given through this language: a concrete courtyard, a monotonous dormitory and a grey education, foul-smelling and well-disciplined, through the prism of their grammar books. As they begin their existence, children will shield their eyes when they raise them towards the patch of sky visible at the top of the well shaft which is their school-prison; we did not need Plato's cave to teach us how painful sunlight can be during our foolish, studious childhood.

If you form their words through the senses, amidst the hawthorn and primrose, if rose, in all its declensions, can be related to the exploding, fragrant bouquet of shapes and hues, if you build their language through the given, then anything can happen. Even a poet. Even a happy adult; even a wise one. Even a philosopher mathematician, free to laugh at the mechanical, fossilized rigidity of intellect; and careful to maintain a distance between the senses and language, for the sake of the safety and vitality of both of them.

Did you find this garden? The architect has concreted over it. Did you discover the thicket, back there? The agronomist has bulldozed it. Any viable spaces now resemble the schoolroom. Outside, Janotus is winning.

There is no point playing truant any more, theory is everywhere. Language has eliminated the given and substituted itself in the latter's place: Marphurius' courtyard. Grammar and logic create a world in their own image. The schoolmaster of this space presides over language and space.

Arriving at the ancient banquet, the statue breaks the glasses and over-turns the platters, kills the living bodies drinking living drink, reproduces itself as marble statues or automata, begins a feast of language with for-mulated drinks, perfectly adapted to the world that these formulae have already rationalized. You know, at symposia we talk about concrete things.

Soon the only places where we will be able to find thickets, will be schools. We will cultivate them for unruly children.

This meditation on chaos and mingling, this attention paid to the sensible, does tend to resemble a philosophy of unruliness. The crowning achieve-ment of a long career as a restless kid, the inauguration of wisdom.

In my language, they who cannot see are called blind; deaf, they who cannot hear; mute, who cannot speak; sometimes we might even use insensitive to describe the loss of sensitivity. But there is no word to express the loss of taste. My language can indicate lack, in the case of blindness, defect in the case of deafness; it admits to these, either because such dis-abilities only affect a small percentage of the population, or because they put its own acts of language at risk or on alert – who knows? The vast majority of us lack a sapient tongue and gets by perfectly well; and our tongue hides the fact, concealing its own defect. It lacks a word to describe what it does not lack. Therefore what it says, without actually saying it, is that speech is all we really need, and anæsthesia will suffice us for the rest. The statue becomes a dictionary, and you would swear that the dictionary, like the statue, has a tongue of marble. It drugs our sense of taste.

Technical discourse alone speaks of anosmia, and even more rarely of ageusia.

Arriving at the banquet, the statue interrupts it, neither sitting down nor drinking, neither smelling nor tasting; it consumes the menu: a mobile dictionary capable of memorizing the list of dishes, recipes and wines, but unable to commemorate a meal. Tomorrow it will talk about vintages, restaurant guides and chefs, effortlessly and competently – you'd swear it had years of experience. It can talk better than anyone about things it has never felt, but it betrays itself through vocabulary. The word uttered by the statue, local, says only rose: odourless because it only exists in logic; the language of the dictionary, global, has no word for the lack of smell or taste. By crosschecking like this, we can recognize a robot.

But a phantom enters behind the automaton, a ghost of sorts. What could be returning to haunt us like a reproach, beneath language, if not empiricism?

We get along quite well without it, what is it doing here? Even so-called philosophers of sensation or perception get along without it in their algebra, logic or phenomenology, all of them literally odourless, colourless, bereft of sensation and flavour, even of words and expressions to describe tastes, aromas or hues; like robots, all they need is language, heard, seen or read, or reduced to code, but doubtless also encoded in our genes or social customs now, as it is in the memory of the statue, automaton or computer; language is all that is required to ensure the genesis or advent of our knowledge. Why would we need things? It is enough to be able to name them.

Yet stubborn empiricism resurfaces, doubtful that the menu tastes as good as the meal itself, that the analysis on a label quenches your thirst as well as the contents of the bottle; only ever devouring lists and books *between* meals. It does not confuse love and loving words. Born of war and deprivation, it is hungry; it is always thirsty, a child of poverty. We can never get enough of the things we had to do without, in the prime of our youth. Nor can it get along without things: it comes from the country, and remains flabbergasted by the flashing signs of the city. Empiricism resurfaces from deep within us: from the sum of all childhoods, from the deep well-spring of deprivations that sentences can never fill. A child of ancient necessity, about which we hear nothing these days, but that I, like many others, experienced in childhood. Empiricism resurfaces from the ruins of Antiquity, not to demonstrate but, beggarly phantom, to make demands.

If necessary, we can do without immediate sensory experience, it says; marble-like grammar or logic work well and demonstrate clearly without it and have long since replaced it in classrooms and in the world around us, which science has peopled with automata. We are beginning to resemble the statues we build. Once, adults would make fun of going to school, having learned from hands, shoulders and skin that the real weighs more heavily than lessons; today the whole classroom can laugh at such people, who no longer understand the codes taught in schoolrooms and which impinge on everything. The polarity of the educational axis has been reversed, it is now the child who must teach the old man about formulae and keyboards. So we can make do without empiricism, our knowledge will not suffer in the least: we will adapt to the new world rather better, but will we be able to live without wisdom? Of course, knowledge comes from language; but what if philosophy came to us through the senses?

We will no longer do without higher knowledge: the philosopher who lives for its sake cannot think without the conceptual work it does. But the further he presses on into this knowledge, the more apparent it becomes that we cannot deprive ourselves of beauty without paying a high price for that knowledge. A new wisdom comes from this. Youth learns, forges ahead with knowledge; the adult loves and practises intelligence – inventive, vibrant and free – creating abundantly; after this comes a time when the need for beauty reigns: a knowing subject while still green about the gills, fertile in adulthood, in search of culture when we reach the age of wisdom. After a certain age, each of us is responsible for our face or appearance, sculpted by our actions and plans, our words and lies, you should always be wary of ugly old men: their ugliness comes from their acts, time strips bare our inner workings and intentions. Behold science, fully developed now, mature, powerful, revelling in its triumphs, celebrated above all else, do you imagine it cares what it looks like, at this stage? What is the good of power and precision if the price we pay is ugliness and death? What is the good of thinking, if we have no idea how to live? There comes a moment when formal knowledge is no longer enough, no matter how powerful it makes us; when, for instance, the universal musicality of language, beneath our utterances, seems to speak to our senses more than the sense of the words themselves; when culture, wisdom and philosophy are worth more than intelligence, and the latter, by virtue of its freedom and tolerance, more than knowledge, and knowledge more than demonstration. Let science have its way, right now: if it excludes the things that temper power, barbarity will resurface. After the age of positivism, an era of serenity?

So, do we learn how to die, how to survive alone through suffering, to sing joyfully when our child recovers from illness, to prefer peace to war, to build our home over time? Or do we take our education in the direction of serenity? In dictionaries, codes, computer memory, logical formulae; or quite simply at the banquet of life? I don't believe, says the beggarly phantom behind the machine, that if there is any sense to life, it lies in the word *life*; it rather seems to me that it arises in the senses of the living body. Here, in the sapience cultivated by fine wine, with as few words as possible; in the sagacity mapped out by scents enhancing our approach to others; there, through vocalizing, sobbing, and what our hearing perceives beneath language; through the aromas that rise up out of indescribable earth and landscapes; from the beauty of the world that leaves us breathless and speechless; from dancing, where the body alone dives freely into deaf and mute senses; from kisses which prevent us from even whispering . . . from the banquet we will have to leave.

Observing the statue sadly, the phantom says: have you noticed how badly people dance when they are talking? How you noticed how ugly thinking people are? Have you ever found yourself ogling someone powerful? Do you see the countryside filling up with ugliness under the reign of automata? Do you believe that one day we will be able to recognize our well-coded society by the unquestionable ugliness of the earth and its population? A culture stands out for the beauty of its women, the delicacy of its bodies, the distinction of its people's gestures, the grace of their faces, the splendour of its landscapes and the accomplishment of some of its cities. The radiance of people's expressions demands such grace, the smoothness of gestures demands such delicacy, there is a secret agreement about beauty. Ugliness knows no shame in a devastated country. Anæsthesia creates hideous bodies, words drug bodies and things alike. I salute you, still-graceful culture, rare remnant of our world, says the phantom.

The more our knowledge grows, the more we fear the absence of grace, and guess that the latter is the seed and nucleus of the former. As though our soul made our body full-bodied. When linguistic messages replace the non-linguistic messages of the senses virginally, our knowledge remains safe, progressing even faster, but our culture loses its grace, you can read its absence on people's faces, in social representations, on the face of the earth. Are we precision engineering our own ugliness?

At the beginnings of science, during the first phase of its evolution, philosophy sought to identify the genesis of knowledge, and claimed that the latter came from the senses. At that time, philosophers, somewhat learned, carried with themselves immense cultivation. The most learned did little learning; the least cultivated people were enormously cultivated. Doubtless they took their culture for science. By believing that they were describing scientific knowledge, they were in fact duplicating the genesis of their traditional knowledge.

We cannot commit the same mistake. Compared to that time, the most cultivated of us remain barbarians, the least learned know a great deal.

While we imagine ourselves to be describing the genesis of knowledge in general, it is in fact the formation of scientific knowledge that we are pursuing. Not so long ago, we took great care to distinguish between gnoseology and epistemology, the theory of knowledge and the theory of science, the latter being a part of the former; these days, we use the latter to describe a theory of all knowledge. As though science had a monopoly over all knowledge. Culture is evaporating. Copying the first genesis, language is now drugging and replacing the senses. As children, we are plunged into language before we have any contact with the harder world. More and more, we inhabit the soft. Some of us even spend our whole lives without realizing that there is a world outside of signs: actions separate from administrative paperwork, acts beyond media spectacles, a climate outside of the library. The first treatises on natural education, reacting against this growing encroachment of language, are exactly contemporaneous, first with the genesis, then the growth of the sciences. Now, at the hour of the latter's triumph, and of our concern over a new culture, the very same questions have resurfaced acutely, precisely because they had disappeared. Just as the formalisms, logicisms and nominalisms of philosophy have expelled empiricism – hence its ghost-like appearance. It emerges from the earth, between the statue's feet.

Efficient knowledge pays homage to language, from which it descends in a direct line, obliterating its more oblique history and submerging it in the anæsthesia of forgetting. We have lost our five senses in this way.

The remembrance of a lost wisdom and culture returns them to us.

The marble automaton exorcizes the spectral apparition by treating the pale, vague, insubstantial figure of the timid, unassuming, indecisive, frightened phantom with steely disdain: it writes off the easily forgotten old impression. The precise moment of tasting perishes, already receding into the distance; the impression left behind by a taste evaporates, it is not preserved in language. What arises on the tongue before words, and then vanishes, is crushed by the statue with the full weight of its memory. But it resurfaces. No impression without wax tablet, said the statue in Antiquity; no impression without printing press, it said in so-called modern times; no impression without software, it tells us once more in the age of computers and artificial intelligence. Nothing new here: no impression without encoding or language, the same word describing writing and the traces left behind. The statue dispels impressionable empiricism, like Don Quixote tilting at windmills that turn in the slightest breeze. Flimsy rotating weather vanes, receptive to any puff of wind, stop dead under the weight of books.

THE FIVE SENSES

Why kill what is already dying? Empiricism is lost, and all we see now are its ruins. What is the point of destroying ruins? Empiricism is destroyed, leaving mere remnants behind. What is the point of eradicating remnants? Empiricism has been eradicated, and only exists in a fleeting state as impression or shadow. Should we exorcize another shadow?

Naturally, we no longer remember the impression left behind by the breeze, the cloud of scent or mouthful of taste; but we have lost our memory of empiricism itself – and what if we had also lost all memory of our five senses? The phantom or ghost plays the role of three people: vanishing sensation, but also the theory that used to speak of it; and finally, alas, the organs that received it.

Who now goes hunting first thing in the morning on an empty stomach, nostrils twitching at the slightest change in the wind? Who sits astern and listens to the sound of the backwash, having been alerted by the first smell of leaves cutting through the thick wall of algae and salt? Who keeps their sense of distant sight and hearing so keen? Who today does not need to be notified by posters or messages of when to hear, feel, watch or taste? Frigid organs, empiricism in ruins, lost impressions, phantoms.

So, how long has the statue reigned like this? Since the time of origin, since the beginning of our memory, since the birth of language. The first of our ancestors described to us – the first hero to be celebrated in song – sets off across the water towards the fragrant Windward Islands or unknown lands somewhere on the violet horizon; the prison of language, poetic, slams shut on the traveller who attempts to lose himself in order to escape; despite the desired storms, the worst perils of the sea and witches who can turn men into beasts, Ulysses falls back into the woven trap through which he threads his journey, into Penelope's shroud, woven by day and unwoven by night, into the textual programme, into language: he sings of all this at the king's banquet; kills the suitors who do not sing at the last feast, after returning home to his wife. And yet, with fists clenched deep in the stinking fleece, he tried to escape from the cave where Polyphemus yelled and screamed, deafened by this proliferation of tongues and intoxicated by wine. Delivered once, twice, a hundred times, he ends up back in the web of language, bound to the neat weft of the poem. Back then you could already explore empiricism the way you might go sightseeing around the world: travel agencies spruiking it, selling it off cheap; a topic for conversation at dinner time; suddenly reeled back to the fantastic Underworld inhabited by vain shades and spectres, already weeping, who vanish when silence descends. On the opposite shore, our first ancestor, quite content to feast on fruit under the trees, naked in the company of his beautiful mate, begins by naming the different species. One in rubrics, the other in poetry, each one feasting, with Alcinous or in the Garden of Eden, and speaking the language of genesis.

Empiricism has been lost in islands of distant images or the spectre-ridden Underworld, since our origin as writing or singing beings, pursuing lists or building statues which wait on us at table. It dates from a more than fabulous Antiquity, because the Antiquity in question comes to us through fables, written or spoken in perfectly adequate tongues, surviving long after death. We have been losing our senses for as long as we have been speaking. Yet as long as it remains forgotten, immemorial empiricism will always resurface, emerging from its own tomb, reawakening with a gesture, a fleeting impression appearing above the last resting place of our black, cold, stiff, fossilized body. We imitate machines, we turn our children into automata, we bury ourselves beneath a skin of marble, and still the spectre reappears in a faint odour, in a taste we rarely encounter but which triggers an emotional response, in an unexpected posture adopted while farming or sailing, through an environment which is rent asunder or undone but which occasionally lets through to us the strange lightness of things themselves.

In Plato's dialogues, hymns to logic, the more recently named Presocratics are given the role of forebears, Parmenides is even called father. Different thinkers and schools of thought descend from this lineage, with one exception. Protagoras, the bearer of sensory turbulence, came out of the ground – which proves that he was buried there. Emerges from the ground, and is sent back there. He is evoked and dismissed. Which proves that empiricism was already a shadow. Wandering through the Underworld, from which it can resurface. The sensible is buried by the tomb-body. What does the name Protagoras mean? Before dialogue, before speech, before language?

Ancient: pre-dating our history as beings who come into being through language. Pre-historic: pre-dating our recorded traditions. Lying amidst the dead, victims of the power of language, who in the last four thousand years have never been raised.

DEATH

Here is the tomb of empiricism, clad in engraved marble. The body, the statue, our knowledges or memories, libraries or cenotaphs: all imprison the phantom by denying its existence.

THE FIVE SENSES

My book is a memorial to empiricism, in the same way that Ravel evoked François Couperin in *Le Tombeau de Couperin*.

Celebration and tears. Commemoration, respect.

Ancestor of philosophy and men, pre-dating all language, a ruin of the time preceding writing and leaving no or almost no remains, hail; hail, enemy of philosophy, outlawed by it and hidden beneath language and steles since the dawn of our histories, abhorred by meetings and dialogues, distrusted by reason, banished by the stone-city that covers up the earth-countryside, expelled from public spaces, sometimes haunting our banquets, a cloud or plume that suddenly bursts forth from bottles, condemned by the voices that emblazon our skin like a tambour, sense on word, word on voice, voice on skin and skin on flesh, covered by multiple layers, the unutterable ancestor of our voices, how to salute you without language?

Silence surrounds the cenotaph: music, murmuring, shades of colour and scents. Our forebears embalmed mummies: the vacant statue was thus enveloped in a perfumed shadow.

Wisdom. Your body should not become a statue or tomb, a cadaver before giving up the ghost, dead before it dies; avoid all anæsthetics, drugs, narcotics; beware the torpedo or torpor of language and philosophy; flee cultures of prohibition. Your body radiates wisdom: the world gives us sapience and our senses receive it; respect the gracious given, embrace the gift.

Ethics. The timeless morality of gratuity. We receive sense data as a gift, without reciprocating. Grace penetrates the fissures of an open body, flooding it with sapience. Statues close themselves off with toll gates and ticket windows.

Upbringing. Child of man, start with the open fissures, eyes, nostrils, pores, lips, pavilions; you'll be talking quite soon enough, rest assured that you will. Quite enough, always too much. Refine your skin, fear the invasion of marble, be scared of stiffness. Awaken your barbarous bard, so hard and harsh that one day you'll get yourself into fights. Soon enough, always too much. Become subtle, sapient, sagacious, keen, lucid, shrewd. Do not be like a dog with cropped ears, quartered like an animal or squared off like a beam. Perforate the statue.

Medicine. Immediate remedy, without medication. Countless illnesses come from not knowing when to be silent or how to live anywhere but inside a hard shell of words that chaff and scratch. Language kills time, silence is more golden than a golden tongue, giving us back duration, our only real treasure, and causing our shocked senses, sealed tight by the thundering of language and the intimidation of sense, to blossom. Taste, listen, sniff, caress, examine – silently. Æsthesis dispels anæsthetics. On the tomb, the recumbent statue beneath the perfumed murmur dies when administered with it. Welcomes the given, the gift, refuses the dose. For in this instance language is using the same word, and admits it; quickly replaces dosage with gift or given: fine wines keep us from alcoholism, delectable foods save us from obesity. Whatever fails to awaken our senses merely drugs them, empiricism needs no medicine cabinet. Immersed as you are in the culture of messages, rendered insensible by them and made ill by language, do not look to formulae for a cure. Drugged on speech, agitated by shouting, dead drunk on information – this is treatment by prescription, coating your tongue with another layer. Rhinoceros, armour-plated hippopotamus, alcoholic or drug addict, statue covered in labels or posters: all of these are mechanisms as predictable as a weekly planner. Undergo the quiet treatment of the five senses. It is enough to accept what is gratuitously given. Statues sleep or die from drugs, money and words; one god, three forms. Free treatment given graciously, certain recovery, this is our salvation.

Wise old man, calm, ancient, tranquil, as subtle as a vapour, delicate, simply healthy, robust; pedagogical and medicinal empiricism carries us far from cenotaphs and funerary statues, even when language would entomb it in song. It stands apart from eternally engraved monoliths.

Hail, giver of good health.

Then the guests at the banquet, awakened from the speech-induced torpor, and every participant at every feast in history, forgetting the tragic side of these performances, rise up and raise their glasses to the phantom which vanishes in daylight and delivers them from the black anguish of death; they clink the goblets of translucid crystal in which the Yquem quivers and gleams: good health! Not death, no, but health! Salvation, joy, jubilant trembling!

Hail, *ave*, joy; a cry, a shout, barely even a word, flying on vowels, an explosion of elation, all coming from bodies in splendid health. The first breath of life? The first word? The birth of language? Hail, O flesh of which the word is born. Hail, flesh full of grace. *Ave, gratia plena*. Phantom or angel? When the word is made flesh, grace abandons our body.

The given comes from language alone: the word invades the body, filling every pocket of our flesh without exception. The word requires that nothing should precede it.

Et incarnatus est: language is made flesh; the latter, virginal, is with the word. Born of the Virgin, the word wipes clean every stain in its path.

The given comes from language alone: it comes to us neither from the world nor from our bodies. Neither from the empty places of the former: the world has not known it; nor from virginal flesh: immaculate body.

Any unutterable traces predating the arrival of the word could only be stains.

They are wiped clean by three dogmas: those of the Immaculate Conception, of logical empiricism and of the virginal conception of the word.

Barely stirring the limpid air with its wing and its voice, the angel hails her, full of grace, before the word comes forth. Before blessing her, before giving her benediction, the envoy finds her occupied, saturated with grace. Only after that does the Lord approach her, and dwell in her. Before she conceives, before the word enters her, before language and concept, before the unstained virginity required by the word and produced by it, she – flesh, mother, woman, bodily sensibility – lived full of grace.

Full: of grace or of language. After: heavy with language. Before: filled with grace.

With grace: gratuity, gratuitous things, the given.

Welcoming the given, beforehand. After, welcoming the word. Be it done to me according to thy word.

The given comes from language alone: nothing moves, exists, or is given outside words, without sentences, beyond concepts. Sensibility is extinguished outside concepts, on their periphery, without them.

What word other than virginal could there be for such a conception?

The Virgin conceives the word.

Without saying so, she sees an apple tree in blossom. Always eternally covered in flowers. Never do we read that this apple tree bears fruit, anywhere. The flesh which has been promised to language, naked beneath the first tree, has never picked any, is free from any original trace of the first sin.

What name could we give this painting or scene other than 'The Immaculate Conception'?

She – flesh, mother, bodily sensibility – conceives the word as a virgin: unaffected by the given, except through the word. Before she could conceive thus, she herself was conceived immaculate.

The given comes from language alone: the body has never received anything except from the word. Before receiving nothing but the word, thus before conceiving, it had never received anything.

To understand the dogma of logical empiricism, you need merely to add together that of virginal conception and that of the Immaculate Conception.

The first says the same thing through the same oxymoron as the two others, which each use the oxymoron to stress a different side of the equation. All three describe the same situation of concept divorced from flesh.

The only philosophy is that of language, the only religion is that of the word.

The woman has no response to the words of the announcement, except that she knows nothing and has known no man.

Hail, empiricism, lost to us the day the word was made flesh, the morning the angel appeared; already forgotten when the mother was born, white virgin flesh.

Hail, flesh full of grace.

Ave, pure-vowelled greeting. With that, the angel alone makes us remember that the body was filled with grace before the word effaced it and rendered the body immaculate, as though in compensation.

Flesh full of grace which the angel alone may speak, through tenuous messages or phenomena coming incomprehensibly from the world towards the senses.

Once saturated by the word, flesh loses these ancient graces, old messages incomprehensible in language; grace, washed out, is forgotten.

When the word is made flesh, the flesh is abandoned by grace.

The words of the Annunciation, barely translated, are quite unexpected here, as clear and limpid as the present thesis: the given comes from language alone.

THE FIVE SENSES

It marks the return of woman, and of the virgin mother abandoned by the venerable reformed theology of which I have already sketched the profile. The return of the foreign woman from Nazareth.

This foreign woman does not speak.

This – what we drink or eat – can be reduced to a sign, a symbol, a word. The given comes from language alone.

This – what we conceive – comes from concepts alone. The word cannot flow from the given.

Our wretched flesh eats nought but language, no-one gives it anything to eat or drink, all they do is spread the good word and nothing else; it falls pregnant without saying a word, after begging for something to eat; impregnated while still a virgin.

Poor flesh.

Taken as a whole, German philosophy since the end of the eighteenth century sounds like a patristics of the Reformation, a counter-counter-reformist theology. It is gradually taking the place of Roman patrology, the touch-stone of so-called classical philosophy and dominant until the end of the Counter-Reformation. One college of fathers expels another, an expulsion which neatly sums up the history of ideas within the import-driven French university system.

The question of language and the senses, innocent and presented anew through an apparatus of sophisticated technical quibbling, both hides and occupies the ancient site of squabbles between the triumphant Anglo-Saxon reformed fathers and the old Greek, mostly Latin, Mediterranean fathers, vanquished and overwhelmed. See reappear anew, in the slightly musty decor of empiricist questions, the quarrel over transubstantiation in the taking of the Eucharist, at the original Last Supper, or of the virginal body of the mother, as incarnation of the word.

The history of ideas seems as slow-moving as tectonic plates moving a few millimetres in a few millennia.

We are still talking about symposia, love, and how a poor woman came to conceive.

I hail thee, full of grace.

The angel is speaking of a woman's grace: charm, attractiveness, delicacy, amiability; I bow before your beauty.

The grace that fills the body before it is filled with the word, is the same as beauty, called gratuity. The gift is not a matter of obligation: the giver does not owe it, it is not the recipient's due. It might be called the given. I hail thee, body filled by the gratuitous given, received as gifts from the world. What enters via the senses or into the body through the senses is not paid for in money, energy or information; not in any currency, thus we agree to designate it given. I hail thee, flesh filled with these gifts.

I hail thee, full of grace, beautiful; greeting full of sensory gratuity. The angel is referring to æsthetics twice over, with the same word: in the sense of what is given, in the sense of beauty.

The angel is proclaiming the unity of æsthetics: I hail thee, unitary grace, charm and gift, sense and beauty. What can we possibly say of this unity, when all we can do is hail it?

As soon as the word arrives, gratuity vanishes. We need to attend to the cost of writing or speaking, to what the word buys or redeems. Yet before the reign of language, the flesh was filled with grace requiring no compensation; unitary, beautiful, gratuitous. When the word is made flesh, the flesh is abandoned by grace.

Here the unity of the æsthetic field is undone.

In the time before the arrival of the word, the flesh is brimming over with grace, intrinsically. It sleeps during the long, wordless night, surrounded by the golden harvest, so full of the given that it leaves some behind for the gleaners, slumbers beneath the ancient, unnamed stars, daydreams while listening absent-mindedly to the oxen ruminating in the rustling stubble; and dreams, amidst the fleeting scents of asphodel, that an enormous tree is sprouting from its stomach, the last branch of which is called the word. Bare-breasted and resting near the patriarch, himself heavy with sleep, she, flesh, dreams in silence of an inconceivable child, in the middle of a peaceful summer night as long as the sum of the length of all the childhoods of all men put together, and whose sky barely illuminates the shadows. Flesh dreams of words; language – fruit – takes root in its womb.

Filled with the given, saturated, it leaves the rest for the gleaners. Poor gleaners, bent over the stubble, gather to their breasts the ears left behind, the tiny overflow from the completely saturated plenty, the defect or excess of the given.

THE FIVE SENSES

The woman receives a benediction at dawn. The angel hails her: *benedicta tu*, well said. She receives her name and the assurance that her name suits her perfectly: well said, *Maria benedicta*. The angel which brings her salvation and language, early morning apparition, phantom floating in the open door or window moving at the whim of the breeze, soon fades away. Heavy, full, hard, the flesh receives softly scattered seed.

Genealogically speaking, good blood branches out. She who, weighed down with gifts, lays herself down in the bed of the patriarch, himself brimming with the given, windmills, lofts, precious metals and forges, only ever gives birth to plump, satisfied children, concrete and as full and round as solid balls, obese with plenty, grazing on their daily grass in between two successful ruminations. The real mother is bent over, following behind carts and picking up the remnants of the bulging sheaves piled up beneath pregnant mothers; she is satisfied with leftovers. The real mother is sown with the seeds that fall from the over-stuffed bushel, by that which persists and will end up rotting at the bottom of the empty silo. Mary, daughter, grand-daughter, great-grand-daughter of gleaners, from the long line of women who have never participated in the banquet of the given, Mary virgin daughter of Anne, welcomes the angel into her bosom; the remnant of a man, barely perceptible, translucid and floating tissue, what remains of a thing when it disappears and none remains, given, sound, call, greeting, benediction, fading glimpse, quickly forgotten scent, caress so delicate that no tissue quivered beneath its touch, Mary, daughter, grand-daughter, great-grand-daughter of the long line of gleaners with broken backs stretching out after Ruth and her carts groaning with wheat, welcomes into her bosom what remains of what remains of what remains of what remains . . . of what remains of the rare grains of wheat in the almost empty ears on fragile stalks, the airborne, transparent, fine, minute seed of the word.

It is born, incarnated. No-one has ever known or understood the secret of this passage, neither the Gospels nor Einstein, astonished that the world should be opening itself up to understanding. A mystery for the former, incomprehensibility for the latter. The heavens are filled with song; and space, filled with words, announces the good news: words redeem the flesh, language purchases what is concrete, occupies it, saturates it, such that the golden wheat harvest paves the way for the bread to be transformed into the flesh of the word, such that the laden grape harvest pours forth the wine to be changed into blood, such that the stars spell out our birthplace in the night sky, such that the nova lingers in our constellations and memory, such that the calendar is organized around the epact, around the Friday of the Passion and the Sunday when the word was revived, such that the ruminating oxen give life to the wailing word and that the winds, scents and noises flying about announce the spirit in every language, another nomination of language and another set of gifts reduced to language, in such a way that the world, filled up with language from its entrails to its dreams, from heavenly bodies to beasts of burden, from ears of wheat and bunches of grapes to the wind, has nothing left over, not the tiniest grain of millet, not a slender stalk, not a breeze, not a sigh with which an evil angel, Hermes or Michael, might touch the flesh.

In the ancient world of the flesh, the word moved in the form of dreams or angels, a stalk waiting for a gleaner, an abandoned remnant, the last branch at the top of a tree growing out of the womb. In the modern world, purchased and redeemed by language, all flesh, every blade of grass and every stone exactly balance out the weight of their names, leaving no tare. Either incomplete spaces or jam-packed universe.

Unable to sneak in through the tare weight of a remnant, whatever purchases or redeems the word itself must therefore come through its passion and death: speculative Good Friday, pronouncements that God is dead.

In the contemporary world where science has taken the place of language, even language and even the subject are taken, even the empty places: the world has been supersaturated, even the abstract has been captured. Science regulates the relationship between words and things with precision: handles things better than words ever did, and moreover handles an algorithm's handle on its object.

We have lived through the time of the redemption of the flesh by the word, we are now living through that of the redemption of language itself by new powers. The word is dying.

The time of gleaners begins anew. Will we find any remnants left after this death?

Language is dying. Having robbed it of precision and rigour, science has taken over its splendid body. It hovers like a phantom which others have plundered of its delights: the other side of splendour, or the forced dictation of facts.

After Good Friday, the Sabbath is a time of repose. The word rests in the tomb. Gone down to the Underworld, they say, where you can enter disembodied.

And the day after the Sabbath, Mary Magdalene and the other Mary, mother of James, accompanied by Salome, carrying jars of spices in their arms, hurried at dawn to the tomb where the body of the word had been lain, in order to embalm the corpse. We will not be able to move the stone blocking the entrance to the sepulchre, they said to one another, too heavy, too hard for our soft strength. When they arrived, they saw it already rolled to one side. There was an angel above it, dressed in a blinding white robe. Or: when they entered the tomb they saw a young man seated on the right, dressed in a white robe, and were struck dumb. The winding sheet lay on the ground, the shroud folded separately in another part of the tomb.

On the Sunday morning, while no-one knew of the Resurrection, the hard was made soft: the heavy stone rolls aside without being pushed, the body fades and disappears, and there remain a winding sheet, an angel in white, appearances, voices in the garden.

You seek language here; it reigns elsewhere, in another world, where it has taken a resplendent body.

We now know that our knowledge has taken, in splendour and power, the body of the word, we know why language has died and of what. It will never return in its first form, we must learn to live without its real presence, hard and strong, its flesh and blood.

It has vanished before our dazzled eyes.

The philosopher writes under the dictation of an archangel, another of Hermes' names, designating the messenger who invented languages and created pathways. What he writes depends on the site through which the announcement passes. Socrates and Descartes each had his demon, appearing at thresholds or invoked in an enclosed space within which a fire is burning, Heraclitus awaits his gods by the fire of dark light. But almost all of them meditate under the influence of the enunciation of the Annunciation. Where the window flaps back and forth, where the shutter is ajar, there stands the angel. You will give birth in misery and beauty, he says, and the fruit of your womb will be called the word. Language will come, he who will appear has promised it, he who is already speaking utters it.

The lesson or image of the announcement: the apparition speaks. Understand by this: the phenomenon brings the word with it, language bears what is to appear. The messenger or angel of the Annunciation displays the face of language, prosopopeia, or the body of language, but because he appears – blinding white robe, resounding or discreet sound, gentle caress, light spirit – he must pass as an element of the phenomenon, small perception, barely sensed differential, what Lucretius calls a simulacrum, a delicate garment flying through the air. The announcement is spoken using apparent language, the angel, at the outer limit of visibility and tangibility, standing on the edge of the threshold, reduces the given to language and speaks the gift, we shall call angels soft. The body, the face of the angel occupy quite precisely the place where the act of appearing becomes language, and vice versa.

The Annunciation remains internal to speech. It begins with appearance, bearing it into the woman's womb in order to give a body of flesh to the word. Whoever writes, receives the archangel: the outer limit of the phenomenon which melds with the outer limit of speech, then seeks to fill space with something other than wind. It conceives, it needs a womb, it seeks a woman. Miraculous if it succeeds, Noël and joy over all the earth.

Everything depends on the womb, then, everything depends on this woman. If she does not come, whoever would write is struggling with the wind.

A rare archangel guards the tomb – rare because it reverses the announcement. The word will no longer be made flesh, the flesh of the word has suffered; dies, disappears. It will come no more, and has gone away: here is the empty hollow where its body lay. Dead, first of all; vanished, even; tortured before dying. Hands and feet shattered, bones broken, it has lost its hardness, its power; flagellated, face and skin lacerated, covered in sweat, spittle, bile, sediment, vinegar, its charm has left it; crowned mockingly with thorns, it has shed its sovereignty. The three-fold power of the word abandons it. The body of language lies in the tomb.

And now on the Sunday morning the women find it deserted. Even the dead body has vanished. No more announcements from angels, the women do not conceive, they move on; it remains, reduced to a remainder: what remains of language is a blinding white robe, a sound resonating in the tomb-box, three women carrying jars of spices, two men on the road to Emmaus recognizing the taste of the last supper, Thomas placing his hand inside the open wound on the body that appears before him; the disappearing archangel of the five senses remains, witness to the fact that one day, the word made flesh, born of woman, came amongst us, died, disappeared, but lives again.

Nowhere are we told what the women did with the spices. The same Mary Magdalene had already poured some on the body of the living word; she approached him carrying an alabaster jar of precious ointment of nard and poured it on to his head, according to some, on to his feet according to others, she anoints the body of language and washes it with her hair. Its perfume fills the house.

Lazarus was there, recently risen from among the dead, death still near; or else it was Simon the leper who presided over the table, another condemned host; the word took its meal there, condemned and soon to be delivered. A last feast not long before the Last Supper, a perfumed feast, a supper of blood and wine at one and the same time, and one after the other in the story of the Passion, a meal in the house of Lazarus or Simon where the guests, Judas Iscariot included, protest: 'This perfume could have been sold and the money given to the poor. – Leave her alone, the word replied. When she poured this perfume on my body, she did it to prepare me for burial. What she has done will also be told, in memory of her.'

The perfume poured on the living word fills the air. The women cannot embalm with spices its dead body, missing from the tomb itself.

Nard or valerian, artemisia or angelica, thyme, vanilla, savory, oregano, cinnamon and benzoin, hyssop or coriander, lemon balm, myrrh, ginger, marjoram, beautiful words with no fragrance, words of taste and smell entirely without smell or taste, does some jar-bearing woman pour a subtle blend on their rhythmic feet so that their fragrance might fill the air? The miracle occurs during the word's rare and exceptional life; more often, in the long course of history and time, it vanishes, and the women with their jars, including she who was once able to anoint language, have no idea what to do with their spices. However there was once, a long time ago, a language made fragrant by the hand of Mary Magdalene. Woman, come and anoint my sentence with nard or valerian, artemisia or angelica, thyme, vanilla, ginger or marjoram, without you your companion cannot write perfumed lines.

The odour of nard, borne by her, is far from the word nard, uttered by him; life arises, for each of them, fragrant spirit, each pouring itself onto the other, mingling, death bringing separation. Absent word and sealed jar; living language and unstopped jug.

Money has no odour, it would have been better to sell the mixture and give the money away. Judas estimates that the perfume is worth three hundred denari, the delivered word is valued at thirty pieces of silver. Has the redemption of the world and men by the word ever been calculated in figures? Was payment made in kind, with life and body and blood? But what price blood?

The word has no odour, it must be anointed; money never has any.

The language of perfumes is vanishing, chased away by the specialization of algorithms; the chemistry of perfumes aligns calculations and molecules.

The word's flesh is drawn from the woman's womb. He has no surname that we know. I will call you Christ, Peter said to him. Man speaks, woman makes: he draws his name from the unction, the balm poured by the woman, the perfume she wipes away with her hair. I will call you Peter, he said, a reference to the hard rock, the foundation. During the penultimate feast on the day before he was delivered, the Lord's anointed was actually anointed by Mary Magdalene. He was called Christ, his body became Christ, a reference to his anointing during the meal at Bethany.

Christ? The word means anointed. But what else?

Christ means: touched gently, brushed. Someone comes as close to you as possible and brushes against you. Thus a woman came up to him and washed his feet with her hair. Soft veil.

It means: touched harder; even scratched and stabbed; more than that, flayed. Thus, later, the body of the word will be flagellated by a whip, pierced by a lance, scarified by countless wounds.

And thus means: marked. Emblazoned.

Marked: different, designated for torture, a victim. In a flock of leaping gazelles, hyenas and tigers pick out the one that is marked.

Marked: the body of the word, of language, bears the trace or scratch of writing. The life and death of the word bring together the written and the spoken.

Marked on the body, marked on the shroud, on scattered cloths, folded, rolled up, abandoned in the tomb. Cloths, veils, skins, parchments written that we should remember them, tactile and legible remnants.

And it further means: rubbed, coated. And then a woman came up to him and poured perfume on to his head. Rubbed: she washed him. Coated: she anointed him. Coated him like a cloth or veil or other kinds of skin.

It means: coated in colours, pictures, coloured pictures, dyed, painted, colourwashed, tattooed. The word bears the ink, dye or paint of writing, abstract on the body and thus concrete, unrepresentative, iconoclastic on the face and thus iconophilic. The brief anointing segments the tattoo, restricts it, but also initiates it, the anointing can pass for an element of the tattoo. Christ: the Lord's many-coloured one. Coated in wine, blood, spittle, bile and vinegar.

It means: coated in perfume, ambrosia, poison. Then the woman who approached him coated him in precious nard. Its perfume filled the house during Lazarus' feast, he who was brought back to life, during the feast of the word, before its passion, its death and resurrection, during the feast of death and immortality.

Scent marks you out from afar and roaring lions on the prowl for their next kill come running, drawn to whatever is coated. Perfume brings death and is transformed into deadly poison and mortal stench.

And thus means: coated, soiled, defiled. Anointed by Mary Magdalene, defiled by the sinner.

Money has no odour. Sell the nard. Distribute three hundred denari in coins amongst the crowd. Do not come near the alabaster jar, take the perfume away, avoid the anointing. Already, Judas wants to save the Saviour for the first time. Avoid giving him the scent that will mark him out and make him noticed. Money is anonymous and designates no-one, is easily scattered in the hands of the multitude, scattered coins substitute for quartered limbs. Do not designate the body for public condemnation with this scented coating, sell it, sell it before it can touch or brush or stigmatize the body.

Judas tries to save the word from stain or defilement, from perfume's inevitable transformation into poison. The result, or rather the repercussion of this is that when the poison changes back into perfume, after the resurrection, Judas takes the stain on to himself. For the second time, glory and praise to Judas.

Finally it means: coated, greased, anointed like a king; like a priest, sacred.

Two resurrected bodies are eating at the table, the word and Lazarus, two victims, Judas and the word; two women, Martha the servant, and Mary Magdalene, who anoints it before burial and will not be able to embalm it after the resurrection; Mary Magdalene who turns Christ into Christ. Who marks him out for death while Judas seeks to save him.

Food, unction, money, words and death are all in circulation around this table. A tragic scene.

Touched, pierced, marked, signed, coated, painted, perfumed: this, ultimately, is what Christ means. A smeared, pierced death.

The word became flesh through a virgin woman, a sinful woman made it tangible and visible and legible and fragrant, during the feast where Martha serves the bread and wine which are tasted. Beyond the tragic table where language, money and death are seated, Mary, who does not take a seat there, occupies an ancient place off-centre: that of the sensible. The first Mary gives flesh, the second Mary gives the senses.

She institutes Extreme Unction.

Christian: a tattooed, drawn, coated, rainbow-coloured, studded, tangible, touched, sensible body, painted in various colours like a map, covered in sweat, in a shroud, in scents and odours. Anointed.

Chrism: oil mixed with balm and used for anointing, but also: cement or mortar used for building. This one and that one are called Peter, but to build with rocks you need, also and at the very least, a binding element, a cement to unify and mix, this element or chrism gives us Christian. The Greek word for binding is preserved in the Latin word religion.

Unction is made through mixture and produces a mixture, there is no mixture that does not bind.

Christ will die because of the unction that transforms him into what his name designates. Anointed: marked, visible, tangible, scented. He will die because of the senses.

Money and words circulate around the table, to the death. Lazarus and Judas, condemned, surround the word, also condemned, playing a game of who will die and who will rise; present, absent, substitutable and unsubstitutable. Money replaces language which replaces the body, which replaces the bread, an interplay of transformations on the tragic stage, where the objective is another world.

The women stand far from the table and beyond the tragedy, outside of the scene of substitutions and transubstantiations. Bearing urns, alabaster jugs or jars of spices, dishes or amphora, bread and wine, they work without making a fuss.

Every meal is about death, encircling it like the steps of an amphitheatre. As he lay dying Socrates continued to speak; now the word itself is dying.

Martha with the bread and wine, Mary with the alabaster jar have always absented themselves from the theatre, they attend to their business nearby, working at what is never said, taste and smell, wordless. Present, the women run to the tomb, the work of death done, urn-bearers.

THE FIVE SENSES

Last scene, last meal: when the flesh no longer exists, the bread remains, when the blood flows no longer, there remains wine. Penultimate act or meal, in the house of Lazarus, far enough from death that burial can be spoken of and the resurrection perceived there, as though the distance from the fatal point of symmetry made it possible to extend the vision of the other side: the word also evokes memory, what she has done will be told later in memory of her, it says.

This is something we have seldom retold, we remember the Last Supper but have little memory of the preceding meal. We always forget about the women: men and women who do not live in the tragic theatre, women and men who never make a scene: who never participate in the action. The only history is that of language.

We are losing our senses.

Once again: what is left when the word withdraws, what is left of the unction, the perfume, the coating, what remains of Christ?

At the back of the tomb, scattered linens: canvases, veils, tissues and the shroud, rolled up separately a little further away. The black box of the empty sepulchre, flooded with light when the stone rolled aside. One last meal on the way to Emmaus. The garden-paradise.

When language dies and enters in to its full glory elsewhere, this book remains.

I hail thee, full of grace.

'Grace' expresses the given – same word, same thing; it is charm, the same word again: beauty received graciously, our receptors astonished.

Is it really given?

No. Gifts are part of an exchange, they set up the expectation of a gift in return, they construct a logic, establish a circuit, relate a story, begin a performance as old as the anthropological era. No. Grace escapes the logic of the gift, it is an exception to the time of performance.

Grace is forgiveness.

Long ago, we entered the time and logic of gift-giving, through purchase and redemption, exchange beating out the rhythm, calculating deviations and equivalences. Grace points to a world or space outside of that time.

A world unknown to us, incomprehensible in our languages, forgotten since the paradise of angels, a utopia in which economics suspends its Iron Law.

I hail thee, gracious, you who gracefully and graciously give redemption its name, its grace; I hail thee, pure gratuity from before the time of gifts. I hail thee, full of grace.

The body receives gratuity. The world gives graciously, disinterestedly, asking for nothing back, expecting nothing in return; it has no scales, no balance sheet. Our senses cede nothing in return for it, can give nothing back to the source of given beauties. What could the eye give back to the sun, or the palate to the vines of Yquem?

The given comes through language, which counter-balances the given and constitutes reciprocity to the world. The word redeems the fruit that the flesh has picked from the tree of the world.

But grace. Sensible æsthetics, the unified field of beauty, seems to be exempt from the iron laws of give and take.

God doesn't cheat, wins nothing, neither plays nor exchanges; in this sense, God does not calculate. He keeps no accounts, neither economical nor an economist, the laws he gives the world map out a space of graciousness. The laws of the universe do not conform to the double-entry system.

The sun is inexhaustible for us: universal and infinite well-spring. Or rather: when it dies, our senses will, come dawn, have lost their place in the sun.

The body receives the given without having to pay for it. The source of the gift, or better said, of grace – God, the world, the environment, air, water, sun, how can we possibly name these things? – is selfless.

They give everything, universally, always, to everyone, everywhere, without exception or pause or omission.

They give to pure sensation, without concept.

They give out of necessity, and the purpose of the given is not always subsistence or knowledge or satisfaction: it is sometimes superfluous, fearsome too, and sometimes ignored by our cultures. They give without purpose, without anyone being able to represent what such a purpose might be.[10]

These four canons on matters of taste, drummed into us in school, are applicable to grace: predictably so when it designates beauty; but they are equally applicable to grace when it comes to the given. The unity of æsthetics is easily demonstrated.

The world – beautiful – offers the sensible graciously.

Empiricism, a wonder-struck philosophy of the inexhaustible, presupposes that the world is beautiful and its treasures infinite. You cannot put a price on the best things. To hell with avarice! No accountant, God is generous; the world, abundant. We can always drink from the fountain of youth, plentiful and irreversible, its level never goes down.

The gods meddle with mortal banquets. Dressed as vagabonds, wayfaring beggars, watchful Hermes and Jupiter knock at the door of Baucis and Philemon, whose love, a child of poverty, grows old. The impoverished mortals proffer food and drink to the insatiable immortals with trembling, wrinkled hands. Even in their reduced circumstances, they still have a ham smoking in the hearth, hanging from a blackened beam. Even in poverty, the world still gives to those who do not need it. And now drink. To the health of old loves and gods in rags, to the health of immortality, of angels come amongst us, hypocritical and unrecognizable, of archangel guests, Hermes or Ishim. Pour, drink, the level never varies. Usually the more you consume, the less there remains. Here, in Philemon's cottage, on that day, the level remained stable and constant. A miracle.

A miracle? We have entered the banquet of the gods where the taste and infinite volume of ambrosia bestow immortality. We have left behind banquets of gifts and exchanges, from Don Juan's donation to the word's gift of flesh, all those suppers you have to pay for in gold, or blood, or death, where a 1947 Château d'Yquem costs a fortune, all those suppers requiring reciprocity, where love is redeemed cheaply; we have entered the feast of grace, hail Baucis, full of grace, Jupiter or Philemon is with thee says Hermes the angel, here we are at the table of immortality, in the paradise where all we need is fruit, in the supralapsarian garden where abundance flows outside of time, the original, fundamental banquet with no possible predecessor – free, gracious. In the world as it is given.

A Château d'Yquem flows from barrel to glass or from bottle to mouth and when the level of one rises the other falls, like the water in any jug. When the fall of one pan leads to the rise of a second, you have a pair of scales. If the levels do not move with the flow of time or water, then you have no balance.

Stability is required: whatever moves over there does not remain here, what stays here does not move over there. Invariants are needed, constants. No-one can act without them, nor think in the absence of their logic, nothing can exist without their sum.

A balance exactly conveys the economics of the world. Whoever bottled the wine has absolutely no expectation of finding full casks. Whoever refines it in his cellars leeches the surrounding space dry. This is how scarcity is organized. Empiricism marvels at profusion, a philosophy of well-springs, whereas economics, the calculation of equilibrium in exchange, suppresses it. The miraculous feast that Philemon serves with Hermes' intervention, Adam's banquet of abundant fruit, ignore balance and precede economics.

A gracious cask can fill countless glasses without revealing its low-water mark.

We need stability, and constants. Whatever flows over there does not remain here. Imbalances always hide an equation, an equivalence, even transformations do. From which we get science, which organizes the thousands upon thousands of ways of writing an equal sign. Philemon's supper with its bottomless pitcher and the utopia of a garden with superabundant produce describe the minimally twofold absurdity of perpetual movement. Out of ignorance of equivalence, and invariance, and balance sheets. Both these stories precede science.

An inventive brain can fill countless attentive brains nearby with its inventions, without ever depleting its own flood of inventiveness.

We need invariance. The wine in a glass is not the wine in the carafe. Quite impossible that the latter should be the same as the former, that it should both be and not be the latter, at the same time and given the same relationship. It isn't merely about drinking or calculating the wine's vintage, it is a question of speech. Of conjugating the dangerous verb 'to be' and playing with negation. If you want to speak, you need stable contracts with others and with things: in this, the identity principle is equivalence or conservation, balance and stability. It is the foundation of logic and of every possible language.

The gracious banquet of empiricism takes place before gifts, exchange and reciprocity; before economics and the scarcity that it constructs; before science, by virtue of the eternally flowing spring; before logic and language. I rest my case.

It assumes the wine already drained from the glass to be still in the bottle. It assumes a world full of grace before the word comes and redeems everything by balancing the scales. It assumes a time so ancient that we have forgotten it, a time so impossible that we can neither think nor speak it.

In the first garden, the tree of knowledge had the form and function of a set of scales: the fall, aptly named, called for a compensatory rise. On the scales of the cross. Paradise is where all kinds of perpetual movement take place.

Hail, Eva, full of grace. Ave.

In the garden of the senses, who pays for the light in your eyes, the florilegium around your lips, the rosy satin hue of your skin, the spirit-like lightness of the scents carried in by the breeze, the primary voices in the foliage?

Hail Eva, Mary, you who love graciously.
Sensible beauty, desire, without counterparts, love without equilibrium.

Mortals and immortals drank wine or ambrosia, long ago, at banquets
on the eastern side of the Mediterranean. Men or gods, these ancestors of
ours, turn to dust underground. In modern Greece their contemporary
counterparts drink a mediocre retsina with their meals: it is a mixture.
A mixture of the fruit of the vine and the resin of pine trees. The wines of
long ago mixed pure water in craters with heavy syrup poured from jugs.
We only ever drink mixtures, even when they come from Yquem.

We have difficulty speaking about mixtures or rationalizing them. They
are resistant to principles. Analysis abhors them. Give the analytical person a glass of sugar water and ask where the water is and where the sugar
is: one is distributed through the other, which is distributed through
the first. Where is the resin in the wine? The former mingles with the
latter which is mingled with the former. Where is the water in the syrup,
where is the Semillon in the Sauvignon? Identities are destabilized, their
precise locations lost in ill-defined surroundings, contradiction itself hesitates in the face of confusion.

Let us invite logicians, linguists and grammarians to drink with us, let
us mix the drinks and raise our glasses to confusion.

Hermes, passing angel with winged feet, stands there in front of the
elderly lovers who will soon intertwine their limbs, Baucis' boughs embrac-
ing Philemon's branches, the wine mixture flows into goblets, twists and
turns as it slips from amphora to pitcher, from crater to glass, its long,
ruby-scaled body slithering as it merges with other serpentine forms.
Hermes pours from his caduceus: a clear and distinct schematic of confluent streams, a graphic representation of the opposite of a balance. Let us
drink to Hermes' caduceus, to confluence, to confusion. Can we think it?
Can we reason about mingled bodies?

Are we talking about a different time?

The empiricist hopes for and believes in resources. Knows nothing of
scarcity, lack, fatigue, exhaustion. Mocks the second principle, laughs
at the fall, neither pays nor speaks.

He haunts banquets. The crucial experience of philosophy is structured
like a feast, which is the best expression of it. For reasons beyond that of
taste. The sun gives us light, shapes, colour, heat and power graciously,

still; thunder and wind offer us scents and sounds, expecting nothing in return, still; bark and rock still do not charge for the feel of their texture; have we ever, since the time of paradise, tasted food or drink without spending a crown or even a farthing? This is the site of scarcity, the source of information, old site of the gods, where economics, the law of our world, is triumphant and where exchange reigns supreme along with its different representations; where speeches are made, organized, distributed, regulated, prioritized; where conversations play out, sophisticated exchanges of speeches and dialogues, this is precisely what the gift-table looks like.

The empiricist enters the banquet as though at the centre of a cross, in search of gratuity where none has found it since the Garden of Eden. Full of grace, he enters amidst the lounging statues: reclining gods, in a state of equilibrium, revelling in the victuals in the city's main square while its inhabitants die of famine and pestilence.

Scarcity is the law of this place, where the Iron Law of economics is triumphant, now the site of sophisticated speeches, of information and science; for these days prizes, scarcity, fortune come from knowledge; for today, less so than tomorrow, we will eat and drink knowledge, this banquet feeds barely a tenth of humanity, and to the point of nausea, a pantheon of gods protected by a ring of apocalyptic fire; site of scarcity, of economics, language and science, well-defined by atomic weapons; surrounded by the starving, deprived of everything and multiplying their offspring, as is always the case in extreme poverty; site where the sated expatiate knowledgably on what is given through language . . . Ask the malnourished, who are excluded from the banquet, whether or not the given is different from words; give them bread on the one hand, words on the other: this is the difference between life and death. Their lives and their deaths. Our lives of satiety and their lives of starvation.

The question is ultimately one of gratuity. Of economics and scarcity. Of the organization of scarcity. Of the organization of the feast. Of the division of space into two zones: that of the banquet, surrounded by that of bushes and hedges where the scrawny run about naked. In the former, you eat and drink to your heart's content because you know, because you know how to speak, calculate, weigh, think; in the latter, wandering through the shapeless and chaotic night, they who are dying of hunger because they cannot take part in the conversation do not know how to participate in the feast of words or the laws of giving.

When did grace enter this space?

Beat the hedges and the paths, let them all come to the wedding feast.

THE FIVE SENSES

The banquet remains the site of philosophy, today as much as in the time of history or myth: today the banquet is the world. An enormous hospice where shadows lie dying of malnutrition, where the table of scarcity and abundance, around which a few obese individuals throw up their excesses, is carved up. Yes, the feast of gods come down to earth highlights the meaning of the word 'mortal'.

When, therefore, will mortal and immortal eat together at the same table, forgetting the scales, for free? Paying as little as our eyes do for daylight.

Like the champion of graciousness, empiricism enters the feast of the statues, all of them recumbent at the tipping point of equilibrium.

It remembers the alliance of the sensible and the gracious, a venerable relic of language, borne by the saving grace of angels. It remembers the Garden of Eden, the sufficient paradise, land of milk and honey, and the desert where manna fell from heaven, and the hut where pitchers, as though they were springs, poured forth their contents.

It is astonished by a world populated by scales, and speeches regulated by multiple weight checks; by a time in which everything requires payment: bread, water and soon the air we breathe and the silence required for sleep and privacy, all graciously given, once. It is astonished that the law of the world is dictated by economics, ungraciously.

It enters the feast of the senses, the only philosophy without an economy, full of grace, trembling with life, shouting out life.

Economics abhors free gifts, thought to be wasteful ceremony. It attacks the sensible. It destroys the beauty of grace, then reinvests gratuities. Everything has a price, it tells us.

Tells us. Speaking, saying, writing: evaluating. Weighing things up.

And what if the word bought and sold every previously free given, at a fixed or variable price, negotiable and fluctuating depending on the location in space or the particular moment in a conversation, reducing it to a datum by the counter-weight of a word. Does language pay for the nature of things with the words it coins? Are we buying up the world through language?

And what if the word came amongst us to redeem the world?

Our economy sells auditory and sound signals, populates space with noises and images while driving out free voices and spectacles in order to make us think that the given comes from language. It trades in æsthetics and anæsthetics, supplanting grace. The scales of scarcity take the place of the caduceus of plenty. We might hail them, devoid as they are of gratuity.

Yet if you take the case of the sun, you would have to say that it gives without charge. Our bodies turn towards it, animals and plants too, stalks bend under its influence, an inexhaustible spring flowing irreversibly in one direction only. Without debt or reimbursement.

And yet it heats us.

And yet it turns, said Galileo before the Church tribunal, founding modern science in a cold culture.

And yet it heats, says the empiricist memory of the gratuitous that we have lost, before the tribunal or scales of economics, thermodynamics and language, in our hot culture.

Sensation is free, it requires no payment in any currency. Never call it given: no reciprocity is called for. Do not call it perception: who plays the part of the taxpayer here, and who the part of the impostor?[11]

Parasites join its banquet: they are fully aware that they take and give nothing in return, we already know them. They pay in words and would have us believe that the given comes through language. Don Juan presides over this feast which neither honours debts and wagers, nor keeps promises. They are all ignorant of scales and equivalence, living off and in a deviation from equilibrium, a deviation that is never redeemed. This is how the world is born for Lucretius, this is how time begins out of the chaos of Genesis, this is the start of history, like a story about the foundation of Rome, for instance, and its departure from the sacred.

For a long time I have been searching for grace. Or for some object that could not be called a prize or fetish or merchandise. Searching not for a gift, but for grace. Not for gravity, but for grace. Not for nature, but for grace.

Certainly neither physics nor science, with their laws of valency. But beyond them, metaphysics. Off-balance in relation to them. But philosophy: wisdom and love which speak grace, also. Hail, philosophy, full of grace.

BIRTH

Anyone who drinks one of those industrial concoctions which are flooding the market and the planet, is swallowing terminology; and is fully aware of what they are drinking. It moves through the mouth like a language:

written on a small label. Everything inside the metal or plastic container is declared on paper, everything printed on the external surface can be found within. These two propositions leave no remainder. The brand announces a finite and quite brief sequence: drinking is as much analysis as reading is; the label and the container carry the same series of words or substances: a formula for refreshment, abstraction in a bottle, pharmacy. The law decrees it. Imposes the fidelity of advertising. The law, written, forces the written label on us, and we are made to drink writing. Concoction or drug, same decree. Sense begins and ends with language. Anæsthesia and numbed mouth. Potion.

Anyone who drinks a good wine will not talk of brands, cannot say fully what flows over the palate, or lingers in the mouth. A finely detailed watered-silk map is drawn there, lacking ready-made words to designate it or sentences to describe it, for want of experience, apart from feeble vocabulary which everyone ridicules. The label carries a drawing of the chateau or the name of the estate, an indication of the vineyard or its location. If we had to set out what the wine contains, the list would be as long as our admiration of the wine was profound, the label would cover the bottle, the cellar, the vines and the surface of the countryside, mapping them all faithfully, point by point. Excellence opens up a descriptive sequence which we can imagine running on to infinity. Drinking envelopes this endless list and endless time: the singularity of the vintage, date and bottle itself wraps this immense series around a smaller, quite literally summary, location. Concreteness resides in such density, reality in this summation, like a singular essence: not a homogeneous purity, reproducible through repetition, analysis or industry, but a manifold mixture of tightly packed implications. The act of tasting anticipates the unfolding of this hard, dense involution, the unfurling of this ball wound around itself, the delectable moment when the bird fans out its tail and struts about, inimitably. Almost beyond analysis, the mingled flux leaves behind, wherever it passes or lingers briefly, a meticulous tattoo, aurora borealis, a shimmering engraving, constellation of assorted ocelli, its singular essence the signature of a sumptuous storm: a manifold, disparate, non-standard ensemble passing above. After having received such detail, the subject concludes that his previous mouth was frigid and numb, smooth and pure beneath the passage of imitable, quickly analysed currents.

Boring books in libraries quote other books in libraries: transcriptive, composite, analytical. Good books come from elsewhere and aim for bookstores. From the moment of their arrival they are surrounded, carved up and analysed by bad ones to show that they too were written using the books in bookstores. Bad authors hate good ones, try to make the latter look more like them and try to tell us that a good book is merely the sum of its analyses.

Children have long been taught that there are infinite libraries, labyrinths that no-one can escape, that there are masons who can build towers of Babel stretching to infinity. In short, that language imprisons us within walls that lock us away from the world by imitating it.

Yet in the space of our short lives we build finite things, all the more finite for having been built with what has already been built. No intersecting corridor can enclose us for more than a relatively brief period. The corner of a wall ends right *there*; fractal, the bottom of a bay can never be completely mapped. You can wander the seas for all time; whoever searches long enough for the exit to a labyrinth is bound to find it. The singular given is never-ending. No-one ever leaves the world, but anyone can easily exit the library; we can enter objects infinitely, a book is quickly finished.

Sometimes a work of art is implicated in itself, manifold, as though interminable, producing the time of history: as though it were a singular essence, non-integrable. Large numbers sit between the finite and the infinite. In philosophical libraries, it is as though they sit diagonally, resolving antinomies.

That industrial concoction passes over the tongue like the lists of boring books and leaves it cold: pure, identical, analytical, reproducible. The tongue has no trouble recognizing its drug, manufactured specifically to be recognized. Good wines are inimitable, and can even confound experts. A desert beneath the sun, on the one hand, a forest of infinitely diverse leaves on the other.

Accustomed to reflex actions, dogs respond to the sound of their master's voice and suffer terribly if they do not hear it, salivate automatically at the sight and sound of their canned food, knowing what to expect and what awaits them: their drug.

Expectation creates anæsthesia. Æsthetics tastes improbability. If you wish to live freely, drink singularly. If you wish to live singularly, drink freely.

Bound to the flesh, but without flesh, language moves through the mouth leaving it intact. The word is conceived in flesh, leaving its virginity intact.

THE FIVE SENSES

Tasteless dishes anæsthetize our tongue as they do language. Language anæsthetizes the mouth as industrial concoctions or pharmaceutical drugs do. Smooth-talkers, golden mouths, metallic and frigid. Language asks everything of the mouth, neither giving nor leaving anything in return, like a parasite.

Taste is a kiss that our mouth gives itself through the intermediary of tasty foods. Suddenly it recognizes itself, becomes conscious of itself, exists for itself.

Born of the mouth, as though its child, language asks to be born, assisted, conceding nothing in return. Tastes give the mouth lingering existence. The man of taste exists in precisely the same place as the frigid megaphone, disgusted and numbed.

I taste therefore I exist locally.

The object of taste exists, concrete and singular outside of any short, finite sequence of technical terms. It carries and gives up the virtually infinite detail which causes us to suspect and guess the presence of the real, the object in the world. The subject of taste exists locally, now, in and around the mouth, which without taste would not exist, virgin, frigid and talkative. Taste determines the existence or non-existence of the local subject and singular object: this inimitable drink and that agglomeration of flesh, mouth, cheek and palate plus centre and edge of the tongue, plus the deployment of our entire sense of smell.

Here the banquet of banquets comes to an end, and we have recognized none of the guests. As there was no roll-call of speakers we do not know who was there. Whoever speaks names himself, whoever names himself has the right to speak: one word designates the speaker of words. Or: the speaker of words ends up speaking a name which speaks the subject.

At the manifold banquet to which many banquets contributed, those in attendance constructed their identity through taste. All told, only three tongues or three mouths were seated around the bottle of Yquem at first; three for a single person no doubt: the one that speaks, the one that receives the liquor, the one that gives and takes kisses. A feast of wine where we talk of love. Once tasted, the Yquem brings the palate and sense of smell into existence, as well as the stitching that tacks mouth to nose, the many layers of glaze painted around the mask. Who sits at the table? Masks: of black velvet, white satin, some old-rose silk, others with tiger or zebra stripes, shimmering, mingled, in every shape and colour. In the end the wine gives each of them a face.

Along the length of the table, stretching into the distance, the masks are moving, drinking, evanescent. Faces without necks, heads without pectoral girdles, napkins floating in front of vacant chests.

I taste, therefore a fragment of my body exists: mouth, head, mask. An ENT model. I sense, therefore patches are formed. Empiricism gives us a localized cogito.

The senses construct our body bit by bit, as we use them. We carry within us the roots of our basting. Empiricism foresees the diasparagmos of Orpheus, life finishes just as it begins. Strings are added to the lute or lyre, they then slacken or break, music harmonizes the arts which then secede, the muses converse peaceably, then the Thracian women scatter into the mountains, screaming. Enough imagery, we're talking about the body. It is constructed from one proximity to the next, from one vicinity to the next, around these sensorial roots. It acquires sight which is quickly lost if not used to see at a distance, in detail, for snapshots, colours and shades, fusing sight to the ear, remembering the birth of hearing and who bestowed it and the delicious, heartrending circumstances in which it felt its triple tongue growing . . . the rag comes together piece by piece, site by site, a tattered body well-sewn here, cobbled together there, scraps more or less attached, fluttering, tacked on hastily . . . a divisible individual, limbs always scattered.

The subject is not united, it has local offices; has no head office, but constitutes a bouquet of delegations. I do not exist all at once, globally, emerging into existence through the act of thinking or speaking . . . or rather: if I think, if I speak, then yes, I do exist, a totality bereft of detail, a neat, coherent but locally frigid block, a cold statue which enters the banquet in order to converse, reclining on a divan like a god, its cup always left untouched, a robot with an anæsthetized mouth, its parts of marble or metal, indifferent, empty, punctured, stoppered, absent. I speak, therefore I exist globally, yes, but virginally. Virginity always accompanies speech. I exist as a block, but with phantom parts. An angel always announces the word. No, I do not exist in localities. Everything is concentrated in the capital, the villages are dead. Like the map of one of those countries ruled solely by the State. A synthesis without parts, therefore uncomplicated, a smooth statue.

Diasparagmos for death most ordinary, for life most ordinary as well. Bodies with half a mouth hover around the everyday table, skinless shadows, some with their auditory canals sealed up, some with no sense of smell, armless men, women with no sense of touch, all of them bodies with phantom limbs, mutilated humanity with a reserved seat at the banquet, all of them spending their time saying I. I speak. Standing in front of my chair to expatiate on love, I raise my always full or always empty glass. Each broken statue has a global unity, thinks and speaks beautifully, but falls down in ruins in spite of its capital unity. You'd think the guests had all been gathered up from an excavation site: a whole collection of broken statues in front of the pristine tablecloth. Global subjects from cities and countryside, under the sun, resembling the pale, indistinct shades surrounding Eurydice in the Underworld. Speaking and thinking easily bypass a difficult construction job.

Following the music, walking slowly, Eurydice constructs her body in patches and fragments, beginning with the æsthetic terminals or sensorial roots, follows the lyre or sum of the arts, the fine arts which no culture can do without, as essential to the construction or modelling of the living totality as the world is; an ear emerges from the darkness, a phantom limb becomes flesh, the pavilion and petrosal bone are incarnated, the tympanum becomes taut – a veritable blacksmith's forge starts to take shape, with its anvil and hammer – a dark mouth emerges from the darkness, a cascade of flowers is already flowing from her lips; the palate will be stitched to the already incarnated ear, at the banquet, the breadth of her skin is tacked onto the islets that have already emerged, her tongue unfolds out of the frozen virtuality where it lay, rolled up, before birth or reappearance; the formation of these parts, one by one, requires joints here and there, bridges, folds, hems, pathways from one sheet to the next, one root to the next, transitions or delegations, scents as soft as souls, tastes as silken as caresses, singing shades of colour, stained-glass harmonies, dance, dance, giving local syntheses in joyous bursts at every stage; Eurydice, emerging from the Underworld, a guest at the banquet of her new nuptials, extricates her forms from the shadows of anæsthesia, of the social pharmacy, of the drug of language, all of which keep virgin flesh impotent or frigid, escapes the labyrinth by crossing unstable bridges, fills in her wells, leaves behind the inn with its banal dinners in order to inhabit her body's own house, breaks out of prison, rises from sensory death; life most ordinary.[12]

Never assured of being able to build a sufficiently connected self, the I thus constructed from bits and pieces risks coming apart in the wind, crumbling, dissolving in the rain; the body only barely divested of the phantom shroud which cloaked it as it emerged from the Underworld is incapable of enduring anything at all – the sight of Orpheus, a hard stone in her path, a too heady wine, a passionate caress – the naked feminine form which emerged from the subterranean chaos vanishes back into the Underworld, a piece at a time, first diasparagmos; just as the male body of her lyre-player will disappear piece by piece on a Bulgarian mountain, under the gaze and claws of the Thracian women, dancing Bacchae; just as mine and yours, built up over the course of a similar labyrinth, following in the wake of a similar lyre will disintegrate under the same old diasparagmos, the disparate bits scattered and unstitched, the pieces collapsing before turning to dust. Sometimes a head remains: Orpheus' head floats downstream, still singing, still speaking, following the sea currents towards distant islands. It says: I speak therefore I am. Capital cogito ignorant of the body's collapse, giving unity or existence, but like a phantom reintegrating phantom limbs. I sing, I speak, I think, the head of an angel on a cloud, or of a prophet on a silver platter.

Statues and ghosts cause quite a commotion at banquets.

The body is constructed as books are composed, its pages come together like pieces and patches. Entirely sewn from skin, at first, naked in its closed bag, as though it had been dressed a sheet at a time – hose, scarves, pants – by an assemblage of pieces of skin or a juxtaposition or stack of assorted garments, sewn together, overlapping, but leaving gaps, because some places repel each other. Skin is no synthesis, but basting, collage or patchwork. What was once called the association of ideas is less true of ideas than it is of fragments of body or skin. Clumsily tied together, loosely knotted, tattered, if you like: bandaged together. Each time you hear someone talking about a living being as a system, you should understand: Harlequin's cape. Books are assembled like touch or garments.

Empiricism is a tailor, working locally, basting, thinking in extensions, from near vicinities to vicinal proximities, from singularity to singularity, from seed to layer, from well to bridge. It draws detailed maps as it traces paths, maps the body, the world and dressmaker's patterns: cuts out, pins, sews. Subtle and refined, it loves detail, its creations fragile. It is a topologist, having a sense for borders and threads, surfaces and reversals, never assuming that things and states of affairs are the same, more than a step in any direction, a weaver of varieties, in detail.

Language on the other hand does not go into detail, instantly occupying a homogeneous space: voice carries and echoes afar. A cymbal within the resonating thorax, it rises like a column above the throat, a whirling cone out front, its base planted behind the uvula, trumpet, clarion, announcing itself and flying into the surrounding volume, unifying it through the mastery of its vibrating force, lending the body a hasty and wide-ranging synthesis, global and urgent, dominant. Acoustics, through its harmonies, erases the seams that came before it and makes us forget them.

THE FIVE SENSES

The speaking subject trembles in geometric space and traces out chains of reasoning which are long, simple, straightforward, bearing their own law, using sound to create a straight path through an isotropic world. A possessive master, it presupposes that the global, distant, does not differ from the local, proximate. Reason, over there, maintains the same relationships as speech, over here.

Empiricism, tailor of our skin, has the same relationship to topology as the sonorous word has to geometry. The latter pair dominates and hides the former. Masons, architects, logicians and geometers construct, rationalists of language all. The empiricist-tailor darns, hems, prefers looseness to hardness, folds to articulations. No, the body is not an instantaneous construction, it folds over and unfurls – puffs and gathers – it stretches out like a landscape.

Subtle, acute, sagacious. The tailor precedes the lyre player, who precedes the cook. The garment is threaded onto the phantom body like a veil or cape. With the striking of a gong, or the clash of a cymbal, or a drum roll, the ghost enters the banquet. Without this acoustic thunder it would fall to pieces, mask and cape, laughable. Phantoms need noise to sustain themselves in the world of the living, which explains the incessant clamouring of our culture of ignorance. By dancing to music, from lyres or voices, the hasty garment can be made flesh, through the medium of language. Small children should be made to dance, often.

Guests, statues and ghostly apparitions, dressed, masked, rustling with language, enter the banquet of life where the harmonic space has been set up by an orchestra, and risk falling to pieces again as soon as the music fades.

They eat and drink, sagaciously or not.

Empiricism, both cook and cupbearer, knows more recipes than laws, for the latter apply to homogeneous states of affairs and the former to mixtures, so frequent as to be commonplace. It has prepared the banquet menu, where mixtures eat mixtures in order to exist as mixtures: this is my body. And where mingled bodies drink mingled bodies: this is my blood.

The body is composed like a book: a topology of tailoring, the pieces are stitched together at first; a geometry of sounds, next, the first global synthesis through the medium of language; and once again a topology of mixtures, the cook makes refinements based on the vicinity of ingredients to one another. Knows how to dissolve liquids into fluids, or solids, as poorly cohesive as flesh, into thin or thick sauces, thereby obtaining subtle liaisons. Where does meat end and stew begin? Sometimes even our sense of taste cannot distinguish. Our body has difficulty knowing where one sense, place or part begins, and where another sense, a second place or nearby patch ends. The striped, mingled body is made up of the proximities between gradations. It moves from one sense to another, imperceptibly. In the same way it is said that in Van Eyck's polyptych panel, *The Adoration of the Mystic Lamb*, in Ghent, the painter applied the subtle glaze over Eve's thigh in fifteen successive layers of gradation, each a different shade of pink. Thus did the Creator. Thus does each of us perceive her leg. And our own mouth, when tasting. An Yquem paints our palate with frescos and polyptychs in a hundred gradations. The eye loses its bearings, as though it were looking into infinity; the mouth tastes until taste itself dissolves; our tongue is lacking in tongues, we do not have fifteen different ways of describing a shade of old rose, our lexicon trembles and stutters, experts invent terms amongst themselves, private and intransmissable. At the sixteenth layer, Van Eyck thought he saw the woman move. Just as he thought that by crushing gemstones to mix new colours he was creating them on the canvas. And Van Eyck created woman. The continuous, differential, imperceptible spectrum that tattoos places invisibly and binds them with knotted, fleeting, transitional ribbons can be said to paste our body together, to mix its parts together, more than it can be said to construct it, or produce a synthesis of it. A fine matador can thus be recognized not by excellent passes, but by the complexity of movements melting into one another within the performance. Happy are the melted bodies. The banquet assists in effacing the tattoo through the fusion or confusion of vicinities, erasing its swirls of colour while preserving its effectiveness. In this way Van Eyck plays God, and matadors play with life and death, each dreaming of perfect liaisons. And thus does the cook.

An art as fragile and evanescent as perfume, fluid empiricism, transitory, forgotten, misunderstood philosophies, left in the kitchen. No-one wants to admit to living in the kitchen, in domestic territory. And yet the body is bound together in such places. Delicious, undervalued empiricism falls silent. Nevertheless, behind the scenes it is the constant companion of life. The banquet has two distinct parts: the performance and the pantry. Now decide where the most important events occur, in the factory or on the stage? In the sauces or the speeches? Mask or life?

Empiricism produces people worth spending time with, people who are alive, with supple, cohesive bodies, recognizable at the first beat of a waltz. It is, without doubt, little given to instruction, leading to neither higher understanding nor great speeches. But it gives small pleasures which make up the uninterrupted tonality of life, the comfort of our body, the rhythm of our gait, adaptation: simple arms in the everyday struggle against the legions of death camped in the theatre. Death is always lurking at the banquet. On the performance side of things: the statue, itself dominating, heralds the death throes of the dominators – thunder and drums. Empiricism takes refuge in the kitchen alongside the kitchen boys smeared with sauce, and the maids, saucy brunettes in white aprons. Quite well-behaved, even simple-minded, it listens to the speeches after the wine, takes fright at the jovial, booming actors, hams, prostitutes, imperious and decorated as they are. It is frightened of philosophy, science and laws, preferring to withdraw. To leave the table before the end.

In the kitchen it learns not to abhor impurity, puts it finger in the soup. It learns about mixtures. Separation reigns on the impeccably set table. In the theatre the law is in charge; in the kitchen they make do with recipes. Language and reason resound during the performance; behind the scenes, what is reasonable is sufficient. What if coarseness ruled the world, like a capricious and inattentive king? What if a certain reticent sophistication, attentive to localized details and caring about nuance, had no place except behind the scenes? Polite empiricism; unified rationalism. The former tells no stories, never makes history. It prefers life.

In the sunshine, the world resembles a banquet, or a sideshow. One-legged men, one-eyed women, eunuchs, smooth heads with no mouth or nose, dressed not in a tattered garment, flayed, but in tattered skin or senses; trunks of men, necks or earless skulls, blind, legless cripples, armless individuals, frigid, impotent, limping, paralysed – these are the creatures eating at the table, the feast is in full swing for them – passers-by, onlookers, coming, going, busily getting drunk, with one sense anæsthetized or a phantom limb, unfinished bodies, poorly constructed, uneducated, oblivious to the defects, deficiencies, random joins, everyone salvaged, redeemed, corrected, completed by a hasty orthopædic intervention, wooden legs, prostheses, bandages, plastic hands or leather noses, false teeth, hooks, dildos, hiding the space of the void beneath artifice, hiding our numbness beneath obesity, each of us shouting, verbose, screaming out our existence or trying to impose our language, speaking our category in the agora, believing that we have achieved the miracle of a unified, finished, harmonious, full, complete body by broadcasting the published word, while nonetheless admitting, almost with a slip of the tongue, that our bodies, in pieces, have been suffering since the dawn of time. A miracle of language at the table of freaks: I'm speaking, I'm speaking, can you hear that I exist? Tragically incomplete cripples obscured by the clamouring, shouting and squabbling. Everyone sees hats and coats and puts their trust in language. But rather than hiding skin, clothing in fact displays its stitching and patchwork. Everyone naked.

I taste; existence for my mouth. I feel; and a piece of me thus comes to exist. There was a blank void in the place which was just born of the sensible. Being settles in my body, a tunic of nothingness. Being patches nothingness. The topologist is a variation on the Harlequinian cogito. The edges of my tongue had no existence of their own until they emerged from underneath a coating of Château Margaux; the broad sides of the body itself remain blank; empty cœnæsthesia suffers or enjoys this multiple birthing, ongoing creation. A new tongue grows. Then touch, a real hand with five real fingers, my very own palm. I grow the top part of a back, a pavilion, enormous and brand new, a precisely sculpted petrosal bone, an unexpected gaze; this improbable skin envelopes me at the zones that see, hear, shiver and fold inwards, to great depths. This vicinity did not exist – it is born. It existed once, it exists differently, it hibernates and reawakens countless times. Is born, wants to be reborn, will soon know how to be reborn, knows how high it is aiming. Learns that, from now on, if it lets itself descend into bad, unworthy or cheap feelings it will return to its initial state of nothingness. Exists, insists and erects itself.

Grows and reinforces itself. Stays soft in order to feel better, becomes strong in order to live on. Knows how to, and is able to cross the tunnel of nothingness where once it lay; the softness of the sensible has hardened it. We learn by linking the fragilities which guarantee receptive accuracy, to the power which lends endurance. Enough imagery, I'm talking about erections. But only if we generalize them properly. Far from being restricted to an organ which is never given a lovely name in any language, an erection describes the everyday, local and global phenomenon of sensation. This partition appears from out of its white nothingness, like Venus above the roiling sea, enlarges, exists, acts, grows like a bud, or sleeps while waiting for the next feast. I feel, therefore a slab of me is erected. The construction of the body is the result of a number of erections. You spoke of love at the banquet: without knowing it, you were giving us the template of what happens in your mouth and on your lips.

The hideous little monster drawn by physiologists when they map nerve endings according to the relative space they occupy in the brain – fat lips, enormous tongue, small torso, boxing gloves for fingers, a hare's ears – quite literally erects its receptors. Studded with tumescences, the homunculus takes out its antennae and deploys them. A template for those masks or models which trace cœnæsthesia, which depict in detail the feeling body, and which we, people of the word, so rarely understand. The topological structure of sensation corresponds, piece for piece and Harlequin's cape for matching tunic, to the rainbow-coloured, blended, striped, ocellated, almost checkerboard space of the sites of our brain. We need no trepan to see this patterned carpet, the world of the senses is enough, along with our variegated skin – or our mouth, erect when faced with a wine fanning out like a peacock's tail. A bird with the same constellation as a brain.

The appearance of the feast at the table of freaks changes according to our sophistication, talents and circumstances. The two preceding tableaux were inventories of the guests' masks and deficiencies: the colour of pieces of nothingness – a mask the colour of invisible, in Couperin's words.[13] Here is a tableau of pieces of being: many-coloured masks or Harlequins.

Now entering and sitting down, getting up and leaving, eating, drinking, screeching and singing: this one here, a chatterbox amidst chatterboxes, a number of hare-like creatures with small eyes and tall ears, useless and pliable, stunned owls with an enormous gaze set in dark-ringed sockets, motionless, studious and stupid, anteaters with long, sticky tongues, a few primates with interminably long arms reaching all the dishes with ease, praying mantises on thin, articulated, almost artificial legs, and the entirety of the shark and tiger families, their terrifying teeth guaranteeing them the tastiest morsel, flanked by pachyderms, slow and cold, with their impregnable hides, scores of defenceless, fleeing rabbits or indestructible rats . . . each of them erects their speciality, whatever it is that defines them as an inferior species, each exhibits its mask of winning colours . . . big eyes gazing down upon immense members, oh Grandma, what big teeth you have . . . Here is spring, here is the feast of metamorphoses, of daily miracles of sensation. Each individual, laughing, surprised and moved, sees new growth appear, reawakens through green grafts, crowned, girt and shod with foliage, floral necklaces sprouting on the skin, bracelets born of velvety touch, a string of petals falling from the mouth, perfumed vine tendrils around the nose, fingers and feet extended by tufts of branches, bushy trunks, fauns, gnomes, tritons, witches, she-devils mounting the first wood they see, all of them, through the din, drinking to the glory of wines born in the glory of autumn.

And what if fairy tales – seven-league boots, beast become beauty, donkey skin, vair slipper, little mermaid with her lower body numb from cold and sheathed in blue-green scales, ogres smelling live flesh – and what if *fêtes galantes*, masked balls, Harlequin theatre, visions and sabbaths were simply brightly coloured representations of the lost, forgotten, disintegrated ruins of the sensible, whose qualities our culture of language and religion of the word will no longer allow us to apprehend?

Saint Anthony, priest of the word, a hermit in the smooth, homogeneous desert under the immutable sun, a space where nothing new can appear beneath the metallic midday brightness, living amidst an infinity of stones, feeding himself on bread and water all day long, drunk on fasting, always chanting his text, his eyes worn out on the Book, his tongue numb from words and hard crusts, suddenly feels his logical anchoritic skin shudder as the multiple traces on him the silent, manifold caresses of its shimmering pattern. The lost paradise, the disparate garden of the senses, with fruits and animals and devils and women, returns to the unitary desert of the word which has never understood or received it, perceiving it rather as a hellish temptation: a banquet resurfacing in the middle of a diet, a feast of phantom sensation amidst the reign of language.

These days saints live and read in cities, surrounded by concrete as far as the eye can see, eating special diets conceived for fragile stomachs and dishes, the taste of which has been removed by the agro-alimentary or pharmaceutical industries, moves about in the unifying light of electricity which prevents even the night from adding something new to the day, breathes only the scent of petrol and kerosene, and most of all knows nothing beyond writing, word-images covering the desert city, walls, screens, billboards, shops, vehicles, even the sky; finally the saint exists in word alone, the word whose existence requires that ascetics know nothing else: logic, media, grammars, announcements, formulae, codes . . . information everywhere you look, cenobites who prove that their grey cities and insipid diets never excite them as much as sentences and syntax do. The victory of reason: the only taste an apricot has is the taste of the word 'apricot' passing over the lips.

Cities are populated by hermits, who have only one tongue.

Which can only speak the sensible monstrously or abnormally or infernally.

The abominable teratology of Saint Anthony's temptations is the product of strange couplings: naked bodies with cauldron bottoms, muzzles grafted onto wings, floral whales: bifurcations of different kingdoms, mingled bodies do not graft well. And yet they can be mixed!

These chimera can be reduced to words, juxtaposed with hyphens: logical fantasies, a digital grammar of senses. Incapable of following the thread, movement, cohesion, continuum, history, graded spectrum, flesh and mixture of the sensible, language uses catch-all terms to describe the exquisite glaze in which it is bathed. There are fifteen monsters contradicting each other on Eve's pink thigh.

Incapable of speaking her, the word damns her instead.

Brueghel, Bosch, Flaubert: banquets translated into language, through words, grammar, erudition and dictionaries, nightmares of damnation, computer-drawn beasts. Just as we hear in symposia these days that p therefore q is a neat substitute for a Château d'Yquem fanning its tail.

No culture ever achieved the degree of asceticism that our so-called consumer society, our banquet, imposes on us today.

Language is threefold dominant: administrations rule through the performative dimension of the word; the media dominate through its seductive dimension; the sciences enjoy mastery through its truth dimension. Trismegistic language produces an abstract dominant class, drunk on codes: legislative, computerized, rigorous, thrice efficient, and in this manner producing a whole world.

Never in the entire course of history have those in power practised austerity to such a degree. Our princes inhabit discourse; of law, illustrative rhetoric, and science. They neither eat nor drink, nor take slow walks nor know anything of the fine arts. But where are the feasts of yesteryear, at the Trianon or Versailles?

Saint Anthony is triumphant, bending subjugated humanity to the word, putting it on a bread and water diet of abstraction, only allowing it access to the given through the three channels of language in the incorporeal desert of administrative, informed, technical cities. He commands, fascinates, speaks true. He is going to reprogramme the world.

Suddenly, we are living in the middle of an enormous, collective Temptation of Saint Anthony. It takes a body and senses to create a culture. Language or artificial intelligence produce a sub-culture, for want of a body. Through this imposed abstraction the sensible returns, a stubborn, infernal shadow, in images and language, but defigured by wasteful contempt. Seated at the banquet, the statues and robots dream of lists and icons. Anchorites exhausted by formal and solitary work, come evening, we seek reclusive sleep; gorged on crimes of red ink, fascinated familiars of those in power, quenched by acrobatic promiscuity, stuffed on junk of disgusting colours, on an entire instantaneous, illusory banquet, passing out at a keystroke. Who described it better, this perpetual, contemptible, imaginary sub-feast, initiated by the pressure of language, than he who signs off with the name we've come to expect: San-Antonio?[14]

In bottles, around the lips, there lies culture. And, absolutely all things considered, knowledge: intelligence and wisdom. *Homo sapiens*: he who knows how to taste. Sagacious: he who knows how to smell. All of these things are vanishing under the weight of logic and grammar, dreary and insane when they deny themselves bodies.

4
Visit

(LOCAL) LANDSCAPE – (GLOBAL) DISPLACEMENT – METHOD AND RAMBLING (THE GLOBAL AND THE LOCAL) – CIRCUMSTANCES – MINGLED PLACE

(LOCAL) LANDSCAPE

And supposing paganism and polytheism assembled a ragged world in the same way the body is constructed, a bit at a time? As if the world did not differ ostensibly from the skin: a tatter-landscape dressing itself piece by piece. Vulgar here, magnificent there. The *pagus*, canton, department, partition of ground or space, is a piece of the country, an element of the countryside: a patch of lucerne, vineyard, plot of land, small meadow, neatish garden and its enclosure, village square, tree-lined walk. Held in tenure by the peasant, the *pagus* – his age-old noble lineage – is where rustic divinities dwell. Gods repose there: in the hollow of the hedge, in the shadow of the elm.

Peasants in their countryside element cohabit with their pagan gods.

The old language has retained memories of the pagan peasant; think of the old *restanques*, terraces that preceded the tangled surroundings; the enclosed fields that preceded urban planning, the checkerboard that you could never have called a panorama: the topology of a map made up of disparate, variously coloured, oddly interlocking slabs, a shabby cape made of vines, meadows, ploughed land, glades, localities, the ruins of polytheism wiped out as soon as the word was born. If you have seen Mother Earth's harlequin costume, you have known Antiquity. It is gradually disappearing, becoming a white, virginal coat again, open fields where monotonous corn, disturbingly, occupies the space as far as the horizon, ugly and greenish. Language and monotheism homogenize the pagan tatter, technology tramples over the altars: the old gods of the byways destroyed, tenure and boundaries abolished. Empiricism respects and nourishes a hundred local divinities, and will even allow the adoration of the word. Monotheism makes global technical intervention possible: to create an isotropic space, it was first of all necessary to kill the idols. Nothing new under the sun across the Mid West. Peasants hounded out, the countryside destroyed.

The body is made up of disparate limbs and organs, a garment is constructed from pieces and seams, should we also believe that the countryside clothes the body of Mother Earth, the demigods of the pagan pantheon pinning jewels here and there for her adornment? Does the peasant veil or violate this body? Stop asking how one sees a landscape. This is the question asked by spoilt children who have never worked. Seek to know rather how the gardener designed it; how the farmer, for thousands of years, has been slowly composing it for the painter who reveals it to the philosopher, in museums or books.

He composed it *pagus* by *pagus*. Now this same Latin word, from the old agrarian language, as well as the verb *pango*, dictate or give us 'page' – the one that I am ploughing with my style in regular furrows this morning, a small plot where the writer's existence settles, puts down its roots and becomes established, where he sings of it. Meadow, hamlet, lucerne, garden or village, the locality where he works, good fortune and habitat; where he has never been able to live without the company of a god. Each page needs at least one god in order to exist, in order to help the person who is slowly creating it to exist: he never leaves a page without having fashioned there the secret sanctuary that he humbly requests the reader or passer-by to acknowledge by stopping for a moment. A god reposes here, hidden and invisible. The page where so much time is concentrated is covered with so much dense writing, with the sole aim of his coming and establishing there his dwelling and hearth. If you make the effort to look, you will find him. Pray to him for an instant, for yourself and for the peasant of the locality.

Like the peasant, the writer composes. Dwells for a considerable time on the page, or patch of land, honours the altar, works at the limits, up to the wall of the enclosed field which separates him from the neighbouring sanctuary, and sometimes meditates on the countryside, seen from a dip in the land: I must plant a poplar, cedar, yew, next year in the upper part of the coomb, between the cemetery and the pond, so that in thirty years' time, there will be an additional note of perfection to enchant the absent-minded passer-by, meditating on perception and nature. An obliquely placed god sometimes brings together in modest harmony twenty separate localities: the circumstantial coat is brought into being.

No countryside, work or history exists without singular accidents or events which spread their influence throughout the canton, an influence that is unexpected for those who come from the locality. The singularity of the accidents or events is difficult to relate to it. It takes work and time to trace the byways separating or linking, stitching together or mingling these neighbouring circumstances. Time flows on these roads. Let us say that circumstance is a state, or rather, a local equilibrium surrounded by an irregular or capricious zone of influence, a star with asymmetrical festoons or deviations, a spiny ball unnecessary in every respect. All over the surface of the circumstantial ball, others crowd, tangential and literally contingent: the latter word signifies that they touch each other individually, and as a whole, without any constraining law. Countryside, work of art and history partially integrate these contingent circumstances, creating a picture, park or garden, excerpt, period or interval. Global integration, a straight road going through the forest, calls for method or science.

A hamlet, houses clustered around the belltower, and a cemetery; a valley descending in a long line emphasized by hedges on the sides of the coomb; a lake crowned with concentric ridges; a wind-swept plateau going who knows where . . . a picture. The traveller describes in detail his breath-taking discoveries, rambles along country roads, quotes contingencies and percolates like time. The sailor is lost in the Bay of Kekova with its multiple inlets, rocky promontories, small islands, straits, outlets and narrow beaches, strange branchings, harbour basins and walls; all he sees of the bay are scenes, he can only comprehend it in its totality at the table of the watch and dreams of a great work, each book of which would describe or illustrate a total, beautiful and sufficient perspective of the bay, opening up and hiding the neighbouring vista, showing and covering its global geometry, longed for as a divine surprise or rejected as too great a task. But the constant level of the water condemns the sailor to rely on abstract thought or the stars, in order to see. He proceeds horizontally. The time of this great work, both unexpected and expected, percolates along the whole length of the navigation route or ramble, as it could be called, up and down, adventurous, but a knot in the volume of space, with repetitions, rediscoveries, novelties, and sudden grandiose visions.

What world is created by the rag stitched patiently from thousands of already ploughed pages and by the thousands we hope are ahead of us, what country is embellished by them, what land do they map, what body do they dress? The variegated, striped skin of the writer, banded with lines and letters, pieces of body, flakes of skin, fields from the countryside, pages of another desired earth, paradise.

How is this map to be stuck on to the countryside, to the ground of moving flesh, to erectile spring growth, in celebration of sensation, for it is thus that each page is erected. A work of art is dead without this conjunction, sterile without this bracketing together. Pages do not sleep in language, they draw their life from the *pagi*: from the countryside, the flesh and the world. When you meet the Harlequin costume of Mother Work, you know Antiquity: the stubborn return of paganism, of solitary peasant work constrained by its own contingencies, of the local countryside, patiently modelled – the attention to lawless neighbourhoods, reality which shines and overwhelms us at every stage of its germination, cries of life.

Creativity is as old as the landscape, lost Antiquity and the senses. Redeemed all at once and integrated through the word.

Do not seek to know how to look at a landscape – compose a garden instead. Learn the æsthetic error of submitting everything to a law: levelling the local event produces boredom and ugliness, a world without landscapes, books without pages, deserts. Take everything away and you will not see. To see space demands time, do not kill time. Avoid the symmetrical error of being satisfied with fragments. A lack of story is as tedious as a singular law, and produces even greater ugliness. Composition requires a tension between the local and the global, the nearby and the far-off, the story and the rule, the uniqueness of the word and the unanalysable pluralism of the senses, monotheism and paganism, the international expressway and remote villages, science and literature. Hold the bridle of the galloping horse firmly, keep a tight rein to prevent his shying, expect a long and steep path. Watch closely, anticipate. Philosophy sometimes requires syntheses. Go visiting.

Suddenly, at the same time, you see both miniature and panorama.

Can the page-units be fixed in time and place?

Take, for instance, the photograph of a beauty: in times gone by we would have called it her portrait, and more recently, her representation: full-length, naked, outlined, in various scalar dimensions . When enlarged to reveal the detail – the grain of the skin, the molecules of the grain, the atoms of the molecule – the beauty becomes an abstraction. Thus did Gulliver, in the course of his journeys into just such a representation, come unexpectedly upon the breast of the giant wet-nurse. Conversely, to carry this beauty easily with you on a journey, you can have her portrait miniaturized, making it smaller and smaller and scaling it down to the point where thousands of beauties can be fitted into a cherry pip. Thus did Gulliver see the Lilliputians, swarming around his stomach-mountain as clusters of angels or lilac, thus does the painter depict a crowd in miniature framed by a window behind two giant faces in prayer.[1] Thus are we able to manufacture electronic chips. Miniature beauties are to be found everywhere.

THE FIVE SENSES

Imagine stacking the representations on top of each other, enlargements on top of miniatures, larger and smaller than the average-sized original scaled portrait; the pile can reach to the moon or even to infinity since there are no limits to size in either direction, except practical ones. This scene displays a sort of prism or astronomically long cylinder, or immensely wide cone or pyramid. The card or photograph right in the middle reveals the full-length portrait of the young lady, the zone above increasingly refined close-ups; the zone below, increasingly distant bird's eye views, leaving room for a growing crowd of beauties.

Imagine pathways going from one portrait to another within the pile, a set of transversal paths in the cone or prism, linking together the various dimensions of a particular place. Each set of tracks, the volume it defines and carves out in this infinite prism or cone, enters dimensions other than those of ordinary space. Dimension must be first of all understood in the sense of size, and then in the sense of a topological invariant defining a space in two or three dimensions, or in a fractional dimension. As a result, our vision is immediately transformed and turned upside down. The beauty lies next to her component parts: tissue, cells, large molecules, or otherwise in the middle of her tiny twin or cloned sisters. In the midst of her elemental composition and her possible reproductions.

Thus the mountain reposes amongst its rocks, the latter amidst their pebbles, the pebbles among molecules or debris, everything producing a vast mixture; the ocean sparkles inside and outside its seas, outside and inside its straits and breezes; the forest slumbers amidst its glades, the plain is next to the clearing; the variably sized *pagus* is composed into others, in spaces with different dimensions. This is what the countryside is, the moving totality of its real fragments, paved with hybrid pages. If you want to *see* this, draw one or more paths *across* its possible representations.

A great work, like a park, is composed of atoms and oceans, drops of water and mountains. The sailor observes the stars and dreams of the shore but he negotiates the wave that strikes the prow of the vessel, makes it disappear beneath the plumes of spray.

Wide pages and tenuous differentials.

Here. The countryside assembles places. A locality is drawn as a singular point surrounded by a neighbourhood: springs or wells, jagged capes jutting out from the shore, islands, a small lake, long braids of streams, narrow necks at the top of a mountain pass, the bank of the river eroding the foot of a hill, clearings, fords, harbours, topographical events, obstacles, limits or catastrophes; someone chooses to live near the singularity already there and endows it with his own. Who has not dreamt of stopping here, in the middle of a circus of arid mountains, in blazing sunlight, of pitching a tent and waiting for death? A habitat or niche, a place for the bed or table, around which footprints trace the countless festoons and garlands of everyday life. Here someone lives, eats, sleeps, keeps to his daily routines, loves, works, suffers and dies. The passerby knowing immediately that he is transiting through a place, stops on the site or in front of the stone identifying it: here lies the unknown person who made marks on the countryside and whose tombstone perpetuates his occupation of it. He has saturated this singular point with his smell, his rubbish, his excrement, his work, his tastes and colours, his corn and vine, buildings, descendants, then finally litters it with the ashes of his corpse, the engraved marble of his tomb. The passerby bows his head, visits the god of the place. Where are you going? To this place. Where do you come from? From my site. Which way are you going? On past here. To reply to each question you would have to tell an infinitely detailed story which would not fill the space, occupied by the tutelary deity of this place, its tones and balms, its tact and silence, its remaining traces that have no name in any language.

The outline of a garden miniaturizes the countryside, assembles places, sites, rooms or squares, composes the heres and nows. A mark facilitates the task of recognition: statuary indicates the singularity of the site. Whether island or cape, pass or lake, the braid of a river alongside a hill, sculpture can take over and assume the position of the local goddess, replacing the tombstone under which lies the founder, mythical or otherwise, of this niche, of this page of countryside.

If you are at all capable of writing you can design a garden.

The path passes through the countryside, strides over obstacles, catastrophes or limits. Pushes the gods of place aside, goes straight ahead. Overcomes obstructions.

Where are you running? Down there, where it is said that milk and honey flow. Where are you coming from? I have lost the original paradise, where the father lies beneath the earth, the road forks there, coming from further away. Which way are you going, where do you not stop? How can you know without signposting and, since the path is straight, without knowing how long it is? Here is the bust of Hermes, the term, the milestone. The walking or goat tracks in the mountains are dotted with cairns, hillocks, pyramids, tumuli . . . What vestal virgin or other victim lies underneath these stones?

Here are the places in the countryside, tombstones mark them.

Here are the sites of the garden, statues indicate them.

Here on the winding road are cairns or tumuli.

Here on the straight path are terms or milestones and busts of Hermes.

Points of accumulation endowed with neighbourhoods or metric reference points, or at the very least identifying stones for a well-established here and now.

Here: the singularity of the world where an individual persists in his tomb. Keep in mind here that the first theorem of measurement came into being in the shadow of the Egyptian pyramidal tomb, at the time of Thales. It is not known whether he compared the shadow of the tomb with his own: to do that he would have had to remain motionless like a statue, in the midday sun.

Can one see a totality-page?

Antique and pagan, the countryside precedes the new architectural language. The landscape artist stitches, juxtaposes, assembles and tries things out. The architect imagines a unitary synthesis: the rooms follow logically from the whole structure whereas gardens are induced from the page. A wall is the sum of stones, and the building is the mason's Euclidian summation of its rooms, in three dimensions; whereas the tree goes from trunk to branches and radicles, ramifies from large to small and bushes out, fractally: and supposing every species of flora grew in its own dimension? This would certainly be in defiance of simple structures. Landscape artists have to deal with individuals and time, the architect rarely pays attention to localities, failing to give the variable *pagus* – pebble, dust or hill – its due. His global space slides into the same dimension as the localized rooms. Le Nôtre and Mansart do not inhabit the same space and do not conceive of the same big picture. And the time of conservation or of degradation has a different rhythm from that of life.

Although a creature of language, the writer does not easily free himself from paganism, subjugated as he is by the same local page and by the infinitesimal miniature of fragile intuition borne by mute sonority, an immense breath that inhabits him. The gardener, like him, sets out gods and statues, altars in each ocellus of the park, raises peacocks and cultivates orange trees, a bejewelled coat, luminous pupils. Two varieties of pagan peasant. The one God was never invoked as a fashioner of landscapes, but often evoked as the architect of the universe. The creator, like a master stonemason, creates a totality. The global design and conception is his alone, he plans and divides.

The gardener lets the multiple eyes of the countryside control his world. The multiplicity of what is seen itself has eyes.

Think of the immense amount of work done by the writer prophets of Israel to construct the Bible, a unique book, binding their pages into monotheism, struggling against an idolatrous people who would scatter them in all directions, making them into a landscape, lost garden or paradise, a land flowing with milk and honey, a promised land, and who, out of dread of the desert, abandon themselves to the world. The declaiming prophet and the chosen people pass for all eternity through the empty white plain between two landscapes, the age-old garden and the garden of hope, their life, that of the austere word that regrets or promises.

Think of the infinite work done by science to found a unitary system across the chaos of its pages, as numerous as grains of sand. Knowledge beats to a systolic, then diastolic rhythm, hesitates, balanced in time, passing from one phase to the other, between the hope of a universe and the irreducible pluralism of a world, between a systematic whole and the irrepressible growth of difference. As though it could not bring itself to leave the earth or garden, with its thousand species, for the lure of a desert.

Think of the impossible work done by the philosopher – caught in architectural, logical, desert systems – in resuscitating the body of the countryside and the countryside of the body vitrified beneath language, so as to create a world from the explosion of fragments. Happiness requires the landscape to hold its own beneath the pale ochre of the desert, as the body holds out against the machine, or the young girl against the greybeard; stubborn grass grows under the cracks in the expressway, myriad angels flinch at times under the domination of the architect God of the universe but drown him in the garden of their eye-spangled wings; the pleasures of the multi-coloured banquet hold their own against the grey cameo of the abstract word. Empiricism carries the unforgettable memory of gardens. Where God himself moves freely amongst the species.

The architect inhabits synthesis; the philosopher seeks it even when he postpones it for a long time, passing lingeringly through empiricism and science to delay it even further, and keeping closer to the landscape artist in order to learn from him, to invent, practise, project with him a concept more elastic than totality, less complete than synthesis, more fluid than addition, looser than integration, more alive than the system, more changing than the concept itself . . . the edifice makes a totality, like the concept, word, scientific law; the countryside assembles: sketch or pattern, for local gods are strongly resistant to federative efforts; sets, groupings, collections, regroupings, bundles, re-memberings remaining more apposite names for a process that commemorates Eurydice's body and the interminable time necessary to emerge from the infernal shadows. The fields depict limbs that stitch and tie themselves together, confluences that flow into each other like the tributaries of a stream. Fluid slip-knots like those of a loose shawl which takes on the movement of the body and gives it a subtle, ethereal grace: the dynamic, instantaneous unity that we call elegance.

When the sciences of life talk of systems, they borrow their terms from other fields of knowledge – music, mechanics or astronomy – which have never understood time, whereas they have before them a countryside to re-member, pieces stuck together with crossed strips of sticking plaster, knots in a shawl. They should seek, as we do here, subtotals, dynamic confluences. But they imagine a soft object in hard terms. The architect conceptualizes hardness, the landscape artist re-members the softness of living matter.

The landscape expresses the page of pages quite precisely, by doubling or exponentially increasing the *pagi*. A book can be shut, completed, a labyrinth, well or prison; the landscape page of pages, always open, displayed, free, readable, stretched out, unfolded, uncovered, manifest and obvious, never hides one page with another. This fragile book is the one we should pursue. The earth's adornment does not lie.

Pango, I write on the page, *pango*, I sing, the hymn begins with a pagan confession, *pange, lingua, gloriosi corporis mysterium*, sing, o tongue, the mystery of the glorious body, *sanguinisque preciosi*, and of the precious blood, a dead body and blood shed for the redemption of the world, *in mundi pretium*. The medieval hymn puts *pange* at the very top of the page, thus putting paganism before language, before the word, its sovereign. The word gives its body and blood as payment for the world; language buys the world for the price of body and blood.

Nobis datus, nobis natus: the world no longer gives us the given, we receive the word as given, language gives it to us, *sparso verbi semine*, it sows its seed in the world. The flesh is made word, the word is made flesh.

Suddenly the word has redeemed the pitiful dismembering of ground, world and body, tendering for every page. You will no longer find the tiniest corner, stray bush, stone, insect or marshland not covered by its categories. The word has recovered every page, whatever its size, from the largest to the smallest, from the most to the least complete. The countryside recedes to a place before language and its glory: *pange, lingua, gloriosi . . .*

Paganism is reduced to an old map, *antiquum documentum*, an ancient document; an illegible, unwritten scrawl; an archaic lesson, example, instruction, education in ruins; transmitted imperfectly, or not at all, through lack of written or spoken language: an aptly prehistoric document leaving room for the new rite. Language is novelty, this instruction dates from Antiquity.

The present volume reveals that antique document, page by page, seeking out its ancient lesson beneath all the so-called new archives of the word. The senses, caught out, are defective, *sensuum defectui*. The tongue sings of the senses in order to enunciate their mistakes. They are in error, not only in relation to the word, but in particular in relation to the body of the word, its flesh and blood. Language finds the senses defective in the body itself. The ancient document falls apart. And philosophy, when it seeks to teach or educate, begins its first lesson by catching the senses red-handed at the very places in which they are making mistakes.

Faith in the word papers over the gaps, makes up for the failings. The word re-members them again, since it is body and blood.

The victory of language over an empiricism which is always in ruins retells the story of new rites which are in a way quite old . . .

O for the time when the ear could hear and the eye could see that the worshipper in his temple, the ploughman toiling on his clay soil, the writer on his page, were working in the same places.

This place dates from such a remote time that even in Antiquity it was called ancient.

The only news we ever announce is news of the word: Advent, coming, baptism, Epiphany, parables, Passion and Resurrection. We have shaped our culture so that it will resound at the birth or rebirths of a language, in whichever language they take place: Greek, Hebrew, Latin, Romance and then Anglo-Saxon languages. Each takes over from the preceding one and resounds again, convinced that it has invented the world. Every tongue believes itself to be the fulfilment of language just as every ethnic group at some moment in history is certain that it is the fullest expression of humanity.

Each tongue celebrates the birth of language in the idiom of its background world. It announces the logos, like a mathematician or metaphysician, voice, law and relationship dictated accordingly in a space drawn, ruled, calculated, measured, known and embellished by that world . . . It speaks the *ruagh,* spirit, wind, breath, voice moving over the waters before the first day of Genesis, the preliminary to creation. It affirms that in the beginning was the word . . . It describes language positively, logically, empirically, or scientifically using algorithms, equations, codes, formulae – in any case it excludes from philosophy everything not related to language . . . The same good news still thrills us, the logos orders and circumscribes, the breath hovers over the primordial waters, the word arrives to redeem and renew, language replaces the given. Pre-Socratic sayings, prophets, priests, scholars, recent philosophers all fall into line behind the same announcement, depending on the mode in which they function (religious, metaphysical, ontological, positive-historical, logical, formal and even mechanistic), they never tire of announcing that they are writing or speaking, that the kingdom of language is at last amongst us. Our Western culture reiterates this fact, is shaped by it, entering into resonance or harmonics with it alone, and dwelling in it. Today we take an active interest in this constant law because today we are beginning to lose it. We are witnessing the last reverberation of the centuries-old shock which caused us to be born at the same time as language: we are witnessing it in its death-throes. Our culture, born of language, modelled by it, vibrant in it and with it, could only rejoice in this ground-breaking emergence and still proclaims the good news in every language: mythic or pious, abstract or scholarly. We could not get over it, we are beginning to emerge from it this morning.

Beneath this ongoing newness that sums up and is celebrated by our culture, Antiquity shows its face. True, not the Antiquity recounted in history books, immersed as they are in the novelty of the word, whatever period or interval they report, but that of the body and countryside, pages composed of dead ocelli and seen by blinded eyes. Great antiquity, engulfed and flooded by the word, lies underneath its clear, transparent covering. Can one uncover a single site beneath this occupation, any dis-occupied flesh? Was there a countryside before the circular rite of newness, before the great liturgical cycle of philosophy, which comes and goes leaving nothing but advents?

Cultivated land displays high or secret places, immediately visible as stations. Equilibrium reigns here. Let us stop, pitch our tent, build walls, wait peacefully for the fatal hour, obviously less harsh in this setting. This is the place to posit my thesis, the Greek word for what Latin calls a statue. In this place a window appears to open, from which light falls, spreading tranquillity. At such stopping points, the countryside creates pathways, dotted with cradles, halts, long pauses, tombs or ports, studded with stone altars. Around these navels or buds, folds or singularities, the habitable locality projects arms, rays or tracks for irrigation, thus festooning the site with local tracks, with pathways sprouting from it and leading back to it, a constellation of senses, a small interchanger. To define place, one usually speaks of its borders, but in fact place is organized like a tied or untied knot, like a star or a living body. As animals that live in houses, we do not position or build them just anywhere, but only here, in these surroundings where the gods sleep and from where they shine, hospitably, from one place to the next, forbidding and incomparable, although close by. Our peculiar body, supplied with a capricious locality that defends and feeds us, like a porous breast-plate that can also stifle us, adapts willingly or blissfully to a local *here*, similar to this. Place, house and body form analogous nuclei and pseudopods – the existence and ascendancy of the local divinity, a home similar to an animal's kennel. And the country-side re-members or consolidates sites into their surroundings, defended or heralded by a voice like a nightingale's nocturnal song. Language, like a chorus of cries, rises from the mottled countryside roughly outlining these places with their irregularly-shaped localities, varying sometimes in width according to the carrying power of the vocal organ. Brilliance, clouds of odours, sound, or a crown of thorns radiate from the individual points. The five senses compete at the contours of the habitat, locality and body itself. Similarly, the latter stinks, cries, scratches and shines in order to define itself, or, welcoming, it caresses, smells good, delights and illuminates. Likewise the body of Mother Earth flashes, sparkles, glistens and dazzles. Consolidated into landscapes, seeds, navels, sites and neighbourhoods, she took shape gradually after emerging from underground Hells, in the geological period when pangea had no eye to see her, her body emerging from the waters, wrinkled, jostled, smashed, raised, covered, eroded, a prey to ice and the depredations of the sea, overrun by changing and adaptable flora, unrecognizable in her new clothes, soon to be over-run by living, seeing beings. The great antiquity of the pagan countryside, shaped countless times by inert forces, cultivated since time immemorial by her peasants, watches us watching her in formidable silence.

The countryside concludes our variations on the theme of variety: thick or thin, light or heavy, inert, living, sensitive, social, touching at the shared or separate edges of air or underground, neighbouring zones made up of collectives or of comfortable individuals, whether remote or in the vicinity, a manifoldly contingent variety in this sense, the countryside keeps numerous astronomical, physical, natural history and human constraints in equilibrium, balancing each sub-total at its origin, in an extraordinarily individual picture, from which in turn byways radiate. We inhabit an interesting place in this variety, an uneven layer that takes a long time to form, that is easily torn and nearly always tattered: a countryside almost as rare as a totally constructed body. We often sleep in its lacks or absences.

The countryside begins when each exact or human science falls silent.

The fractal face of the earth reveals itself as fragile, often ravaged. The earth turns its ravaged visage towards the sky; all manner of populations, armies, industry, tourism and invasions, have changed it into a valley of tears. Pillaged by those who pass but do not stay, its ruins are all we see. All we have before us are the remnants of a waste land, we live amongst memories.

Like the body, the skin, the senses or empiricism, the landscape is clothed in a patchwork of tatters. As frail as paradise itself, lost as often and for as long, it is found or revealed in fragments. Bits from the here and now, the detritus of places. Paradise becomes green like a landscaped garden.

In a certain dead language so closely related that it is still alive in ours, devastation and ravage are expressed by the word population. What earth are we soon going to see as a result of the immense growth of populations? The populating of the countryside is a delicate enterprise. What havoc is in store for us from methods that bulldoze their way through, without heeding places, or localities or elegantly knotted pathways now made straight?

Pity the frail earth, torn, or covered in violent remains and unspeakable garbage.

The word discovery is used in mining terminology to describe the pushing back and then removal of the plant or animal humus, the sand and rocks, the more or less thick coat that lies on top of the sand, stone, metal, diamond or ore to be exploited.

Nothing seems more humble than the earth; when language wanted to express humility it chose humus, compost, the face of the landscape that we never see when we pass by or remain there, occupied as we are with our passions and business. Grass, hedges, forest and flowers hide the earth's face from the most perceptive, and they who pay attention to deep things remove it to reach the copper or gold. It goes to ground under floral phenomena, it melts into language, underlying reality eliminates it. Our greatest philosophies do not pay humility its due.

It is rediscovered by the attention and also the nostalgia inspired by blind lives which skim over the world, our only possession: just as when flying over Siberia on a clear night we see no lights. Lucidity comes, nonetheless, as if a door were suddenly opening, as though rebirth were channelled by humility.

. . . In Brazil, on the heights of Congonhas; in Turkey, in the ruins of Pinara; and in the middle of the Entre-deux-Mers region . . .

The vineyard was bathed in the first light of September, the glory of August was coming to an end. We enter the gentle hills as if into another world; an intense silence reigns; sounds carry in the still, clear air. Hard scales fall from our eyes; the earth in all its density rises up, everything goes upwards towards the sun which floods everything with tranquillity. We are seeing blue and green, a grape-vine, for the first time, the visible is embodied there, peaceful and serene, tangible and tacit, spiritual and perfumed. The paths running along the rows go nowhere, they are a part of the garden, like garlands. Without shadows, the brown earth, warm vine-stocks, black, sweet-smelling grapes, low sheds, local stones, odd trees, all the small, particular, familiar or unrecognizable details rise gently with us, towards the sky, as on the day before our baptism.

The levitating countryside, our nascent bodies, discover each other in that place; the joint creation of visionary and winemaker who for a thousand years have been preparing what we see here, a paradise between two rivers.

In front of the window the sun twinkles with a hundred sparkling stars through the moving branches of the wind-tossed apple tree – blond, tawny, copper, golden, straw-yellow, orange, ochre, sand or tan, multi-plying the straight, centred, short rays, piercing and sharp like the trill of a bird; the Indian summer has erased the palette of greens: no more lime, almond, emerald, celadon, apple, bottle, olive, those restful shades of the hot August summer; the foliage of the maples is blotched with madder, carmine, cinnabar, coral, scarlet and poppy, brick and dark-red, tangerine, maroon, crimson, blood and ruby; this weathering, with its wealth of reds, garnets, purples and vermilions, glazes the world in a rosy hue beneath the supernaturally blue sky in which the dry wind whistles like a blade, making the branches twist in the solar light that they diffuse in dancing fragments, a bath of intoxicating violence; are there any ideas or words to describe this moment of bedazzlement?

Brutally reduced to primary colours – the yellow dwarf of the sun, the blazing trees, the perfect blue sky – space sinks into oppressively funda-mental beauty, as in Greece or Provence. Deprived of all its subtlety, the body, blinded, flees towards the abstract, in painting or in geometry. It invents black and white graphics, colourless and formless concepts, con-sciousness or demonstration, it escapes into inner worlds.

THE FIVE SENSES

A child of the South, although carrying the abstract baggage of my distant youth, I have learned to prefer Flanders or the north of France, the mysteries of misty seas, places where light disappears beneath low-lying vapours and absent stars; a grey, hazy plain, the black texture of sparse tree-trunks, where a sudden ray of light, as though trapped, lights up an odd area, works its enchantment on some specific place, a clearing or kitchen, not merely defining it, but rather by suspending objects in a bath of delicate brilliance: an evanescent pinkish-grey pearl or chaste emerald, cushioned on velvet, cherries and melons mounted like beryls or jade on platters of soft silver, lengths of dress material with colours melting into the fabric, so-called still lifes on the verge of movement, portraits in which the eyes are turned away, the spectator being subjected to the lucidity of a jewelled eye, tones broken up into tiny ocelli, azure, lavender, indigo, blue, turquoise, periwinkle, forget-me-not, navy-blue, ultramarine. Few languages have an equivalent word for *vergogne*, a form of modesty, it takes Aquitanian tenderness and shades of reticence to coax things into existence.

Twenty years ago deep sea fishermen were required to present for inspection a complete set of sea charts and their navigation instruments in good working order. Does this requirement, a matter of insurance and safety, still exist? Or is it accompanied now by a multitude of irritating procedures, administrative parasitism having spread like the plague?

One day back then, the equipment seemed to the inspector to be in too good a state of repair. The unmarked, new, white charts were superbly arranged in a large, painted chest of drawers the key of which, at first difficult to find, was then hard to turn because of excessive rust. The required technique had disappeared beneath the paint. It all seemed a bit artificial. The whole company had gotten ready for the fray and responded to the caprices of the law, rather as one runs a standard up the masthead, so that it will be seen. That is the flag's only purpose.

'You never use these things!' exclaimed the inspector in a surly tone. The mariner was crestfallen, he shuffled nervously. The inspector chose to smile, he wanted to know and he promised not to report him. So how do you go about finding Murmansk or Newfoundland in both cod-fishing seasons? The answer took some time; they had to sit down, uncork an aged bottle, arrange the glasses, chat for a long time about their children. Vessels of the high seas do not surrender immediately. There must always be conversation before the speaking begins. So, how do you get there?

You have to imagine the countryside without signposts. What peasant would lose his way when going to a neighbouring farm? He turns left at the end of the evergreen shrubbery, goes straight to the walnut tree, then down along the stone wall, and from there he glimpses the neighbour's red roof, at the bottom of the valley behind the cedars. You don't ask those questions. You learn the answers at the same time as you learn to walk, speak or see.

That is how one used to go to Saint-Pierre: sail towards the setting sun until you see a particular kind of seaweed, veer slightly left, when the sea becomes an intense blue; you cannot mistake it, the preferred haunts of porpoises are there, there are other spots where a strong, constant current carries you north, others still where the dominant wind blows in low, small gusts and where there is always a low swell; then comes the immense, grey expanse, and after that you cross the route that the large packets follow, and after you've seen them, that's where the first bank is, leeward. Sometimes furrowed by the white choppiness of the river.

The captain went on and on, he would have kept on talking, revealing everything, until nightfall. And what he was describing, what he had seen from the time of his adolescence, the changes he had observed during his travels, he had never really been told by anyone, since his two successive masters would not utter a word all day long, but would point out on occasion, when they were changing direction or speed, all the things that he was blurting out now, at the table with its rum-stained lace tablecloth: the watered-silk surface of the sea, this complex surface as differentiated as our age-old landscapes, with their squares of lucerne, their glades, marshlands, rows of vines beneath pear trees. He described everything in precise detail – the colours, fish, wind, sky, the constant surge of the sea – exactly recreating this ancient document, an encyclopædia, sunken like the great cathedral. That day, a body of knowledge died, empiricism gave up the ghost. Let us listen now to its sound rising above the waters.

Where the old scholar could only see monotony, the master obviously saw a streaked, colour-blended, tiger or zebra-striped, marled, precisely differentiated body, a surface on which he identified local regions, where the boat's position, at every moment and even in a fog, had already been plotted; where the old scholar only saw instability, the master perceived a space which changed little.

But why was one body of knowledge inspecting and monitoring the other that day. Did it have the power to administer sanctions, to command obedience? In the oldest dialogue in modern philosophy, that of reason and the senses – no matter what it is called – reason inspects the oldest knowledge in the world and torpedoes it. The day of these last confessions heralded the ethnology of the conquered. Now it is of no more use, except as the subject of a popular novel or of a fashionable university humanities course, where one goes to learn about the vernacular of savages.

We learn from earliest childhood that science can make the invisible visible. And, in fact, the sea chart does indicate depths, the distance of a rock hidden by fog. The instruments inspected by the official are even more effective, they give warning of the coast, map the bottom of the sea and, if required, calculate a location automatically. We all bow to such efficiency, but we are obliged to bow to the inspector also. Why is reason alone not enough, why does it choose to impose itself through force? Conversely, and more importantly, how does it make the visible invisible? This watered-silk body, as stable and changeable as a mountain meadow in springtime, this recognizable and mingled space, disappears. Yes, the surface of oceans and their landscapes are swallowed up and disappear.

We learn from earliest childhood that the senses deceive us. No-one says whose senses. The inspector sees nothing on the high meadows where the frigates graze, reason perceives only monotony on the surface of the sea, the master, on the other hand, sees clearly, precisely and in detail. The senses rarely deceive when they are used, reason is often wrong when it has not been trained. These principles, the same in both cases, must judge in the same way everywhere.

The senses do not deceive. The palate of the discriminating taster makes more precise judgements than a thousand machines, the most sophisticated machine is made from the flesh of a living being, the only failing of artificial intelligence is its lack of a body; a given organ, insect or snake perceives mixtures at the molecular level. We only ever judge empiricism scientifically; now, suppose we began to judge rationalism empirically? Descartes' methodical doubt is not reducible to a schoolchild's exercise, nor to solitary ascesis. Once again, force was intimately involved in that immense historical turning-point. The visible disappeared, faded into the invisible. Qualities were despised. Another invisible swam into view. No-one saw the watered silk of the sea any more, everyone looked for the distant and the deep and made them into objects of the senses. We might say that what was immediate and close by was erased. And the cod fisherman had nothing to say. The sea became a blank page.

Thus the makers of maps could say that they had discovered America, convince others and take credit for it, when countless fishermen, following the paths traced across the watered silk, had already reached it without proclaiming it loudly as historical fact. The triumph of the written word resulted in a catastrophe of perception. The age of science created new iconoclasts, this time of the senses, and totally destroyed a prodigious body of knowledge in the realm of the perceived. All we have preserved are ruins, remains, fossils.

Our reasoning and sciences have become sufficiently refined for us to understand at last the extent to which the senses are capable of subtle kinds of knowledge. After centuries of simple maps, those of the inspector; or violent maps that wipe out the fisherman's differential perceptions, substituting for them a blank sheet of paper covered in sporadic figures. Let us draw the immediate map of those senses that have been called the practices of place, let us map the surface scenography of the seas: blended colours, striped, marled, damask.

I had never seen the sea before that night in La Rochelle, when, after spending hours listening to the old cod fisherman, we left the smoky saloon untidy, and the lace tablecloth spangled with ashes, stains and splashes.

My region remained until quite recently tightly planted with vines in rows, nonetheless far enough apart for corn or wheat to be planted between them, depending on the years. Alongside the vines, alternating fruit trees – plums mostly, yellow or white peaches and cherries, in counterpoint to the rows of grape vines. The wine sometimes retained the flavour of the two different peaches or the smell of the cherries, the cattle found shade in which to protect themselves from work and flies, the herdsman would already be sleeping there, stretched out with his hat over his face and his legs crossed. I don't know whose invisible hand tore up the immense garden thirty or forty years ago; now children do not know how the plain of the Garonne was a patchwork of squares. It looked like a complex, variegated carpet; now the corn, its hundreds of hectares watered by revolving water jets, makes it look as though it is imitating the American Mid West. A hundred peasants used to live where now only the odd driver passes, sitting astride his hundred-horsepower engine, a primary producer, as he is called in the papers, preferably of one thing only and only ever unprocessed at that. Between monoculture and economics on the one hand and the two last wars on the other, peasants have been eliminated and the countryside wiped out.

They have been subject to the same attacks and assaults as our towns and language. Like Haussmann, urban planners have created straight boulevards by destroying, not far from the Seine, dozens of Gothic chapels and Renaissance mansions: troops charge unhindered and cannon fire is more effective. Linnaeus uses one Greek or Latin word to express three hundred vernacular names for a plant or animal. Vernacular: a scientific term to designate the people, declared thus to be uneducated; note here the word *verna*, a slave born at home, ignorant, vulgar, speaking the local farm dialect poorly. When a scientific term becomes fashionable or commonly used, who counts the words, patiently developed by the people over time, that it destroys as it replaces them on the page? An avenue of meaning covering the countryside in a straight line. We never say of a countryside that it has had a change of scenery or lost its bearings: yet it could be said about nearly the whole earth. How can we likewise describe our languages and towns?

A complex tangle of dark, twisting streets; languages, names changing from one village to the next, a multi-coloured atlas; vines in rows with changing notes of fruit trees, forming a spectrum or musical score: the age-old obstructions of empiricism, cleverly opposing the global abstract, posing local circumstances.

In this green desert the driver, alone in a monoculture, has only one job and one idea.

They began with the most difficult, subtle and fragile things: with patently non-linear problems – those with a thousand limitations and a hundred unknowns. Ten varieties of fruit, vegetables and animals, a grape vine and a trellis with white grapes, geese and their livers, a squawking guinea fowl sleeping amid branches, techniques born of the inert (ground and weather), the living (flora and fauna), the social (work, family, with its festivals and rituals, and in addition hunting, love, mushrooms) – a hundred occupations, a thousand ideas, twenty gods, as well as awkward gaps in knowledge, pain, stupidity: a mixed, multi-coloured, bedizened world, in the mind as well as on earth; a culture amazingly like that of the *Essais:* the random, felicitous juxtaposition of large or small fields, like the chapters where Montaigne speaks of Hesiod or quince trees, Virgil or hazel trees; odd, artistic proximities which inject a bitter, dry, astringent note into boringly smooth monotony. The intellect is in its element when detecting variety. Let us cultivate the varied so that the intellect remains alive and active. Everything flashes and changes beneath a cloud-covered sun in the voluble April sky; God disappears somewhat behind all those saints and angels. Polyculture, polytheism.

Monoculture. Nothing new under the solitary sun. Never-ending, homogeneous rows prevent or efface the watered-silk effect; the isotrope excludes the unexpected; agronomy replaces agriculture; a small number of laws replace tiny, incremental, pointillist permutations. In the place of culture, chemistry, administration, profit and writing hold sway. A rational or abstract panorama expels the combinatory spectra of a thousand landscapes.

Beneath our gaze two visions of reason or intelligence put on their performance.

Non-linear difficulties subject to a thousand constraints soon collapse in the face of the long, simple, easy chains of wheat and maize. The single takes the place of the multiple. And pure disorder, faced with the order of homogeneity, drives out refined mixtures. By this chaos I mean the industrial solution, that of movement or heat. What engines require of molecular disorder is that the bird's-eye view of the world be one of singular order. Here we have two kinds of facility: the fragile lace maintained at the cost of great discernment and many men, moves left to right, from the varied to the unitary, and from front to back, from the variable to the disordered. Twice over it goes from one extreme to the other. The difficult, mixed landscape lies between these limits.

Are we now reaching a third era when we will dine at the marriage of the global and the local, without ejecting from the nuptial feast those who were once despised, according to the norms of the day, as being empirical or abstract? We are contemplating specifically the segment going from chaos to unitary or monochrome order and passing through an infinite number of intermediary multiplicities. Why would we consider boundaries separately from what they encompass? We have forged the intellectual and practical means to choose with ease the appropriate solution, the place in the segment adapted to our constraints and needs. Sometimes we use a combinatory spectrum and sometimes a universal one, we prefer to travel on the abstract expressway, the global boulevard and the formal concept, along the homogeneous rows of maize whizzing by, but we also like to dawdle along twisting back roads, to lose ourselves in the countryside, in order to understand and to know. Why not become rational and intelligent, knowledgeable and cultured, variable and wise, all at the same time? In many cases peace is only achieved by the one God, in just as many cases angels are better. One-track reason has its place in the countryside; irony of ironies, non-linear thought tolerates linear thought as an individual case.

(GLOBAL) DISPLACEMENT

Who am I when the aeroplane descends slowly into a voluble landscape of turbulent clouds or a deadening mist, a tropical cyclone, or a blizzard where the snow scuds along the ground, or into the middle of a dry furnace, when an indifferent, disembodied voice announces Atlanta, Christchurch, Shanghai, Copenhagen or Dakar? What displaced wanderer today – exile, migrant or citizen of the world swept up in wind and weather – could ask himself the Cartesian question without anxiety?

Descartes, a minor nobleman, therefore a peasant, a soldier posted a few leagues away from the German border, sitting inside his blue ceramic stove, protected from the winter; motionless, seeking a fixed point, only losing his bearings in a dream about swimming,[2] locating himself in space and time, the centrepoint of these coordinates, before God, enjoys bringing into being the word and the subject which is an off-shoot of this stable situation. He will die as the result of a voyage to Sweden.

Our unstable lives suffer at least three displacements after encountering three difficult forks in our road. We had to leave our birthplace, swapping red tiles for black slate and grey zinc; one language and its accent for another with a different word for yes. Born in the heartland of legitimate French, Descartes' idiom never changed and he never had in himself that double voice which always makes one prone to doubt. We then had to move briefly away from the French centre itself: after three wars with millions of dead we learned to love the Po, the Spree and the Thames as much as the Garonne and the Seine; and then the Saint Lawrence, the Amazon, the Congo and the Huanghe. Other languages enter the body and make the head vibrate differently when one's eyes gaze on fields of snow or rice. We no longer remember the lost happiness of being: being here, stable and constant in familiar surroundings in the countryside, age-old communities and trades, the river's edge, gravel, reeds, floods, patches of cress, willows and poplars, convolvulus, vipers, sing-song dialects, sweet proper names, usages and customs – the speechless delight of being me. Displaced twice, by having moved from one countryside to another and then by wandering in numerous countries, continual emigrants or homeless fires, we are unmoored now and it is a matter of painful indifference to us whether we inhabit the pack ice or the Pacific, an island or a desert, provided that every morning we are at the service of the page.

This fire, flying, lost, wandering, wild, unstable, frantic, rapid and anxious, with its rubbed, worn, threadbare, shabby soul reduced to nothing, its names progressively obliterated by the pronunciations of foreign throats, reduced to *nemo*, no-one, and with an almost transparent body, looked at and through so many times, with gestures made fluid through adaptation to a thousand habits, this inexistent, dancing fire occupies its place, and the page, not the stove, is its most recent landscape.

The true displacement, the third kind, now concerns humanity. It is losing its place and its self, like me, detached from its countries and the whole earth. Not only because of its fluctuating movements and its chance felicitous mixtures, begun before the Neolithic age, but because of its new global emigration from space to signs, from the countryside to the image, from languages to codes and from cultures to science. It leaves behind places of work – mines, quarries, rivers, building sites, grassland, ploughed fields – for interiors without windows; sitting and counting, it transforms its muscular body and its numb, callused fingers into a nervous system which fails to recognize any physical relationship with the space outside. Soon it will no longer inhabit anything but schemas, messages and numbers, all digital. The new humanity without earth, blind now to what we called the real – drugged or lucid, who can tell? A new earth, without landscapes, without bearings?

Are we now entering the universal, having lived and thought through three similar displacements, and seen a hundred countrysides displaced one after the other? Do we inhabit it through our wanderings across the terraqueous globe, or as we engrave a valid page for every piece of world?

Once mathematics alone was able to provide us with universals. Yet it has been teaching us for at least a century that the global is merely the local puffed up. Hence new kinds of prudence: he who claims to be universal hides the fact that he won the last war, through language or force, the singular becoming widespread, an individual expanding the channels of publicity through his voice. Nothing new under the sun: King Solomon's so-called wise pronouncement celebrates the victory of a star preventing any change within its barren space that would put it in the shade. But the sun, a small yellow dwarf, drawing close to its deadly supernova, borders on a thousand similar, diverse and even strange stars. The utterance of a minor king.

Wandering takes you from one landscape to another, the pages make headway. What great truth is obstructed by long chains of reasoning, lines on the page, wheat or vines on the face of the earth? What rapid lightning flashes or world-shattering messages do expressways, airlines and communication satellites compete with, all under the control of a relatively small number of men? What gracious confessions of love? What equitable sharing of power?

We had already become familiar with such abuse of power for the sake of the idea or name of man, reduced to a singularity proposed as a model because it had been victorious in abominable battles and blocked all other languages or notions. The exact and the human sciences agree for once about these abuses.

If you have never spent harsh April nights on the Garonne as its waters swell terrifyingly, how can you understand the Chinese anxiety about the flooding and destruction that the Huanghe wreaks on the loess plain; how can you speak to the Bambaras, the peasant boat-men in the loop of the Niger, if you are not familiar with the close association between river and bank from the landscapes of your own childhood and work; how would sailors recognize the Saint Lawrence, in spite of its cover of collapsing ice making it difficult for them to adapt . . . experience means that localities visited are added to the places where one has lived, whereas the universal passes by, retaining from all these places nothing but the universal, such a local global that all the other places are forgotten: grand principles locked into their wish for power. The body hybridizes, slowly accumulating the gestures necessary to live on the Huanghe, the Niger or the Saint Lawrence. The wanderer, the exile, adapting to and travelling across all manner of waters, with so little identity that he recognizes that his name is no-one, accumulates in his body passages, landscapes, customs, languages and mixes them: mulatto, quadroon, hybrid, cross-bred, octoroon . . . the mingled waters of all the rivers of the world beating in his arteries.

The hideous, deadly passion for belonging, responsible for just about all the crimes in history, has never been an object of study, since even those who study need to belong to a sect, jargon, party or scientific discipline, in short a pressure group, in order to hold ground that is immune to all possible criticism. Likewise corporeal mixture and mixture in general are foreign to philosophy which is a discourse promoting separation and purity, enveloped by a hideous and mortal passion for belonging.

Who am I? No-one. Who am I, again? A hybrid or octoroon, a mixture as precise and refined as bar codes specifying things in a combined spectrum of bands and numbers. Displacements, confusing allegiances bringing together and totalizing ancient, retained, local experience, have turned my visible fluctuating body into a long, striped, banded, many-toned, shimmering, multi-hued, marled, damask spectre, through the subtle accumulation of a thousand operations; it must be possible to represent my blood by a similar code. This brightly-coloured tissue, curiously enough, is used by Plato as an ironic metaphor to define and mock democracy in the eighth book of his *Republic*. A gaily-coloured mish-mash of others is not a being. Who am I? This many-toned, brightly-coloured thing. So something always makes me resemble a man: a gesture or colour; ritual and smile; a way of navigating or my relation to the earth; usage and work. We lack a fully developed philosophy of mixture and hybridization, or of identity as the sum or combination of varieties of otherness: discourse and abstraction lag behind the body which knows how to act and practises what the mouth cannot say. Who am I? What does this curious word mean for the displaced, mixed, hybridized person, for the wanderer who tries to fit in? What can it mean besides fateful belonging?

The philosophy that will come from mixture connects the global and the local irenically, and presupposes a different ontology.

METHOD AND RAMBLING (THE GLOBAL AND THE LOCAL)

The countryside brings together places, a page of pages. The desert, with neither hearth nor home, tends towards the global, nothing new ever appearing in its homogeneous space. Method crosses the desert easily but is hindered by the countryside, every place is an obstacle. A walk through the countryside is called a ramble.

In the old French hunting lexicon, *courir à randon* meant to force the game: for example, to ride in pursuit of a deer following its movements from the beginning of the chase to the kill. Rapid and impetuous, the animal must often have changed direction, attempting to throw the pack off the scent with sudden, unpredictable leaps. The dogs, however, brought things back on track: the music, riders and the whole din of the hunt. *Randon*, in equilibrium in the middle of the English Channel or the Saint Lawrence River, is equally divided between the French and English languages. In French, *randonnée* ended up meaning a quite long and difficult walk. In English, in memory of the irregular and unexpected course of the quarry, random means chance. I should like to use *randonnée* in a sense close to its origin, but inflected here and there, as chance would have it, according to the direction I take and how long I ramble. Weather conditions, difficult terrain and wayward currents often turn the Odyssey into a *randonnée*. Ulysses eschews the best way because of a combination of circumstances.

A method traces a route, a way, a path. Where are we going, where do we come from and which way are we going, questions that must be asked if we are to know and live, in theory and in practice, in tribulations and in love. Why hurry, trying to use or use up time? But we do not master it all the time.

Here, first of all, are the straight paths. The one that most expeditiously delivers the fearful traveller from the forest, the one taken by weightless, blinding light – the Cartesian path. A succession of links in a chain, a sequence or series of proportions, an algebra structured by the relationship of order. A straight path means a maximally efficient one, under the rules of the *Method* superlatives hold sway. First, not to include anything other . . . than that which presents itself so clearly and distinctly to my mind that I have no reason to doubt it. Secondly, to divide each of the difficulties into as many parts as possible and as would be required to resolve them. Thirdly, to follow the order from the simplest to the most complex. Finally, to make everywhere such general and complete reviews and lists that I can be sure I omit nothing. This certainly looks like a function serving as a criterion, maximized by constraints. Leibniz was right in deriding such an accumulated litany of requirements, but was nevertheless wrong in failing to discern here a design, the laws of which he had already attempted to formulate. For to pile up in this way superlatives upon comparatives is to propose an extremal strategy. It is to minimize the constraints dictated by doubt, difficulty, composition and omission in order to trace the optimal path, the Leibnizian path par excellence, *de maximis et minimis*. Descartes, who did not like the infinitesimal, reduces the minimum to nothing: no opportunity, omit nothing, if he cannot with good reason make something out of the maximum. And this is how light travels, so as metaphorically to flood intuition with clarity, taking the best path, and this is how the lost traveller emerges from the wood, taking the shortest, straightest path. It is in this way, Leibniz will say, that the world comes into existence, just as bodies fall. Arriving at the best result with the least effort: managing one's heritage like a good paterfamilias, earning the maximum by paying the minimum. The economy of the laws of nature, or the supposedly natural laws of economics. The classical age has triumphed here; this most direct strategy, which has become reason, is the only one we know. Whether we travel by land, sea or air, learn mathematics, with its axioms and deductions, make the most of our own time or that of others, engage in conflict or war, we always apply the tactics of the *extrema*, thereby priding ourselves on optimizing our practices. Reason, efficiency, investment, violence together underpin this economic law – by economy I mean this strategic relationship of *extremum-optimum*. This economy becomes our norm: when morals become knowledge, the traditional set of paths that determine our rationality and rectitude. In a way, we reduce to nothing any disturbance or fluctuation that would make us stray to any extent from this path which our culture as a whole tells us is necessary.

This is the talweg of our rationalist culture. But we have also inherited non-economic paths that are not concerned with this equilibrium between extremes. It could be said that Ulysses was a Cartesian before his time. That as soon as he set sail, and once Troy had been taken, destroyed and pillaged, he thought of taking the shortest route to Ithaca, his heart's desire; and that he had decided and planned his return journey with this in mind. It would probably not have followed a straight line, a thousand constraints preventing and hindering such a path. But a skilled sailor was also responsible for optimizing the journey: following this coast, then avoiding that area, taking advantage of this regular wind, entering that strait at a different point, calmly dropping anchor further off according to the season, and so forth, finessing with the constraints. Hence a winding route, admittedly, but one chosen cunningly from amongst the possible twists and turns, a route where obstacles define the choices made. But in another way they don't. The *Odyssey* traces pathways outside this order, wasteful paths. The ship approaches Penelope and likewise moves away from her, sometimes it is on track but just as often it strays from the beaten path. The scalloped arc of its navigation goes beyond the boundaries of the normal path. It is a path enabling the discovery of unknown lands, inventing when cunning fails.

Method clearly traces a journey, a pathway through a space. Knows where it comes from and where it is going. Running between both these situations, the methodical line passes through the middle and is defined, and of course constrained, in terms of these extremes. The Odyssean path never, or at least rarely, thinks of itself as being methodical in the sense canonized before the classical age in the philosophy of Plato, in which dichotomy also passes through the middle and where articulation seeks economy. The Odyssean path is an exodus rather than a method. An exodus in the sense that the path deviates from the path and the track goes off track. Where the route taken and followed locally, even if not chosen, is an exception to the predetermined choice. The Mosaic exodus marks a different outside: Moses leaves Egypt with his people; subjected to the constraints of the desert, he never reaches the promised land. So that the path itself, whatever its nature, remains outside both his departure and arrival: open to the possibilities inherent in its endpoints. Ulysses makes his exodus differently, he leaves Troy and returns to Ithaca, he goes home, resumes his royal rights, and closes the circle. The exodus and deviations inflect the path itself, not the stable places on the route. When you have a method, you say: a methodical approach – a tautology. But when you are speaking about an exodus, you can say: a discourse of exodus – equivalence. The discourse deviates in relation to the path travelled, just as the exodus moves away from the middle, from equilibrium and from the extremity of method.

Ulysses thus submits to fluctuations: those of the sea and wind, fluctuations of the waves. His boat subjected to moments of calm, tornadoes and the whirlpools of Scylla and Charybdis. Off the beaten track, he is immobilized, becalmed or trapped in other forms of stability. As if there existed some form of stability off the beaten track which is itself stable and well-defined in its course. As if a river, diverted from its customary bed, were to meet a plateau and form a lake, remaining there for a certain time before returning to its preordained course. As if there existed an order outside order, original or singular equilibria outside the well-balanced middle road. Strange attractors. As if there existed types of order, unpredictable in relation to the normal laws of equilibrium, to the ordinary laws of order. As if chance fluctuation, unexpected storms or atmospheric disturbances, spread stochastically through the space of the high seas, suddenly led to (the formation of) a temporarily stable locality, an island where another time would come into being, a local time forgetting the past, the ordinary and the time of the journey. Remote in relation to the methodical path, these islands create order through fluctuation, a different order that could well be called exodic. You will never find these islands with a methodical approach. Exodic, exotic, ergodic, they lie outside the global equilibria of the episteme. Method minimizes constraints and cancels them out; exodus throws itself into their disorder.

I am no longer seeking to entertain you with the story of an old man, or even worse, of an old blind man. My discourse is scientific and at odds with epistemology; it breaks with two millennia of method. Or rather, this old fiction is saturated with a different, incredible kind of knowledge. New knowledge. It is not fiction and not a true story I seek, but the exodic discourse or, more exactly, the entertainment, the diverting, diversionary path of most cunning Ulysses who had in his baggage all of the twists and turns of the new science, the theory of blind knowledge, obscure evidence, evidence hidden by several centuries of method. By millennia of useless method. Useless with respect to the new.

Ulysses has an interesting relationship with the strange attractors dotted along his pseudo-path. He attempts to avoid the sonorous seductions of the Sirens, is frightened by the deep whirlpools of Scylla and Charybdis; he passes them by, seeking to move in a straight line. But throws himself, is thrown, at the feet of Nausicaa, the girl with the ball. Seductive, so they say, and certainly cunning, Ulysses is never anything other than seduced or indefinitely seducible, by Circe or others – seduced, that is, led outside his normal orbit, the straight, normal or ordered path. And, because he knows this, he sometimes blocks his ears. Because he knows that at the fork in the road he takes the wrong branch, fascinated and disoriented by it.

It is said that Hercules always chooses the right branch, virtue and not vice. Consequently vice always has the face of Ulysses or cunning, and virtue that of strength. Hercules, a virtuous, powerful, strong, heroic, classical god uses his paths to their best advantage, as do our sciences, practices and morals. And if he goes so far as to divert a river from its normal course, he has good reason for doing so, namely to clean out the piles of manure in the filthy stables. Always the good, invariably successful strategy. But, it must be remembered, he kills: kills the lion, wild boar, bull, birds. Kills the living and dies on the funeral pyre, amidst the twin flames of the wood and his poison tunic. Hercules, the perfect soldier, always uses the correct method and has the best strategy, making the right choice at the fork in the road. He is thus the strongest and is always right; he wins, conquers, kills, the optimal method of maximal violence, a balanced path towards death. I suspect Ulysses, on the other hand, of postponing his return to Ithaca where bloody carnage awaits him beside the conjugal bed, and of postponing by choosing, *nolens volens,* a path other than the optimal one when faced with the choice, by discovering forms of stability other than general equilibrium. Knowledge tricks death, its exodus forms a set of anabases: leaving the coast, avoiding the talweg, going against the flow, deviating as much as one can from the shortest path. Thereby not negating the effect of fluctuations. Life trusts in chance which loathes reason.

The story of the *Odyssey,* a discourse on exodus, then becomes an encyclopædia of knowledge. Greek children learned from it their culture and techniques, from cooking to the repairing of ships, their history, myths and geography. Greek children: Plato as a child, Theodorus and Eudoxus as children. They read in it the inventive dynamism of the anabasis. Not, as we believe it to be, an archaic and savage science, but highly refined knowledge, of which we are only beginning to conceive. Not a method using the shortest route, but a long, winding, intricate, brightly-coloured path. In that way they were getting ready to demonstrate the rationality of the irrational, for example, or to map unknown lands.

I regret, as soon as I've said it, the term encyclopædia, which is not a concept formulated by the Greeks. Had they thought so for a moment, they would have told us if knowledge traced a cycle within a circle, if pedagogy closed a cycle of cycles, believing as they did that the circle was the optimal figure. But they did not, by virtue of the Homeric exodus. The encyclopædic schema can be applied, on this point, to the paths taken by methods. It takes the shortest path, as does the extremal cycle or circle which contains the largest surface with the smallest curve. Stock and capital, or accumulation of knowledge, follow the same laws as the encyclopædia, the same economic laws. In this sense, all encyclopædias remains method-ical, and these notions are both maximal. The discourse of the first exodus of Greek knowledge is not economical, but chooses long, interesting paths, insofar as interest supposes an interval, a distance, a gap that is not cancelled out; it chooses intersections and conjunctions. Here knowledge is dispersed and distributed, but not integrated into a totality, nor con-ceived under the category of the optimal figure. Always deviating from itself. As soon as knowledge can be equated with method and the ency-clopædia, with straight lines and circles, it is immediately overwhelmed by redundancy: repetitive, ordered, normalized. It attracts local laws of decreasing output. The *Odyssey* does not therefore represent an encyclopæ-dia, but rather a scalenopædia. Scalene, as one says of a scalene triangle, rather than an isosceles, right-angled or equilateral triangle. Unbalanced in parts, scalene signifies lameness, like Hephaistos, an inventor and the husband of Aphrodite, lame like several relatives of Œdipus, with sore feet, like him; scalene describes an oblique, twisting, complicated path. Baroque, just like the period in which the encyclopædia was conceived but not yet realized. Ulysses takes scalene routes and thus discovers and invents, routes of Greekness, those of non-redundant cultures. Cultures with history. Non-recycled history, not recyclable into a balanced or preconceived model, into a model in the two senses of the word, both theoretical and optimal. The first words of history are an exodus. There are cultures in which that history forms a scenario rehearsing legislation or structures, self-evidently present, or buried and yet to be revealed, a characteristic scenario, a methodical journey. We are beginning to know how to construct them, these schemas are no longer unfamiliar to us. One or two cultures came along in which history freed itself from this equilibrium, and began to fluctuate outside the cycles, to branch outside repetitive schemas, to abandon itself to scalene paths. Ulysses navigating without a care in the world leaves behind closed knowledge and histories constrained by structures, he invents inventive knowledge and open his-tory, a new time.

Smaller expanses of water do not require the same kinds of sailors as large oceans. The former force Ulysses to maintain a level of vigilance and skill in handling his vessel unknown to Christopher Columbus, an astronomer. The *Odyssey* provides lessons despised and forgotten by the Renaissance, as it sets sail beyond the Pillars of Hercules in caravels.

The Concorde flies across the water in two hours; from Cape Canaveral or Kourou, rockets blast off towards space, the sun or Venus, leaving behind earthly gravity. We see a different space through the window of any vehicle. Is our knowledge changing?

The Atlantic swell flattens out sufficiently to contain any vessel in its wave length; however high the breakers, they are spaced far enough apart for boats or liners, aircraft carriers or frigates, cargo-ships, to nestle and sleep in a sort of cradle. Even when it is wild, the ocean is easy to handle. Narrow seas with a short swell, the Irish, Ægean and Iroise, cruelly endanger ships of any size, caiques or coastal steamers: the keel scrapes against reefs of pebbles. The spatial element changes, the hollows are not bordered by the same walls.

Odyssean rambling within sight of land requires neither the same strength or patience nor the same talents as the route to India or the American adventure. By dint of long days over immense stretches of water with a gentle swell, travel in a straight line remains mandatory and possible. Ulysses tries and yields, takes a turn and abandons it, runs under the wind from the shelter of this headland towards some unprotected port, takes a hundred constraints into account, must use cunning. If he goes in a straight line, he will wreck his ship. As late as the beginning of the last century, Chateaubriand, consumed with rage against his patron, was obliged to spend months getting to Tunis from Egypt; he often had to leave in a hurry and seek refuge. Thirty years ago, in the same vicinity, despite its thousands of horses, my disoriented boat was likewise at the mercy of the winds. Seen from an aeroplane, the ocean appears simple, wrinkled and striped with a broad brush; the Iroise or Ægean Sea, in a gale, appear misty, tiger-striped, ocellated in parts, disrupted – a horrible mixture. Ulysses embarks in this mingled body with its many variables, Columbus carves out his route in the simplicity of the high seas: a long chain of easy reasons, a thousand short detours around difficult ruses.

When a constraint or variable is so much more significant than all others that they seem negligible by comparison, a straight line or simple curve appears and everything becomes clear. Take away everything so that only one thing is visible; what is neglected falls by the wayside as though a mere detail. On the other hand, one can be obliged or wish to take account of a hundred constraints, but their net seizes or binds us; the knitted fabric with its threads running in many directions represents a place in the sea, bound in the swell, a turbulence of competing winds, a circumstantial cell with as many dimensions; in this singularity, Ulysses loses his linear head.

Did he ever have it? Descartes and Bacon, after Columbus, gave it to us, but we are losing it today. Or rather, without losing it we are taking on a second one causing us to embrace Ulysses again, willingly. We consider the linear head a little stiff and lacking in subtlety, effective and optimal in days gone by, but rather old-fashioned today.

Ulysses, a peasant or sailor with his oar or grain shovel, is involved in non-linear industry subject to the multiple constraints of necessity; intelligence with its many twists and turns – skill in manoeuvring, the rapid and energetic invention of expedients adapted to the circumstances that crowd and batter it – is born of the Ægean Sea, as it is of other small expanses of water; or from the agrarian landscape with its individual allotments, checkerboard or mosaic of places modelled by the breeze, jumping suddenly from one to another; from capricious currents and threads of breakers, mermaids and weather. These monsters rule localities as hammadryads do the trees. Circumstances make places; they require an intelligence, which inhabits the places and populates them with gods who preside over the circumstances.

The necessity of the peasants and sailors of Antiquity – by Antiquity we mean the age in the course of which humanity drew its subsistence from just such a set of non-standard cells, an age which has been drawing to an end in certain parts of France since the Second World War, but which may subsist elsewhere today – a variable necessity, multiple rather than massive, local rather than global, imposing itself through a mixture of current laws and chance blows of fate; it uncannily resembles the odd character of women, or the social behaviour in certain towns: the moods of the weather, the impulses of tyrants, political shenanigans . . . Bays, glades, caves and beaches submit themselves to the fluctuating, colourful caprices of enticing, but terrifying heroines. The landscape displays the same complexity as the famous North-West passage, and for the same reasons: nature and culture are displayed there in the same structure. You need to manipulate the current as you do a woman, to duck and weave when the wind gusts or when the king disowns you, to become multiple when faced with a hydra-headed crowd or hurricane, or to be no-one in order better to resist fate. When it has a thousand faces or variables, it can appear behind the mask of a goddess, a natural or political law or temperament, its multiplicity, rather than its appearance, being the essential element. Multiple twists and turns on the path, appearances under many guises, innumerable places on earth and sea, a thousand cunning ruses.

Classical mastery of the world and things selects a single constraint or variable and ignores all others. Sheer force of will steers a straight course, crosses the ocean by means of rhumb lines or the arc of the great circle, and goes through the forest in a straight line – nothing distinguishes the local from the global. The age of the great voyages implies monotheism, the dissolution of the countryside, the drawing of immense maps, stubborn disregard for circumstances, and the supremacy of the will over intelligence. The scholar, sailor, philosopher or traveller gets carried away with linearity and confuses it with reason. Forced simplicity, fine victories; non-linear, unexpected or unrecognizable necessity, with its hundred faces and thousand detours, is forgotten, together with its corresponding intelligence and the antique and polytheistic world. It has to be said that on the Atlantic, in the season of the trade winds, anyone at all, with twelve metres of wood and a tailwind can travel west effortlessly and runs the risk of confusing the stable regime of a single variable with the mastery and possession of compliant nature. His resolve and stubbornness are to be applauded more than his adaptability. But beware of the return journey.

Who in Antiquity would have believed in the existence of a universal law, when no olive tree twisted in the same way as another and no gust of wind resembled that of the previous day? Before imagining such a possibility Plato had to conceive of a smooth, colourless, invisible, insensible space. Before being converted to its existence, the Hebrew people journeyed through the invariant, isotropic and homogeneous space of the desert. Mathematics is born in the shadow of the pyramids, the solitary sun marking the smooth sand with the trace of death, or the other world. Intuition is obliged to see without accidents. A single God again brings about the birth of knowledge.

The eye sees countryside or space: perceives one and forgets the other. The cartography of Antiquity expresses the danger of the journey, the multitude of obstacles, the difficulty of seeing globally when one finds oneself deep in a varied countryside. The Cartesian forest, on the other hand, becomes a totality where the direct path of the traveller ignores species and varieties: the traveller no longer bows down before the golden bough. One does not record the coordinates of every wave. Sometimes it takes centuries, a few geniuses and the so-called crises of history to cross the border of a local area, or the limits or catastrophe of the clearing in which the whole group believes itself to be imprisoned.

Could we not say that what we call understanding and sensibility, and even reason, those secret compartments in the subject of knowing, the existence and location of which has never been demonstrated (but in which, according to manuals and treatises, operations take place which change detail into synthesis or processes of subsumption), are simply layers or strata of memory, memories of past cultures lost by history? We can see the Atlantic by means of a sextant or with the practised gaze of an old sea salt, nothing obliges us to call ourselves empirical or abstract in either case. Does the blindness preventing us from reading accurately the breeze printed on the page of the sea come from our failure to conceive fractal turbulence, or from our insensitivity to the minor buffeting within the gusts of a downpour? It has long been said that vision is the model for knowledge and all our languages still express this idea, but supposing vision carried with it its memory and its forgetting?

We are entering a third state that destabilizes both of the others: the countryside can pass for an abstract, formal model on the same basis as the uniform space of classical geometry or mechanics, the abstraction of which strikes us as being somewhat hasty and rough and of which the practical and concrete virtues in particular impress us. Euclid comes from the same direction as the mason and Lagrange from that of the engineer. Local, singular vision is revealed not to be an accidental detail to dismiss – global vision is not alone in imposing law. We would no longer understand why the first belongs to the order of the sensible: abstraction has its subtleties; in opposition to the other, situated on the side of understanding: the concrete has its geometry. Both seem to our eyes to be as concrete or abstract as data can possibly be. The distribution of digital, homogeneous or diverse multiplicities triumphs over the distinction between the felt and the conceived, or tends to erase it, making us all believe that everything is played out at the level of language.

Now that we can go around the world in a few hours and travel to certain heavenly bodies more rapidly than we could to distant islands a hundred years ago, we tend to think that a detailed journey around a vegetable garden can offer us information that is just as surprising. When the universe widens, the countryside returns. We maintain a better balance between world and place now, whereas Antiquity or what I call thus, stifled by the local, could not aspire to the global; whereas the modern age wilfully despised all local obstruction to global laws. As a result, we are re-establishing an equilibrium between what our predecessors called the empirical and the abstract, the sensible and the intellectual, data and synthesis. We will probably have to redefine quickly the abstract thus, carefully distinguishing it from its seamless counterpart.

Besides, every great change in knowledge, intuition or our relationship to the world, corresponds to a crisis over the concept or reality of necessity, that formidable bit-player in our age-old struggles. It no longer crushes us with its universal law or with its continued buffeting, be it unexpected or foreseeable. It left the battle, after the fifties, right in the middle of the century, and the combat ceased without our having really been aware of it. Many still lash out at empty space and arm themselves to the teeth for the last war. It will no longer take place. Yes, we have won. Let us not overstep victory. The old need for mastery now returns as though it were in a feedback loop with our definitively acquired mastery. We have transformed things, so we must understand them, or rather: we understood things in order to possess and transform them as we wished, we have to understand them in order to protect them. To pass through the forest without considering the trees, without seeing what we are doing to the trees through the very fact of our passing, appears to us today uneducated and impolite. We encounter the local again through the necessity we impose on it. Our ancient adversity has changed camp: it is now embodied in our politicians. We have to regulate the law of our collective wishes which have become as global and incomprehensible as the laws of the world once were.

From there we can re-evaluate Ulysses and Columbus with new eyes, the ancient and the modern, the fathers of this new third state.

Ulysses must have had a thousand tricks in his bag, to cope with the unexpected and the unscripted; you have to make do with forethought, if you are not good at making predictions. Prediction assumes the predictability of a global, homogeneous space on which the law can be written; forethought involves the countryside, the intuition of a historiated space with circumstantial cells, a set of localities: the person with foresight does not know what the neighbouring cell has in store for him tomorrow, hence this bag of a hundred tricks, at his side or in his head. Now it so happens that Ulysses is caught short by events, an unusual set of circumstances leaving him ill-prepared and helpless – he is short of a trick. Does he deviate from the designated route? No, this route would have to be drawn like a law on smooth, global space, a straight line in the forest or rhumb line across the ocean. No, Ulysses adds braids or loops to his route, which will count as a new trick in his bag and will add a new element to the countryside. The itinerary is scalloped with as many twists and turns as the sailor winds loops of cable around his duffle-bag, as his memory mulls over grievances, as space is enriched with unexpected places, as the pantheon burgeons with gods, as the story branches into episodes. The word polymechanistic accurately describes circumnavigation, or the quality of intelligence, or the drift of a poem: the vision of a space and its fabrication. On the balance-sheet of life, Ulysses wins and loses, trying his luck, but not always effectively, taking each thing as it comes, picking this fork or that one, throwing dice at the cross-roads. Scallops and bushes: countryside. Twists and turns and branchings: limits and summits of cells of circumstances. Ulysses follows exactly the geodesics of his space, his place in the countryside, his non-linear head is drawn thus. The gods come together thus.

Bacon, Descartes, Columbus leave the bag of tricks: no cleverness or cunning. Reason favours will over intelligence. The non-linear cultures and peoples of the Mediterranean give way to the new Atlantic and linearity. Method passes through the forest considering the trees of no account; it crosses the wide sea. Thus the farmer ploughs the field to kill all plants and roots and to coax it so that a single plant may flourish without rivals; he despises as a savage the woodsman who is expert in trees and vines, in the places and times of each, finding his way in the forest with no paths or compass, by means of markers so ingrained that they become instinctive. Taking the straight path out of the woods without seeing anything is equivalent to liberating oneself from savagery or wilderness. These two relationships to places and space are still the distinguishing mark today of the distance between the man of science and the man who is called, disparagingly, a literary man or poet – wild – the distance between the landscape and the panorama.

Let us design a polytropic, polymechanistic ramble with a thousand twists, turns and connections, Ulysses' bag of tricks. It resembles a labyrinth, as if the Cretan hero had traced on the sea the maze of the land. The direct method, impatient with roundabout ways of doing things, preferring optimum or best practice, crosses through and upsets this tangled web. The Odyssean journey, the ramble, becomes obsolete, adaptive or empirical, while method claims to be intentional and abstract: one follows the path of rectitude, the other is crooked and skewed.

What justification is there for favouring one side of the body when judging what is the most direct path? In the name of what outlandish underlying values does one condemn the variable, and what is related to it as being a deviation or gauche, belonging to the left hand; and a constant direction as right, or adroit? The latter, misnamed, never goes right.

So the Odyssean journey or rambling now looks like an electronic chip with portals and pathways, or one of those circuits that we manufacture today to enhance our calculations and formal strategies. The new industry, Cartesian of course but also Odyssean, brings together practice and abstraction in that the computer can be described as a universal tool: a constructed instrument, concrete to the touch, but of open and indefinite application like a theorem. Will the circuit replace the straight line in our methodical paradise? Rambling also like one of those (universal?) curves passing through all points on a plane, on which every conceivable curve can be defined as a local sample? Introduce into it a few chance happenings, the term rambling will be even more appropriate.

Let us design an interesting itinerary, one that leaves its optimal talweg and begins to explore a place: one which does not reach a foreseeable resolution, but searches; seems to wander; not deliberate or sure of itself, but rather anxious, off balance and relentless; questing, on the watch, it moves over the whole space, probes, checks things out, reconnoitres, beats about the bush, skips all over the place; few things in the space escape its sweep; whoever follows or invents this itinerary runs the risk of losing everything or inventing; if he makes discoveries, it will be said of his route that he has left the talweg to follow strange attractors.

If you happen upon a fertile method, forge straight ahead with it. It will be productive. You will soon have a notion of the sort of questions it resolves. Then stop because you are heading rapidly towards boredom, rigidity, old age and idiocy. To be sure, repetition and results, canonizing a place, give it the aura of what one knows: money, power, knowledge, things already accomplished. Dead, imitable, desirable. In the beginning, however, the wondrous idea promised life.

Leap sideways. Keep the recognizable method or methods in reserve, in case of illness, misery, fatigue; go rambling again. Explore space, a flying insect, a stag at bay, a stroller always chased off his habitual path by guard dogs growling around familiar places. Observe your own electroencephalogram jumping all over the place and sweeping across the page. Wander as free as a cloud, cast your gaze in every direction, improvise. Improvisation is a source of wonder for the eye. Think of anxiety as good fortune, self-assurance as poverty. Lose your balance, leave the beaten track, chase birds out of the hedges. *Débrouillez-vous*, muddle through, a perfect popular expression meaning literally to unscramble yourself. It supposes a tangled skein, a certain disorder and that vital confidence in the impromptu event that characterizes healthy innocents, lovers, æsthetes and the lonely.

This research regimen distinguishes us from machines and brings us close to what the body is capable of. It is the latter, more than the mind that separates us from artifice.

On Sundays method rests; rambling saves lives every day. If what you need is victory, everything in its place, battles, banks or institutions, go by way of the first. The other is there for time and intelligence, the well-being of thought, freedom, peace: the creation of unexpected places.

But take both paths, condemn neither; those who love the countryside sometimes need expressways. So leave outlandish thought which, with no good reason, privileged the straight and narrow. Those who would orient themselves intellectually have to head east.

THE FIVE SENSES

Even space ships do not follow a simple, straight, monotonous, Cartesian path. They do not travel towards the Moon, Mars, Venus or Halley's Comet along the paths of method, like the lost traveller hastening to escape from the forest as quickly as possible, proceeding straight ahead in a constant direction. A battery of computers ceaselessly oversees, controls, corrects their direction in real time, with the result that their pathway is quite irregular in its detail. If they always kept to the same direction, they would diverge, and get lost among the stars. The dialogue of computers, on earth and in flight, leaves long tables of numbers in the archives.

Remember Jules Verne. On the whole, that old dreamer was not often mistaken. He goes to the heart of the enterprise, calculates precisely the point of departure, locates in advance the splashdown; certainly naive, but never ridiculous; his comical social analysis remains true however: the astronautical project is of too much importance to be left to any but military men; the Baltimore Gun Club resembles a club of elderly hunters. Jules Verne was wrong on one point, the straight line; let us emphasize his memorable, canonical error. The *Columbiad,* dedicated to Christopher Columbus, a monstrous medieval bombard dug into the earth like a well, loaded with tons of guncotton, shoots straight, straight into the system, straight into the image, but misses the real.

The spaceships of the present often change direction while heading towards their goal. Forget about the initial explosion and the ship's separation into stages to stop it from melting before it even lifts off, we are only concerned with the course. Shells make straight for their target, ships negotiate, hesitate, falter. Bombs are confident, gliding speedily along in a smooth system, with no interest in the local state, like the lost, frightened traveller who has no interest in the rich medley of colours in the countryside through which he passes. More aware, spaceships observe their positions: we observe them, we do not allow them to fly alone. We do not know how to plot their course with precision at the moment of their departure, we fear that they will go wildly off course if we let them continue on their initial trajectory. We distrust memory and complex systems.

In other words, Verne's shell, because of a slight error in aim, will not go around the Moon, it is more probable that it will depart on an erratic and ornamental path: which is what happens to any lost traveller who persists in walking straight ahead in the middle of the forest following the precept of method – he diverges and deviates to an increasing degree. Just as the shell, fired according to a simple system and travelling in a theoretical straight line is sure to go astray, whereas our prudent, meticulous space-ships are oriented directly in and by the phenomenon of which they are a part. The tables of numbers recorded here resemble the old Alphonsine and Toledan tables of observations, judged by the laws of modern astronomy to be highly empirical.

For once calculation falls on the same side as phenomenon and practice, and all three deviate from the simple, stable system of principles and general laws. If the computer were to plot, as we know it can, the landscape implied by the tables of numbers and criss-crossed by spaceships, one would see a mingled, marled, striped, striated, damask body, so different from the abstract void rejected by the canonical vector. The countryside returns unexpectedly, to the void or system, like a rainbow in a meadow. The spaceship travels from one locality to the next as if it were encountering twists and turns rather than straightforwardness. Who would have thought that geography was so close to mechanics?

The object of geography is the countryside. It is said that the countryside hides and displays physics: geography would therefore have decoration as its only object. Ashamed of its indefinite status, it attempts to give itself a basis by penetrating the earth's entrails in order to find, in the black box, the measurable depths and the simplicity of geology, then geophysics: sciences that become increasingly exact the deeper one descends and that one can only finally perceive by using instruments. In addition, it prefers the invisible to the visible and the large fault between the Atlantic plates to the tortured earth of Iceland, the former explaining the latter; rising towards the visible – the lacy coastline or rock chiselled by squalls or waves – it turns again towards the contingency of localities, without always seeing that they carry as many powerful, abstract concepts as the simple: general and hidden. Just as we are identified by our thumbprint, the earth's identity card, a veritable map of the world, can become the model for highly formal meditations. Once again, we find that æsthetics constitutes a body of knowledge, in this case topological, without always having to invoke the reality to which it refers. A necessary invocation, to be sure, but not a sufficient one. If we find the countryside in the system of the three bodies and in relation to its unintegratable equations, we no longer have to believe that a single system exhausts our reading of it. Nothing as deep as the countryside, face or skin.

This is the exact site of the countryside or work of the geographer, on a new map on which are drawn the vast ocean of the exact sciences, and physics: systems, experiments and laws, an immense sea in the vast plain of water, and geophysics, a middle-sized sea in the heart of immensity . . . there, palæomagnetism amid the theory of fields, here, ecology in the theory of living beings . . . as one carves out more precise subsets in larger ones, neglecting neither overlaps, nor interference producing more complicated distinctions, the exact sciences slowly fade into the human sciences . . . living beings work and change the inert; collectives fashion and transform the inert and living environments that they inhabit, or through which they pass . . . ecology, rural sociology . . . straits and gulfs carved out by new seas, and seas belonging once again to the great ocean of the 'soft' sciences – we have just crossed the bar with geography. If it is defined as the intersection of ten or twenty fields of knowledge, we can say of it what all sciences say about themselves, that its singularity has not been defined. It transports us, in fact, from one major body of knowledge to the opposite one through the North-West passage. In geography, the carillon of the hard sciences finally falls silent, when that of the human sciences is barely beginning. In this almost silent space lies the landscape.

An intermediary state from which originate on the one hand estimations and measurements, and on the other stories and history, both feeding ultimately into wide encyclopædic seas; a mixed state, the countryside is immediate and fragile, the foundation of our knowledge, both theoretical and practical. Since it feeds us and gives us pleasure, Pomona and Flora, we had not the slightest suspicion that it was transcendental; and since we can destroy it, it did not occur to us that it was fundamental. A mix of contingent localities where scientific knowledges blend and fall silent by reciprocal disposition; concrete, abstract, whatever you will, it provides the model for models: what schema is not reducible to a simplified cross-section of the countryside? As if the most immediate concreteness were to be found in the greatest abstraction, as if the purest abstraction were immediately readable.

Which goes to prove that this new map of knowledge reproduces the old world map, or a present-day view of the North-West passage: great oceans invaginated into seas, then straits and gulfs or bays, scattered archipelagos and islands redrawing immensity on a small scale; ice flows, variable through freezing and melting, projecting into time the complexities of space, overlaps and dead-ends, reliable passages and obstacles, a mixed landscape in a fluctuating state, an intermediate and complex state between two plains of water on which constant, methodical routes are ensured.

The Beaufort Sea or Davis Strait can be approached from afar using a rhumb line or the arc of the great circle, but between these two places rambling is the order of the day. The countryside can be approached from the point of view of physics, or in local detail using sociology or history, but once you have arrived there rambling is the order of the day. Now meditate on this model of simple, easy methods, suddenly connected to a tangled web.

The name geographer is given to those who write about the earth: for peasants are the only ones who really write on it. It would be better to call geography the writing of the earth about itself. For things – resistant, hard, sharp, elastic, loose – mark, hollow each other out and wear each other away. Our exceptional style makes use of this general property. What the earth reveals results from what should be called the reciprocal marquetry of things.

Carried away by torrents and their own weight, halted by obstacles or their own shape, stones descend and break, carve into the talweg the long path of their fall or movement. Masses of sand, driven by the wind, file away at the mountain. Ice cracks and breaks stones and trees, cliffs and the earth on the plain, as does drought. Who is writing? Water, snow, the return to gentler weather, ophite, granite, equilibrium, density, energy, sun, flora and fauna. This covers, that stains. On what do they write? On snow and water, on fauna or flora, on marble or ice. What the earth displays results from the wrinkles it gives itself. A page.

What we reveal to others is a consequence of the erosion that others and things leave on our faces and skin, or from the shrinking of the harder skeleton, a worn-out frame on the edge of ruin. Whether we write, or are written on, our case is no different from the everyday concerns of geography. The constituent parts of flesh wear each other out: biography.

Talwegs, erosion, wrinkles, these reciprocal scarifications create a clock. The countryside, mapped, marked by the wear and tear that each thing imposes on, and in turn receives from, the things around it and its environment, is studded and cluttered with memories, a collection of remains, monuments, memory. Every place can be dated by this mutual hollowing, and by these ruins, literally by these details: what remains from the cutting and slicing. The antiquity of the countryside comes from the fact that it bears, exhibits and retains the beat of time past, the clock of wear and tear and of durable, hard things cutting each other – duration. Thus geography, the writing of earth on itself, precedes history and all imaginable prehistory, it determines it here and now, accessing the fundamental time of things, marked by the trace of each thing on the others and of several others on each thing, and shortly afterwards by the trace of men, furrows, dredging and style.

THE FIVE SENSES

The relationship of the word to the world leaves less trace than the lightest touch. The soft does not affect the hard, it leaves it intact. Naming makes no mark, sets no seal on the named. Baptismal water, the chrism of anointing, mime the gentle caress of the conferring of a name, whereas circumcision mimes the harsh bite of biography, the latter on the side of things, the former on the side of the word, one definitive like a feature in the antique countryside, the others labile and temporary like contracts. Hard, durable things engrave each other and this relationship brings about their duration. The soft, in relation to things, ignores duration, which explains why we are always announcing the novelty of the word.

Geography, a hard science of hard things, is related to duration; history, coming later, new and light, follows the word. It begins with writing, the engraving of the soft on the hard: a new, unwritten time.

Ulysses and Columbus, Bougainville or Cook share, together with all sea populations, the rare chance of inhabiting and travelling simultaneously.

No-one knows a place until he has built on it with hard materials, dug his grave there, for the wall is supported in the foundation trench, that of fertility, treasure and the grave. First surround trenches with chairs, and you have a cathedral; and leave your sweat, the skin of your hands, your time, a memory in lime and sand, and the porch curved hollow like your anxiety. The house, at first a fleshless skeleton, then dressed and decorated, consolidates its motionless body supported by your corpse and your exhaustion, looks at the landscape from its immense bay windows; likewise in certain cemeteries the grave stones are decorated with small houses, behind the windows of which bouquets of flowers decay. A stable body attached to an earthly place, as if to flesh. The former will never know whether it was built in honour of a local god or whether it yielded to the ridiculous ambition of a modest apotheosis.

To build, then to inhabit, teaches one that the sphere of influence of the constructed goes from the stand of chestnut trees – white on the left, looking towards the stream, and pink on the right, beyond which the land falls away, steeply sloping – into foreign, almost untouchable places. We do not go there out of respect for the neighbouring gods. A bestial, pagan and vital topology of the immediate and the mediate, in which the locality of the locality quickly appears as strange as the immensely far distant. The homebody or peasant that the creole tongue graces with the name of inhabitant is as much, or as ill at ease on the borders of his commune or parish as at the outer limits of the universe. He lives on a large, gaudy spot, the contours of which closely follow the uneven contours of the ground and the circumstances of history, surrounded, at a short distance, by a thin, homogeneous, geometric crown, where the distance separating Australia from the White Sea rapidly approaches zero. Then again he may become, from the moment he leaves his region, an intrepid traveller, not caring whether he establishes himself near Seattle, Manila or Timbuctoo. For the inhabitant of the house rooted in divine death and giving its tonality to the locality, as for his twin wandering from one airport to another, everything lies equidistant from paradise, where deviations vanish.

The mason's Euclidean space is grounded in the topological space of the inhabitant. Or: surrounding the Epicurean sphere of the garden and as soon as one leaves through the exit porch, begins the crown or torus of the Stoic universe of isotropic causes or harmonic series, the site of communication. Or: the dense ball of concreteness where the habitat touches its localities and where the constructed measures out its dividing lines, surpasses life in its superabundant detail, whereas one can understand in three minutes the laws that govern the remaining space. Or even: the individual gaudy paving-stone of a site punctuates an empty, infinite, simple, boring volume, criss-crossed by the vectorial arrows of journeys. Better still: the countryside through which the rambling takes place along scalloped paths, braids, loops and detours, regrouping paving stones and balls; the extreme ways of method traverse the homogeneous universe of communication. Best of all: why on earth should one world exclude the other?

Question: where are we? *Ubi?* We, the stable inhabitants, Latin statues, Greek theses, logical positions, situations, affirmations. Answer: in the garden, a circumstantial cell in the countryside. No, I, a redundant element in the universe, see only desert, through which I pass. Where are we? Here, in a place. Individual, surrounded by neighbourhoods, a locality scalloped with foliations. We come from such a place, we remember it; our body, like an animal's, experiences this memory, we go towards it, our bodies quiver with this hope, even if we cross a smooth, vectorially naked space, even if we take the expressway cutting through places strewn with refuse.

The claim of the double body, of the motionless and moving animal, with its complex, varied, unstable, agitated, inert, lively, verbal niche concerns the passage from the local to the global. It wants to run and to rest at the same time. It wants to navigate.

I sing of the happiness given by a boat calling in at ports after having planed the knotted plank of the ocean, the delightful pleasure of going to sleep amidst familiar things, but in the vicinity of strangeness. China, pack-ice, tropics, visited in one's own habitat. No, sailors do not travel now; in the age of the great discoveries they alone risked life and limb. They return every evening to the same bolthole and the same hammock, what ignorant person would have the effrontery to contrast life at sea and peasant stability, as wandering and immobility? A boat: a small hamlet with several hearths in a fragile shell. Welded to the helm, the mariner does not move, incorporated in the vessel, his nose the prow, his back the stern, moustache wrapped around the stem, hair streaming at the masthead. His village moves. It seems to travel across a strange space, but the agrarian vessel also is immersed in a hazy halo. Mooring his vessel securely on a fine evening, the sailor goes ashore just as the farmer goes hunting, secure in the knowledge that he will soon return to sup from the same warm dish, that he will come home to the same smells and familiar gangways. A stay-at-home sailor.

Voyaging begins when one burns one's boats, adventures begin with a shipwreck. Only then do the gods foresake the sailor who has abandoned them, then he smashes his hut twenty thousand leagues from his home just as the conscripted peasant leaves the farm for war. In God's hands. But before that, he saw without expending himself. As at the theatre or cinema or in a picture book. Comfortably seated in the pitching, curled up in the tossing, rocked by the maternal waters, behind the wave-washed scuttle, he observes, safe. He will tell the story.

In the Euclidian sea or sky he takes with him his topological and voluble niche.

We become attached to the odorous, flavoursome, colourful place, we establish our dwelling there, but together they form only our half-niche, like a sort of dead land, dotted with tombs, criss-crossed with foundations. We free ourselves and arrive at the other limitless half-niche, on the other side of the borders; it has no limits. Kernel, ribbons. On the road we sleep just as well, exhilarated about leaving the equilibrium of being a statue, about abandoning the thesis, in order to embrace deviation. Leaving your house behind is the beginning of metaphysics – what exists beyond; but as fear takes hold of him, the adventurer builds a boat. He will not leave behind his cradle. The first truly metaphysical object holds the promise of elsewhere without leaving the here and now. Invents a moving equilibrium, stability around its fluctuations, but also movement into the open half-niche from the half-closed niche, a kind of fixed agitation. As long as the caravel moves beneath his feet, his self-confidence is intact. The beyond is revealed when you consign your shoes to the flames, with your clothes and habits, the beams of the old cart and the shepherd's hut. You will find it if, and only if, you do not turn back towards the statue of the old philosophy.

Thus the earth displays the collective traces of this 'niche'-totality with its kernels or heads from which threads radiate. We cannot do without gardens and journeys, tempering the sometimes desperate austerity of the latter with the delights of the former, or the tediousness of plants by jumping over the garden wall. Wandering is part of the human landscape; history forms the boat's stable hull, the pitch of the vessel and the metaphysical adventure. Peasants who stay put want to forget the long period of emigration of their forebears, always from somewhere else; voyagers want to remember their forefathers rooted in the glebe. The complete niche of human collectives – earth, water, terraqueous globe – adds gardens to exoduses, mixes circumnavigations with islands, extends edenic or hellish valleys into endless pathways, expels apple thieves, turning them into runners. From the park, endless pathways burst forth in a scalene star – the former probably accumulating energies, memories, fauna, flora and Pomona, all of which come from the latter. Space, considered lucidly, bears a striking resemblance to a medium for thought, studded with narrow, dense cells with fringed markings and endowed with gigantic, threadlike axons which extend and connect it with what is near and far. There is nothing in the intellect that you cannot see in the world: disciplinary places which often result from atypical wandering and from which those who wish to resume the methodic or exodic road are excluded. The same drawings, similar fates; toss a coin to decide where the concrete or abstract is.

Universe and place are connected in a knot as difficult to form as to imagine. On the one hand, the local sees obstructions on its borders, causing neighbouring areas to be inaccessible; the extremal path on the other hand knows no obstacle and recognizes no place. The countryside assembles *pagi*, the universe sends vectors through it, the real difficulty being to stitch the local peculiarities onto the global pathway, or to trace convenient paths in the landscape. Whence the temptation to dip into one culture or another: a multiplicity of stories, meanings and hamlets; a scholarly, formal, rapid, transversal uniqueness – taking one to be ancient and the other modern.

The Greek adjective catholic means universal, but those who use it mostly ignore this sense and speak of a religion with rites and saints, virgins and martyrs – a figurative monotheism in a sea of angels. The memory of its linguistic origin combines with its current meaning to display a rare and delicate synthesis – a source of beauty and art – between absent unity, with which to open a dialogue or relationship of submissive love, and the pagan countryside, resurfacing and dotted with localities, statues, stopping places, altars and localities, slightly skewed by the unitary field; between the local and the global, existence and law, the one God and one's neighbour. This difficult union or communion, in which tolerance protects polytheism, exposes Catholicism to the sight of itself constantly torn between the exclusive monotheism of the desert, the universe of empty space whose name it bears – nothing new under such a sun – and the proliferation of pagan odds and ends, small leafy rites in a variable spring, such that it must work ceaselessly, heroically, in a climate of general incomprehension, at the paradoxical – and suddenly highly contemporary – knot of the infinitely far and near: the love of God and of one's neighbour.

I now contemplate the double commandment of the Christian religion and the double person that it requires us to love. To love both the absent universal and our individual neighbour. The proximity of one's neighbour tempers the savagery of monotheism, that radical violence that empties space so that a single law prospers. The unexpected set of connections between proximities repopulates this space with colourful individualities. I contemplate the wholly reasonable asymmetry of the law of reason and the surrounding circumstances, for every instance of the given.

An unequal balance, with its sloping beam: justice does not separate here the true from the false, the just from the unjust, reason from unreason. Dualism and the dual have faded away. The balance swings towards peace. I love the absence of him who alone has been invested with power and glory, which here are tantamount to crime, and to crime alone. I love the immediate presence of him who is in possession of no space other than that in which I exist. Peace descends, twice. The universal and the singular with whom I communicate are dual but do not oppose each other. Is God to be found in the incremental extensions of our neighbour? What is the latter's relationship with God?

I contemplate the strange prescience of what our sciences are beginning to understand: the ancient figure of a new reason, called good news in Antiquity. Universal reason is tempered under pressure from local knowledge. Topology, fluctuations, small deviations and circumstances, mixtures, singularities again crowd into the empty, monotonous space of law. Yet we cannot, indeed must not, dismiss pure reason, rigour, nor exactitude. We must welcome this overpopulated place. This is reason reconciled: God and one's neighbour, pure and perfect reason as well as local singularities. The world is made of systems and mixtures.

Who would have believed that reason and pathos together would lead us today to this asymmetry, a lesson from the old Christian commandment?

Now is the time to revise, or revisit the connection between the global and the local. Method passes through the panorama, a uniform universe. Rambling travels across places, landscapes.

Here we have a ball with fuzzy outlines, a singular event, turbulence or whirlpool. A starburst of methodical pathways, transformed into a complexity of lanes because of the contours they must cross, converges on or diverges from this place.

We shall call these circumstances, and the connecting points exchangers or interchanges.

CIRCUMSTANCES

The shade of a tree; for all things, their shadow is a function of the sun, clouds, wind; the height of a tree and its form depending in turn on its shadows. A tangle of overlapping footprints around a water source, layers of the past, the meeting place of the lost. The border of a well and its position on a plain where it draws herds of animals and their keepers. The surroundings of the building, access paths to the bridge. The hedges on the embankment, with or without a row of shrubs, surrounding an enclosed field. Marches protecting the kingdom. Sounds announcing something important: the followers of the powerful man intercept news. Glacis. The square of the gentiles, where Notre-Dame presents its face to the world. A district, suburb or ancient meeting place, on the outskirts of towns. Thresholds where intimacies are hidden. Areolæ. Reflections, dullness, brilliance; sounds; suffocating heat from a place of flame or ice, coolness; fragrant perfumes. Follow tracks of game animals, discover the island before seeing it, guess from the changing marks around it. Intuitions that latch on to ill-defined surroundings. The garden of the dead next to the walls of the church, with vacancies. The crowd milling around the gates of the stadium in the evening. Clamour. Tidal land on the flat coast, a space shared by earth and water, according to the phases of the moon, the breeze, the season and the syzygies. The sun so brilliant that we are living inside the star and not at an immense distance from unattainable borders. The halo around the moon, the Rings of Saturn. An aqueous coating, gas like hair surrounding certain celestial objects, a tail of comet dust. Glory preceding the body, nude, saints, stars, face, eye, skin, thought; glory using new words that knock your socks off. The great power of hate, on the ground and in history, the dense odour of resentment. One sex beseeching the other, attraction to the maelstrom, voices around the Sirens. Belts. Wayward and swift-flowing water upstream of small waterfalls, stretches of turbulence downstream. Our fragility is defended by a double or triple invisible skin, a breastplate repulsing even the gentlest aggressor. Far-reaching intoxication projected by productive intelligence, a work of art, charm. Vertigo. Corolli that fall from the lips of she who will say yes. Emotion and silence that follow and precede the event. Snow flakes blowing about, flights of archangels before God, petals floating down in the shade of the tree.

Bark, membranes, porous walls, skins, crowns, hues, haloes, in space, time, force fields, phases, causes, pretexts, conditions . . . surroundings, deviations, indecisiveness, areas neighbouring what is more strictly defined: places through which sense messages pass, circumstances.

Logic. – The principle of reason acknowledges some existing thing by affirming that it exists more than it doesn't exist. And as a singular entity, rather than as nothing. Now it could be said that existing, more or less, is a redundancy and repeats, using a verb and adverb, a discrepancy or excess, a deviation from a state of equilibrium. Existence expresses this deviation, since the radical expresses the static, and more or less vaguely quantifies the counterweight. As if the beam of the balance were not quite level. Existence indicates a state outside the zero state, or better still, a state outside states. On the other hand, Greek science, named episteme since its beginnings, expresses equilibrium through this word, a sort of state above a state. The word system roughly expresses the same thing. The traditional opposition, the relative strangeness of existence and the episteme, become clearly legible. The general something or other is a deviation that science reduces to zero. Rigorous or precise knowledge fashions the scales of existence. Or its state. Its reduction to equilibrium. Its abolition. Science considers existence as a counterweight, a defect. A balance between accuracy and justice, between equilibrium and moral and mortal politics. Existence then functions in a different mode to that of science.

I think, therefore I exist, a contradiction in terms. I think: I weigh, I press down on a plinth, base, seat – I am immobile and fixed, at rest;

I exist, here I am pulled off balance, off-balance in relation to rest, almost mobile and literally disquieted. In other words, a tautology: I weigh therefore the needle of the balance moves.

Aristotle posits the identity principle as the founding necessity of science. From its first formulation, this principle is defined in relation to contradiction. It is impossible for the same attribute to belong and not to belong at the same time to the same subject, in the same relationship, without prejudicing all the other determinations which can be added to deal with the other logical difficulties. Let us forget for a moment the attributive character of the Aristotelian definition and say with Leibniz, for example, what is A cannot be non-A, at the same time and in the same relationship etc. Always the double negation, identity as the impossible contemporaneity of itself and its contrary, or else its contradictory. We can observe in passing that the Greek term for determinations that can be casually added, διορισμοί, evidently designates something like a limit. The meeting of A and non-A is carefully described using a set of identities: at the same time, in the same relationship, in general, conditioned by the same determinations. A curious necessity that can only be imposed in a universe made up entirely of conditions. The identity principle comes into play if, and only if, other identities – time, relationship, determinations in general – are observed. A curious definition because it requires as a condition the very thing defined. Could the first principle be merely a begging of the question? A circular identity?

Thus we can go back to Aristotle and Leibniz again by saying: in the same circumstances, it is impossible for A to be non-A. It can immediately be observed that the famous principle, the universality or supposed necessity of which is eroded under the pressure of conditions, borders on another more familiar one, that of determinism: in the same circumstances the same causes produce the same effects. Now, as no-one knows the status of causes and effects, as the philosophy of causality can just as easily be put aside as the attributive logic discussed above, it remains that: in the same circumstances, the same x produces the same y. Or rather: through the identity of the circumstances, there is identity, or stability of experience, the possibility of repeating it at will. Or: through identical allocations, experiments are invariant. Thus in both cases, physical here and metaphysical there, the formal identity of any A, or factual or phenomenal identity, or that of experience, only take place under the express condition of reducing the set, or a set of what surrounds them, to the identical. In both cases, the identity of the circumstances is a primary consideration or condition, in theory as in practice. Without it, no logic, no manipulation or philosophy.

Philosophy has worked to cancel out, deflect or overturn this condition. The history of philosophy or science causes us to forget it in order to maintain the independence and isolation of the universality of these necessary principles. Leibniz, therefore, follows Aristotle and first of all redefines factual truths and those of reason. Among the latter, the primitive truths of reason merely repeat the same thing, without teaching us anything. Either affirmative: A is A; or negative: what is A cannot be non-A, for the same proposition. Having said this, it remains to carry out experiments. In the field of logic and algebra – pure discourses, as we say – the functioning of these principles remains clear and distinct, on condition, of course, that there is no variation in the propositions, which is precisely identity of circumstance, in any language. But everything changes very rapidly, even without going outside mathematics: it is sufficient to immerse discourse in space and time, geometry and mechanics. And the rest follows from there. Let us suppose, he said, that there exists a multiplicity of states of things, and that these states do not include anything opposed to them: it can then be said that they exist simultaneously. For Aristotle, contradiction or identity can only be defined with the minimal condition of simultaneity at the same time. Leibniz reverses Aristotle's contention and defines the simultaneous as a state of things in which contradiction is neither present nor included. This reversal would appear to be conclusive.

It allows space and time to be defined. Not as conditions for these principles, but, on the contrary, as things produced by them. Space becomes the order of coexistences, the order of simultaneities, or the order of non-contradictories since they could not exist simultaneously. Conversely, time becomes the order of non-simultaneous things, which can therefore be contradictory. Those that were produced last year contain or imply opposite states of the same thing, in relation to those that are produced this year. It is sufficient to reverse the condition in order to produce it by the thing conditioned. There can only be contradiction if there is simultaneity. If there is no simultaneity then a contradiction may exist. Then time, the order of the successive, enters the implied order of the contradictory. Reverse the proposition again and you have: if there is a contradictory, then there is time. This is Hegel – who forgets in passing that the object can imply a contradictory, in time. It passes from the possible to the necessary and sufficient. And the dialectic begins to produce history. On the cheap.

The double reversal of the condition of these principles launches a one-track time where the object never remains the same. Thus the doubling of the negation does not necessarily return to the same point. The process of negation transforms the essence of A. The old language with two values then moves down into living or historic objects. It produces them. And the real is rational, the rational real.

All the conditions of the principle have been repressed by this clever trick. It has chosen one, time, and uses it to hide the others from view. Through a subtle reversal, the principles produce time or history. So history produces itself in and through the principles and, consequently, abolishes the other conditions. There is no longer even a relationship, nor the other determinations, nor the set of circumstances: falling back on time, they are produced, in turn, by the functioning of the contradictory and identity. Everything disappears in the machinery of disjunctive or binary logic. From the angle of time and history – gone from being the condition to the thing conditioned, as they have gone from being the possible to the necessary – reason produces fact. Reason is identical to existence, and produces it dynamically. The imperialism of the rational absorbs into the logos the deviations from the equilibrium of existence.

Now the real surpasses through the rational. Through the remnants of chance, about which I have no information and never will: the unknown, profusion, noise, proliferation and difference.

Given this, it remains true that there is not, and that no-one can conceive of, identity or contradiction except in specific circumstances of place, time, position, site, relationship, without prejudging the other innumerable determinations or limits. That the philosophy of circumstances conditions the first principles without which no-one can think, speak or transform the world. That only errors of logic, begging the question, and hypocrisy induced by the instinct for power have managed to reverse this condition and cause it to be produced by the rational principles conditioned by it. Existence is not deduced from identity, as modal logics are not produced by a logic of double values.

Quite the contrary. Existence, a deviation from equilibrium, refers to circumstances. The circumstance creates the total set – without the possibility of a balance sheet or accounting – of existences themselves, of deviations, imbalances; the total set of the 'somewhats', as the principle of reason states, or of what remains a state outside states.

This vast set, real and intimation of the real, surrounds the highest point of a singular mountain pass, like contour lines, far removed or in closest proximity. At this quite exceptional point are to be found balance, equality, congruence, parallelism or countless things of the same kind – that is, identity. $A=A$ or $A\equiv A$. A rare case of stability at the top of the pass, surrounded by circumstances. Identity and contradiction, rarely to be found, are exceptional, ultrastructural singularities on the infinite variety of deviations, discrepancies, imbalances and so on – existences and circumstances.

Philosophy has only ever taken note, or wished to see these crests, making the flood-tide of terror rise to drown the contours of the land. Those who drag themselves on to these islands say that they have control over the fury of the waves, poor shipwrecked creatures that they are.

Institutional language, logic and science – improbable archipelagos or miracles on the manifold deviations from equilibrium or the rule, on the polymorphy of circumstances – produce nothing, but are on the contrary conditioned. Not by another rule but by its absence. Whether you say infrastructure or superstructure, it always comes down to an ultra-structure. Maxima or minima are equivalent to extrema. Passes, peaks and islands.

The countryside, pages surrounded by rambling paths, becomes a logical model, and logic, conversely, redraws the landscape.

Grammar. – Classical grammars distinguished, in their syntax, between subordinate substantival or noun phrases and circumstantial or adverbial ones. The first posit a direct link from the subject to the object or the converse, focused on one or the other, or on both. Action, passivity, discourse or thought: the whole programme of the philosophy class. The so-called secondary adverbial propositions shift this focus and describe time, place, condition, consequence, the concessive, either comparable or causal and so on. As soon as he saw a rose he thought that spring had returned; the river had swollen to such an extent that one could no longer ford it; I could if I wished, or when and because I should like to, or at the place I choose. The world plus several emotions return in force to crowd around the austere, meagre substantival axis. This multiple is abolished if reduced to identity or repetition: in the same circumstances, the same . . . complete the sentence yourself.

In the usual morphology of these grammars, neither adjectives nor adverbs have a very good reputation. Less is more, one used to say. Always God, never the angels – a circumstance of angels, said Tertullien; get to the point, don't dilly dally. Style and philosophy in black and white – morning coat and dicky – thought, action, science and transformation of the world: we have not a minute to lose. Adjectives throw us sideways, off-course – seductive, bifurcating, diverted. Literally parasitic,[3] like static: surplus noise, beside the master devouring the substantive master's share; blood-sucker. Adverbs cause action to deviate, to lose its balance. Both denote circumstances, limit and bring the act, person or thing into existence. A small deviation begins with corners, moments, qualities or restrictions, weather conditions; why don't we take our time? So rare and precious, often enslaved, miraculously freed, superb, ecstatic, never monotonous, beside us, far away, secret, available, rich, full, tasty, free, mixed.

Like adverbs or adjectives, adverbial phrases add a leafy, sensual and sensible dimension to the ascetic, puritanical or austere meaning of the sensate. If you wish to make an honest statement about the sensible, an epithet of Colette's is better than ten statements by a logician; as is a visit to, or better still the creation in detail of, a garden.

Academic philosophies fail to say this in their substantival or attributive alignment, through their exclusive use of verbs and nouns: of the abominable verb to be, unknown or invasive, of motionless predication, of predication with its horns of dilemma . . . how boring the rhyming dualist results: realism-idealism, empiricism-formalism, dialectic-analytic . . . the rigidity of nouns: ontology, phenomenology, epistemology, molo, nolo, tolo, internal rhymes, can thought ring true in such ugly writing? I plead guilty.

Visit the environment. Traverse circumstances floating like crowns around the instance or substance, around the axis of the act. Make use of what is cast aside. Describe the parasites in signals, the collective or the living: it is always to be found eating right next to you. Study neighbourhoods, travel along country roads which surround and give shape to the countryside. Consider the fluctuations, deviations or inclinations, in the estimations or concepts of science. Atoms are sometimes cast aside. Do not despise conjunctions or passages. Hermes often veers off as he goes along. And detaches himself. Observe the mingled flows and the places of exchange and you will understand time better. Hermes gradually finds his language and his messages, sounds and music, landscapes and paths, knowledge and wisdom. He leaps sideways, to the places where the senses murmur and tremble, the neighbouring turbulence of bodies – sensation. He loves and knows the spot where place deviates from place and leads to the universe, where the latter deviates from the law to invaginate into singularity: circumstance.

Static. – A statue is set on a pedestal and does not move from it. Immobility, rest, fixity: thesis.

A balance comes to rest through a relationship of equality or exchange between its arms, trays and weights. It cancels out the virtual movement of each one by compensating it with that of the other: equilibrium.

A spinning top, a miniature planetary globe, remains upright, a vibrating statue, a whirling balance, because of its rapid rotation, and the earth, stars, the whole solar system remain constant in the composite periodicity of their variations. The word system is generally used when a complex moving set is ordered around an invariant.

Statue or thesis: singular; equilibrium: duality; system: plurality.

Zero movement, movement around a position: rotation, trajectory, orbit, vibrations, rhythms, diverse compositions.

Reversible time.

We think in theses, affirmations, equilibria, systems, thinking or pondering means quite literally weighing, weighing up. I think therefore a balance exists. I could not think without it. There exists a statue or system. A thesis, an antithesis, a point around which the beam of the balance resolves their exchange or agreement or does not resolve their inequalities. If it wobbles or hesitates, am I still thinking? If it lacks constancy, fluctuates, if it keeps on deviating from stability . . . Montaigne expresses excellently the locality of non-thought by the double balancing act of doubt and the eternal wobble of the world in its course. I cannot think without referring to stability in general. The affirmation of the 'I think' and its requirement of constancy in the subject is translated into the reality of things by the principle of equilibrium. Subject, object, I don't know; I know in any case that language always says the same thing, we know nothing more. I affirm – that statement remains firm on its base, be it thesis or statue, thought, table or basin. I think – I weigh, on that base. Who, I? It is of no importance.

The work of thought or history advances on a stable front into fields where at first glance it has no place or time. The unthinkable equals the unstable. The unknowable is equivalent to fluctuation. Identity remains the explicit or implicit condition of science. We must be able to repeat what is said, find the statue again in the same place, recognize the thesis, solid, affirmed, unchanged, repeat the experiment – determined, determinist, as stable as a terminus.

That being the case, the said work consists in recognizing the stable in the unstable, equilibrium in movement, the spinning top upright as it whirls around, the system stable even when it is animated by a variety of irregular rhythms – the invariant in variation.

I think if and only if I take my disquiet into places where ponderation brings with it risks.

In the heat which stirs up the smallest elements; among the insubstantial fluids and turbulence; on the inclination of atoms; in the midst of the atmospheric disturbance; in qualities belonging entirely to the senses; among mixtures and landscapes; in the human sciences and history. The programme of conceptual work to be done follows the infamous North-West Passage. A ramble rather than a method. Wanderings, journeys, dangers.

The example of the river is appealing to us: flowing from one source or several, it descends the talweg towards the sea or lake, it looks at first glance as though it runs, turbulent or calm, towards its equilibrium; true for each drop of water, is this affirmation true for the river? It moves of course; but stable, it lies in repose in its aptly named bed. It appears to run, but sleeps after a fashion. If some Hercules should pass by, if some civil engineering project should for whatever reason change its course, the river will return to it. The river hollows out an overall stability, from its source to its mouth. Homeorrhesis. Do we follow the course of a river as we do the formation of the embryo, from fertilization to birth, and the river bed in the same way, until the hour of its death?

One illustrious example among many, for the progress of thought: we ought to direct our restlessness, the deviation from rest, towards obviously restless things, the equilibrium of which seems unthinkable. Chance often lies in wait for us there, opposing its disorder to our identity: with reason or without, who can tell? Who can guess, without thinking, without believing oneself to be God, that the real is rational and vice versa? Thinking doubtless consists in wandering, restlessly, in a place where this principle has not yet been enunciated.

The Seine and the Garonne display homeorrhesis; there is no sign of it in either the Yukon or the Mackenzie. The latter deviate incessantly from their equilibrium. Sometimes they flow with a hundred arms, sometimes not at all, frozen, blocked, barred by obstacles and gravel, have one bed at dawn, ten at midday, twenty at another moment and at the same spot, or at another spot at the same moment. Do they march to the rhythm of a different drum? It could be said that they write on the earth or country-side the whole programme of their circumstances: constancy, instability, consistencies, inconsistencies, circumstances.

What order is carried away by their fluctuations? The effort of thought must be directed towards these latitudes: fixed paths in a random environment or random paths in a determined place. Time no longer flows like water but percolates like it.

Celestial mechanics. – Laplace deduces the celestial movements from Newton's law and thus makes the world into a system. He needs no other hypothesis. And yet an idea other than attraction dominates his argument. Everyone remembers the famous passage in the *Republic* where Plato describes a spinning top. It remains in equilibrium on its base, but moves in respect to all points not on this axis. Plato finds this inseparability of movement and repose contradictory. He does not say that the base can move, move forward, backward, that the axis can nutate, etc. This contradiction, in the eyes of modern mechanists, defines a new equilibrium, constancy through movement, invariance through variations, immobility through mobility. In the preface to the second part of his *Celestial Mechanics*, Laplace indulges in a hundred linguistic variations on the pair in question: celestial objects display oscillations, librations, nutations, vibrations, periods – annual inequalities, one or many centuries old, going up to nine hundred years etc. – around equilibrium.

The system of the world can be named thus not only because the totality of appearances are deduced from one law – the word phenomenology has its origin in astronomical observations – but because of its stability. A large number of objects remain together in equilibrium. They move ('and yet it moves').[4] Indeed – but all apparent anomalies, nutations or librations, return to their point of repose, all variations are restored over time. Constancy. World harmony comes from the composition of vibratory movements; a set of tops in periodic equilibrium. A sound, after all, certainly indicates a constant for the complex movements of a string, plate or column of air.

On the other hand celestial objects do not present themselves in a homogeneous manner; the earth has a solid core, covered in places by a liquid magnifying glass – oceans and seas – enveloped entirely in a gaseous mass, the atmosphere; three states which make it somewhat viscous. Plato's top moves in the same way, solid at every point. The mantle of the seas can slide, take on its own rhythmic movements which, in return, can influence the rhythms of the moving solid. The atmospheric envelope is traversed by vibrations also, the periodicity of which we have not yet discovered, if it exists.

The question of movement gives rise to the law of constancy.

That of composition gives rise to the concept of consistency.

Consistency is a characteristic of the solid, but also of rigorous deductive reasoning: non-contradiction within a system. In celestial mechanics, as practised by Laplace, mathematics corresponds to the world: two consistent systems. But when it comes to the solid, we hesitate and vacillate. Solid mechanics gives enough guarantees; for the aqueous mantle, we can go on to a theory of tides: we'll leave aside weather, fire and air. Too complex to fit into the system.

But carrying with it the framework of its formation. Following its usual regime, with which we are familiar, the world obeys reversible time, that of the pendulum: nothing in either our equations or rhythmic phenomena would change if time were counted backwards. A new question: how was this system formed, how did it arrive at this regime of equilibrium through its movements? Laplace moves from cosmology to cosmogony in *Note VII*, attached to his *Exposition of the System of the World*. Observe language just as Laplace observes the planets: 'exposing' pulls off balance the set of things that are positioned there – the 'system' or composition. The astronomer reasons and begins a new topic; Auguste Comte,[5] following Laplace, says that five general circumstances characterize the constitution of the solar system; circulation, rotation and satellites all move from West to East, never the other way round, they are quite literally oriented; all orbits display eccentricity, although it is very slight, in planes which deviate from each other ever so slightly.

It is indeed a question of circumstances: phenomena not included in the strict definition of the system, not deducible from the general equilibrium, apart. No balance compensates for the general directions of movements I would call 'occidented', nor deviations from equilibrium, excentricities or inclinations, by symmetrical obliquities. Reversible time does not integrate these exceptions into a rhythmic totality. Lucretius' *clinamen* returns, in gigantic dimensions. He projects us into the irreversible time of genesis, the time of fire: in cosmogony, the sun abandons its role as central mass in order to become again a source of heat. The spatial or temporal distance that separates us from it, the original nebula, is not counted in terms of forces, but in terms of the cooling process. Hence the linear history in which the circular system will function: the said circumstances, fossils of the rotating hot nebula, initial conditions in both senses of the expression – mathematically, when it comes to equations, and in terms of mechanical systems, when it comes to evolution – surround many constancies or equilibria with their given disequilibrium, with their lack of consistency. In cooling, the system becomes harder, less viscous. Irreversible history and time send their roots deep into strange substances. They are born from circumstances.

Thermodynamics. – Carnot distinguishes between machines dependent on fire and those whose movement is not produced by heat. Error: men and beasts of burden, waterfalls and draughts of air always draw their strength from heat and ultimately from the sun. Mechanical theory studies the latter cases and explains them, says Carnot, by general principles applicable in all circumstances.

Such a complete theory, both global and local, is lacking for machines dependent on fire. They have not yet found their Lagrange for the system, or their Belidor for manufacturing principles. To arrive at a desirable level of generality, the principles must be independent of the mechanism concerned. Lagrange does not speak of Belidor. Carnot says nothing about applications or circumstances.

He reasons for every possible machine using fire, whatever the substance brought into play, whatever the manner it is acted upon. Substance is no longer important.

'The production of movement in steam engines is always accompanied by a circumstance on which we should fix our attention.' Accompanied: he who accompanies travels beside; of no real importance, he defers to the instance, which is the principal traveller. It could be said: movement and its production would continue if this companion were removed. Hence the name circumstance: it stands about in the surrounding area. But the text had said that it would avoid such circumstances, and in spite of that, here we have one.

It is a question of 'restoring calorific equilibrium, that is its passage from one body where the temperature is more or less high, to another where it is lower'. Here Carnot posits the two sources, hot and cold, and the transfer of heat from one to the other. Motive power is produced by this transfer, being equivalent to the restoration of equilibrium between the two sources, an equilibrium supposedly interrupted by combustion or any other action. The term circumstance describes the process with splendid accuracy.

Here we have two bodies in equilibrium, not according to their mass or weight, but in the new relationship of heat. As nothing in the world can be said to be neutral in relation to heat, this quality can be said to be universal. First state: stability, thesis or stance. When one of the bodies or substances begins to combust, it consequently deviates from the state of equilibrium. Instability. One hardly dares say that the two sources, confronting each other, hot and cold, and deviating for this reason, are antithetical to each other. If stability or synthesis is to return, a transfer must take place from one body or source to the other, in this case transfer of heat, like that of water or air, or tare elsewhere. It takes place; it produces movement. Now combustion continues in the warm body, the deviation from equilibrium is again produced, the transfer is perpetuated. We all recognize a familiar cycle, that we will accurately call circumstance. A given equilibrium, upset, then restored – cyclically so.

Circumstance becomes the whole motor. Substance is no longer important: it is burnt in the fire.

But it doubly expresses a cycle or circle: not only that of the breaking and resumption of stability, but the definition or closure of the process. For the second principle, also discovered by Carnot in this context, precludes any kind of dialectic, the latter being reduced to an absurd or trivial perpetual motion, or worse still, to a faulty connection between the global and the local. With little effort it becomes universal. Meditating a century later on the two sources, equilibrium and movement, or dynamism, Bergson, like all scholars who preceded and followed him, stumbles across the conditioning question of the open and closed. Carnot's description, his cycle of equilibria, interruptions or circumstance applies to a closed system – closed by a frame, inside which in fact another equilibrium is forming. The enclosure could also be called circumstance, for this reason. The question, neglected by Bergson and taken up again recently in the sciences as well as here, is how to connect the closed and the open, the local and another local, or the beginning of a global; is how to extend the equilibria over deviations or precarities, by crossing the threshold of the wall of circumstance. What happens there, by which I mean on the other side?

Circumstance is a splendid description of the productive work of the local and its temporary movement, space and time; plus the periphery which encloses it and inside which an equilibrium is at last established and holds sway; plus the set of fluctuations surrounding the open windows in the membrane or skin or frontier or wall or enclosure. What is exchanged there, by which I mean in the vicinity of this aperture?

You can be sure that the sun always manages to filter through a hole somewhere . . .

Circumstance enters science just as it was being eliminated from it; it enters philosophy as a topical question; and here we find it in the realm of the senses: does it define that too?

Seeing: from the open or closed, from the local or global, from islands or access pathways, from mixtures . . . Seeing: from an open or closed eye, an island-eye and pathway-aperture, a local organ or general perception, fabrics or veils through which photons, enzymes and other elements pass and are exchanged.

Zoology. – Vertebrates have eyes. Those of the mole are very small, hardly apparent. The aspalax, a Persian mole, has none, neither does the olm, a small aquatic reptile living in deep, underground waters. Vertebrates have teeth: but not the whale or the ant-eater; birds have horny beaks.

Without exception all vertebrates have ears. That can be explained: sound is propagated universally, unlike light: sight is local and hearing is global. Lamarck wrote a memoir dealing with sound and its vibrations. We will come back to the banquet of the birds.

Life displays an overall plan, says Lamarck, composed, perfected or complicated progressively, by and over time. But extraneous causes here and there have interfered with the execution of the plan, albeit without destroying it: it has given rise to significant gaps in the series, or anomalies in organic systems. This cause lies in the circumstances in which the different animals find themselves: climate, soil, location and environment, ambient or surrounding fluids, weather conditions . . . When they move from one place to another, animals change.

The plan of life unfolds in order and generality, like a global law. If we describe in local detail the organs of animals, we do not always find development of increasing complexity. Circumstances have thrown up obstacles and introduced accidents, variations, deviations, irregularities in its unfolding, which then display disorder and contingency. Lamarck takes on the task of conceptualizing the connection between the local and the global as being the greatest problem posed by living creatures: the simplicity of a law is deflected or disturbed, here and there; this is the product of circumstances.

Circumstances express multiplicity, irreducible to unity: not in number alone, but as regards site, form, time, colour or shade, matter, phase, locality . . . contingency. When we can, we reduce them to zero, nullifying and excluding them: the reign of a logic that never gets its hands dirty. Take everything away so that I can see: I can see if and only if I always look at the same thing. Nothing new under the sun. 'In the same circumstances' is a fine oxymoron, would one really use the word circumstances if they presented themselves in the same way? In which case, we would already have law or unity.

In their ramifying chaos they are resistant – a technicolour sunburst opposed to order. All intellectual effort in the past consisted in negotiating multiplicity from the point of view of unity or law. A simultaneously rational and irrational negotiation, even within the processes of reason. In methods and protocols disgust is sometimes a factor. Acclimatize or tame circumstances or, indeed, exclude them, in any case clearly distinguish them from thinkable knowledge – and consider them with horror or benevolence according to the state of your skin: as an object or obstacle.

You can see this negotiation in action, as though knowledge were signing successive agreements with an increasingly significant adversary. We have just read the contract of total expulsion: we must not laugh when logic speaks about the sensible – or grammar. You can see the intelligent and meticulous approach of complex cases of equilibrium in which the deviations cancel each other out or compensate for each other in an equally compensated time, you can see the circumstantial maintenance of certain deviations. You can see Laplace grouping together the circumstances which are irreducible to periodic, reversible laws and attaching all deviations and discrepancies to a hypothesis outside of the agreed scientific wisdom of the time, thus accelerating the paradoxical formation of a cosmogony. You can see Carnot finding equilibrium in a cycle and a new disequilibrium in this closed equilibrium, you can admire his invention of the motor within circumstance itself. Subtle negotiations on the sharp edge of knowledge and non-knowledge: could circumstances, always present, constitute the privileged object of their contact?

You can see Lamarck continue to negotiate. Life for him is a plan, law, unity, order. Every scientist, every politician and indeed every individual considers himself to be on the side of law and order. A common position: meaning what is general, global, vulgar and stupid. The science that I practise lays down the rules. Lamarck: life unfolds its unique plan, of increasing complexity. Why irregularities? You can group them, relegate them to another order: the world, context, climate and weather, in short the conditions of life, the inert and living environment also; in their multiplicity these rediscovered circumstances striate or marble the space and time in which unitary life is immersed. Life in turn negotiates circumstances and adapts to them for it cannot nullify them, or consider them unworthy of note, or assume that they will always, everywhere be the same, or group them into classes. It is immersed in their mixture and changes. It visits a technicolour world. Lamarck enunciates laws: great changes in needs produce great changes in actions, and if these actions endure they give rise to habits which produce new, transformed organs. In other words: in other circumstances, the same causes produce different effects. True? False?

You will discover hidden teeth in the jawbone of the whale foetus, and their indentations in the beaks of birds: law leaves behind traces of itself. The aspalax retains traces of an eye under its skin and likewise the olm, whose fossilized organ no longer even has access to light. But birds live in circumstances where they need not masticate, and moles wander about in deep pits.

Whether Lamarck is right or wrong is of no importance; the essential thing is that he distinguishes between a technicolour, detailed, multiple world, and a unitary life unfolding its legalistic plan. The latter descends into the former, as elsewhere the spirit into history, hence the variety of local avatars.

In turn, biology advances by negotiating multiplicities. The circumstantial cloud – outside life for Lamarck – somehow finds it way inside with Darwin and his successors: mixture pervades genetics and genetic material. Life itself produces circumstances that it once merely reflected. Skilful, delicate negotiation continues. It reduces the separation between the global and the local, life and the world. The connection between the local and the global is much better described as mutation and selection.

Thought visits circumstances, whereas our mind finds them hellish.

Love. – Julien has just taken Madame de Rênal's hand: 'The hours spent under that tall lime tree, that is said locally to have been planted by Charles the Bold, were for her a time of happiness. She enjoyed listening to the keening of the wind in the thick foliage of the tree, and the sound of scattered drops which began falling on its lowest leaves. Julien did not notice a circumstance which would have completely reassured him; Madame de Rênal, who had had to withdraw her hand from his, because she had risen to help her cousin set upright a vase of flowers that the wind had blown over at their feet, had hardly sat down again when her hand reached out for his almost naturally, and as if it had already been a convention between them'.[6]

They stand like a group statue; each one sitting, hand in hand, the vase standing there, a system in equilibrium. Now a gust of wind knocks over the flowers: the lowest object leaves it place, both women rise from their seats, unclasping their hands, the three elements in the system lose their equilibrium because of the chance and, it could be said, unpredictable breeze. Yet from this very circumstance genuine assurance follows. The vase returns to its upright position; instead of going off to bed, the two friends sit down again; their hands resume contact. The same equilibrium as before the wind, but quite different at the same time: convention has emerged from circumstance. A new order is produced by the chance wind. The two hands coming into contact through a physical or literal agreement return together to sign a contractual convention. The breeze brings contact, the unexpected flurry propelling the women, vase and hands from a state of rest to one of anxiety. Circumstance traces equilibrium as well as a deviation coming from the perimeter.

On the periphery of the system, its shadow: the thick foliage of the lime tree, together with a crown of sound; the moaning of the wind in the branches, the pattering of the drops of rain on the lower branches. The halo of circumstance emits background noise. Louise listens delightedly to the murmur. From this environment comes the wind, from this din comes disequilibrium, the contractual agreement is a result of the background noise.

Let us trace the genesis of the convention. Let us go back, to the same spot, in the evening, under the lime tree, on the day before. 'Julien was speaking energetically; gesticulating, he touched Madame de Rênal's hand which was resting on the back of one of those painted wooden chairs that one puts in gardens. The hand quickly drew back . . .' The first contact takes place by chance, unintentionally, unplanned on both sides, because the boy was waving his arms about. The abstract word describes it no better than the concrete word: contingency literally describes a moment of contact, as if the tactile or material meeting were accompanied by opportunity, fortune, accident and uncertainty. To say, then, that contact takes place accidentally is redundant. When Cournot defines chance as the intersection of two independent causal series, he is merely describing the term contingency, he is not going beyond the word itself, or its meaning. Two sequences encounter each other, two hands touch, two paths cross: this is a combination of circumstances. That the hand is quickly withdrawn means that the unexpected gesture could not give rise to a state. The meeting cannot be reproduced and does not result in equilibrium.

Movement goes from contingency to convention. The difference between the former and the latter is hardly visible, for the two words have almost the same sense: two hands, after meeting, will come together. Ironically, from chance to intention, the path still goes by way of chance: conjunction or fortuitous coincidence is transformed into a convention by a gust of wind that confirms the equilibrium. The height of derision for someone who, reading and imitating Bonaparte, implacably follows his will: aims, duty, constant unswerving ambition, equality, all those things. The purposeful curve that tolerates no deviation is divided into differential pizzicati by chance occurrences; whereas fortune integrates minor turns of fate.

Circumstance describes three things superlatively: the imprecise surroundings of subjects, objects or substances, even more remote than the accidental; highly unpredictable chance occurrences; a tricky history of stasis and equilibrium, disturbances and returns to the original state, deviations towards the fluctuating environment. Thus the lime tree and its thick foliage, the profound darkness when evening comes, the clouds, wind, weather, the sudden breeze knocking the vase over, the gesticulation of hands and arms between bodies, the pattering of the rain, the voice of someone getting excited, conventional silence.

Attributes, which are implied in the substantial subject, are distributed around the stable substance. Around the attributes, there can be a variety of accidents. Circumstance hovers above like a third crown. From this remote ring a detail suddenly swoops down, disturbing the stable subject or system, changing them or not changing them; if it does, it transforms them considerably, slightly or totally. The circumstantial cloud, like a labile torus, bombards the centre with imperceptible, negligible, eliminated elements, which at times can be quite decisive. A philosophy which fails to recognize this crown would be like accounting before the invention of large numbers, medicine before germs and viruses, mechanics ignorant of atoms or particles, a message without information or sound. The cloud or torus of circumstances sometimes approaches the substantial core and destroys it as well as its attendant dependent attributes or accidents; so-called causal series can also be drowned out by it. Multiplicity prevents us from identifying subject or object, just as the morning fog hides the valley, as the burgeoning brambles in the hedgerows proliferate in the countryside, degenerating into scrub or desert when the fields are neglected.

As the moaning of wind and rain begins, the boy's gesticulation disturbs the precise chain of the deliberate project, or deflects it, or splinters it; just as mud, sleep and greenery hide the grand strategy of Waterloo from the eyes of those who pass by.

Between the contingent moment or the chance caress and the hand given according to convention, a day goes by; a multitude of disequilibria mark the waiting with slight deviations. She loses her head, he feels his heart beating; her voice is strained, his trembles; he is beside himself with emotion. Like a river leaving its bed, the story seeks new points of stability, is churned up only to settle into a new stability. A new whole is reorganized as if from vibrations, sounds of words and heart, movements and wind: a storm is brewing, the warm breeze chases the clouds in the sky; the two women, like clouds, go for a walk: a ramble.

Imagine several marbles lodged at rest, as they are to be found in certain children's games; a shock or vibration shakes them out of the groove, or indentation, in which they lie. Gently tilting the game this way and that you have to get them into pre-determined hollows. The random movement of the marbles on the level surface follows an interesting although unpredictable path: so little determined by simple laws that each attempt is probably like no other, original and impossible to repeat. Circumstantial bombardment makes every situation unique while the methodical pathway crosses a homogeneous desert. Thus the hours that pass between contingency and convention, marked by deviations from equilibrium or by unstable states of bewilderment and agitation, are loaded with singularity: glances, cardiac arhythmia, every action that day appears strange, unpredictable, rare, unique.

The system returns to its final state through a host of small, fortuitous jolts which cause each element to lose it local stability and push them all towards intensified repose.

Moment after moment, life, gloriously improbable, advances. Probably programmed, deliberate, ambitious, tense, in such a case, but immersed in a turbulent cloud of solicitations that we'd have to call meteorological. Lucid, with our voluble crown of circumstances, we understand or know better, our daily happiness increases – that is the adventure.

In this halo, torus or border the global plugs its connections into the local, and conversely. For a general law to apply, here and now, repetitively and predictably, we require first of all the same circumstances: proof that we distrust them and that together they constitute the totality of conditions for the said experiment. They might disturb the thread of the causal chain; in other circumstances the same causes would not produce the same effects. Elements coming from this crown have the power to disrupt the determinist system and cause it to veer off towards other consequences. In other words, the very principle of determinism implies, in its initial conditions, its own generalization, or even better, displays the world in which it is immersed and shows how it cuts it down to size in order to cross it. The legitimate series transits via the crown and negotiates its passage there before reaching its proper place. Thus the sun's rays cross the Van Allen belt and the atmosphere, currents, clouds, moisture, and are transformed by these objects or filters, before touching us. If you change this mantle significantly, life on earth perishes. Like identity, determinism could be conceived of as stable states, at the bottom of a hole or depression: each well has its coping, its surroundings, the encompassing plain where traffic can move towards other low-lying places. Or as rare states, on the highest point of some island: every shoreline has its reefs, the sea-floor around it, the churning sea from which we might navigate towards other archipelagos.

Roads radiate out from towns – coming from remote and neighbouring cities or going towards them; forming a lattice on the ground, they channel the elements of space. They set traffic and flux in motion on the periphery where mixtures, sorting, exchanges and deals take place. The capital, the head or centre, seems to owe its existence to these outer layers, as if equilibrium were being created on a plateau or in a depression, an acropolis surrounded by a fluctuating belt that bombards the state, destroys, then shores it up again; in short, causes it to vary. The points or places of sorting and mixtures, the exchangers, may or may not be marked; the site of the centre may or may not be isolated, it being possible for the exchangers to fill the whole space. No capital? We at least have the palace. No central castle? We have the king or secretary general. Knight harbingers pass emissaries on the steps of the kingdom or throne, but does the lonely head of the president himself contain anything other than thousands of neurones and axons humming with messages like any intersection and perpetuating exchanges? Place is invaded by exchangers and the crown of circumstances; where is the subject, substratum, centre or capital to be found now? Iris wears a long trailing scarf, Hermes is recognized by his intertwined snakes: ringed with communication, a totally decentred space invading the centre.

The global (matter, energy, information . . . law) comes to a locality (cell, body, town . . . an element of the countryside) through its surroundings (membrane, skin, peripheral walls, borders . . . circumstances) where it negotiates its transit or passage through an exchanger.

Exchanger. A path allows movement in a band and in a line. Method results from an optimizing calculation. Go straight ahead but above all do not multiply senses and directions beyond necessity; choose. From several possible paths, you must choose one and stick to it. Even before making this choice, you must in addition decide on a dimension, and only one, and stick to it. Do not disperse yourself across planes or in volume; the traveller lost in the wood wanders into the clearing and climbs the trees but sees nothing but foliage. A fork in the road, like a loop or braid, defines a plane by two straight lines, or a surface by two curves; the moving object fragments. The same thing in very fine detail: optimization requires a smooth line and not bands with holes and protuberances where the moving object disintegrates through a multiplicity of minute shifts in the same space: jolts.

So the exchanger splits one line into two, and so as to avoid an intersection on the same plane, also into three dimensions, efflorescent. Left, right, between, loop, braid, up and down, over, under, knots explore places. An orderly ramble. Here optimization does not require you to cross rapidly, but rather to thread your way between: instead of abolishing space, movement creates it or makes it flourish. We would never have believed the sky so voluminous until we had seen the aurora borealis displaying its festoons: the display celebrates and creates immensity; we would never have believed our plot of earth so large before building there. The pathway passes between two others and in the process creates other paths between. Knots fashion places through which a thousand new knots can be threaded. Conveying messages gives rise to new messages. Space proliferates.

Proliferation becomes a condition for analysis or the result of its practice. To untie is to create profusion. Everyone knows that transporting a heap of sand, with spades or cranes, or moving it about, keeps on increasing its volume. Jolts create interstices between the grains like those found in the threads composing knots. What difference is there between a traffic interchange and the network of pathways that cover a country? Proliferation alone, the emptiness of the intervals. Although inflation has a bad reputation amongst thinkers, no-one can analyse without untying, no-one can untie without bringing deviations into play, nor loosen without causing an increase in volume. You sometimes write a volume on one page, three volumes on a line, a whole treatise on a single word.

The knot or exchanger, analytical itself, invents the local through similar profusion. It invents intervals between the walls of the pathways through which it passes; as a result, passing through an interstice, the passage itself gives rise to others: between its own flank and the wall. Turning back on itself, the path therefore offers new return pathways. Implication abounds and multiplies of itself. Creates its space, localities and intervals, open and closed, frontiers and continuity, and thus fills the volume that a taut, abstract thread denies by intersecting it. Splicing gives rise to a ball or doll. Cat's paw, clove hitch, granny knot, lark's head, sheepshank, lariat loop, eye splice, figure of eight or reef knot: the emergence of a thing in a place. I no longer think of names of knots in terms of images: how is it possible to express what a head or rose owe to the invagination of a thousand pathways? They burgeon.

The converse operation of proliferation is that of constriction. A well-tied knot can be tightened as much as you like but can still be untied. Analysis does not require us to undo knots: the old language is unhelpful, one can constrict while remaining analytical. An excellent work of art likewise constricts: creates its space, fills a volume, proliferates leaving no gaps. It is clear from this that global motion by its force creates pockets and that local implications by their richness look further afield: like a landscape of the world.

Like a bodily organ. When it looks at atlases of anatomy or embryology, the eye is reluctant to recognize the proliferation of exchangers or tight knots, in every size, filling a local volume with their branching or folds, braids and loops, envelopes or tears, windows.

Can every inert, living, crafted thing be defined as a turbulence organized into an exchanger?

In the beginning, it merely serves as a global conduit. Soon, in some corner where there is not so much traffic, a sort of garage takes shape; long queues of trucks rest at night in the whirlpool, the drivers sleep there in spite of the din. The police have constructed site offices on a traffic island, to deal with wrecks and for their own services. Trees have grown in the circles of grass in the hollow of braids and bends, where the birds nest; tramps have found paradise there, protected from the world by the turbulent circumstance, frontiers you do not cross on pain of death. They live, drink, copulate and carry out small transactions with the long-distance lorry drivers under the fatherly eye of the law. The interchange, or exchanger, is now surrounded by a tall, opaque fence protecting the surroundings from noise, with the result that one sees vehicles exiting or entering through doors and windows set into the fence, the sum of the exits no longer equals that of the entries in a box that becomes blacker and blacker; are we witnessing the emergence of a place comparable to a hive, town, palace, organism, cell . . .? The interchange has invented a place through weaving knots and passages, it is creating another with stases and emboli, these stabilities creating other exchanges that . . .

A hand creates with thread or cable an eye or aperture through which to pass, thereby opens up a distinct interval. Clear, in other words neither obstructed nor blocked: the thread passes as many times as it wishes or is able, in every direction or dimension invented by the passage itself. And the gesture repeats the open eye and the between-path. This is analysis, but it ties without untying, or prepares to untie while tying tightly, clearly and distinctly. Knots create place by multiplying these between-spaces clearly and distinctly. Here, far from destroying, analysis constructs, the dichotomy or cut being constantly repaired. The in-between is superabundant there, it brings things closer to each other rather than tearing them apart.

These gestures of weaving, knitting or knot-tying have been ours since body and time immemorial: even the birds in the sky know how to knot or weave with their beaks or legs when making their nests. These are the buried origins of topology and therefore of geometry; beginnings where sight disappears into touch, where touch, sensitive and delicate, sees contours, the smooth and the separate: origins preceding the arrival of speech by an entire era.

In tying, weaving or knot-making, hand and gaze devote themselves to connecting the far and the near, or to creating varieties from a simple line: flat or voluminous, tight or loose, dense or scattered. Place begins to proliferate by the very same element that denies place, cutting through the global economically. It attaches itself to other places as it goes along, as the tacking point passes to the bowline and through it connects with the whole rigging of the ship leaving for the other end of the world.

Through their topological design, their friction and their strength, in distinction and clarity, knots weld the local to the global and conversely.

We speak with several voices. The world can be seen as localities surrounded by their neighbourhoods: circumstances, connected with each other by exchangers that themselves become places, linked to each other by pathways that radiate into the global, the more or less local status of which is difficult to determine. These propositions are valid for the inert, the living – either simple or complex – the hundred kinds of collective, formal or beautiful works of art and thought, surrounded by conditions or garlands; we should move towards a global theory of exchangers and circumstances, localities and mixtures, crowns of exchanges around the ocellated place, valid for the countryside but seeking universality. Where in all this is the passage from local to global to be found?

The sensible, the subject of this book, which paradoxically refuses to reduce it to speech – experimental science likewise owes its very birth and existence, its success in apprehending things themselves and deducing their laws, to a comparably paradoxical defence against the imperialist ascendancy of the philosophy of language which held sway in the Middle Ages – the sensible is in general both the constant presence and fluctuation of changing circumstances in the crown or halo bordering our bodies, around its limits or edges, inside and outside our skin, an active cloud, an aura in which take place mixtures, sorting, bifurcations, exchanges, changes in dimension, transitions from energy to information, attachments and untying – in short it is everything that connects a local and particular individual to the global laws of the world and to the manifold shifting of the mobile niche. Through the sensible, this unique and unpredictable place tames or acclimatizes reigns of heat, light, shock and so forth. Weight itself, or gravity passing through our posture, determines the symmetry of the sensorium and sculpts a body which would no doubt have a radial form without it. In this peripheral whirlpool in which exchangers proliferate, themselves to some extent like whirlpools, our moving relationship to the world is knotted together: a stable base, unstable audacities, the chance slight buffeting it gives the periphery, the metastability of our lives that from now on will have to be called circumstable.

Sensible, has a meaning similar to that of other adjectives with the same ending. It indicates an always possible change in meaning. The magnetic needle can thus be said to be sensible as it vibrates or seeks equilibrium around a fragile bearing. Minute promptings coming from everywhere, in quality, dimension or intensity, on every wave-length make sensibility tremble, fluctuate and sweep and dance randomly over the spaces through which things, the world and others bombard or summon it. Thus the electroencephalogram seems to look everywhere for possible calls in a white expanse, sweeping back and forth, paying no fixed attention, complete, open and intelligent because of its instability: if an ear of wheat remains to be gleaned here or there, its cautious, inconstant movement is unmissable. A thousand vibratile lashes swarm randomly around strange attractors. Both act and thought, fascinated, choose an aim and an orbit; the sensible, open like a star or almost closed like a knot to every direction, mobile in all dimensions and sweeping over the entire neighbourhood, devotes itself indefatigably to its random dance, playing its role as an exchanger until the flat hour of death.

The term visit and the French verb *visiter*, to visit or inspect, mean first of all sight and seeing; added to this is the idea of a distance travelled; if you visit, you go and see, and with some active emphasis, you examine and scrutinize, show benevolence or authority. Generally, in traditional philosophy, the bearer of the gaze does not move, but seated by the window, sees a tree in flower. A statue set upon affirmations and theses. Yet it is quite rare for us to keep watch while transfixed, our ecological niche includes a thousand movements, sometimes we even travel around the world out of admiration for the visible. The earth turns, our global lookout post has long since left stability behind, the sun itself, the giver of light, mobile, is apparently rushing towards another place in the universe. In most cases, the observer moves far or near, at greater or lesser speeds, and moves around the thing observed at least once. Bodies, boats, spaceships, our planet, all move; and photons set the upper speed limit; the world passes from landscape to panorama, from local to universal, rambling changes into method and vice versa. God no doubt saw the world and things, we on the other hand merely visit them: not only because of the site occupied by the body; not only by means of tools, instruments and machines; but also intellectually: each discipline, experiment or theorem, provides a view that has to be sought after, another movement. We visit the encyclopædia, if it exists, like the world, if it exists. And the speed of light limits the visible and the knowable alike, as well as our technical successes. Thus the act of visiting is equally valid for the empirical, the machine and abstraction. The visit we are just finishing here had no wish to separate them.

Nor did it separate research, control or inspection, legal and juridical activities sometimes invoked during punctilious and detailed examination. Thus warships have visiting rights on merchant ships, according to certain conventions and circumstances. Our visit did not separate scientific meaning from that imposed by force or law; nor the objects of the visit: landscapes, living bodies, persons whose visit it is appropriate to return. We have just crossed the North-West passage again, from crude or medical observation to social exchange and even to the God of theology when he wishes to manifest himself: the first attested meaning of the verb to visit.

In order to see, movements take paths, crossroads, interchanges, so that the examination goes into detail or moves on to a global synopsis: changes in dimension, sense and direction. Now the sensible, in general, holds together all the senses, dimensions and contents, like a knot or generalized exchanger. It is understood that by content we mean the different terrains through which the visit passes: places, world, statues and gardens, deserts, oceans and seas, weather, scenery at home and abroad, meadows changed into pages, the stated concrete or the claimed abstraction, the law and laws, mediæval hymns and the commandments of love, the topology of knots and the spectrum of colours . . . visits explore and detail all the senses of the sensible implicated or gripped in its knot. How could we see the compact capacity of the senses if we separated them? We have visited without dissociating the senses from the word visit. Analytical language alone unties the knot, but consequently the sensible is lost. It cannot have it both ways: separable elements and their interconnected totality.

But what must we do so that the senses are not separated? We could have visited them as a group: the group does not ever visit anything but itself and its noise, although it sometimes perceives a few fragments of what it has come to see. We would have had to assign proper names to all the participants in the journey and a character and identity to each one.

THE FIVE SENSES

Each character, with that title or name, would have discoursed, as you do, on a particular subject. Have you ever heard anyone depart from his script? A Latin name would have been given to someone holding forth on pages, a Christian first name to someone unveiling an ancient document, a Jewish name to someone describing the desert in the sun, a university title to the topologist and astronomer; a Greek would have recited the *Odyssey*, a Gascon would have celebrated the Garonne, and Stendhal, returning to the fray, would have told of the loves of Louise, one windy evening. Plato writes no differently. The contents in question untie themselves, one body at a time, each one burdened by speech like a wooden panel on its shoulders, on which its discourse would be written. Callicles, whose name means violence, speaks in Calliclean tones, handsome Alcibiades argues and disrupts, like the badly-behaved son of a rich man. Socrates exemplifies and interrupts, an elementary school teacher, Theetete dies as a geometer, none of them deviates from his role. A colloquium. Its subject: The Sensible. There, a psychoanalyst only ever speaks about his own institution, a representative of the analytic school discourses on the meaning or non-meaning of discourse, the resident Marxist is careful not to step outside class struggle, each one embodies his discipline, all of the named bodies fit neatly into tombs of wood or marble on which the details of their membership are engraved. Into each of these boxes, insert a cassette pre-recorded in the discipline box. The organizers of the conference press play on the control panel and everything is underway in the best possible way in the best of all possible conferences – the different disciplines express themselves. The analysis of the contents is already 'untied' by the separation of the bodies, the totality or set of bodies being the equivalent of the totality or set of languages. As a result, our bodies are taken out of the equation. The sensible is expressed by colloquia or language. Socrates and his friends die as soon as they hold a colloquium on the sensible, long before the *Phaedo*.

The mind sees, language sees, the body visits. It always goes beyond its site, by shifting position. The subject sees, the body visits, goes beyond its place, and quits its role and speech. In other terms: no body has ever smelt and smelt only the unique perfume of a rose. The intellect, perhaps, and language most certainly, carry out this performance of isolation and selection. The body smells a rose and a thousand surrounding odours at the same time as it touches wool, sees a complex landscape and quivers beneath waves of sound; at the same time as it refuses the gaudy sensible to imagine at will, meditate abstractly or fall into ecstasy, to work actively or interpret its state in ten different ways without ceasing to experience it. The body leaves the body in all senses, the sensible ties that knot, the sensible or the body never remains in the same territory or content but plunges into and lives in a perpetual exchanger, turbulence, whirlpool, circumstances, maintained as such until the moment of death, when the knot is untied, loosened and analysed, when turbulence unties its bond and vanishes into the floodtide. The body exceeds the body or fails, the most recent self goes beyond the previous one, identity is freed at every moment from such dependency; I feel therefore I pass, a cameleon in a gaudy multiplicity, I become a half-caste, quadroon, mulatto, octoroon, hybrid. How is the sensible I to be described by naming a fixed speaker for each discipline represented or role played in a science or colloquium? The sensible I splinters and changes direction, wavering and various, losing its self, unlocatable rather than hateful.[7] If I am legion, how do I give versions of myself, and to whom? The word slides, falters, flows from description to story, or from reasoning to evocation, fiercely loyal to the state of things that the body lives and knows, visits the exchanger, knot, whirlpool, circumstances.

With the massive, floating given of the sensible, philosophy cannot be divided: into bodies, which are statues; or names, which are funeral masks; or into roles in dialogues or conferences which are useless theatre and politics; or disciplines, which are knowledge. Philosophy protects this infinitely precious treasure, still to be discovered in spite of millennia of fervent attention: the density of meaning knotted on itself and deployed in the world, seeking without finding another patiently deferred word.

We have visited the compactness of the given.

MINGLED PLACE

Not so long ago, in *Rome: The Book of Foundations*,[8] I described a moiré and precisely historiated landscape of blended colours – striped, brightly-coloured, damask – called the transcendental place of history, made up of bits and pieces, localities. Master and slave struggle there, or blues against greens, a stadium contains the struggle; at the doors of the stadium the ticket offices open, one must pay to enter; the person who wins, inside, blue or green, slave or master, differs from the person who wins at the periphery because the latter is in possession of the cash register: his law is not dependent on the struggle nor on the game. The game changes its rules according to place. When you move through the marbled country-side, you find that it is heterogeneous in its rules and laws, a tissue of individual localities. Of course there are long moments of homogeneity when a single law is propagated over a considerable distance, but on balance these are quite rare. In general, laws are not generalized. While the Sabine men, philosophers, are entranced by the local struggle in the stadium between master and slave, the Romans swiftly kidnap the Sabine women. The law of the street differs from the rules of the game on the field. The stadium delimits a spatial area, its periphery provides the transition towards a quite different element, the neighbouring streets introduce a third one; three laws are in operation on this chequer-board – struggle, taxation and kidnapping.

This blended, striped, mixed place reappears in this book which speaks of it alone, describes it, attempts to see it and make it more clearly visible. A transcendental space again: a diverse, differentiated, variable moiré on which a thousand shapes and colours play, in every imaginable relief; studded with splotches, criss-crossed by long and short, open, closed and broken curves; pitted with wells and valleys, pleated by mountain passes and protuberances; you must imagine this pluridimensional variety, overload it with properties. A journey becomes an adventure there, with many encounters and most unexpected happenings – there, to see is to visit. The countryside is revealed, magnificent, beneath seamless, homogeneous spaces, pillars of the law where pure reason wanders, as the precondition of these smooth volumes. A bedizened, transcendental space, conditional but not general.

The term transcendental means general in the tradition preceding Kant: the latter gives the sense of conditional and general at the same time. Kant describes the habitat of classical science, the conditions of its possibility in the subject; yet the foundation in this subject of the Newtonian world of universal laws, drawn from experience, is informed by the same generality as these laws.

We have abandoned or lost such a habitat; the same science no longer offers subjects the same consensus; the conditional figures in a range of varied circumstances. We have learned to doubt water-tight generality, we have not often, nor with the same ease, come across other universal laws. Newton was lucky, with his serendipitous discovery: we no longer mistake a winning combination for the full set of numbers.

The global appears to us as an inflated local: thus Euclidian space, or mechanical time, or time taking its rhythm from numerical series; the sun shines, nothing new happening beneath it, a yellow dwarf in a little canton where the Copernican revolution has stirred up the neighbourhood; did the one God run the same risk amongst the small individual gods, as numerous as archangels, thrones and dominions? The general hides an inflated local, in the two unities, heaven and earth; but equally so for the self: I am legion and will remain so for a long time. Can this observation be called an astrophysical revolution?

We see a pudding of localities, a tatter, a damask chequer-board; if the transcendental exists we can only describe it as a patchwork of individual places. It is true that the general, an infrequent case, sometimes occurs, but by chance, like a winning number: beneath this seamless event, the conditional remains a motley assembly of local pages, a detailed, circumstantial landscape. This blended, shimmering, bedizened place lies beneath the Kantian transcendental, which covers it with its language: a particular dilated case of the general moiré, reason ignorant of its own luck. We see seamless, homogeneous, solar, theologal, verbal space as a sudden inflation, extension or erection, a straight path. Brightly-coloured non-standard multiplicity, hyper-abstract under the usual simplified abstraction, becomes, dare I say it, the general case.

This general moiré vibrates beneath our eyes, and dazzles us with richness and inexhaustible novelty: an infinite number of shades, strange reliefs, mountains and tunnels, valleys or watersheds, unexpected events on monotonous plateaux . . . Supposing we were to call it universal variety?

Transcendental place of history in the *Book of Foundations* where Rome, a township or local *pagus*, spreads its empire over the Mediterranean universe; transcendental place of geography in the course of the visit finishing: here this shimmering place can be seen, touched on the tattooed, ocellated skin, a supple plain of common sense, the underpinning of the senses where their peculiarities mingle; it is revealed or implied in the state of things, canvases, veils, varieties; is deployed in the totality of the arts that we call music, the multiple house of the Muses; it is here when the peacock's tail of taste or the glowing fan of aromas opens; it is here, all in all, a body in its own right stitched together with many seams, a patched, thread-bare tatter; it is here as a pagan countryside, tissue, rag, formed of diverse *pagi* joined together with sticking plaster, an antique document visible on land and at sea, and that one can encounter by sounding the depths of space; it is here marked on the pages of this book, written with the express aim of redesigning it; moults of skin, the quivers of hearing, fans of taste, landscapes of sight, this is the sensorial – in other words, the common sense. Here is the underpinning for an empire of empiricism.

This transcendental, excessively formal, abstract conditional, this varied set with its individual peculiarities which is the basis for the sciences, does not reside, it seems, in the subject – we do not know the path that leads there – has no resonance in our languages, but constitutes, quite simply, the common place discovered in the exercise of the senses when they attempt to forget the anæsthetizing effect of language and the social constraints of knowledge.

The transcendental presents like our world: the most abstract as well as the most immediate thing. The real – touched, tasted, seen, heard – bears a striking resemblance, as though it were its twin, to the apex of abstraction. It could even be said that language and knowledge delay the moment of their nuptials, like obligatory ticket counters at which we have to fulfil an infinite number of formalities.

After the nuptials of body and mind, we shall now celebrate that of space and time.

5
Joy

STAINED GLASS

You can die of either heat or cold. Although it is the most beautiful object produced by human hands and even has something of the sacred about it, a boat is nothing but a metal shell, its exterior set ablaze by the sun, which makes a fiery furnace of its interior. In the middle of the port of Djibouti, or along the axis of the Red Sea, not far from Cape Guardafui, west of Aden, at the height of the hot season, even dawn is oppressive and night gives no respite. What's more, bread has to be baked on board, and working at the boilers down in the hold, or next to the oven, suffocates you. Outside it is no more comfortable. In the fifties, when a ship reached land, at least one sailor a day would be taken to hospital to be rehydrated; we had to separate those who, intoxicated by fire, fought each other with knives. How were we to cool down? Sea water or water from the hold would burn our skin. Yet if we visited American liners, we caught bad colds from the air-conditioning. We despised such luxury and bodies ignorant of the terrible conditions of the world. The real is so highly prized that those who live in comfort, however powerful they are, cannot imagine the disdain in which they are held by those who live in harsh conditions. Lethargic officers in the cool air of the wardroom would leaf through geographic periodicals as they consumed iced drinks and glanced absent-mindedly at the brick-red land beyond the scuttle. This was how the new world came to visit, a cosy shelter for fragile skins.

The keen, constant, implacable wind combs the Canadian plain beneath the motionless winter sun, the immaculate dark-blue sky. The snow brings clemency. Or lacerating knives: ear-piercers, nose-shapers, cheek-slashers. They cut right to the skeleton, bones separate, the body falls: cold, death; death, cold.

311

THE FIVE SENSES

In temperate regions, where the sea currents have a warming effect, there are sensations that affect the epidermis; others go straight to the muscles and exert pressure on them, and still others disturb the nervous system, dilate veins or shrivel them with cold; the most fearsome of them attack the last citadel: the skeletal structure. You have to have been cold, even beyond your bones, deep into the axis of the spinal cord, to know that this is not merely a figure of speech. The hard turns to liquid, you fall, the mounted police pick up what's left. On days of wrath in Quebec, a public warning imprisons everyone indoors – wherever they are – to avoid certain death outdoors. Here and there, on roads and around villages at dawn in Siberia, cadavers block the path: from the hard drug of alcohol, taken to forget the drug of politics, they go straight to being frozen solid – humiliated bones in the valley where tears themselves freeze.

How were our ancestors able to survive, from Labrador to Wisconsin, with only wood fires to keep them warm? All the children born at the beginning of autumn died. On James Bay, the base of the foundations for the dam to be built on the Grande Rivière – a wall so heavy that it makes the earth shake – revealed the remains of Indian dwellings, almost as ancient as the Neolithic. Our skin, now so sensitive to the cold, prevents us from understanding those naked bodies in animal skins, battered by the blizzard. The ancient world, from which we fragile creatures are sheltered, is revealed anew when we contemplate these ashes.

Heat inspires fear; cold, pure anguish. At sea, fewer deaths are caused by water than by the chance wind that whips it up – one can freeze to death in it; but before you fall over in one last shudder that shakes you to your very roots and makes you lose your grip, fear comes and kills you. It precedes ice and signals its coming. At high latitudes, in the dreamy grey of the Arctic, long whaling ships have been found with fixed, stiff, open-eyed corpses, still sitting on their thwart, their hands on the oars, poised to row hard, the sides of the skiff piled high with supplies and furs – everything was going well on board; dead with fright, the ghosts glide on the calm sea, shipwrecked through sheer terror. I shall die of cold, I am frightened of white, I love winter.

I have been agonizingly cold when going no further than the mountains of Auvergne. One of my books, written at that altitude, died there of the spring: my hands numb, shivering under seven layers of rough blankets, my feet hard and lifeless, a hastily knitted bonnet on my burning head, in a room without heating, in the bitter April rain mixed with snow and the harsh North wind. A book on Plato's mathematics and philosophy was turned to stone after three hundred pages, like a succession of statues, beneath the frozen, trembling immobility of all my senses. There is nothing in the mind that has not first of all been set free by the senses. If they become rigid, then that's the end of mathematics. Mental rigour requires a back that is not shivering. That spring, the sun was hiding behind the mountains that stopped me seeing my loves, beyond the realm of being. Who can talk about Plato in the cold? The condition for intellectual work, as far as the senses are concerned, is to be found in a warm room, the transcendental glows red in the stove – I learned this from my humiliated bones.

Hot-cold. Sitting hunched over the burning bricks, with my arms around my legs, naked, covered in sweat, motionless, near suffocation; calmer, adapted to the furnace, feeling as though I were swimming in its water, as if wrapped in a shroud, with my eyes shut; deep in a damp torpor, listening distractedly to the desultory conversations of my companions, drowning in the heat, but far from sleep; suddenly, after a freezing shower, diving into an ice-cold swimming pool, my skin is objectivized: comes unstuck, detaches itself, floats in the water like a coat, separated, at a distance from my body; the subject curls up within, anxious but calm, dense like a small black diamond in the centre of the plexus, leaving all the rest to become, independently of it, an object there in the world – stable, motionless, relaxed, pliant, blissful in the liquid.

We left paradise for the tree of knowledge; because of knowledge and in imitation of God, we shall never again enter the garden on the river's edge. All night long, night after night, on the plain of the mid-Garonne, an area with a temperate environment, at a little less than forty-five degrees latitude North and a little more than the Greenwich meridian in longitude, the temperature is so moderate, after the prune and peach trees have lost their flowers, that bare skin cannot tell whether the weather is hot or cold, or even mild, cool or warm. The body does not seek to clothe itself, it passes, like an angel, in the dark. Only when the breeze traces on it a pattern like watered silk does it notice that it is running out of doors. Why did we leave the garden where the water murmured?

Awakening takes place in a bath of skin and bed; you are buried in a double thickness of flesh and wool; the sheet is a continuation of the epidermis, the body spreads into its soft pockets and folds. A tip emerges from the shadow, heat and strangeness, the end of a journey under water, the swimmer bumps against the bank, carried there by the current. Bones and tendons inside the calves and thighs; the small of the back thrusts forward in a satisfying stretch; weightless food passes the solar plexus; a calm symmetry settles there. The interior, lived, explored and discovered in the blindness of sleep, folds in, invaginates to leave room for the exterior; the soft, now outside, will have to strut its stuff on the stage, pretending to be hard.

To fall asleep is to acquiesce, waking tends towards refusal. To dive is to consent; to drag oneself up on to the rocky coast. To be born each morning with the day. Joy.

The body is far from behaving as a simple passive receptor. Philosophy should not offer it to the given of the world in its recent repulsive manifestation, sitting or slumped over, apathetic or ugly. It exercises, trains, it can't help itself. It loves movement, goes looking for it, rejoices on becoming active, jumps, runs or dances, only knows itself, immediately and without language, in and through its passionate energy. It discovers its existence when its muscles are on fire, when it is out of breath – at the limits of exhaustion.

It breathes. Breathing, both voluntary and involuntary, can take different forms, transforming itself by working like the bellows of a forge. After the piercing cry of a baby's first breath, its first sigh, the body begins to enjoy breathing, its first pleasure. It enjoys it so much that it tries to lose its breath and get it back again – like a desired woman who flees and reappears – enjoys getting its second wind and beginning again, so as to achieve, through successive, breathless stages, a new rhythm, another world, a space in which everything becomes easy. There is nothing wider than a generous thorax. The first utterance of Genesis, at the dawn of the world, above the hubbub, says God, *ruagh*, a hoarse, alliterative breath, on the soft palate, at the back of the throat, before language, in front of the root of the tongue, where the gasping intake of breath acknowledges the divine; *ruagh*, breath, breathing, wind, breeze of the spirit, at its last gasp, dominating the wild beating of the heart.

The precursors of death are suffocation and choking, and the precursor of those is the kind of anguish that takes your breath away.

Jumping, first of all an elemental part of running, constitutes the second bodily pleasure after breathing, after the rituals of early childhood and the joy of our first steps. The animal makes itself as small as possible, crouches ready to spring. The build-up for the standing or running jump brings together the conditions for potential flight, the zero point at its apex, the decision to jump, hoped-for success, anxiety – the momentary loss of balance. The build-up, more pleasurable than the actual jump, thrills the muscles more intensely than does the jump itself – as if the force of the potential, on the ground, outweighed that of the act, in the air – the promise of intoxication being more intoxicating than the ecstasy itself. In a long race, ecstasy, strictly speaking, comes at the end of the sequence of small repeated jumps, low to the ground – it is the rapid intermediary leap; or the throwing of the ball into the basket, the goal keeper's flying catch, at the top corner of the net; but most especially the slow marriage of the stomach and back with the taut wire in the jumping pit. Have you ever seen an angel with your own eyes? Tradition defines an angel as a body that can instantaneously do everything that the mind conceives, projects or desires. If the angel thinks, for example, that it is alighting in a particular place, then it is immediately to be found there. The archangel I saw was named Tracanelli – the name is significant and if he is reading this, I greet him and, for once, it is not an angel doing the greeting. A spiritual being, he flew, with no apparent effort, over the fine, slender, flexible bar, and his arms, which had just let go of the pole, sprouted wings. When he launched himself and in his flight, there was no evidence of gravity, the universal action of which seemed for a moment to be suspended: a seraphic miracle. No effort, no sweat, we were surprised when he fell back down again. You could say that in that moment an angel passed – you could have heard a pin drop in the stadium.

I did not choose Hermes as my totem, emblem or theorem for speculative reasons alone. Nor with the historical foresight, necessary in philosophy, that made me say a quarter of a century ago that we were at the beginning of an era in which Hermes would occupy the dominant position over Prometheus, although the latter had held sway over our world and thinking for more than a hundred years. I took him for my ensign also because he flies, the first angel, with wings on his feet. Hermes precedes all other angels, just as they leave traces of Hermes in their wake.

He should always be depicted with wings on his feet: the lower limbs launch flight. What a mistake to attach those vast wings to the back! Ecstasy builds up in the dark core of the lower muscles, quivering and trembling before bursting forth. Death comes as a collapse, you fall, the tension in your legs, your life support, is released.

You who profess to speak – professors, actors, solicitors, all kinds of rhetors – you whose daily activity uses song, who must make your voice carry outside your body to fill a space stretching as far as the back wall and who have to lift a vibrating column, concentrated sounds and exquisite inflections, like a whirlpool of fire above your throat, be aware that everything comes from your base, positioning and posture on the earth, from your balance, from your instinctive gripping of the ground with the soles of your feet, from your grasping hold of long roots with your toes; be aware that a mysterious, burning spring comes from a mysterious chthonic current and rises along the muscular columns of the legs, thighs, buttocks and abdomen; that this voice that shouts or speaks or signifies owes its deep inspiration to these foundations, and that today, this evening or tonight you resemble the ancient prophetess, Pythia, who could not say or signify except when above the vapours emanating from the depths of the earth; you can tap into them with the lower limbs: the voice takes off if the wings of the word sprout from your ankles; you will observe that you can speak, sing, incarnate the word in your body, thanks to the knees and metatarsals. Music and meaning, like ecstasy, are products of these forces. The soaring voice comes from the earth, through the intermediary of the volcano-body. The soul is a life-sized wind instrument.

Nothing is more fun that jumping on a hard, bouncy bed. All children have enjoyed doing this until the mattress collapsed – a bad memory. The double ecstasy of the muscular effort in the thighs and calves, a powerful, almost metallic leap, a pause in the air that seems eternal, during which the body assumes positions and performs.

Nothing brought my brother and me closer to each other than this pleasure enjoyed together. We had never laughed so much in our lives. Do you remember? We made faces at each other mid-air. Coming down, we rarely hit the bed in unison, one of us would collapse, losing momentum, while the other, in the air, opened out like a star. A delightful lesson in circumstances.

Civilization sometimes makes minor progress: does there exist on the earth any object more marvellous than the trampoline, has human technology ever invented a device more divine? Pity me, young people, pity the man unfortunate enough to have missed, because of the burden of his years, a trampolinian upbringing.

Two beautiful, statuesque women, with narrow waists, jutting breasts, firm bottoms and strong legs, in strict navy-blue one-piece swimming costumes with the national coat of arms (they belong to the Olympic diving team), are training on the trampoline. They train as they do every day: they jump together, facing each other, just like my brother and me all those years ago, slowly assuming positions at the apex of their flight and carefully breaking up gestures and postures into their component parts, glancing sideways at each other, symmetrically, as if they were imitating each other, as if a mirror were separating them.

As everything – spins, jack-knife and swallow dives, or somersaults – follows on in a sequence governed by habit and their virtuosity, they become bored with this mechanical exercise, however difficult it is, and talk. I don't know what about, but they appear interested, involved and chat to each other – indifferent to their bodies, as though nothing were happening. A dialogue more than two metres in the air, where speaking bodies are flying, immobile in acrobatic and natural positions, demonstrates how angels speak. They were chatting about love, confidently, happily, like little *putti* laughing and skylarking.

This is where speech comes from.

There still exist, thank God, those simple merry-go-rounds with small seats, suspended from chains, which carry a single person. Around you, you can sometimes count twenty-five of these hanging armchairs. The machine spins like a top, the chains fly outwards through centrifugal force, like a crown, around the merry-go-round, and seek the horizontal; anyone riding on it loses his gravity. He has the impression he is flying, weightlessly. He has exchanged one force for another, he weighs differently, a false flight, a second chain, flight-footed.

The real begins when my friend sitting in front of me, and within my orbit, allows herself to be drawn into my arms, or pushed with my feet: she takes off in an epicycle and, in return, I move backwards or regress, aberrant planets in the sunny, circular system. I become weightless and, instead of a simple centrifuge, the movements seem to me to come from both my friend's strength and mine, from our special relationship: she pulls me, throws me, catches me, intercepts me; I leave her, find her again, fragile and dishevelled, hardly corporeal; I fly if she wants me to, she flies if I want her to, we fly at will, effortless, eye to eye, toe to toe, weightless, our interconnection alone creates our ecstasy, we alone are responsible for our existence, the rest has disappeared. Here is seraphic love.

We were a band of six or seven kids, in search more of amusement than study, the merry-go-round was set up on the gravelled area between our houses and the Garonne. Off we went, off we flew. In groups of three or four, we stuck together, we let go of each other, we burst apart like a bomb, one suddenly leapt up on all fours, another slid along on his back, this one rolled like a ball, that one, a jumping jack with his arms outstretched, did the splits; all together in a row, separately or opposite each other – star jumps, back flips, festoons, whizzing around frenetically on the spot – we were like angels, *putti* skylarking in the clouds in groups or laughing clusters. It was much more fun than jumping up and down in the morning on your parents' bed, alone – a rather dismal activity.

I saw this merry-go-round again forty years later in a mountain village in the valley of Livigno, where Latins laugh, dance and mingle in close proximity to the frosty morality of Swiss Germanophone Upper Engadine – a Romansch mixture. Six or seven kids were playing at chasing one another; two lovers, like serious cherubims, were flying. I knew then that I was born of a group of skylarking angels, occupying the clouds, going past in a crowd or suddenly, as a joke, bursting forth in a single ornamental orbit. Now over the age of fifty, seeing this spectacle again, all my knowledge of astronomy enters my body, and the adult returns to his childhood, when he was a planet. The child, becoming serious, provides the adult with a new, levitating body – living, archangelic love.

Counteract weight with another force, so as to do what you wish at last, by means of a weak third force – that is what spirit is.

Walking creates rhythm, accompanies the voice with cymbals, drums – a whole percussion section; walking also gives rhythm to silence. The double beat of the foot and heart, of walking and blood. We can never know our bodies unless we take them miles away from their birthplace. Look at statues dating back three centuries or more: wide feet, solid thighs; we are forgetting how to walk, an activity which used to give us a nobility of gait and carriage. The world has given up walking, our forebears from Asia crossed the Bering Strait and distributed themselves all over America; one great-grandfather of mine, a grenadier in the Imperial guard, marched from Granada to Moscow. Aeroplanes, it is said, have shrunk the world; on the contrary, all means of locomotion have increased its size out of all proportion to our footsteps. Our feeble legs no longer seek to cross space.

But it is better to walk in the mountains so that our legs become almost like arms, our body imitating the quadrumane; climbing up steep gradients and feeling our feet gripping the ground, to a certain extent the lower limbs enjoy no longer having to carry us, and discover another function. Feet make the best hands and hands the most reliable feet. The lowest muscles always aim highest: pillars, launching pads, towards the spiritual part. Hermes always has wings on his feet.

Running: a third pleasure – a combination of breathing and jumping. When the wheels of a train pass over the expansion joints that occur at regular intervals in the rails, the shock makes a sound which, at the beginning, is a rhythmic accompaniment to the progress of the train; as the train gathers speed, it appears to fly silently over the gap, the journey becomes smoother. It is the same thing with our foot on the ground. Those who are not used to running imagine that those who do so regularly touch the ground with their feet, and in fact, they are not far wrong: the foot fleetingly strikes the ground. The runner does not perceive it in this way, but has rather the same experience as the passenger suddenly riding smoothly in the train carriage. At a certain moment during his run, he could swear that his shoes are no longer touching the ground, he flies through the air, parallel to the horizon, his lower limbs have melted into silence or absence; both sprinting and long-distance running project him into the new world of birds, which skim along the surface of the track, high and low. Running does not speed up walking but rather generalizes jumping. What the supporting elements of the body, the lower limbs, those moving forces and columns of life, are able to achieve differentially in jumping, is fully integrated in the act of running. They work without drawing attention to themselves, they carry but are absent. Like the subject that thinks but is not there. They do, without being. This is what the wings on your feet say – this is the message of Hermes the runner.

Young people find it easier to run than to walk. As you get older, you think rather than acting instinctively, or you learn how to throw away your crutches and legs.

It is commonly believed that porterage turns people into slaves. Indians crushed by bales of jute or Chinese doubled over under their yokes – have you ever been a porter? We are losing the habit of carrying. You do not know your body if your pectoral girdle has never been subjected to weight and been under pressure.

A piano produces sound, but bends under the constraint of several tons, hard and soft. This philosopher pays homage to the master with the sensitive hands, but also to the builder, and to the removalist as well.

If you ever have to carry someone on your shoulders from the top of a mountain, down to the valley, you will think at first that you are dying, the torture endured by muscles that do not know how to work when walking down a slope is unbearable; then you get your strength back, as is always the case, a second wind and addiction to this new labour, gradually and for the first time previously unknown muscle fibres, unaccustomed angles, slumbering joints, zones of silence in the middle of your flesh make strange yet familiar music, never before heard yet immediately recognized, the mobile, non-homogeneous porterage column separates into its component parts, a whole world comes to life within it, arranges and adapts itself, redistributes its responsibilities under the implacable, crushing weight; the body becomes an architectural structure, moving masonry, a ship; the skeleton becomes a firm framework, with tie-beams and rafters; the muscles form the wall and partitions, a whole fluid network of flexible woodwork; the tendons, changing their angles through time, supply supple, pneumatic, almost liquid, foundations, running the risk at any moment of toppling over; the body becomes a tripod, armchair, sedan chair, hammock, triumphal arch, cathedral, boat, cradle and tower, a strong and solid foundation for a building, a fluid support for a ship or ball; the body, then, throws itself underneath, *sub-jects* itself, knows suddenly what one must *sub-ject*, and how to do it, recognizes itself as thrown beneath – *sub-jectus*, subject. I carry therefore I am.

Porter, ensign-bearer, voice tube: bearing a burden, an ensign, a voice.

How happy you are when transporting your dancing partner or beloved, flying is nothing if you cannot make others fly, ecstasy is completed by the static moment of ecstasy, the call to flight. Gravity brings a couple together.

He who lays down his burden grows taller.

Weighed down for so long by sciences and books, great authors with immense corpuses, weighed down by so very many fathers, living and dead languages, hard science and soft knowledge, weighed down for so long by memory and history; when the burden is at last laid down, at our feet, we become children again. Immediately happy in the sensible world.

I took a girl, my child, to the summit of the mountain covered with ice, all the way down to the valley where the mountain streams sing.

This incorporated educational duo does a *pas de deux* in the happy valley.

Male, weaker sex, do you know how to carry? Only women have this knowledge, and on occasion, experience incorporated porterage when two ages are added together.

The *ruagh* was uttered from the depths of the throat in breathless gasps before the latter thought of speaking; like fire and wind the thorax escapes from its lake of tears; each leap is torn out of the belly of the earth; walking is in cadence with the rhythms of the heart; running cancels out the lower muscles that launch you on your way; the body acquires bearing when it lays down its weight of knowledge and self-awareness and begins to dance, a compendium of all the primary pleasures – total elation. Joy inspires, quivers, dances. Life dances like a curtain of flames, death stiffens; intelligence dances; stupidity, repetitive, stands still; intuition dances, logic and memory merely programme robots; words dance at their birth and collapse into stereotypes; desire dances, indifference sleeps.

Dancing, the music of the body, reigns before language. It measures the beginning of time: runs and jumps to a repetitive rhythm, becomes redundant, makes the same movements again, takes new steps, rolls up into a ball and from time to time surprises you with a sudden attitude, the body inventing a new figure; dancing sows the eternal return of rhythm with the seeds of the unexpected – this is the beginning of time.

A body is not born until it has danced.

The lift for which, in your usual form of locomotion, the sole of the foot alone is responsible, is distributed over the whole surface of the skin when we swim. The responsibility for porterage, in a medium that would offer no resistance to weight if it were concentrated on the banal polygon, is transferred to the body which suddenly, in its entirety, becomes a foot. Sandal, in Turkish, means a boat. The head, above water, in the lighter air, sits on a skin, the leather of the submerged shoe. Thus the skin rejoices and negotiates, one area at a time, the weak support provided by the fluid, integrating all these small impressions, each of which relies on the others for overall flotation. Swimming involves the whole skin, every tiny part of it, and all at once. A baptism that takes us back to a time before we were born. Should we, conversely, rethink the feet as scale models of the whole body, providing it with floats when fluid becomes hard? Freed from any obligation, the whole skin will touch, differentially, not carrying any weight, complete in itself. Therefore tattooed.

It could be said that standing and walking, because of gravity, impose on us the axial symmetry that sculpts our form and appearance, linking us all to the centre of the earth. Swimming in water and dancing in air release us from this commonplace, and replace the straight line with a point in that indeterminate place, constituted by passing through the birth scuttle, that I previously called the soul. All our symmetries change. Breaststroke, glissades, jetés, diving, transform us into radiant beings – or rather radiolaria. If we lived in the water for several million years, would we become starfish? We've all seen dancers whose torso disappeared as they moved. Cylinders set on the ground, eyes and knees as symmetrical as backs and breasts: the solid imposes a heavy architectural angularity, whereas we become spheres around a point in the voluble fluid which naturally inclines towards roundness. Everything that decreases gravity, or nullifies it, leads back to this centre that comes out of the earth and is incorporated in our autonomy, that is encircled by our movements in the water and controls jumping. The head and tarsi on the axis lay claim to centrality, but there they are on the periphery, neither base nor summit; everything is reordered in relation to the solar plexus, not far from the sexual organs: if we were to float or dive for a million years, would we become a little less rational – emotive and tender?

So, curled up, slowly swimming in the mother's womb, the fœtus is wrapped around the same point; curls around its soul before birth, determines it at the moment of birth, rediscovers it when swimming or dancing, in the magic of a thousand spherical symmetries. Don't swim overarm, don't dogpaddle, don't obediently maintain the competitive and proud posture of axial symmetry; coil up in the liquid you remember from your embryonic days, in search of the buried soul – it is there that true progress is to be found.

Attentiveness bends the body into a convex arc that places this point at the focus, or centre of the circle. The point leaves me and goes to seek its fortune in the world.

The point of spherical symmetry, around which swimming, diving or dance unfold their flight, and the existence or soul of which is revealed by birth, or by passing through the crack opened up in the side of the burning boat, moves outside the body as a result of positions, movements, exercises. From our fœtal origin, we have known how to move around this pole, we know how to bring it into existence outside ourselves. We are born, we give birth. My soul, a pole of subjectivity; soon to become a pole of objectivity.

A clumsy person plays ball by moving it around himself, an aberrant planet receiving its law from the subject sun; discordant, rigid, wilful, controlling, he will never learn anything. He does not know how to bring things into being. He refers things to himself. A statue, a robot. The ball, on the other hand, plays with the clever players as they pass by, wandering planets around the small new sun, harmonious, flexible objects around the ball-subject. These players will be able to learn everything because they have abandoned their own law and given up controlling things in order to adapt, becoming submissive, and therefore subjects in this new sense to the law of what is fleeting, and already far away, and in which they recognize their former soul. A soul that is soft to the touch up close; visible, sonorous and sometimes perfumed from afar. These players have given birth to the relationship and the object. The almost-subject point becomes an almost-object, a relationship and soon, a thing. These players know how to give. As a result, they know how to receive the given. Clever and attentive, quickly catching on.

To know how to be born and to bring things into being, to recognize a place of schizogenesis, in the body, around which the subject is organized, and which leaves the body and becomes relationship and object, my inner core suddenly taking up position a certain distance away, absenting itself from my generous self in whom the totally alien and remote can, when it wishes, also receive shelter and lurk nearby and inside . . . The space of the five senses constructs the distances around it into a set, close to taste and touch, far from hearing, perfumes and sight, within which this place moves and gets it bearings.

If you ever played team sports in your youth you will be familiar with the personal state in which your body suddenly becomes angelic and succeeds in everything it undertakes: without fatigue, without experiencing any obvious effort, you can jump higher, go everywhere, run tirelessly and reach every goal. I remind you again of the tradition according to which angels can immediately bend their bodies to their will. So you will remember having been given an angel's body for a few seasons, having passed without knowing how into another world, into a space without error or weakness, where the craziest plans were effortlessly successful, precise gestures, subtle movements, delicate and always accurate decisions – life lived a metre off the ground, in a state of levitation. The ball itself pulls the arm to the goal. Music composes for the author without his doing anything.

Individual ecstasy leaves an imperishable memory – of sport and one's body, of the intellect or emotions – it is the best thing that happens in your life. You can even spend your time collecting such highs – a good and fruitful existence; ecstasy *à deux* is rarer and through modesty I leave it to your imagination. Do you know that a seraphic state can suddenly alight upon a whole group?

I shall remember until my dying day the two times this bolt out of the blue happened: to five of us and a round ball, and to fifteen and an oval ball. I remember particularly the dense silence in the narrow, compact space in which we danced together, a certain deafness or blindness as we entered the world of miracles. Usually, when the ball is passed – and it flies quickly so as not to be intercepted – it moves from one pair of skilful hands to another; acute, vigilant glances are exchanged, often preceded by a call, word, cry, brief interjection, vowel and even a coded hand gesture. The ball runs with them, after these signals, at the same time as they do, along the network of fluctuating channels that they trace out. Suddenly the ball takes their place, all other signals are extinguished. The whole team enters a box, a dim cave, the clamour of the spectators becomes distant like the far-off seashore, the opposing team dances like a group of shadows without strength, ghosts; it is at that moment that my body positions itself at the point where the ball will pass, I throw it into the vacuum that another cherubim will fill, immediately and unquestionably, we no longer look at each other, no longer hear each other, no longer speak to each other or call to each other – our eyes are shut, our mouths closed, our ears blocked, we have no language, we are monads – we know, anticipate, love each other; we anticipate each other at lightning speed, we cannot go wrong, the whole team cannot go wrong, *it* is playing: not me or my partners but the team itself. I move to the right, I know that another player knows that I have done so, that the ball will await me. The ball is travelling so fast that it weaves between us bonds of unassailable certainty; as this certainty is seamless, the ball can travel around even more rapidly, and as it travels more rapidly it weaves . . . No-one who has not experienced such ecstasy can know what being together means. I have the impression of knowing from the inside, as if by intuition, how a part or element of an organism must live. But in the case of the latter, where does the ball go, and where do balls come from? And again, what is a ball in a collective that does not play, and where does it go? And who, unlike angels, is blabbering on?

Sublime dancers are encountered rarely in one's life. Who can express the wordless ecstasy of what is always a little like a *pas de deux*? How is it that one raised hand immediately encounters the other's raised hand, that legs bend at exactly the same moment, that one foot anticipates the other's foot, that the supple body joins in with precision, that the two bodies conspire – speechless, silent, unprogrammed – eyes lowered and abandoning themselves to the pleasure of harmony, rhythm and music: music has taken over both bodies, has invaded them and the dancers, seraphic, have become music-made-flesh. But when they make love in so many exact and tacit encounters, tell me, where does the ball go, where does the music come from?

Wordless God of perfect harmony.

There is nothing to equal a great philosophy because it opens up a grandiose landscape, leaving on it a gaudy, moiré surface – the miraculous exhilaration of achieving better understanding expands the dwelling of those who sleep in average rooms and suddenly creates for them a palace the size of the world; there is nothing to equal an elegant proof, that combines subtlety with reason; an intuition that makes the body fly at the speed of thought which seems to us swifter than light; deep meditation, altitude, slowness, the serene plain of wisdom; there is nothing to equal trying or waiting, and if I am mistaken I will at least not have hurt anyone, and if I am not, we will exult joyfully; nothing as good as a piquant, incisive, off-centre idea, attaching its movement to the long, crooked chain of ideal grains winding their paradoxical path through the air around us; most valuable of all is apt expression, literal language, the calm and transparent water of style, a diamond with a hard but diffuse sparkle, the life of the intellect gives you the opportunity to be totally joyful, those who enter its temple fall on their knees and no longer wish to leave.

But the deep-blue, autumn sky, as grave as someone who has few days left to live and is not wasting them; but the coppery light of the last fine afternoons, trembling timidly in the red trees, the crunching sound of feet dragged through the leaves intermingled with the still-green grass, the indeterminately cold or cool breeze, the very last hot days or the first signs of winter; but opened and still bitter walnuts with their membranes, rotten grapes, prunes cooked six times, caramelized on the racks taken out of the oven, the acrid harshness of new wine, almost as blue as skin, almost as green as grape pulp; but the high forest in Auvergne in the glory of October, grapes harvested in low-lying areas, the supernatural peace of the countryside at the end of September, a plenitude in which divinities, tangible, come down to earth, between the not-yet and the already-over – dense minutes when the body understands more than the mind does – is there any sentence to equal the delights of the given?

The knowing subject dilates and extends itself over the whole body; the previous subject was condensed into a simple abstraction, existing somewhere, but in the background, unknown, in a transparent place, leaving the rest of the body in shadow; the body, now knowing, becomes a hypercomplex spirit, leaves ancient, forgotten knowledge to its brutal simplicity, takes it as read, and travels towards a totally new conquest: I know or understand through my skin, as fine as any iris or pupil, and they in turn as fine as intuition, in a bath of sounds or noises, anharmonic. I understand or know through sapience – taste finally has the name it deserves, that of art and wisdom – and through sagacity, intuition at last regaining its cognitive dignity; but I apprehend and conceive also through my muscles and joints, my bones becoming transparent, my stance off-balance in the hurly-burly of the world, an attentive and flexible posture – the rhythm of my heart and the tunic of my arteries beating against its rocky obstacles. Through assimilation and inspiration, through running and jumping, walking and dancing, love, the knowing subject at last occupies its house, its true house, its entire house, the whole of its old, dark, black box. By what idiotic cruelty was it reduced to this absent hole, why was it excluded, without home or hearth, exiled from its body, evicted from its home? Why, in short, was it forced to detest its ancestral territory and to bring about its inevitable destruction by reason and science? The knowing subject, the prodigal son, returns home after travelling at length through the empty world and abstract spaces. The house is decorated with white tablecloths and flowers in the vases, garlands on the walls, burning torches, lavender-scented sheets on the beds for the feasts of the Prodigal Son's return, the knowing subject occupies the entire body – the luxurious headquarters of broad and complete knowledge – founded and based on the sweetness and competence of the senses, knowledge attuned to its limbs and to the world, toned-down and pacified, ready to agree, delivered from resentment, consenting, a luminous, transparent, vibrant, spiritual, flexible, quick, lively subject body – a body that thinks.

HEALING IN FRANCE

France has rarely produced an empiricist philosophy: entirely given over to sensuality, it had no need. Those who are living don't talk much, those who talk don't act. Traditionally, French culture is one of taste, it busies itself at tasting and works hard at tasting. This still life of cheeses, wines, game, pastry and cooking is its identity card. On the sparkling cloth, transparent glasses and carafes, wines with ruby legs, a table runner and conversation. The latter emerges from the most exquisite taste. Is there any culture or agriculture, except for that of China, that has to such an extent and for so long worked on refining its taste? Neighbouring cultures are more hesitant: amazed or disgusted. When you condemn those who live to eat, you who speak of eating to live, have you worked out why you are living?

Is there any culture that has, to such an extent and for so long, worked on refining perfumes? Strong, heavy fragrances in the past; subtle and evanescent ones more recently, rose has replaced musk. Perfume is to aroma what forgiving is to giving or what per-fect-ion can be to fact – quintessence. If what is given to our bodies is reduced to language, what does the forgiven person say? The bouquet, a composite, brings together taste and smell – French culture excels at creating it.

The ebb and flow of conversation fades away. The bouquet does not produce language, but brings about conversation – the consummate, perfumed art of the ephemeral, fleeting, indestructible spirit. It is lost, floats and disappears into the air; in ruins, tattered, it sometimes returns in a lightning flash, in the way that blinking lights do. Paradise lost is rediscovered in snatches. Dialogue is obstinate, struggles making its dialectical clickety-clack audible, as stubborn and stupid as a couple of goats locking horns; conversation awakes and languishes, begins, fades, murmurs on, expresses living intelligence, like a thin mist in space.

There is nothing in conversation which has not first been in this bouquet. Fireworks which temporarily streak the night with shimmering and stripes.

Language is preserved in dictionaries, knowledge in encyclopædias, money in safes. Written signs remain. Conservatories or museums are the haunts of the arts – precious pieces: paintings, busts, stones, icons, shut away in boxes, protected from thieves. Theory is interested in what remains. In the invariant. There is nothing in the intellect that has not first been in the senses: something of the sensible remains. Although it has undergone a transformation, there is something of the invariant in it. In general we are only interested in what remains, in what survives of the sensual in the intellect. The word flies, the written remains. The bouquet does not remain, neither does taste or perfume; the supreme human art, conversation, which derives from them, drifting over lovers in clouds of signs, is lost in the air. All of that fades away, nothing is preserved or exchanged for long, nothing of it is compared or reduced to money, everything vanishes when inflation strikes. There's no interest, so goes the theory, in counting on interest from capital which is concentrated in specific places, or in our heads.

The given can arrive in fits and starts, the art that derives from it is fleeting; language remains, like money. A flow without reserves in the first case, circulation with capital in the second. If the given, therefore, is reduced to language, then data banks are easily constituted. It is not possible to set them up for the ephemeral. Knowledge, science, languages can be put into data banks, but not the sensual, by nature evanescent. There is nothing in the intellect that has not first been in the senses: this means that the intellect has collected what has remained of the senses, that it therefore becomes a memory, a reserve, a data bank. Conversely, any data bank is quite precisely what classical philosophies have always dreamed of. Now what do we call someone who, in the place of intelligence, carries such a data bank in his head, constructed like a beehive with labelled cells? A perfect fool.

THE FIVE SENSES

There is in the sensual a delicacy that does not remain, a bouquet, a conversation – a joy that does not linger. All the finer and more intense for being transitory; crude when it comes to rest. Is there any culture lighter than mine, that has attracted more accusations of levity? Weightless, priceless, doubly graceful. Grace passes by, too modest to assert itself. The intellect does not register, does not recognize graceful sensuality, nothing of which can be put in the bank. Hence the contempt in which my culture is now held. It does not produce any theoretical, social or pecuniary interest, but speeds along on its capricious path. Our culture is made up of what our graceful senses do not leave behind: the capricious, the light, the transitory; what does remain of the senses is accumulated like money, the venal theory of knowledge accumulates and calculates. The latter, an epistemology devoid of pleasure and grace; the former, a gift of sensuality. So the given slips through language and there is no such thing as a data bank, there is never anything but banks of money, even in the realm of theory. I do not know of any culture lighter, more attractive, less abstract than mine, less calculating.

Even the French language has a certain piquancy, especially when speaking about what does not concern it. It calls given what comes from the world to the body, it calls perceived[1] what is apprehended by us as coming from the world. We take what is given to us, it says. As if we were demanding, as if we were perceiving – in the manner of tax, through a levy – what is free, what is simply on offer. A strange paradox. What is the use of levying, collecting the given, what is the use of making grace pay tax? Furthermore, why would we bother?

We have covered over the given with language; the world, bought out, is hidden beneath its price. We must now tax priceless, gracious, gratuitous data.

Coming after sensation, perception remains at an economical distance. The former registers grace, the latter pays for it with language. French expresses and teaches us this, having quite precisely perceived the relation of language to the world.

Generous are they who give themselves over to what passes, forgetting to count, ignoring the bank, taking their time, and taking pleasure in the ephemeral. The given passes by, gratuitous because it is instantaneous. Pleasure, a differential of time, lasts a moment. The fleeting sensorial contains the infinitesimal eclipse of time. Æsthetics gives brilliance to the moment or sets it on fire, brings together all the inchoatives. It does not know how to totalize them, it is incapable of integrating or retaining them.

The bank retains them, language retains them, but while apparently successful, both in fact lose them. Time accumulates in data banks, but you never find the time you've put into them. We believe that we are grasping at least a sub-total of time, a sort of total, when in fact we are deep in the chaotic ebb and flow of its inchoatives, of its fragmentation. Æsthetics confronts this cloud, or noisy sea. The intellect, language and data banks attempt pseudo-integration of small sensorial, non-integrable, perceptions of time. Has any culture ever come closer to this cloud, this pleasure – the instantaneous? Has any culture ever left time?

Courageous are they who give themselves over, in abandonment, to this chaos, who dive into this mixture. Fear, horror or economics urge you to distance yourself from it, to enter the bank. Accounting wants to triumph; avarice is intellectual vice. The intellect has a horror of the extravagant senses. But it miscalculates, like all misers. If you want to waste your time, attempt to save it; if you want to save time, be prepared to waste it. You will never find in the bank all the time that you have put into it. It is there, but has frozen into signs. Whereas the bouquet, perfume, shade, conversation which are lost in the air subtly marry themselves to the disappearing differentials of time; they flow, pass, fade away, return, blink and percolate. The senses play hide-and-seek with time, which is lost, found again, recovered at an unexpected moment. Absent from the place where you believe it to be, missing from where you put it. I know of no culture less miserly than mine, less fearful and less horrified. There is nothing in its mind that does not move or adapt as if it were a sense. There is nothing in the intellect that is not as rapid, gentle, vigilant, capricious as a sense. The senses are models for the mind, which, without them, risks understanding nothing about time.

All wisdoms have celebrated the instant, the wise man leaves aside memory; he has few projects, makes himself at home in the present, inhabits its differential. Is there any culture more sapiential than mine, light and immersed in the evanescent? Æsthetics, the pleasure of the senses, refinement, beauty of fleeting forms, flight of time, opportunistic life, all laugh at the morals of history. The wise man, living in the moment, knows no bank.

Is there any culture that has to such an extent, and for so long, refined the art of love? This loving has been ruined by theoretical bombardment, by the attack from clichéd language; behold three generations whose fleeting encounters with love are pitiless, and who have abandoned its bouquet for a sick language; the flowers of yesteryear have disappeared into the black box of the word. Nothing in the unconscious bank has ever enjoyed the briefest encounter with the senses. The wise man forgets in a moment the long memory of his sad childhood. I have never known such a loving culture, one so free of ponderousness.

This is a people that cannot help being lighthearted. Even though we weigh it down with knowledge or money, overload it with history, bore it to tears with wooden language, this nation, incapable of boredom, has kept on, and will keep on laughing. It smiles and will keep on smiling, it mocks. It doesn't care for power, loves the moment, the everyday. Irredeemably lighthearted, with a culture that is mobile, frivolous, delicate, trivial, flighty – even superficial, lively, relaxed, vague. We are not deep, serious, logical or abstract, we prefer the bouquet, the slight lingering odour; we prefer shades to colours; to comfort, elegance; to truth, wit; harmony is hidden beneath the grace of appoggiaturas, construction is buried beneath swags of leaves. Charm passes before pleasure, taste before judgement, life above all the rest, the cheeky little duchess in old rose before the black-clad, unattractive scholar; we have the superfluous, why would we need the necessary?

If we happened to become burdened with an embarrassment of riches, power, knowledge or reason, we would modestly hide the fact, frivolous to the end. Women – as light here as intelligence, and intelligence here as light as a sense – have a velvety touch, a subtle sense of smell, a delicate palate, acute hearing, an eye that matches a skirt with a scarf, as light as the soaring dove, augural, carried by wind currents in the clear morning sky: in short, our tongue must be used in a light, lively repartee, moments of immodesty; so hide your heavy publicity-laden science – our feminine tongue, muffled and veiled, is studded with mute vowels.

A people such as this cannot help being woman, its culture reveals the modest femininity of the world.

Sites organized around public speaking, built to serve speech, and surrounded by places for listening, usually favour monologues: the pulpit raised for sacred eloquence in the middle of the nave, the rostrum of the specialist scientist at the front of the amphitheatre, now a stage with microphones and cameras. Silence, he is speaking. He speaks, and in order to be understood, obeys rules of logic and rhetoric. At the very least to please the audience and not to contradict himself.

We have all known places where dialogue flourished: two people in search of the truth struggle to exclude the noise between them that prevents their hearing each other, and try to include in their midst the meaning born from the intersection of their vocabularies and the interlacing of their good will. Dialogue is played out between four people, the two who appear to speak, plus the excluded third, their demon, plus the included third – their hope – the god who descends into their midst.

In Paris, there were salons presided over by certain women. No-one made speeches, there were no couples in dialogue, they were places of conversation. No announcements, no thundering prophecies, no teaching, much less discipline – none of this took place, on pain of desperate boredom. The women of that time did not tolerate boredom in their houses. As far as I know, philosophy, in spite of its brilliance in the French XVIIIth century and its diet of conversation, never applied a methodical term to this multi-polar networking, as it did for discourse, choosing the terms logic and rhetoric, and for dialectics, choosing the term dialogue.

Conversation must be understood as it is said or written – or better still, practised, under the courteous ægis of women – as the set of conversions and frequent repetitions of the bodily, verbal and theoretical repositionings of its participants. It resembles the configuration of the famous non-integrable problem of n bodies: the arrangement of a cluster of stars obeys the law of gravity, minute after minute. Nothing is more complicated, since each one is influenced by the gravity of all the others and each responds to the gravity of the others. Conversion, rare and simple in the case of sacred eloquence and in scientific lectures, is frequently repeated here in a complex fashion: multiple, rapid, instantaneous. We have never conceptualized the hyper-Platonic state of conversation: a set of applications, translations, interferences, communications, passages and distributions which would draw its fluctuating map, sometimes its labyrinth, its metastable network, its becoming, when Hermes passes.

In the *salons*, a mechanist, doctor, composer, duchess, economist and diplomat could all converse together. Let us call conversation the activity whereby the doctor, speaking to the mechanist, is obliged to speak of the man-machine and immerse his knowledge in that of the other; but that conversely or vice versa, the mechanist will dream of extending his knowledge into physiology, while the economist describes circulation in terms of hydraulics and so forth. Conversation is the set of applications of a body of knowledge into or onto another, the set of their conversions. These applications multiply rapidly, excluding none, bringing all possible variations; this swift movement or multiplication, not the discipline, becomes the object of thought.

Sacred eloquence institutes, the specialist scientist instructs, both emit without receiving; the *salon* is not a place of instruction and has no discipline. It produces an object of thought: this set of passages. And its condition is tolerance. A condition and an object unthinkable within the academy.

THE FIVE SENSES

The epistemology of conversation died, I believe, when the great universities took the place of the myriad churches. Academies presuppose disciplinary territories, sectarian conflict, in which the exclusion of heretics begins anew, through either words or ideas.

Can we integrate this multi-planet problem? Yes, under the name of philosophy. The philosophy that we despise called French literature.

I am delighted at the extent to which French writers shun learning. They are frightened of pedants, fearing their anger and resentment: as a result, they are quick to make fun of those who correct manners, bodies, words and reasoning. The non-correcting writer encourages freedom. I have spoken sufficiently about literature from a scholarly point of view to enjoy putting on a different hat and listening to the words it uses when describing the learned. It riddles them with arrows. Rabelais makes fun of them, Montaigne is suspicious, Molière ridicules them, Marivaux sends them packing – our literature, or rather our culture fears teachers. Observe the long sequence of doddery and hateful, argumentative and bossy idiots: Janotus, Marphurius, Honorius . . . Blazius is called Wetwhistle by the immortal Labiche. The Latin names make it clear that their language is dying.

Hear the names footnoted in scholarly quotations. Footnotes point to the fossilization of language. The writer of French laughs at these proper names because he's frightened of them; despotic, they dominate, devour, destroy, deface and appropriate texts, sucking the life out of them. In displaying your knowledge, you censor your language. Beauty and elegance in a work is the result of a joyous liberation: getting rid of dead wood, paring down. Write a text in plain language and you will begin to live freely.

How I should like to describe, turning things inside out like a glove, the perspective that opens up for literature, philosophy and art when the pedant leaves. When weighty knowledge is laid down. When clichés are cast aside. If the prison of language opens. Free at last, free to speak as we wish, without harsh rules or canonical references, to think at ease, light, unencumbered by prior dogma, or interminable criticism, to write gallantly, away from that heavy presence. To write for a woman, never again in order to please a proof reader.

I have learned more, working the earth beside my father on the edges of the Garonne or on his barge, I have learned more at Pinara, under the cliff with its five hundred burial places, or at the theatre of Epidaurus, alone; flying over the Yukon or the Mackenzie, or in a fierce storm in the south of Crete, between two distress calls, on the cliff of the bird-man on Easter Island, facing the Pacific, with my back to the volcano; I have learned more, thirsty for knowledge about the world, when on a slow walk through the meadows of Auvergne or the forests of Brazil than in any book I have ever read. No, I do not despise books, I love them so much that I have devoted my life to them. I love my language so much that I have given it all my time, but we cannot bring a culture, a philosophy, to life without feeding it with what it is not. Language is closed on the language side, shut in on its qualities of exactness, precision, rigour; on the world side, on the other hand, it opens out. Inchoative and inexact, undecided but full of promise. Professors, critics, theoreticians and politicians live on the closed side, the writer takes up residence on its outskirts, in the open, facing things that are sometimes hard.

Æsthetics comes into play on the open side of language, overlooking the garden.

I have learned more by working the earth as a peasant boy, in road and construction works, as a labourer, mason, road-mender, I have learned more on boats, as a sailor on fresh or salt water, and in *salons* in the company of the last real duchesses; in huts in the forest speaking to old Bambaras whose language I did not speak and who did not know mine; beneath the gilded panelling of palaces at the side of those in temporary power, amazed at their customs; in hospitals with those who suffer, before altars with those who pray; in gun turrets or facing missile launchers with those who are going to kill or to die; playing in teams, where the balls move quickly without anyone speaking; in theatrical performances where all applaud, in front of deathbeds where eyes implore; with children who do not yet speak; I have learned more during my tacit voyage in the social body or humankind, I have learned more amongst the poor, the simple-minded and the humiliated than in any book I have ever read, in any learned discourse.

Language is born in the emotion of the encounter, words are born when you don't expect them. I have learned more with you than in all the books of philosophy, you who gave me my body, to whom I offer the last words of this book, humbly, in return.

SIGNATURE

Language has taken the place of the given, science is taking that of language. What does the word 'place' signify in this exchange?

THE FIVE SENSES

The history of science is finally catching up with the avatars of literary interpretation, another interpretive discipline; it is merely a matter of changing texts. It has its more or less pure historians, internal and external, its schools of interpreters, its world-famous stars, its theatre. Likewise for epistemology, at least in the old French sense of the term. A single discipline is created, criticism in general, the objects of which vary. You can at least be certain that you are doing history and philosophy of science if you remain in the sciences, if you consider them as objects.

I confess that I have never enjoyed this certainty. I had a sort of intuitive certainty that I was working in this field, yet I was sure that I was not in it. The unanimous judgement of my peers, also, led me to think that my practice lay elsewhere. Where? I did not know.

This is the space that the Greeks began to map, through definition and exclusion – let none but geometers enter here – that the European seventeenth century recognized and even strove to define, the space of science. We have been fascinated ever since, by the following judgement: this belongs to science and that does not, this inside, that outside. Inclusion, exclusion, the strategies of schools of thought, but originally a religious gesture: just as the haruspex carefully divided up the holy ground, marked out its plinths. This is the profane, that is the sacred. Science and non-science do not mix their respective terrains any more than the civil and the religious, to avoid risk of defilement. Yet the frontiers of knowledge shift about, philosophies of knowledge suffer and are transformed as a result of these changes. It is a simple fact that things foreign to science will be embraced by it tomorrow and that things that are a part of it today will be expelled. Time cares naught for dogma or the excluded third.

Schoolchildren, academics or priests can be recognized by this sign: they all ask the question of proper place – they ask: where? In what place does a certain discourse attract a certain consensus? Orthodox, heretical, anathema – choose. Where do you live?

The space of science fascinates us: and for this reason it is compared to a temple, to the zone meticulously outlined by the priest using a ritual baton that no-one may touch. Here is the object, here is the thing that must command our maximum attention. A whole group yields to this fascination, agrees to this objectivity.

Our age has not yet been able to distance itself from science, is not yet secularized in relation to it. The space of science preserves our ultimate values; it exercised on our fathers, and still exercises on certain of our contemporaries, the pull of the sacred. The whole thrust of the epistemology or history of science can be read in this light. We are still feeling the repercussions of the astonishing appearance amongst us of exact knowledge. This gives rise to interpretation, just as the divine word did.

For more than a quarter of a century, I have taken a secular position on this point. I never consider science as an object or as an exterior space to describe, analyse, judge, justify, a town to defend or a place to occupy, a temple to protect from all impurity – I *suppose* it. Not only do I suppose it as acquired, admitted or known, but I suppose it, in absolute terms. The place of objects is in front of us. We are surrounded by a space into which we can immerse ourselves. But to suppose science puts it in the position of *subject*.

We know science in quite a different way. First of all we encountered it. Then we found ourselves immersed in it. Now it is immersed in us. It thought outside us, it thinks in us. We had made our dwelling in it, it now has its dwelling in us.

Let my reader suppose that this author is the most knowledgeable possible; the author knows that his reader is the most knowledgeable possible. To display or show one's knowledge indicates a failure of secularity, or a digestive problem. I therefore do not work on science, in my texts it is science that is at work. Science could work on science: it does so in scientific texts, that philosophy can copy, that it can also consider useless to copy, as a matter of redundancy or honesty. In my texts, science works actively, on things other than itself.

A profoundly secret revolution that has no name: supposed, objective knowledge has taken the place of the subject. This transformation gives rise to a new world, to new texts, to another form of thought.

We know science in a new way: we have digested it. In the past, an instance foreign to it conceptualized it as object. It has taken up residence in this instance. And so we use it as the basis and subject of thought.

We use it as we do language. Language does not constitute an ordinary object, it lives with the personal or collective subject, but plays at disappearing from the object side of the equation.

Language has taken the place of the subject since the dawn of humanity, since the dawning of philosophy, and the beginning of religions, since the philosophy of today. We have taken thousands of years to understand the appearance of language amongst us and in us, our thought is still undergoing the repercussions of its astonishing advent. Language has taken the place of the subject since the dawn of the subject.

Our religions and philosophies speak of this coup.

We had put science in front of us, as one object among others, exceptional only in its behaviour and performance. Likewise, we had put language in front of us as one object among others, exceptional only in its sweetness and transparency.

We always take a long time to understand what it means to understand.

We have taken a long time to digest language. Coming amongst us and into us, the word inhabited a world into which no-one had invited it. Its light shone in the darkness and the darkness comprehended it not. Before the word penetrated our flesh, became our flesh, space preserved the divide between blindness and clarity. Before the word became subject, the luminous sacred was separated from the profane darkness, unpenetrated by light. Now we have received the word, we have eaten and digested it; it has arrived in our midst, into us, and has become us – a subject. Philosophies and religions have been resounding for the last three millennia with the repercussions of this long incomprehensible event, this reversal that traverses and creates our history, or even better, our hominity.

An equally significant phenomenon has been evolving slowly from the time of the Greeks to that of our fathers, speeding up suddenly in recent times. We have at last been receptive to science. We have digested it. It no longer designates an exterior space, a stage set with light and darkness, a battlefield or sacred place, horror or attraction, expulsion or welcome, as if the Age of the Enlightenment had rehearsed for it the tragedy of the birth and death of the word; it enters us, comes amongst us, becomes collective or individual flesh, the subject of conditional or reflexive thought.

In me, sharp, active, hard-working, vigilant; in us and amongst us, saturating the objective world and that of our relationships. Those who were subjects endowed with language become new subjects endowed with science. The known becomes our unknown, the latter is structured like knowledge.

Religions and philosophies of language still construct our age-old dwelling. All that remains now is to construct the house of today.

It is not a matter of a cultural or historical state. To be sure, we all have a smattering of science, just as everyone, in the Middle Ages, no doubt knew something about Christendom, lived immersed in it, even if he didn't walk every day in the shadow of Jumièges Abbey; to be sure, we live immersed in science, just as the Greeks in the Vth century no doubt carried in themselves, as fragments of memory, the sung stories of Homer or the myths of Olympus. But these comparisons could be counter-productive.

Seeing our knowledge outside ourselves, learning it in snatches, living it in the objects that are born of it, we forget that it lies within us. That, without it, we could not learn it. We forget more and more that we are forgetting it.

For the passerby in the Middle Ages, Christendom, present, remained in his memory; for the Greek of the Classical Age, the pantheon of Gods remained impossible to ignore. But language is ignored by everyone. When I am aware that I am speaking in a foreign language, I speak it badly or don't speak it at all. I only ever really manage to speak it when I don't know that I am doing so. Whereas it rarely occurs to me that I am speaking in my mother tongue. This state of awareness or memory is a thousand times more fundamental and obvious when it is no longer a question of one's own tongue, but of language, by the very fact that we are speaking. We almost always forget that we are speaking. The subject is defined by language without memory, however high or low our level of culture, at whatever moment we are living in history.

Science, in turn, is losing its memory today in the same manner. The subject is defined by forgotten knowledge. We live and think now through science, not as we thought or lived as Olympians or Christians – we are becoming subjects of science as we have been subjects of language ever since we became human.

To speak a language other than the one to which our fœtal skin would quiver when our mother's voice used it, remains a cultural or historical event; our skin begins to vibrate differently. The transition to science cannot simply be reduced to a change of language, but should be more broadly thought of as the acquisition of language when, in our unformed state, we had none, our skin trembling for the first time. Science has never had, does not and will never have the dimensions, weight or status of a culture: to impose itself it has set aside cultures or set up its influence beside them; science does not have the status of a language, but that of language itself: it transforms evolution rather than history and affects the process of hominization. Universal in space and for every culture, this transhistorical sweep also marks its universality in time.

These processes that shape the speaking or knowing subject lie in a more deeply forgotten past than that with which history daily satisfies its hunger.

THE FIVE SENSES

Socrates asked a slave child to demonstrate simple reasoning to him using a geometrical figure and concluded that the ignorant person remembered knowledge that was presented to him. That kind of memory is only the first stage of knowledge: when I remember what Socrates said and demonstrated, I mobilize a school child's knowledge. Afterwards, we blissfully forget and true knowledge begins. We would otherwise be as burdened with our remembrances as the boat that has just hunted down two whales and that, having secured them on the port side and starbord side, still thinks it can get home faster if it rows.

Speaking consists of forgetting that one knows how to speak, implies that we leap naked into meaning, or the object, or reasoning, into totally forgetting that we are using language as a medium. True eloquence cares nothing for eloquence, not because it finds the rules and discipline of oratory useless and derisory but because, listening to silence intensely, it immerses itself in the living reservoir of what it can find to say. Swimming supposes that we ignore that we can swim; likewise for walking, jumping, making love, thinking. Culture can be reduced to this amnesis: learn codes of social behaviour so as to behave naturally, was the advice of the duchesses of yore, learn everything possible so as not to display it, the only gaps in your culture will be the vulgarities that you remember, that encumber your language. Quotation is the mark of an uncultivated person, delayed digestion, the flatulent burp of the dyspeptic afflicted with aerophagia.

I think if and only if I am speaking in my own name. Knowing demands that one forget oneself. Thought cares nothing for these memories. Science loses consciousness in the consciousness of the scholar-subject and, through this loss, the latter thinks and invents.

This is what I have sought passionately: that knowledge and science be forgotten in my books, written so that their very loss might elaborate new objects, so that their loss might bring into being a new subject.

The question of philosophy today could therefore be formulated thus: what do we think when we know? What can we think when we know as we speak, when we know science in the sense in which, active and alive, it blends into thought, in the sense in which, having learned it, our flesh has incorporated it?

Not: what is there to think in science? Objective or collective science, as far as I know, answers this question by its very nature.

Not: what is there to think outside it? Or, if science is dismissed or reduced, what is there to think?

That would again suppose a partitioned space, an interior and an exterior, the old inaugural ground that the haruspex marks out with his stick; and that we can easily sideline science or leave it out of the loop, a simple gesture when we knew nothing.

Either we ask the questions that were valid before the dawn of our era, and have been ever since, eternal until this morning – as if science had never been thought of: the royal road of metaphysics.

Or we consider science as an object, without ever evaluating the knowledge of the person practising it, we question knowledge and understanding, their basis and functioning: the royal road of epistemology.

In the case of both of these royal roads, practice, we observe, is designated by a prefix: beyond or above. Somewhat haughty or grand. Epistemology or metaphysics: beyond physics, above knowledge. How we admire the altitude of such scholarly and profound sites, always remote, higher up than all our houses, hanging over vertiginous drops.

Or alternatively, we acknowledge that science constitutes what we know, that it is now becoming what language became in us at our birth, and we ask, humbly, with no thought of surpassing it: what remains to be thought?

We are well aware that everything remains to be thought, reassessed, that there remains a world to construct. We can clearly see that everything remains to be done. What are we going to do, we who know, and who are actively engaged in the thinking that depends on science?

We have said over and over again that science is transforming the world and our bodies; we say, considerably less often, that it is becoming our destiny even more than our history, or the sum of our hopes; we have not yet said that it is displacing languages, and worse still, language, by replacing it with true algorithms. We can no longer speak the common language. Precision and rigour have definitively abandoned it to emigrate towards knowledge with its countless disciplines; it has been robbed of its charm and enchantments by the gigantic machines of communication and show business. Crushed and sandwiched between the Babel of scholarship and networks of information, humming with noise, language is dying, my book celebrates the death of the word.

And yet since we have been men, we have not been able to grow to adulthood without feeding on the word. In days gone by, the greatest of us became the word through having glorified it. We have lost, without recourse, the memory of a heard, seen, perceived world, experienced by a body devoid of language. That forgotten, unknown man became man by speaking, and the word has moulded his flesh, not only his collective flesh of exchanges or perception, use or domination, but also and especially his corporeal flesh: thighs, feet, chest and neck vibrate, dense with the word. This stable period of hominization – note that I don't say of history – is drawing to an end. Tomorrow, we speaking beasts will no longer see the world or the powers at work in it in the same way.

Science uproots language after having shaken it, this event disrupts our bodies, the collective and the world. Our flesh dense, no longer with language but with science, we begin to see, to hear a world – our body knows more than it says, it used to speak more than it knew. It knows, forgetting that it knows, just as it used to speak, forgetting that it was doing so. In both cases, it is flesh, transparent and obscure. And knowledgeable, in the case of those who barely or imperfectly know that flesh spoke for the timid, inexpert, dumb, or tongue-tied. As the deepest level of the subjective, the collective and the carnal, a substitution takes place, in which science eradicates language – this explains our time.

This brutal diminution of the word, this loss or death have given us a fleeting glimpse of the world and each other, as they could doubtless have been seen before language was incarnated in us. Between two reigns, a rapid lightning flash illuminating the five senses.

Today we are living through an acute crisis of languages. Once held to be treasures, they are falling into disrepute, everyone pillages his own, as we do the earth. Our peasant ancestors, whose letters we sometimes discover, expressed themselves with greater elegance and clarity than the dominant class of the day. In moving from agriculture to academia, where clichéd language abounds, I rather seem to have lost some of the verve of my story-telling and my delight in finding just the right word. The most famous of our scholars don't know how to write, and publishing houses rewrite their books. The media broadcasts hundreds of words and deliberately uses ungrammatical or vulgar language to show it has the common touch. Poets are losing their ear for language, the intelligentsia has long since driven them away. Teachers find twenty dunces in groups in which, once, there would only have been two or three – by dunces I mean those who cannot be taught to read or write, however hard the teacher tries. The crafting of language is becoming rare, no-one is inclined to take the trouble. Those who say, or believe, that they hold our fate in their hands have never appeared so barbaric – by barbaric I mean those whose utterance consists of belching and stomach rumbling, usually the sound of a dominant language.

You are not reading the same old lament here, I am making a precise diagnosis. In this age of science language, even more than languages, is collapsing; our relationship to the world and others, and to ourselves, no longer passes preferentially through language.

An example. If we use the word star, we designate a luminous point amongst those that vibrate above our heads on bright nights. Connoisseurs, we called the largest Sirius, in Canis; the blue star, close to the zenith on long summer evenings, Vega; the head of Medusa was the name we gave to Antares, the unstable star in the middle of Scorpio, that even changes colour. We guessed that the confrontation with Mars, God of War, was responsible for these two names for a face over which so many storms pass. We have abandoned that category, as vague or arbitrary as a baptismal name; night has lost its giants and animals. But, as practitioners, we knew their position, in order to determine ours, at twilight, using a sextant; we had to predict the place where they would become visible, early, when all the others were still eclipsed by the sunset, and to observe the visible horizon and the new light all at the same time. Satellites have extinguished these ancient signals. Exact and precise, faithful to things, we now call Rigel, which lies at old Orion's foot, a blue supergiant; the star that overwhelms us at midday, approaching its nova, a yellow dwarf. Still more rigorously, we write equations. The thing once called a star is classified, distinguished and divided into new families, or assembled into gigantic galaxies; is in any case designated by a corpus of codes or catalogues, by a collection of calculations and theories. Stars as such, or things simply called stars, hardly exist any more, astrophysics is no more concerned with them than is the biology of life or the physics of matter. They have disqualified these words, by making these things disappear. Life, matter or star belong less to philosophy or history than to the old language abandoned because of the demands of precision and the dynamics of objective knowledge. RR Lyrae variables and dwarf galaxy NGC 1036 are no longer part of any language and are detached from language as are the formulae that are discussed in connection to them.

Those who use the word star abandon exactitude or focus on the thing in itself. Calculations and codes are replacing terms. All that is left of them are shapeless and empty carcasses, slowly sinking into obsolescence. We and our ancestors spoke of life, or stars; voices we shall no longer hear, of naive lovers carving into the bark of trees.

If we speak of grass, insects, gladioli, fuchsias or emeralds in the same way . . . the same logic asserts itself. Scientific codes gobble up our old languages, harness the aspects of them that are the beginnings of coherence or faithfulness to the real; all that remains is a shapeless tatter. We shall no longer find, in the woods, what our fathers and mothers meant by 'grass' or 'insect', we shall no longer visit the woods from which species are disappearing. Science has not only changed the depth of the world or the relationships between men, through fertilizers, motors, aspirin or the atomic bomb, but has also derealized the things designated by language: we can no longer speak. We would have difficulty in finding matter where we speak of particles and nuclei, in finding life where we speak of acids or enzymes, in finding grass or wheat where clones or mutants of a given stock, produced by genetic engineering and resistant to a given constraint, proliferate. The new farmers of this new Neolithic create new forests in their laboratories by the branching of possibilities, the woods in which plant cuttings are encoded are the only ones we shall visit from now on.

Since the beginning of our history, the global and local world – from the glory of the heavens down to its smallest details and folds, furrows, marshy places and small pebbles – has slumbered beneath the waters of language, inaccessible and swallowed up like the great cathedral. No-one could go to the object without passing through it, just as no-one gathers seaweed, without, in some unimaginable space, getting his arm wet.

Likewise everything today is swallowed up by the scholarly avalanche, nothing escapes the control of science. Nothing. Neither grass nor the word grass, not stars nor the word stars, nor our connections: our emotional relationships, our collective obligations, the withholding of information or confessions, the humble terms we exchange without too much concern about their meaning. Love, abuse, gift, speaking, war, tax, devotion, here again are objects of science subject to transferences of language, where we move from rhetoric to a sort of algebra. When they work on our relationships, the human sciences uproot language by going behind it – as do the exact sciences with objects – replacing it with a true algorithm. Language itself is subjected to equations or formulæ. To conclude, the self, in times gone by, the thinking self, and more recently the speaking self, is now forgetting that it knows. The result is this: language had under its control the subjects of the world, the connections between them, the relationship between subjects and objects, as well as the solitary subject itself and, no doubt, the collective we. It enunciated the totality of the world that we can still call historical and in which no-one could grow up without living intimately within his language. But now science controls all these subjects or objects, as well as their exchanges, as well as the language that controlled them.

The elderly speaker of exact and correct language finds himself crushed between the monstrous growth of true algorithms, which have robbed him of his precision, and the monstrous growth of the remaining mediatized tatters, which have robbed him of his charm.

Why have I written about the five senses in a language long disqualified by so many true algorithms: without biophysics, biochemistry, physiology, psycho-physiology, acoustics, optics or logic . . . depriving myself of the long series of experiments, formulæ, models, schemas, analytical calculations? Why write about an object that is disappearing, in a language that is dying?

Or, why not write in the din of the circus?

The three powers of today, unopposed, have robbed language of its constituent parts. Science has seized its true relationship with reality; the media have taken hold of its seductive relationship with the other; and administration has taken on its performative power: what it says or writes, exists and imposes itself, precisely because it writes or says. These three new powers occupy space and the only opposition they encounter is one or the other of the two others.

There are three sorts of books that remain to be written in these components of language – if you love power over things or men.

My beautiful, strong, relevant old language has lost its power to science, has abandoned its charm and enchantments to the gigantic information and entertainment businesses, leaves its utterances to those who dictate facts.

All that is left of it now are tatters. This phantom in rags retains a vaguely æsthetic function. Æsthetic?

So let it talk about the five senses, let it celebrate the beauty of the world.

The adventure of philosophy is beginning anew, in exactly the same place from which it has always sprung.

Present or absent, sciences are forgotten in the subject, who now knows. He knows, and therefore does not need to display his knowledge. He knows the addresses of the data banks he can mine, if he wants to remember. We are no longer living in the age of rare libraries. Information, available everywhere, makes forgetting possible. It circulates through the air we breathe. What is the use of quoting or copying a list of disciplines or articles that anyone can procure in an instant? Why burden an already long list with a new item that includes the list itself all over again? When memory becomes objective, the thinking subject becomes forgetful. When access to knowledge encounters no obstacle, the status of knowledge itself changes. When language is transformed, all is transformed.

Memory and language are set free. The first, by machines and networks – we shall no longer write theses. We are going to think, directly, light-heartedly, freed from references stored in the bank – out of the text, out of the body, out of the subject.

And language leaves behind its main components, three times.

You could have said that it was dead – or you could say that it is free. Released from its obligations at last.

Each time an organ – or function – is liberated from an old duty, it invents. Freed by the standing position from the weighty duty of support or locomotion, the paw or hand changes, apprehends and finally fashions tools; freed by our verticality from the vital necessity to grasp, the mouth, jaw or maw begins to speak words. Memory is liberated three times: at the advent of writing, by the discovery of printing, now with computers. Who can tell what the invention of geometry owes to the first, the coming of experimental science to the second, or what will emerge from our third forgetting?

And to what new use our regenerated language will be put.

I am seeking to release the book that I am writing and he who is writing it from objective lists, from mechanical memory, from specific algorithms, in order to give them to a new subject or to relaunch the adventure of philosophy. To the new thinking subject, both free to forget and knowledgeable, equipped with artificial intelligences and stores of information, with screens and software, arranging them and depositing them far from himself, therefore detached by a new distance from his former functions surrendered to artefacts or algorithms, I give the first object at hand: the given.

Once the primary object of traditional philosophy which claimed to construct knowledge from it, the given is now a primary object for us, because a remnant of the competence of what remains of language when it has lost everything – an exterior abandoned by our memories when all the data has been dealt with. Primary, therefore, today because it is the last remaining thing – we no longer have the same ambitions. Crumbs from the feast of language which is taking place elsewhere.

The subject, forgetful, detached, immerses itself in the unforgettable world.

The five senses, still on the verge of departure towards another adventure, a ghost of the real timidly described in a ghost of language – this is my essay.

I should have liked to call it resurrection – or rebirth.

Notes

INTRODUCTION

[1] Michel Serres and Bruno Latour, *Conversations on Science, Culture, and Time*, trans. Roxanne Lapidus (Ann Arbor: University of Michigan Press, 1995), p. 165.

[2] Michel Serres, *Hermes: Literature, Science, Philosophy*, ed. Josué V. Harari and David F. Bell (Baltimore: Johns Hopkins University Press, 1983).

[3] *De sensu et sensibili*, trans. J. I. Beare, in *The Works of Aristotle*, trans. W. D. Ross et al. (Oxford: Clarendon Press, 1931), Vol. 3, sig. B4r, B7v.

[4] *The 'Theaetetus' of Plato*, trans. M. J. Levett (Glasgow: University of Glasgow Press, 1977), 156b, p. 29.

[5] Étienne Bonnot de Condillac, *Traité des sensations: Traité des animaux* (Paris: Fayard, 1984), pp. 88, 89 (my translation).

[6] J. Cranefield, 'On The Origin of the Phrase NIHIL EST IN INTELLECTU QUOD NON PRIUS FUERIT IN SENSU', *Journal of the History of Medicine and Allied Sciences*, 25 (1970); 77–80.

[7] John Locke, *An Essay Concerning Human Understanding*, ed. Peter H. Nidditch (Oxford: Clarendon, 1975), 2.1.23, p. 117; G. W. Leibniz, *New Essays Concerning Human Understanding*, trans. A. G. Langley (LaSalle, Ill.: Open Court Publishing Co., 1916), 2.1 p. 111.

[8] *Titi Livi ab urbe condita*, Vol. 1, Books I-V, ed. Robert Maxwell Ogilvie (Oxford: Clarendon Press, 1974), I.36.3, p. 47.

[9] Friedrich Nietzsche, *The Gay Science*, ed. Bernard Williams, trans. Josefine Nauckhoff (Cambridge: Cambridge University Press, 2001), 340, pp. 193–4; Edgar Allan Poe, 'The Facts in the Case of M. Valdemar', *Complete Poems and Stories of Edgar Allan Poe*, ed. Arthur Hobson Quinn and Edward H. O'Neill, 2 Vols (New York: Alfred A. Knopf, 1946), Vol. 2, pp. 656–63.

[10] Michel Serres, *Variations sur le corps* (Paris: Le Pommier-Fayard, 1999), p. 96 (my translation).

[11] Michael Serres, *Hominescence* (Paris: Le Pommier, 2001), p. 47 (my translation).

CHAPTER 1

[1] A reference to the *Carte du tendre*: an allegorical map of the region of the tender sentiments, composed by Mlle de Scudéry in her novel, *Clélie* (1664–1660).

[2] A reference to the distinction Blaise Pascal (1623–1662) makes in his *Pensées* between the *esprit de finesse* (the subtle or intuitive mind) and the *esprit de géométrie* (geometric mind).

[3] In Balzac's tale, *Le Chef d'œuvre inconnu* (1837), the seventeenth-century painter Frenhofer has been working on his *Belle Noiseuse* for ten years and can only finish it when he finds the right model. The finished painting consists of a riot of colour, from which a foot partially emerges. Seeing his friends' disappointment, the painter destroys his painting and commits suicide. Jacques Rivette's eponymous film is a loose adaptation of the story.

[4] Vair is a heraldic term and originally meant fur of two different colours, such as squirrel fur. In Perrault's version of the fairytale *Cinderella*, the slipper was made of glass, eliminating the ambiguity of the oral tradition in which the French words *verre* (glass) and *vair* (fur) might have been confused.

[5] Denis Diderot, *Lettre sur les aveugles à l'usage de ceux qui voient* (1749).

[6] Serres is playing on the French word for armadillo, *tatou*, which is juxtaposed with *tabou* in the original.

CHAPTER 2

[1] This sentence draws on two expressions: (i) *Vivre d'amour et d'eau fraîche* (which translates roughly as 'to live on love and cold water'. However its usual equivalent is the expression 'to live on love alone' which elides the reference to drinking cold water); (ii) *Lascia le donne, e studia la matematica* (Forget about women and study mathematics instead).

[2] Cf. Jules Verne, *Le Château des Carpathes* (1892).

CHAPTER 3

[1] The reader should bear in mind, throughout this chapter, that the standard French translation of *The Symposium* is *Le banquet*. We have rendered *banquet* variously, as banquet and symposium, depending on the context, but the associations Serres draws between gorging and speaking are present in both usages.

[2] *Messidor* was a month in the French revolutionary calendar, which drew the names of the months from seasonal and natural, rather than mythological, associations.

[3] Cf. Diderot, *Les bijoux indiscrets* (1748).

[4] *Oïl* and *oc* were, respectively, the words for 'yes' in the old northern and southern languages of France.

[5] The link Serres is making between the Ishim and the bottle of Château d'Yquem is clearer is French, where the Ishim are designated by the name 'ychim'.

[6] Molière, *Dom Juan ou le Festin de Pierre* (1665).

[7] *Floréal*, *prairial* and *vendémiaire* are also months in the French revolutionary calendar.

NOTES

8   Cf. 'élan vital' in Bergson's *Creative Evolution*.

9   Victor Hugo, 'Ce qui se passait aux Feuillantines vers 1813'.

10 Serres is drawing an analogy with the criteria for an æsthetics of beauty given by Immanuel Kant in *The Critique of Judgement*.

11 An awkward pun, in English, relying on the dual senses of perception (sensation and taxation or collection) and impostor (deception and taxation). Whereas the root sense of collection, from the Latin *perceptio*, is now obsolete in English, it remains in active usage in contemporary French.

12 The labyrinth, the bridge, the well and the inn are all stages in *Le Jeu de l'Oie* (*The Game of the Goose*), a traditional French board game analogous to *Snakes and Ladders*.

13 A reference to François Couperin's harpsichord piece 'Les Folies françoises, ou les Dominos: La Virginité sous le Domino couleur d'invisible', from *Pieces de Clavecin, Book 3, 13th Order in B minor*.

14 San-Antonio is the pen-name of French writer Frédéric Dard, and also the name of the bon vivant chief protagonist in his many thrillers.

CHAPTER 4

1   Jan Van Eyck, *Virgin of Chancellor Rollin*, Musée du Louvre (c. 1435).

2   René Descartes, *Second Meditation*.

3   The French word *parasite* means both 'static' and 'parasite' and Serres plays here on this double meaning. See also his book *The Parasite*, University of Minnesota Press, 2007 (*Le parasite*, Paris, Bernard Grasset, 1980).

4   A reference to Galileo Galilei's reputed *sotto voce* response to the Inquisition in Rome (1633) when required to recant his belief that the earth moved around the sun.

5   Author's note: Auguste Comte, *Cours de philosophie positive*, 27th Lesson, Hermann, Vol. 1, p. 434. Note also how the word *circumstance* is used for the tide: Ibid., 25th Lesson, pp. 405 and 406.

6   Henri Stendhal, *Le Rouge et le Noir* (1831).

7   Refers to Blaise Pascal's aphorism in his *Pensées*, 'le moi est haïssable' [the I is hateful].

8   Stanford University Press, 1991 (*Rome: le livre des fondations*, Grasset, 1983).

CHAPTER 5

1   See note 11, Chapter 3 for the dual sense, to tax or to perceive, of the verb *percevoir* in French.

Made in the USA
Lexington, KY
04 February 2015